RUPTURING
ᵀᴴᴱ DIALECTIC

**The Struggle against Work,
Money, and Financialization**

Advance praise for *Rupturing the Dialectic*:

"Harry Cleaver does battle divine against capitalism. His sword and shield are Less Work and More Time. He rides into battle mounted on a thoroughbred of theory. He carries a banner proclaiming what we— students, housewives, farmers, workers of office, shop, and mine—have already done as we do diligently our parts against the demon. He blows a golden horn summoning us to assemble and to cash in our chits for mutual aid. Here is Marxist interpretation we can use. Now, on with the practices!" —Peter Linebaugh, author of *The Magna Carta Manifesto: Liberties and Commons for All*

"In this timely and long-awaited book, Harry Cleaver illuminates Marx's categories of class struggle and sharpens our critical understanding of contemporary processes of financialization. Harry never loses focus on two grounding aspects of our lives in common: the struggle against capital's imposition of work, and the creation of non-commodified alternatives... Read this book and add it to the fundamental toolbox of radical commoners." —Massimo De Angelis, author of *The Beginning of History: Value Struggles and Global Capital*

"In the midst of a crisis-inspired revival of interest in Marx's work, especially the labor theory of value, comes Harry Cleaver's *Rupturing the Dialectic*. It is a major step beyond Cleaver's now classic text, *Reading* Capital *Politically*. By boldly displaying the lineaments of the class struggle in Capital's monetary categories, he charts a way out of capitalism. A remarkable performance by a leading scholar-activist. Don't miss it." —George Caffentzis, author of *In Letters of Blood and Fire: Work, Machines, and the Crisis of Capitalism*

"Cleaver's theory of the value of labor to capital, explanation of money as a critical mediator of class conflicts and discussion of strategies for resistance and transformation are remarkable. *Rupturing the Dialectic* offers emancipating ways to understand everyday life and financial crises in capitalism today." —Anitra Nelson, author of *Marx's Concept of Money*

"*Rupturing the Dialectic* rejects the quietism inherent in all economistic approaches to the current crises within capitalism, and furnishes working people with a clear, concrete, sensible program for how to move forward. This is a fine book, and it is one from which activists will greatly benefit." —David Sherman, author of *Sartre and Adorno*

"*Rupturing the Dialectic* shows us how we may use Marx's labor theory of value to resist the subordination of our lives to labor. Cleaver's incisive analysis offers the prospect getting beyond the capitalist dialectic rather than merely idealizing it." —Brett Caraway, The University of Toronto

Harry Cleaver

RUPTURING
THE DIALECTIC

The Struggle against Work,
Money, and Financialization

Rupturing the Dialectic:
The Struggle against Work, Money, and Financialization

© 2017 Harry Cleaver
This edition © 2017 AK Press (Chico, Oakland, Edinburgh, Baltimore)

ISBN: 978-1-84935-270-3
E-ISBN: 978-1-84935-271-0
Library of Congress Control Number: 2016954842

AK Press   AK Press
370 Ryan Ave. #100   33 Tower St.
Chico, CA 95973   Edinburgh EH6 7BN
USA   Scotland
www.akpress.org   www.akuk.com
akpress@akpress.org   ak@akedin.demon.co.uk

The above addresses would be delighted to provide you with the latest
AK Press distribution catalog, which features books, pamphlets, zines,
and stylish apparel published and/or distributed by AK Press. Alterna-
tively, visit our websites for the complete catalog, latest news, and secure
ordering.

Cover design by Kate Khatib / Owl Grammar Press
Exit icon by Rediffusion from the Noun Project
Index by Chris Dodge

Printed in the USA on acid-free, recycled paper

TABLE OF CONTENTS

PREFACE

My objective with this book is to share some thoughts. I wrote it, not to convince and convert those whose ideas differ, but to contribute to an ongoing conversation about the world we live in, what we don't like about it and how we would like to change it. That said, the thoughts I share here are by no means comprehensive; they do not deal with everything we don't like or with all possible means of change. Nor do they specify many details about the nature of the new worlds we are striving to create as we experiment with ways to transcend the present situation. Their focus, rather, is fairly narrow. They are preoccupied with what I consider fundamental elements of the existing system that confines and limits us, elements that must be eliminated if we are to achieve more comprehensive change that will craft worlds closer to our hearts' desires.

Frequently in this book I use the first-person plural pronouns "we" and "our"—despite recognizing them as problematic. Sometimes they refer to all living beings, as in "our very existence is threatened by the way capitalist industry poisons land, air, and water"; sometimes they refer to all of us who struggle against the way capitalism organizes society, as in "we struggle against the subordination of our lives to capitalist imposed work." My use of these terms, however, should not be read as a reductionism that ignores the complex heterogeneity of either living beings or of those of us who struggle. As I hope will be clear in what follows, I am acutely aware of those complexities and make no pretense of speaking *for* specific groups of which I am clearly not a member. Yet I use these terms because I want to avoid the academic practice of analyzing conflict from outside and above, as if an objective observer, by being clear that what I have to say here is one expression of my political stance among those opposed to capitalism and striving to create alternatives. I also use these pronouns, where it seems reasonable to do so, to emphasize how capitalist ways of organizing the world impose common problems on us and how we have often found in the past, and can hopefully find in the future, complementary ways to struggle. I juxtapose *complementarity* in struggle to more traditional evocations of *unity*. For me, complementarity implies the critical embrace of differences (not just acceptance or tolerance), both in situation and in goals. It implies the eventual replacement of capitalism, not with a singular new world (socialist or communist) but with new worlds in which we are free of all kinds of domination and can elaborate many different ways of being and living together, while minimizing antagonism and conflict.

As I see it, we live in a capitalist world—that is to say, a world in which business, or the government operating as a business, controls the vast majority of resources and tools required to produce what we need to live and, through that control, has enough power to force most of us to work for it.[1] They force some of us directly, by enslaving us in sweatshops, in brothels, in prisons, or on fishing boats. They force most of us, however, indirectly. By controlling the means of production, capitalists also control the products we produce for them—including most of what we need—and the only way we are allowed legal access to them is through purchase—with money that, for the most part, we can obtain only by working for them. To maintain this indirect coercion, business and government maintain extensive police, surveillance, judiciary, military, and paramilitary apparatuses to violently prevent us from taking what we need directly and to make sure that we keep working.[2]

Working for them involves doing what they tell us to do, using the resources and tools they give us, producing whatever they tell

---

[1] For Marx, being forced to work for capitalists makes us members of the working class "in-itself." If we resist, however, particularly in collaboration with each other, he considered that we become participants in the struggles of the working class "for-itself." This was a distinction he made in his analysis of the French peasantry after the 1848 revolution. While they were all clearly being exploited, he argued, and therefore formed a class "in-itself" by having common characteristics, their failure to act in concert to defend their common interests meant that they could not be considered a class "for-itself." See Karl Marx, "The Eighteenth Brumaire of Louis Bonaparte," Karl Marx and Friedrich Engels, *Collected Works*, vol. 11 (New York: International Publishers, 1978), 99–197.

[2] In the wake of the central city uprisings of the mid-1960s in the United States, sociologists were forced to recognize that the rebellions were not just responses to systemic racism and injustice, but constituted "commodity riots" in which the effective slogan in the streets was "Always loot before you burn!" That recognition was one reason for the rapid expansion of food stamps and welfare programs in the wake of the police and military suppression of the risings.

us to produce, in the ways they specify. This top-down control is dehumanizing; it strips us of a vital aspect of our humanity by subordinating our will to theirs. This subordination alienates us from work that might—in other circumstances and depending on its nature—provide satisfying modes of self-realization, both individual and collective. It also alienates us from each other, as our employers force us to compete, and from the things and services that we produce—that are owned by those we work for, who use them to control us.

Our employers also force us to work far more than is necessary to produce what we need. For individual businesses, our extra labor generates profits that are then invested to impose more work. Collectively we are forced to produce what capitalists need to continue to subordinate us: not only the tools and raw materials necessary to keep us working and to put more of us to work, but also everything required by their various other methods of control, from police and military equipment to prisons, schools, and mass media designed to divert and misinform. Imposing more work than we require to meet our needs constitutes exploitation.

Unless we're too young, too sick, or too old—and sometimes even when we are—either we work at waged or salaried jobs, more or less alienating and exploitative, or we work, unwaged and unsalaried, in schools and at home producing and reproducing our, or our loved ones', ability and willingness to look for jobs or return to them. When we are young, incarceration in schools reduces whole years of our lives to being disciplined and trained for some uncertain, future job. Even when we get jobs, far too many of those jobs are poorly paid and precarious—they don't last long—and very soon we find ourselves, once more, anxious about whether we can find another one—because we need the income that comes with it. Will it pay enough? How long will it last? How bad will it be? A lucky few find steady, satisfying jobs doing something that we would do even if we weren't paid; most do not. Satisfying jobs or bad jobs, we have to work long hours, most days of the week, most weeks of the year, and most years of our lives. To keep costs down and maximize their profits, our employers use machines to measure and regulate the speed and rhythm of our work, while often refusing to spend money on safety measures—from protective masks for those digging into the earth and building things above it, to ergonomic office furniture for those harnessed to desks and computers. Suddenly or slowly, bit by bit, work kills far too many of us. Always, always they pit us against each other—young against old, white against black, men against women, locals against immigrants, faith against faith, one ethnicity against another, waged against wageless—in a hierarchy of billionaires at the top and starvation at the bottom. This is no way to live.

Moreover, subordinating so much of our time to work also results in much of our supposed free or leisure time becoming work. For those with waged or salaried jobs, getting to and from them is work, preparing for and recuperating from them is work; all this usurps hours, every day, at least five days a week. In the few hours when we can escape from our jobs, we barely have time to recuperate and re-create our ability and willingness to go back to work. All too often, work-related email and cell phone calls disrupt and steal our free time. For those without paid jobs, the work of reproducing our ability and willingness to work can be virtually endless.

Everywhere we look, we find this capitalist world—now encompassing most of the earth—a global work machine. By demanding so much of our time and energy, on the job and off, that machine grinds us up and drains our energy—dramatically limiting our chances at any kind of autonomous self-realization, either individual or collective.[3]

Yet we are not just victims. Yes, capitalists do their best to oppress and exploit us by subordinating our lives to endless labor, but the rest of us—except for a few workaholics, who could use some serious therapy—not only struggle against that subordination but also fight to develop alternative ways of organizing our lives, both individual and collective. Overworked, we find ourselves frustrated or angry, so we resist; we struggle against work and against the subordination of our lives to work, on and off the job. In bad jobs, we work as little as possible, either by out-and-out shirking or by exerting our own will against those of our bosses (for example, by reshaping our jobs to make them safer or more interesting). In more satisfying jobs, we have even greater leeway to reshape, even subvert, what we do. Off the job, we struggle to minimize the time and energy given up to reproducing our ability and willingness to work and maximizing the

---

3   The mechanism was different, but the portrayal in the film *Matrix* of a machine intelligence draining human energy for its own purposes provides an all-too-accurate science fiction vision of our own world.

time and energy we devote to self-determined activities. Sometimes those activities are individual ones, such as reading a book, carving some wood, playing a little music, trying out a new recipe, or contemplating the meaning of our lives. Sometimes they are collective, such as figuring out new and better ways to live together. Often our collective efforts undermine how they pit us against each other. Recognizing such efforts reveals the capitalist world to be one of antagonistic conflicts between the constraints imposed by their rules of the game, our resistance to those rules, and our search for better ones.

If we really want to change things, we must place these struggles to escape our status as mere workers at the center of our analysis and our politics. While capitalists try to confine us within their dialectic—limiting and constraining our struggles to activities compatible with the growth of their system—we have repeatedly subverted and ruptured those dynamics. Instead of always portraying capitalism as the driving force of history—a story in which we appear only as victims or sometime as merely annoying irritants—let us see capitalism and the efforts of capitalists as unacceptable constraints on *our* efforts to live free and reshape the world to our liking. This seems particularly appropriate today, when—in every dimension of contemporary society—we find friends inventing, innovating, and crafting alternatives to the way capitalists have organized the world.

We experience these constraints both externally and internally. Externally, we usually know who our most immediate bosses are, and with a little effort we can usually identify those who shape rules, laws, and institutions to keep us working and competing with each other. Internally, while we experience the imposition of work on ourselves, with all the pain, frustration, and anxiety involved, we also, all too frequently, find ourselves in jobs in which we impose it on others and on ourselves. This is true both on the job and off.

If our job imposes any managerial responsibilities, we are obligated to force work on those over whom we have been given power. As a salaried professor for some forty years, I was regularly obligated to impose work on my mostly unwaged students and partially waged teaching assistants—readings, papers, and above all tests, where I, like all my colleagues, were responsible for exercising quality control by imposing a hierarchy of grades. If we are part of a traditional patriarchal marriage, with its usual organization of gendered relationships, we force work on our spouses. If a waged husband, we tend to impose housework on our wife, if an unwaged housewife—dependent on our husband's income—we pressure them to work, to "bring home the bacon." If both are waged, a struggle ensues over who does how much unwaged housework. If parents, we often force our kids to share the housework and are usually under legal obligation to force our kids to go to school—an obligation we usually accept, rationalizing it as "for their own good." So customary are these roles that they are often replicated by spouses and parents of the same sex.

Accompanying these interpersonal impositions of work, the capitalist institutions that shape our lives also condition us to impose work on ourselves. For those of us with jobs, blatantly exterior force is usually not necessary to force most of us to work each day. We force ourselves to get up, prepare for work, get to work, and work. This is true both for those of us with immediate supervisors and bosses and those without. The waged assembly-line worker—as portrayed in Charlie Chaplin's film *Modern Times* (1936)—is typical of the former. Although subjected to frequent observation and pressure, those of us in such jobs still force ourselves to carry on even when our supervisors are off harassing someone else. The salaried job of being a professor is typical of the latter. Although sometimes subjected to periodic evaluation (those of us who are untenured and adjunct more frequently than those of us who are tenured), daily we show up for work, teach our classes, grade our students, and in many cases, research, write, and publish (or perish)—all without direct oversight. If parents, we tend to replicate our own experiences, rewarding behaviors we have been taught are appropriate—such as chores and schoolwork—and punishing inappropriate ones—such as shirking such work. As children, we gradually internalize the pressures initially imposed upon us by our parents and then, as students, by our teachers. Toilet training at home is followed by learning to ask permission to go to the bathroom in school. Chores at home are followed by homework in school and finally—if we get that far—with PhD research and dissertations that are traditionally expected to involve individually conceived and crafted "original contributions to knowledge."

In all of the above cases, on the job and off, most of us, I warrant, also resist, at least from time to time. In *Modern Times*, Charlie sneaks a smoke while pretending to take a bathroom break. As waged workers we either shirk when we can get away with it or organize collectively to subvert our work on the job—through play or sabotage—or we down tools and walk away from it in strikes. As salaried workers, the less we are subject to immediate oversight, the easier to subvert our work. Thus within universities those few of us who achieve tenure generally have greater freedom to structure our courses in ways that subvert our profession's dominant paradigms and minimize the amount of work we impose on our students. Increasingly, the ever growing number of us deprived of any chance at such freedom, such as those of us in non-tenure-track jobs as lecturers and adjuncts, learn to organize ourselves collectively in self-defense—often adopting the familiar strategy of waged workers: unionization. As spouses, the rise of women's struggles have revealed—for both wives and husbands—myriad ways to subvert or cast off internalized gendered roles as well as the advantages of doing so. As children, conditioning to "self-discipline" accelerates our differentiation from our parents and the assertion of our independent wills, often in contradiction to their efforts to impose work. As students, the very structures of schools that impose work on us collectively—like the factories they so resemble—provide a terrain in which we can recognize our common interests and learn how to act collectively to refuse the work imposed on us. Individual shirking (failing to pay attention in class or to do homework) can mutate into collective action—we can play around in class to subvert lectures. Or, in extremis, as during the student uprisings of the 1960s or the more recent twenty-first-century "¡Sí, se puede!" immigrant rights protests, we can walk out of schools all together.

Recognizing these dynamics should clear away any tendency to think of class in terms of sociological categories into which individuals can or should be placed. It is counterproductive to identify individuals as members of this class or that class, in the manner of Madame Defarge in Dicken's *A Tale of Two Cities* (1859).[4] We

---

4   In *A Tale of Two Cities*, which unfolds in the midst of the French Revolution, Madame Defarge identifies individuals as nobles and knits their names into a list of those to be beheaded. Stalinists did something similar by branding some peasants as "kulaks" and making them the first to be dispossessed and liquidated "as a class." Mao had his own classification scheme. See his "How to Differentiate the Classes in the Rural Areas" (October 1933).

need to recognize that the real substance of the class structure of capitalist society is the subordination of life to work and the resistance to it—and that the degree to which individuals act as agents of each of these tendencies varies enormously.[5] This includes how we parse and understand our own actions. Self-reflection on how work is imposed on us, and on the ways and degrees to which we impose work on others and on ourselves, can not only reveal the forces that plague our lives but also help free us from them. Becoming conscious of these forces and analyzing them with care can both sharpen and facilitate our struggles, including our efforts to escape the conditioned, internalized self-discipline to impose work on ourselves. Once we recognize the little internal, capitalist devil urging us to get to work, and the equally internal but often long suppressed spirit of autonomy urging us to act on our own and with our friends, it is easier to resist the proddings of the former and follow the calls of the latter. Yes, I think it's an "us versus them" world, even when Pogo is right that "We have met the enemy, and he is us." Being clear about these pressures that impoverish our lives and poison our relationships with each other can help us figure out how to both resist and get beyond them. In the body of this book I present an interpretation of the labor theory of value that I think helps in both clarifying those pressures and figuring out how to fight and escape them.

*****

The main text in this book is a revised and expanded version of an essay I wrote for a conference, "Hegel, Marx and Global Crisis," held at the University of Warsaw, Poland, October 22–23, 2012. That conference was the first stop in a wider visit to Poland,

---

5   Varies enormously among individuals and varies enormously for each individual over time, as one's circumstances and one's position in the capitalist hierarchy of command change. One of Marty Glaberman's more enlightening essays, based on his experience as an autoworker, was *Union Committeemen and Wildcat Strikes* (Detroit: Correspondence, 1955), where he discussed how the roles of rank-and-file workers in the class struggle change if they become shop stewards or union committeemen and thus enforcers of contracts. An unwillingness to play such a role and suffer the ire of former friends is one reason many workers, both waged and salaried, refuse promotion to managerial positions, whether for a union or for their employer, despite offers of higher pay and benefits.

Austria, Slovenia, and Germany, where I gave a series of lectures and participated in discussions with local activists.

Unfamiliar with the work of the academics who invited me to the conference, I searched the Web and discovered that most participants would be academics from eastern Europe and likely to have more background in studying Georg Wilhelm Friedrich Hegel (1770–1831) than in studying Karl Marx (1813–83). After decades under Soviet-style socialism, during which Marxism served primarily as an ideology justifying domination and exploitation, while Hegel's theory of civil society nourished alternatives to an omnipresent state apparatus, both academics and activists have been understandably slow to explore alternative interpretations and uses of Marx.

Given what I could gather of the intellectual, philosophical, and probable political diversity of those who would be at that conference, I guessed that most would be unfamiliar with my work or the particular tradition of Marxism within which I have worked for many years. Therefore, I decided to emphasize in my contribution why I feel that Marx's work is still useful in helping us understand and get beyond capitalism, more so than Hegel's. The title of the essay—"Rupturing the Dialectic"—was chosen to signal that intent, because for Hegel "the dialectic" cannot be terminally ruptured or gotten beyond, while for Marx, in my reading, the dialectical relationships that bind us are those of capitalism, and the whole point of understanding them is to rupture and transcend them. Given our very different backgrounds, I also decided that the other conference participants might find it useful for me to include, at the outset, some prefatory remarks on how my own personal trajectory, through science and economics and a variety of social struggles, had led me beyond Hegel to Marx. When the editors at AK Press expressed an interest in publishing my conference essay as a book, we agreed that it might also be useful to include those remarks as background for the general reader. These follow.

*****

Although I entered college bent on refining my scientific skills in biochemistry, I wound up with a PhD in economics. Finding the path from the one to the other resulted from my participation in the American civil rights and antiwar movements of the 1960s. Those struggles drew me out of the laboratory, into the streets, and into a search for some intellectual framework for grasping the tumultuous events in which I was involved. I was drawn to economics because it seemed to deal most directly with the capitalist structures of economic, social, and political inequality—organized, in part, through racial and imperial hierarchies—against which those of us in the civil rights and antiwar movements mobilized. We saw and fought the racial component of inequality within the United States and what we saw as the efforts of American imperialism to restructure the postcolonial world as a new Pax Americana—within which pacified pools of ex-colonial labor could be pitted against militant ones at home.

Unfortunately, economics turned out to provide, indeed to have always provided, since its beginnings in the self-serving writings of the mercantilists in the seventeenth and eighteenth centuries, not only justifications for such an unequal capitalist world but also strategies and tactics for creating and managing it.[6] What it lacked, in the 1960s when I was studying the subject in school, were any direct ways of grasping the struggles *against* that world—the struggles in which I, and millions of others, were engaged. Eventually some economists would try to adapt game theory, operations research, thermodynamics, and chaos theory to handle the contestation that repeatedly frustrated the strategies implied by their elegant, theoretical models, but never with much success. Even before I completed my PhD, I decided that economics was very much part of the problem and not part of the solution.

---

[6]   Accepting capitalism, as economists do, has not prevented many from seeing its shortcomings and seeking in both their theories and policy recommendations to find ways to ameliorate them. Perhaps most obvious have been many economists' efforts to find ways to reduce the dramatic inequalities in income and wealth characteristic of capitalism as it spread across the world. In the Global North, while some economists—most notoriously the Reverend Thomas Malthus (1766–1834) and his followers—have argued against any effort to help "the poor," many other economists have been preoccupied with solving "the problem" of poverty. With regard to the Global South, certainly a great many of those who have specialized in "development economics" have also been sincerely concerned with reducing poverty. That the implementation of the policies they have suggested have often merely made things worse doesn't necessarily mean that was their intention. The road to other people's Hell has often been paved with economists' good intentions.

Casting about for alternative approaches, I wound up studying first Hegel, then Marx, both of whom provided critical analyses of what economists call the classical political economy of the
eighteenth and nineteenth centuries. My interest in Hegel was ac-
cidental. While spending an undergraduate year in France, curios-
ity drew me into a course on his *Phenomenology of Spirit* (1807) at
the Université de Montpellier. There I discovered his analysis of the
master-slave relationship.[7] Having already been involved in the civil
rights movement against the legacy of slavery, that analysis was immediately appealing. But because those relationships of master and
slave, so powerfully analyzed by Hegel, had long since, for the most
part, become those of capitalists and workers, I soon turned to Marx.
In retrospect, that turn seems inevitable. Because he dedicated his
life and work to overthrowing capitalism, his analysis was far more
detailed and informative about struggles that subverted and threatened to transcend that world. Yet I did not completely abandon Hegel. In trying to understand Marx's exposition of his labor theory of
value in the early chapters of the first volume of *Capital*, I discovered
how he had also drawn on Hegel's two *Logics* and his *Philosophy of
Right* (1821); studying those works helped me understand Marx.[8] In

---

7   My introduction to Hegel was in French, and I still refer first to Jean Hyppolite's two-volume translation *Phénoménologie de L'Esprit* (Paris: Editions Montaigne, 1947) before checking the English translation by A. V. Miller (New York:
Oxford University Press, 1977).

8   Written after the *Phenomenology*, his "two *Logics*" are sometimes referred to
as "Greater" and "Lesser." The "Greater" is his primary, massive *Wissenschaft der
Logik*, or *The Science of Logic*, published in three parts in 1812, 1813, 1816, and
later revised and expanded in 1831. I use the W. H. Johnston and L. G. Struthers
two-volume, English translation published in 1929 (New York: Macmillan). There
are also more recent translations by A. V. Miller (New York: Humanities Press,
1969) and George di Giovanni (Cambridge: Cambridge University Press, 2010).
The "Lesser" is his much shorter version, written for students: *Enzyklopädie der
philosophischen Wissenschaften*, or *Encyclopedia of the Philosophical Sciences*, part
1, *On Logic*, published in 1817, with a second edition in 1827 and a third in 1830. I
have used the English translation by William Wallace: *Hegel's Logic* (Oxford: Clarendon Press, 1975). The *Encyclopedia* version contains brief synopses of his main
arguments followed by explanatory commentary. As for his *Grundlinien der Philosophie des Rechts* (1821), or, *Philosophy of Right*, I have used T. M. Knox's translation

the process, I discovered how both of these authors grasped, in their different ways, the dialectics of class struggle, including the tendencies of capital to mediation, infinite expansion, and totalization.[9]

As a result of these studies, I came to read Hegel's analysis— and that produced by some Marxists under the rubric of dialectical materialism—as a sometimes perceptive analysis of the dialectical character of capitalist development but formulated as a quasi- science fiction cosmology that celebrated those tendencies as elements of an endless, omnipresent dialectic. Opposed to this, I found in Marx not only an analysis of capital's efforts to endlessly impose *its* dialectic but also, more importantly, an analysis of struggles that repeatedly ruptured, subverted, and sometimes looked beyond it, striving to create post-capitalist futures in the present. Therefore, although studying Hegel's detailed philosophical disquisitions on various moments of his dialectic could sometimes help to parse Marx's analysis, in the end I found that the latter illuminated the former by revealing it as one of the more optimistic moments of bourgeois thought—optimistic in its belief that all ruptures could, and would, be internalized through dialectical processes.

The first fruit of those studies was a set of notes, written in the summer of 1975 and eventually reworked and published as a book, *Reading* Capital *Politically* (1979). There I offered a new interpretation of Marx's labor theory of value. That interpretation argued that he constructed his theory as a weapon that helps us perceive

(Oxford: Clarendon Press, 1952) and the revised and edited version by Stephen Houlgate (Oxford: Oxford University Press, 2008).

9   Here and elsewhere in this essay I use the term "capital"—unless otherwise indicated—as a personification of capitalism or to mean the capitalist class as a whole. Some dislike this use because they feel that it glosses over internal divisions within the capitalist class. However, although such divisions are always present, it is nevertheless true that in most periods it is possible to discern the general thrust of capitalist strategy, policy, and actions—even if some capitalists disagree, would prefer different policies, and are pursuing alternative lines of conduct. On the other hand, a detailed study of any particular historical moment does require identifying various factions and contradictions within the capitalist class. As examples of these two different modes of analysis, compare and contrast Marx's treatment of the class struggle over the length of the working day in chapter 10 of the first volume of *Capital* with his much more detailed studies of the 1848 revolutions in France, *Class Struggles in France* (1850).

how the fundamental organizing method of the capitalist social order in which we find ourselves exploited and alienated is the endless imposition of work. This perspective has led me to characterize his labor theory of value as a theory of the value of labor to capital—that is, the value of labor in providing the fundamental means of social organization and control—a theory of the capitalist project of reducing the world to a global work machine. Integral to this interpretation is the centrality of the struggle against work as the most fundamental threat to that machine—a threat with the demonstrated power to throw it into crisis, opening the way for its abolition and replacement by alternative ways of being with which we are already experimenting. In the thirty-odd years since that book was published, I have been refining the interpretation and using it to decode both capitalist policies and struggles against them that have repeatedly plunged the system into crisis.

Therefore, I crafted my participation in the Warsaw conference ("Hegel, Marx and Global Crisis") with two purposes: to present my interpretation of Marx's theory and to illustrate its usefulness for analyzing one aspect of the "global crisis." The first two parts of this book reflect those two purposes. The first part sketches how the most recent crisis has been only the latest in a long series. It also argues that each crisis in that series has been the product of our struggles. Finally, it argues, in considerable detail, how my reading of Marx's labor theory of value can be useful in understanding those struggles and the resulting crises. The second part applies that reading to decoding neoliberal financialization as a response to our struggles and illustrates how that response continues to be resisted. For this book-length expansion of my original essay, I have added a third part that discusses the implications of the foregoing analysis for present and future struggle. Originally written in the fall of 2012, much of the text that follows was composed amid growing resistance throughout Europe to state- and bank-imposed austerity—that is to say drastic cutbacks in government spending and social services that were (and are) dramatically reducing standards of living. Although the "hot spots" receiving the most attention at the time lay along the shores of the Mediterranean, I found resistance in all the countries I visited during that trip.

INTRODUCTION

Mass protests in Portugal in 2012 against the latest austerity measures seemed to be writing the opening paragraphs of a new chapter in the unfolding Eurozone debt crisis. After putting up with earlier attacks on their standard of living, growing numbers of Portuguese citizens took to the streets—following the lead of Spanish and Greek protesters—revolting against government policies (reduced spending and increased taxes) that were causing depression, increased unemployment, and lower standards of living. As a result, many other Europeans began to ask themselves why such vicious measures continued to be imposed by the European Central Bank (ECB) and the International Monetary Fund (IMF) with the backing of political leaders. Those of us who live in the United States must ask similar questions of government policy makers at home about their response to the depression brought on by the global financial crisis after 2008. Why, for instance, did the US government bail out the very financial institutions whose speculations and fraud brought on the crisis—while doing little for the millions who have suffered the consequences? By the fall of 2014, continuing depression and the threat of spreading revolt by angry citizens all across Europe had frightened governing elites to begin to push back, at least rhetorically, against ECB demands for continuing austerity.

Leading that pushback was the French government. Under attack from within his own Socialist Party as well as from the right-wing, populist National Front, President François Hollande proposed a new budget based, he announced, on the rejection of austerity. But the attacks continued; the new budget still contained huge cuts in health care, family subsidies, and government jobs, while giving tax breaks to business and making it easier to fire workers—the very stuff of austerity! Hollande's rhetoric was soon followed in the winter of 2015 by that of Alexis Tsipras, newly elected president of Greece, and Yanis Varoufakis, his newly appointed minister of finance and self-styled "erratic Marxist."[1] Riding the wave of popular support from angry, exhausted Greeks who voted

---

1 Yanis Varoufakis, "How I Became an Erratic Marxist," *Guardian*, February 18, 2015.

the SYRIZA Party into power, both men announced that the new government rejected the continuation of austerity desired by Greek creditors and promised to reverse many previously imposed austerity measures.[2] Since coming to power, however, they have made concession after concession to the demands of European creditor banks and governments. Despite the results of a referendum that gave overwhelming support for the rejection of the austerity demanded by the ECB and the IMF for a rollover of Greek debt, Tsipras and the majority of SYRIZA members of parliament caved in, and Varoufakis resigned in protest. To what degree any of SYRIZA's promises to the Greek electorate will be fulfilled remains to be seen.

The severity of such austerity measures has varied, of course, from country to country. Policy makers have sought to convince those less severely affected that those being more harshly punished have deserved it. This has been the approach, for example, of the Angela Merkel government in Germany that has worked consistently to convince Germans—themselves facing limits on efforts to improve their standard of living—that the profligate Greeks, Spanish, and Portuguese have only been getting what they deserve for trying to live extravagantly beyond their means. Certainly, this is also the way policy makers in the United States have portrayed the situation, not only in Europe but also at home, especially those who continue to call for more extreme austerity measures at both state and federal levels—despite the spread of protest that followed the Occupy Wall Street movement.[3]

---

2   SYRIZA is an acronym for Synaspismós Rizospastikís Aristerá, itself a rendering of Συνασ℗ισμός Ριζοσ℗αστικής Αριστεράς, which translates as Coalition of the Radical Left.

3   Capitalist demands for the imposition of austerity throughout the United States long predated the recent financial crisis. Perhaps most notorious were those by Peter G. Petersen put forward in the midst of a previous financial crisis, that of 1987. See Peterson, "The Morning After," *Atlantic*, October 1987, 43–65. In Peterson's essay and a Keynesian counterattack by Jeff Faux you can find virtually every element in current debates between liberals and conservatives over debt and austerity. See Jeff Faux, "The Austerity Trap and the Growth Alternative," *World Policy Review* 5, no. 3, Summer 1988, 387–413. Peterson followed this with a book-length version of his argument, *Facing Up: How to Rescue the Economy from Crushing Debt and Restore the American Dream* (New York: Simon & Schuster, 1993).

Three Theses on Financial Crises

Each particular, local situation certainly deserves detailed historical analysis to reveal the dynamics of these unfolding dramas.
However, I think the last forty years have provided us with more
than enough experience to reveal some general characteristics of
the nature and sources of such debt crises and of the punishing
policies that have generally been adopted to deal with them. About
this history, I propose three theses.

THESIS #1: What most people think of as the current global crisis, commonly dated from the onset of financial crisis in
2007, is only the latest phase of a much longer and more
general *global crisis of capitalist command* that has been
going on for over forty years and has involved *a whole series of financial crises.*

THESIS #2: That longer, general crisis has been brought about
by a panoply of struggles that have ruptured the fundamental substance and sinew of capitalist society: its subordination of peoples' lives to work (or labor). The depth
of the crisis—for capital—is the reason for the brutality of
its responses, responses that have included, but have by no
means been limited to, the imposition of austerity.

THESIS #3: Marx's labor theory of value, by providing a theory of
the value of labor to capital, continues to provide insights
into what it means to subordinate life to work and the roles
money, finance, and debt play in that subordination. It also
reveals the *possibilities of rupture* in both those roles and
in subordination itself. Moreover, the struggles that have
generated the current global crisis—and have repeatedly
thwarted capitalist counterattacks—have also sometimes
crafted alternative ways of being in which work ceases to be
a vehicle of social control and becomes one of many modes
of human self-realization, both individual and collective.

Although I elaborate briefly on the first and second theses, part I
of this book deals primarily with Marx's labor theory of value. Part

II deploys that theory in an analysis of money, finance, and financialization. Part III also draws upon that theory to begin to answer the recurring question "What is to be done?"

Thesis #1: What most people think of as the current global crisis, commonly dated from the onset of financial crisis in 2007, is only the latest phase of a much longer and more general global crisis of capitalist command that has been going on for over forty years and has involved a whole series of financial crises.

This understanding or interpretation of that global crisis was formulated in the early 1970s on both sides of the Atlantic—among the Italian theorists of workers' autonomy and kindred spirits in England, France, and North America—and elaborated in a large number of articles and books. The preface and introduction to the second edition of my book *Reading* Capital *Politically* (2000) provide brief overviews of this interpretation and the theories on which it is based. Here I want to make just two points.

First, this understanding differs from most traditional Marxist theories of crisis. Some have explained the causes of the tumultuous events of the last forty years with such theories as the tendency of the rate of profit to fall, chronic under-consumption, over-accumulation, disproportionality, or the inherent tendency of monopoly (or oligopolistic) capital to run out of profitable investment outlets. Others of us have argued that the varieties of evidence usually provided in support of such theories have been, instead, by-products of a cycle of working-class struggle in the late 1960s and early 1970s that ruptured capitalist modes of managing the economy and the society more generally. In that period profits did fall but as a result of workers pushing up wages and benefits while also undermining the growth of productivity through various methods of refusing work—both on the job and off. Such struggles—varying in intensity and effectiveness across time and space—also repeatedly disrupted the proportionalities that multinational capital sought to manage across different sectors of society. Such ruptures certainly reduced the number of profitable investment outlets. But all these phenomena, I argue, are better understood as the result of struggles that effectively ruptured the dynamics and institutions of capitalist control characteristic of the Keynesian or Fordist era.[4] Ever since then, despite eventual success in hammering down wages and imposing deep hardship on millions of people, capitalist efforts have failed to restore control adequate to reestablish a stable new regime of accumulation. As a result, the underlying crisis has continued.

Second, understanding recent financial crisis and subsequent depression requires grasping them as only the latest in four decades of financial, debt, and monetary crises. Here is a brief list of the crises of those decades, which is by no means exhaustive. A growing international monetary crisis of the late 1960s led in 1971 to the abandonment of the Bretton Woods system of fixed exchange rates and the replacement of fixed by flexible exchange rates among major currencies. A fiscal crisis in New York City of the mid-1970s led to the imposition of austerity—cutbacks in wages and social services. Repeated "dirty floats" and crises in the flexible exchange rate system drove European policy makers to search for stability through a return to at least locally fixed rates.[5] Accelerating inflation in the 1970s led the IMF to declare it the biggest problem of the global economy. By the end of that decade, inflation rose to the point of producing negative real interest rates, undermining bank profits.[6] A

---

4   "Keynesian era" because the ideas of the British economist John Maynard Keynes dominated macroeconomic thinking and policy making in this period. "Fordist era" because Henry Ford's practices of assembly-line mass production and paying relatively high wages became the archetypical mode of manufacturing and social management in this period.

5   In principle, flexible or floating exchange rates are supposed to change only in response to spontaneous changes in supply and demand. The system came to be called "dirty" because of repeated central bank interventions—often coordinated among several such banks—to buy or sell currencies, with the explicit goal of manipulating the supply or demand for particular currencies and thus exchange rates.

6   Negative real interest rates occurred in that period when inflation outstripped interest rates. With zero inflation, money loaned at 5 percent interest will earn lenders 5 percent more money and 5 percent more buying power. With inflation at 5 percent, money loaned at 5 percent will generate 5 percent more money, but the buying power of that money (principal plus interest earned) will remain the same. With any increase in inflation *above* 5 percent, the buying power of money loaned at 5 percent will *decrease*. In the period in question, banks were prohibited by anti-usury regulations from raising their interest rates faster than inflation to

sudden tightening of US monetary policy, aimed at stemming global inflation, triggered a global depression in the early 1980s. That tightening also produced an international debt crisis that began in 1982 when Mexico effectively defaulted on its international debts. In 1987, the US stock market and the US savings and loan industry collapsed. Efforts by European policy makers to stabilize exchange rates through a new European Exchange Rate Mechanism (ERM) was thrown into crisis in 1992. Flexible exchange rates and the imposition of open capital markets by the IMF resulted in a whole series of currency and financial crises, including the Mexican peso crisis of 1994, the Asia crisis of 1997, and the Russian financial crisis of 1998. Efforts to implement a European monetary union—to finally achieve monetary stability through a common currency—saw repeated failure in the late 1990s. Financial crises continued to haunt the capitalist world as the new century began—for example, the Turkish financial crisis in 2000 and the 2001–2002 financial crisis in Argentina.[7] Such was the history leading up to the most recent global crisis of 2007–2008 whose effects still plague the world.

Thesis #2: That longer, general global crisis has been brought about by a panoply of struggles that have ruptured the fundamental substance and sinew of capitalist society: its subordination of peoples' lives to work. The depth of the crisis—for capital—is the reason for the brutality of its responses, responses that have included, but have by no means been limited to, the imposition of austerity.

As will become obvious, I use the terms "work" and "labor" interchangeably. In this I differ from some—for example, Friedrich Engels (1820–95) and Hannah Arendt (1906-75)—who distinguished sharply between the two. In Engels's case, in a footnote to chapter 1 of the first volume of *Capital*, in the fourth German edition, he wrote, "The English language has the advantage of possessing two separate words for these two different aspects of labor. Labor which creates use-values and is qualitatively determined is called 'work'

---

keep them positive. The removal of such prohibitions was among the first steps in deregulating the financial sector in the early 1980s.

7   This list is adapted from the preface to the German edition of *Reading* Capital *Politically* (»*Das Kapital« Politisch Lesen: Eine alternative Interpretation des Marxschen Hauptwerks* [2012]).

as opposed to 'labor'; labor which creates value and is only measured quantitatively is called 'labor' as opposed to 'work.'"[8] Arendt, in her book *The Human Condition* (1958) devotes two entire chapters to distinguishing between labor and work. Labor, she argues, is an inevitable and eternal part of "the human condition" and designates the activity of humans qua *animal laborans* who produce everything that is quickly consumed as part of "the ever-recurring cycle of biological life." There is, she says, a compulsory repetition in labor "where one must eat in order to labor and must labor in order to eat."[9] Work, on the other hand, she associates with more durable production that occurs when humans qua *homo faber* violently transform elements of nature (e.g., cutting down trees for lumber, quarrying and mining the earth for stone and minerals) in the process of fabricating the physical things and world that humans share and that give continuity to human society through time and generational changes.[10] The reasons why I reject both of these formulations will become apparent in what follows.

To begin with, I find Marx's definition of what he means by labor (or work) in *Capital*, volume 1, chapter 7, a satisfactory starting point. He defines it generically as human beings using tools to transform raw materials into new use-values, which in capitalism are generally commodities. While such activities have occurred throughout history, I have argued that he violated his own methodology by regrouping all historical instances of such activity under the singular rubric of labor (or work) independently of social context.[11] At the same time, I do think such regrouping appropriate within capitalism because—as I explain below—all of those various activities serve the same purpose within capitalism—social control. The struggle against work, therefore, strikes at the heart of capitalist command and has repeatedly thrown its control into crisis.

---

8   Karl Marx, *Capital*, vol. 1 (New York: Penguin, 1990), 138.

9   Hannah Arendt, *The Human Condition* (Chicago: The University of Chicago Press, 1958), 143.

10   Ibid., chapter 4, "Work."

11   H. Cleaver, "Work Is Still the Central Issue! New Words for New Worlds" (1999), in Ana Dinerstein and Michael Leary, eds., *The Labour Debate: An Investigation into the Theory and Reality of Capitalist Work* (Hampshire: Ashgate, 2002), 135–48.

The true depth of the overall crisis only became apparent with the repeated failure of policy measures aimed at restoring growth by undermining the struggles that created the crisis in the first place. Those measures—essentially counterattacks in an open class war—were undercut again and again by such fierce worker resistance as to cause recurrence, or continuation, of crisis throughout this period.

The 1971 abandonment of the Bretton Woods system of fixed exchange rates signaled the onset of crisis. Fixed rates depended upon the ability of Keynesian policies to keep wage growth in line with productivity increases. The failure of such policies in the late 1960s was manifest in accelerating inflation as business sought to protect profits by raising prices in the face of accelerating wage growth and diminished productivity.[12] The replacement of fixed rates with flexible rate adjustments would, policy makers hoped, shift their counterattacks from the relatively transparent realm of government monetary and fiscal policy to the more obscure world of foreign exchange rate markets. But changes occurring there, such as a rise in the value of a currency that undermined export industries by making their products more expensive, resulted in increased unemployment and popular resistance. Such resistance forced repeated central bank interventions to moderate both adjustments and their consequences. The resulting "dirty float" lurched from crisis to crisis.

The New York City fiscal crisis that emerged in the mid-1970s was the direct result of the successful struggles of both the waged (especially public employees) and the unwaged in that city. City workers were able to force up wages and benefits, including pensions, while the welfare rights movement achieved the highest payments in the country. Such gains undermined business control of the metropolis and led to a business exodus that reduced employment by over a half-million jobs and undercut the city's tax base—forcing the city to borrow more and more from the huge New York banking establishment. The counterattack began with

---

12 As struggles against work intensified, the growth in productivity at first slowed and then actually became negative, with productivity falling dramatically in some sectors (e.g., mining). See William Cleaver, "Wildcats in the Appalachian Coal Fields," *Zerowork*, no. 1 (1975), 113–26.

banks refusing to roll over the city's debt and continued with the imposition of cuts in city worker wages and benefits and reduced welfare and social services. These attacks on working-class income and living standards presaged the austerity policies that have characterized the capitalist response to "debt" crises ever since.[13]

More generally, the 1970s saw a whole series of counterattacks against the ability of workers to raise wages and benefits faster than productivity, thus provoking businesses to raise prices. Every effort to "fight inflation" hid an attack on the power of workers to raise wages and benefits. At first, capital sought to use inflation to undermine real wages. The US government engineered an increase in grain prices by combining a reduction in grain production with a secret 1972 deal allowing the Soviet Union to buy millions of tons. The public rationale was that rising grain export prices would help offset declining trade surpluses. That artificial increase in grain prices soon produced a rise in meat prices and other food prices that so enraged the US working class as to produce a dockworker refusal to load grain on Soviet ships and a widespread beef boycott.

A second use of inflation against wages was the acceptance by the US government of the quadrupling of oil prices in 1973–74 by the Organization of Petroleum Exporting Countries (OPEC). That sudden increase, ostensibly a response to Western support for Israel in its 1973 war with Arab states, was actually driven by two conflicting trends. The OPEC governments desperately needed greater income to cope with the rising demands of their own oil-producing proletariat, but, for more than a decade, ever higher import prices had been undermining the value of a barrel of crude oil. By accepting the price increases—and refusing to join European governments in organizing an importers' cartel—US policy makers not only supported OPEC but also sought to undermine real wages at home while giving business access to hundreds of billions in new petrodollars deposited by the oil-exporting countries in the international banking system. The US government also accepted the

---

13   For more detailed historical analysis of New York City fiscal crisis, see Donna Demac and Philip Mattera, "Developing and Underdeveloping New York: The 'Fiscal Crisis' and the Imposition of Austerity," *Zerowork*, no. 2 (1977), 113–39; Eric Lichten, *Class, Power and Austerity: The New York City Fiscal Crisis* (South Hadley, Mass.: Bergin & Garvey, 1986).

second great jump in oil prices at the end of the 1970s, triggered by the revolution against the US-installed shah in Iran, despite the danger of its spreading throughout the region and further heightening the needs of regional governments for more revenue to cope with discontent.

Unfortunately for US policy makers, both of these anti-wage policies failed. Workers proved to be well enough organized to continue to raise wages and benefits as fast as prices increased, thus preventing any substantial fall in average real wages.[14] The net result was a rapid acceleration in inflation that when combined with reduced business borrowing to cope with their ever-recalcitrant workers, produced negative real interest rates and a crisis for the financial sector.

In response, at the end of the 1970s and early 1980s, the Carter and Reagan administrations abandoned the previous policies in favor of their exact opposite: severe anti-inflation (anti-wage) contraction. This they achieved through legislative cooperation that deregulated constraints on interest rates, and Federal Reserve cooperation, led by Chairman Paul Volcker that tightened US monetary policy enough to produce positive and sharply increased real interest rates.

The deregulation of the banking industry—that began under Carter and continued under Reagan and subsequent regimes—allowed banks to divert money into speculative investments in ways that had previously been outlawed. By removing previous anti-usury caps on interest rates, deregulation also made it possible to earn higher and higher interest on loans. Such changes led directly to a financial boom both within the United States and internationally. Deregulation made speculation more profitable for private industry than engaging in real investment hiring troublesome workers. With hundreds of billions of OPEC petrodollars pouring into the international banking system, vast funds were available for speculation at home in the stock market and real

14   The fall in *average* real wages over the decade of the 1970s was only about .01 percent. Of course, that average hides big differences between those workers well enough organized to achieve wage and benefit increases that kept up with or exceeded inflation and those less well organized (e.g., older workers on fixed income or those on welfare).

estate and for foreign loans—even in the midst of ongoing crisis. Banks make no profit on deposited funds they do not loan out. The resulting speculative boom unfolded in all these markets; when it burst in 1987, the stock market collapsed and the US savings and loan (S&L) industry was crippled. Many S&L associations had speculated heavily in real estate and in some cases tried to survive using fraud and Ponzi schemes. Almost a third of those institutions failed. Despite a cleanup, costing taxpayers over $120 billion, within less than a decade half of the S&L's had closed.[15]

The dramatic increase in US interest rates quickly led to rate increases in all major financial centers. The sudden big increase in interest rates on international loans bludgeoned the world economy in two ways. First, debt service obligations—made up mostly of payments on interest charges—suddenly skyrocketed to impossible-to-pay levels, creating an international debt crisis. Second, the dramatically higher costs of borrowing money resulted in such drops in real investment, consumer spending, and trade as to plunge the world into depression. Although touted as a responsible attempt to stem global inflation, this dramatic shift in policy was actually a scorched-earth capitalist counterattack against the success of workers in defending real wages despite high unemployment and rising prices. Everywhere the plunge in economic activity resulted in production cutbacks, millions of waged workers laid off, soaring unemployment, and—finally—capitalist success in cutting wages, benefits, and social services. The refusal of work was finally met by the refusal to hire and falling wages. In such manner did capital seize the offensive.

The international debt crisis of the 1980s—known in Latin America as the "lost decade"—although triggered by high interest rates and consequently impossibly higher debt repayment obligations, was rooted in all those struggles that had driven local capitalists and governments to borrow hundreds of billions of petrodollars to finance both concessions and repression. Neoliberal policies of austerity and "structural adjustment" were imposed on debtors in countries such as Mexico by creditor banks under the aegis of the International Monetary Fund and World Bank as

---

15 See Timothy Curry and Lynn Shibut, "The Cost of the Savings and Loan Crisis," *FDIC Banking Review* 13, no. 2 (2000), 26–35.

conditions necessary for further loans. Thus were the conditions imposed on New York City spread abroad.

Those conditions mandated a whole series of local government attacks on previous concessions to workers. Debtor governments must end wage indexation—the tying of nominal wage increases to inflation to protect their real value. They must devalue their currency, raising import prices of consumer goods, thus undermining real wages. They must slash expenditures that sustain consumption—such as bread and cooking oil subsidies. They must sell off, or privatize, state enterprises—such as publicly owned utility companies, water systems, and even schools and prisons—that had cut deals conceding too much to workers. By passing control to the private sector, such deals could be broken—costing workers income and producing big profits for their new owners. Debtor governments must open local capital markets to foreign investors and remove obstacles to 100 percent foreign ownership. Like privatization, foreign takeovers permit canceling previous deals with workers, slashing wages, and increasing profits. Such openings to foreign investors have been rationalized as necessary to increase investment resources—which, of course, take advantage of the attacks on local labor and facilitate the integration and subordination of local conditions to the global plans of multinational corporations. Finally, the big banks and the IMF pressured local governments to continue to borrow huge sums of petrodollars to finance infrastructure development—roads, dams, hydroelectric projects—in support of expanded private investment. Unsurprisingly, workers actively and fiercely resisted all these attacks. As a result, there were repeated failures to implement the mandated changes, repeated crises, and repeated renegotiations among local governments, the banks, and the IMF.

The opening by hard-pressed local governments of capital markets to foreign investors—not only those taking over local businesses but also those speculating in local stocks, bonds, and currencies—laid the basis for the Mexican, Asian, and Russian crises of the 1990s. Any sudden surge in popular unrest could spark capital flight. For example, the Zapatista uprising on January 1, 1994, threw the stability of the Mexican peso into question. When President Carlos Salinas de Gortari left power in the fall of 1994 and the new government of Ernesto Zedillo revealed that the Mexican government's foreign currency reserves had all been used up in hidden support for the threatened peso, "hot money" fled the country and the value of the peso plummeted.

The repeated failures of European governments to meet the monetary and fiscal targets agreed upon in the Maastricht Treaty of 1992 as necessary for monetary union and the creation of a common currency were the direct result of widespread popular resistance to the required policy moves. Those moves included reducing inflation by tightening the growth of the money supply and reducing budget deficits by cutting spending and raising taxes. In practice, governments chose spending cuts and tax increases that reduced wages, benefits, and social services. Progress from informal exchange rate ties, through the more formal European Exchange Rate Mechanism to monetary union, was set back again and again by widespread grassroots opposition. Because of all this resistance, monetary union was only achieved in 1999 when national currencies ceased to exist and the euro became the common money. Since then, resistance to government attempts to impose or maintain the agreed-upon conditions have continued, repeatedly throwing the future of the Economic and Monetary Union into question.

Capitalist politicians, policy makers, and corporate media do their best to erase this history from our memories. Remembering it reveals how the recent protests in Greece, Spain, and Portugal against the imposition of austerity measures—aimed at reducing standards of living to the point where people will accept to work at dramatically lower wages with far fewer benefits—are nothing new. They are but recent episodes in an all too familiar drama we have witnessed and participated in for many years.

Thesis #3: Marx's labor theory of value, by providing a theory of the value of labor to capital, continues to provide insights into what it means to subordinate life to work and the roles money plays in that subordination. It also reveals the possibilities of rupture in both the roles of money and in subordination itself.

The elaboration that follows provides a theoretical defense and to some degree a historical defense of Marx's labor theory of value and its continuing relevance to our understanding of the current crisis and our thinking about strategies to be followed in dealing with it. This defense takes the form of a reinterpretation of that theory justified partly by logic and partly by appeals to experience.

Although in my first comment on Thesis #1 above I associate my-
self with others who have argued that the long crisis of the last forty
years has been caused and perpetuated by working-class struggle,
many of them do not share the interpretation that follows—as will
become clear in the exposition.

Even though the analysis in this essay draws upon the interpretation of the labor theory of value laid out in *Reading* Capital
Politically (*RCP*), here emphasis is on the relationship between
work and money in the class struggle. *RCP* dealt mostly with theory; here I both elaborate the theory and use it to analyze the mediation of class conflicts through money and to indicate possible
paths of struggle. Elaboration of the theory in Part I is offered in
four sections: first an overview of my interpretation of the labor
theory of value, set against the background and critiques of previous interpretations and of various arguments that have been put
forward for rejecting Marx's theory, then a detailed examination
of each aspect of Marx's analysis of value—its substance, its measure, and its form. This organization follows that of *RCP*, which
itself follows the structure of chapter 1 of volume 1 of *Capital*.
In three sections the path of analysis runs through the theory of
value to money, explaining how various aspects of the former illuminate the latter. I reverse this approach in Part II and analyze
the current capitalist use of money and finance against us. There
I use my interpretation of Marx's labor theory of value to decode—
in class terms—the usual economic concepts of finance, financial
crisis, and financialization. Then in Part III, in the light of the
previous two parts, I examine the possibilities of resistance and
escape. In other words, I draw on the theory and history to examine the implications of the class analysis for strategies and tactics
that we might use against the capitalist deployment of money and
finance against us.

PART I

On the Usefulness of Marx's Labor Theory of Value

Pretty much all economists and a surprising number of folks who call themselves Marxists have dismissed Marx's labor theory of value. The former are easy to understand, the latter less so. As a prelude to explaining why I think that theory is still of use in understanding capitalism and in figuring out what must be done to get beyond it, allow me to explain briefly some of the reasoning used by those who have set the theory aside. In what follows, I will treat economists and Marxists as separate sets of people—although I am well aware that a few economists understand Marx as a kindred, if misguided, spirit and that some Marxists call themselves "Marxist economists." Elsewhere I have argued that Marx was not an economist and that his analysis of capitalism was both methodologically and substantively diametrically opposed to economics.[1]

---

1   See Harry Cleaver, "Karl Marx: Economist or Revolutionary?," in Suzanne W. Helburn and David F. Bramhall, eds., *Marx, Schumpeter and Keynes* (Armonk, N.Y.: M.E. Sharpe, 1986).

WHY AND HOW ECONOMISTS GOT RID OF THE LABOR THEORY OF VALUE

For roughly a century, in the era of what historians of economic thought now call "classical political economy," a period dominated by the thought of Adam Smith (1723–1790) and David Ricardo (1772–1823), the labor theory of value provided the theoretical basis for economic reasoning and policy. Late in the nineteenth century, however, for a very concrete historical and political reason, economists got rid of that theory. To successfully carry out this abandonment, they had to offer both theoretical critiques of the theory and an alternative that could provide a new ground for thinking about and managing the economy.

The historical and political reason for the abandonment of the labor theory of value was the rise of the organizational power of the working class and the way workers were able to appropriate the theory for their own purposes.[1] During the period of rapid industrialization, the labor theory of value provided a theory of why the capitalist imposition of as much work on people as possible was the most effective way to augment the wealth of nations as well as a rationale for government policies supporting that approach to economic development. Thanks in large part to the work of Karl Marx and other critics of capitalism, however, workers not only came to understand the theory but realized that by its own logic they, and not their employers, should be the owners of their products. If the source of value is labor and they have done all the work—both in the present and in the past, creating machines and raw materials—then all the value produced by their work should rightly come to them. Such reasoning delegitimized the appropriation of value by industrial capitalists in the form of profits, by landlords in the form of rent, and by financial institutions in the form of interest. From a guide to capitalist industrial policy, they converted the labor theory of value into a justification for the expropriation of the expropriators.

---

1 A rare but insightful analysis of this abandonment can be found in Cheeyaka-puvanda Cariappa's PhD dissertation, "The Unruly Masses in the Development of Economic Thought," University of Texas at Austin, August 2003.

Without a doubt, the most thoroughly developed and influential formulation of the labor theory of value that provided support for such conclusions was that of Karl Marx. He pointed out how the previous versions—those of the classical political economists—had served capitalist purposes by guiding and justifying the expropriation of people from independent means of life and their exploitation as workers. The result, he argued, was a capitalist society riven by antagonism. People resisted their expropriation, their exploitation, and the alienation that resulted from the imposition of capitalist-controlled work. Moreover, pointing to the growing ability of workers to organize and fight against the ills inflicted upon them by capitalists, he concluded that they had the potential to overthrow capitalist control and build a new society free of exploitation and alienation. Faced with this *détournement* of their theory, economists abandoned it in favor of a new theory—a theory of value based not on labor but on utility.

Because economists have always developed their theories to facilitate the promulgation of capitalism and solve its problems, the abandonment of the labor theory of value had to be justified and a practical alternative had to be developed to replace it. The justification was twofold. First, they argued that the labor theory of value had certain deficiencies. Second, they also argued that their alternative theory of value based on utility could overcome those deficiencies and provide tools better suited to capitalist purposes. A major deficiency of the labor theory of value, they emphasized repeatedly, was its inability to determine relative prices—something capitalists needed for their calculations of costs and revenues, calculations essential to their goal of maximizing profit. This, they argued, was true both in the case of the classical political economists' formulations and in the case of Karl Marx's version of the theory. Although adherents to the labor theory admitted that actual prices rarely equaled the labor values of commodities, they tended to argue that market prices fluctuated around those values. In discussing real world prices, however, Marx utilized the notions of supply and demand common among political economists of the time.[2] Although some followers of Marx have argued that this rec-

---

2   Concepts of supply and demand functions, such as those discussed below, had yet to be formulated in the late eighteenth and early nineteenth centuries. So

ognized discrepancy between value and price was solved by him in the materials Engels assembled as volume 3 of *Capital*, economists rejected the solution. They rejected not just his supposed solution but also the very need for a solution. Their alternative theory discarded the idea that the value of commodities was determined objectively by one of the inputs into their production, labor, and posited instead that it only made sense to speak of the value of commodities in two distinct senses. In the first sense, they argued, the value of things is their value to those who consume them, and that value is determined subjectively and uniquely for each individual according to varying tastes and circumstances. The second, and ultimately for economists the most important sense, was the "market value" or the price of commodities measured by money.

During the first decades in which they were formulating this alternative theory, economists also argued that those unique values could be conceived in terms of the utility (U) that consumers derived from them. Consumers, acting solely with regard to individual preferences, were posited as having mathematically specified "utility functions" in which the amount of utility gained from consuming a variety of goods was determined by the amount of each good (q_i) consumed: $U = f(q_1, q_2, \ldots q_n)$. This function, coupled with consumers' disposable income, along with a number of narrow mathematical assumptions, made it possible to derive functions specifying each individual's demand for each good as a function of its price, $d_i = f(p_i)$. The quantities demanded by all consumers, at each price, were then added up to obtain *aggregate* demand functions for each good, $D = f(p)$.

Such demand functions, they argued, could be complemented with similar supply functions. Assuming capitalists would always act to maximize profits, supply functions, $S = f(p)$, were obtained by combining a "production function," available costs of inputs, and the amount of money available for investment. The coup

---

political economists thought of supply and demand more simply in terms of goods being supplied to and demanded in markets. In the same manner, Marx recognized that some goods, such as unworked land being bought and sold, could have a market price even though no labor had been incorporated into it. More generally, he recognized how fluctuations in supply and demand could alter market prices quite independently of the amount of labor incorporated into commodities.

de grace for the labor theory of value was the reduction of labor from its privileged position as the unique source of value to one "input" among others in those production functions. In the production function **Q** = **f(L, K, N)**, the output of each commodity **Q** is a function of inputs labor (**L**), capital (**K**) and others (**N**), with the function representing the feasible combinations of **L**, **K**, and **N** as determined by some specific technology. By combining demand functions and supply functions, they obtained the market value of goods—their price—with no recourse to labor value.[3]

Parallel reasoning permitted the calculation of supply and demand functions for each input (e.g., labor) and thus *their* market prices (e.g., the wage). As with the demand for consumer goods, the supply of labor would be the result of the preferences of each worker with regard to trading off desired leisure time for available wages. (The higher the wage, it was generally believed, the more leisure time workers would be willing to give up.)[4] The demand for labor, as with other inputs, would be determined by its productivity (given existing technology as represented in the production function) and its cost (wage level). (The higher the wage, the fewer workers would be hired.) As with final goods, the supply and demand for labor could be aggregated and combined to determine the market wage. Thus, in neoclassical microeconomics, labor appears as a one-dimensional, purely quantitative variable inside production functions and inside the functions representing the supply of labor and the demand for it.

In other words, their alternative theory provided what they

---

3   This theory of production also led to the conclusion that workers' wages could rise with the marginal productivity of labor and thus share in the fruits of rising productivity without undermining profits. When Alfred Marshall and his wife Mary Paley pointed this out in 1879, it appeared heretical in a nineteenth century where both economists and businessmen had long seen any rise in wages above subsistence as a threat to profits. The new understanding, however, did become a key element of Fordism and the Keynesian productivity deals of the twentieth century. See Alfred and Mary Paley Marshall, *The Economics of Industry* (London: Macmillan, 1879), chapter 11 (on wages).

4   Eventually, empirical evidence revealed that this is not necessarily true. As wages rise, there comes a point where more leisure is desired to be able to actually enjoy higher income.

needed to help capitalists understand and manage the economy. So the labor theory of value could be comfortably set aside as a historically understandable but outmoded approach. Eighteenth- and nineteenth-century political economy was renamed "classical economics," and the new utility-based theory was dubbed "neo-classical economics"—or, more pretentiously in French, *la science économique*.[5]

Along the way, all other aspects of labor—many of which were central to both Adam Smith's and Karl Marx's analyses of capital-ism—were shunted out of economics and left to sociologists, psy-chologists, and industrial engineers. Those other social scientists would, for the most part, follow economists in placing their skills at the disposal of capitalists to help them identify, understand, and manage workers' discontent and struggles.[6]

---

5   Fairly quickly, as they had done with respect to the labor theory of value, workers discovered a political vulnerability in utility theory that led to its abandonment by economists. Integral to the new utility theory of value was the notion of "declining marginal utility," the idea that the utility one obtains from the consumption of any good declines as you consume more of it. But if, as utility theorists often claimed, the object of economic policy should be the maximization of the utility of society as a whole, then, workers argued, the theory supported the redistribution of income and wealth from the rich to the poor. Workers said, "If there's declining marginal utility, then we should take some dollars from the rich who have lots of them and give them to the poor who have few—because the increased utility of the latter will outweigh the reduced utility of the former and that of society will increase!" Needless to say, that argument didn't sit well with pro-capitalist economists, so they got rid of utility. They replaced utility with individual choice based on one's "preferences." Henceforth it has been impossible in their theories to make the kinds of claims workers had made based on utility. John Hicks explained and justified this key theoretical shift in the first chapter of his book *Value and Capital* published in 1939. Note well: despite this dismissal, utility still appears in various formulations of neoclassical microeconomics because of the practical usefulness of the mathematics involved.

6   Industrial engineers were created as a separate profession by stripping most skilled workers of their ability to exercise their creativity in the creation and han-dling of their tools and handing those roles over to that new class of worker. Socio-logy and psychology evolved subfields—the sociology and psychology of work—where specialists have studied such things as worker alienation and tried to figure out how to minimize worker disaffection and resultant disruption of production.

An exception to this narrowness was the work of Joseph
Schumpeter (1883–1950), a close reader of Marx, who placed the
"entrepreneur" at the center of his theories of economic development.[7] Entrepreneurs, he argued, were those who innovated, who
discovered new ways of doing things and in their implementation
brought about far-reaching changes. Although those who paid
homage to his ideas tended to think of entrepreneurs mainly in
terms of manager-capitalists such as Henry Ford, innovation is a
quality of labor—a quality ignored in the production functions of
neoclassical economics. Where entrepreneurs have emerged from
laboratories or garages, as in the case of Steve Jobs (1955–2011)
this has been obvious.

Eventually, in the years following World War II, the poverty
of neoclassical economists' theoretical treatment of labor—which
for the most part trailed behind New Deal programs to generalize
Fordist changes in the organization of both labor and its reproduction—became clear even to them.[8] Efforts to understand growth
in that period led to a recognition that most of it could only be
accounted for by improvements in the *quality* of labor (and capital) rather than their quantity.[9] That recognition suggested the

---

7   Joseph Schumpeter, *The Theory of Economic Development* (1912) and *Capitalism, Socialism and Democracy* (1942).

8   So-called institutionalist economists, less wedded to the neoclassical preoccupation with markets, also played important roles in the formulation and implementation of New Deal policies. On the role of institutional economists in the New
Deal, see the writings of Rex Tugwell, a member of Roosevelt's "Brain Trust," and
more generally William Barber, *Designs within Disorder: Franklin D. Roosevelt, the
Economists, and the Shaping of American Economic Policy, 1933–1945* (New York:
Cambridge University Press, 1996).

9   One key moment in this shift was the publication by Robert Solow of his "Technical Change and the Aggregate Production Function," *Review of Economics and
Statistics* 39, no. 3 (August 1957), 312–20. Solow's innovation in the formulation of
production functions explicitly included "technological change," and the application
of his new formulations to the US economy showed that some seven-eighths of the
increase in output per worker over a forty-year period was attributable to technological change—as opposed to mere increases in the quantities of capital and labor—change that could be embodied either in the improvement of capital or in that
of labor. Work by economists Theodore Schultz and Gary Becker, among others,

usefulness of investments in improving the quality of labor (e.g., through increased spending on education and welfare). This new concern was geared to improving its productivity—an improvement necessary to pay for concessions to the demands of workers. Neoclassical economists thus recognized a new dimension to labor, even as they continued to view labor as only one input among other factors of production. More recently, beginning in the 1980s, neo-Schumpeterians generalized Joseph Schumpeter's insights into the importance of innovation by pointing out how the ability to innovate was distributed far more widely than he had recognized. This recognition paralleled changes in managerial practices designed to solicit innovations from all kinds of workers.[10]

focused on improving the quality of labor. For example, Theodore W. Schultz, "Investment in Human Capital," *American Economic Review* 51, no. 1 (March 1961), 1–17; Gary S. Becker, *Human Capital: A Theoretical and Empirical Analysis, with Special Reference to Education* (National Bureau of Economic Research, 1964).

10   See Horst Hanusch and Andreas Pyka, eds., *Elgar Companion to Neo-Schumpeterian Economics* (Northampton, Mass.: Edward Elgar, 2007).

WHY AND HOW SOME MARXISTS ABANDONED THE LABOR THEORY OF VALUE

We can divide Marxists, as with the followers of some religions, into two nebulous sets: those who adhere to some more or less well-defined orthodoxy regardless of the changes they perceive in the world around them and those who respond to changing circumstances by modifying their theory and practice in light of the changes. In a few cases, those Marxists who have felt compelled to modify their theory have done so by abandoning the labor theory of value. Given the centrality of the theory to Marx's analysis of capitalism, such abandonment raises the issue of the degree to which those who have done so remain Marxists. Because Marxism has always involved both theory and political practice, changes in theory have often been closely interwoven with changes in Marxists' political practices.

Some Background

With Marxism, as in the case of Christianity, orthodoxy has been largely defined by the groups with the greatest organizational and political clout.[1] In the twentieth century, the success of the Bolsheviks in seizing power during the Russian Revolution not only allowed them to take over the czarist empire but to establish their Leninist interpretation of Marx as the dominant orthodoxy among Marxists. That orthodoxy had both a theoretical and organizational component. A key element of the theoretical component was adherence to the labor theory of value in analyzing capitalism.[2] Key aspects of the organizational component were adherence to the "democratic centralism" of the Communist Party and commitment to the taking of state power—through violent

---

1   Which is to say, regardless of how much they actually modify their doctrine and practices, they continue to set it forward as the true dogma and sometimes label it as such (e.g., the [Eastern] Orthodox Catholic Church).

2   That said, it is also true that the manner in which the theory was interpreted changed over time, as did the official position on the circumstances in which it was relevant.

revolution if necessary.[3] With the power and wealth of the Soviet state financing the Marx-Engels Institute (later the Marx-Engels-Lenin Institute) and its publication of Karl Marx and Frederick Engels's *Collected Works*, Lenin's *Complete Collected Works*, and eventually *Stalin's Works*, Soviet-style Marxism-Leninism was spread throughout the world, in many languages. Despite dramatic internal changes—Lenin dying in 1924 and Joseph Stalin (1878–1953) seizing power and exiling Leon Trotsky (1879–1940) in 1929—Marxism-Leninism survived, albeit divided into two camps: that of the Soviet-dominated Third, or Communist, International and the Trotskyist (but still Marxist-Leninist) Fourth International.[4] Eventually the evolution of events in China led to the emergence of a third camp: that of Maoism. Marxist-Leninists of all stripes asserted the core characteristic of orthodoxy as adherence to Lenin's interpretation of Marx and his concept of the revolutionary party, while denouncing all other Marxists as heretics.

Those heretics who continued to draw upon Marx for inspiration but rejected both orthodox interpretations of Marx's theory and democratic centralism included at least four more or less distinct groupings. First were the social democrats who had opposed the Bolsheviks during the Second International (1898–1914). Second were the council communists who refused to fall in line in the wake of World War I and the aborted German Revolution of 1918–1919. Third were the so-called Western Marxists who sought to extend Marx's analysis of capitalist domination in the sphere of production to its methods in the sphere of culture. Fourth were those Marxists willing to draw upon innovations in economic theory to analyze what they saw as important changes in the structure of capitalism.

---

3   Here again, the position taken by the Central Committee of the Communist Party of the Soviet Union depended on its own interests at the time. In many instances, for example, local communist parties aligned with Moscow were ordered to play a social democratic rather than a revolutionary role. The way they at times were forced to flip-flop according to Moscow's needs often undermined their local credibility. It also provided support for those who branded all groups fighting against capitalist control agents of an "international communist conspiracy."

4   The Trotskyist movement subsequently split many times but adhered, at least at first, to Trotsky's version of Marxism-Leninism.

Social democrats have defined themselves less in terms of theory and more in terms of their dedication to realizing the hopes of the Second International that the transcendence of capitalism could be achieved peaceably via the formation of socialist political parties supported by an ever larger number of working-class voters. Such parties compete for the power to shape social policy through electoral politics, with the stated aim of replacing capitalism with a better set of socialist institutions. Within such parties, such theoretical preoccupations as the validity of the labor theory of value largely gave way to practical worries over winning elections. In the process, both strategists and candidates have largely argued against their pro-capitalist opponents and in favor of policies favoring the working class using economic rather than Marxian categories. Such socialist parties organized themselves in 1923 into a Labor and Socialist International and later, in 1940, into the Socialist International, in opposition to both the Third and Fourth Internationals.[5] Over time, capitalist success at structuring an ever-widening wage and income hierarchy, fractured by race, gender, and ethnicity—often interpreted as the rise of the middle class—undermined working-class cohesion and reduced the goals of both socialist and many communist parties to marginal reforms. Today the aspirations of most socialist and communist parties fall within the framework of capitalism and, in principle if not always in practice, support policies that amount to capitalism with a human face—a capitalism of more or less full employment, of social security against structural changes, of reduced poverty, and of greater protection for the environment.

Those who became "council communists" did so largely because of how impressed they were by two historical moments of working-class struggle: the autonomous formation of *soviets* by workers during the Russian Revolution and the formation of *workers' councils* during the revolts in Germany following World War I. These experiences, they argued, showed that workers did not need to be led by a Marxist-Leninist party but had the ability to set their own agenda and organize to enact it. Lenin, of course, attacked this heresy, most notably in his *"Left-Wing" Communism: An Infantile Disorder*

---

5   As of 2015, the Socialist International claims full member parties in over eighty countries around the world—around half of which are either governing or part of a governing coalition.

(1920). Despite being denounced by Moscow, Marxists such as Herman Gorter (1864–1927), Anton Pannekoek (1873–1960), Otto Rühle (1874–1943), and Paul Mattick (1904–1981) produced a sizable literature arguing for bottom-up revolutionary politics against democratic centralism. They also supported their politics by elaborating various aspects of Marxist theory, especially theories of crisis in capitalism—albeit often in ways similar to Marxist-Leninist orthodoxy.[6]

Best known among the so-called Western Marxists who concentrated on exposing how capitalists manipulate culture for purposes of domination were those associated with the Institut für Sozialforschung (Institute for Social Research) at the University of Frankfurt in Germany—also known as the Frankfurt School—and Antonio Gramsci (1891–1937), one of the founders of the Italian Communist Party. Among those who participated in the institute and focused on cultural domination were Max Horkheimer (1895–1973), Theodor Adorno (1903–69), Walter Benjamin (1892–1940), Leo Lowenthal (1900–93), and Herbert Marcuse (1898–1979). Although a founding member of a Moscow-oriented Communist Party, Gramsci—who spent much of his life in prison—wrote extensively on cultural domination and is best known for his concept of cultural hegemony, how a dominant class organizes social and cultural life so as to make its worldview and rules seem normal.[7] The implication, of course, is the need to elaborate a counter-hegemonic proletarian culture to undermine and replace capitalist hegemony. None of these authors, to my knowledge, based their analyses of cultural domination on any

---

6   There is, for example, a strange contradiction in Paul Mattick's work between his bottom-up politics and his rather mechanical crisis theory. The former was built on his assessment of workers' ability to organize themselves, whereas, in the latter, workers' struggles play no part—except to take advantage of crisis when it occurs.

7   This work amounted to an elaboration of the point made by Marx and Engels early on in their unpublished *German Ideology* (1845–46): "The ideas of the ruling class are in every epoch the ruling ideas, i.e. the class which is the ruling *material* force of society, is at the same time its ruling *intellectual* force. . . . Insofar, therefore, as they rule as a class and determine the extent and compass of an epoch, it is self-evident that they do this in its whole range, hence among other things rule also as thinkers, as producers of ideas, and regulate the production and distribution of the ideas of their age: thus their ideas are the ruling ideas of the epoch." Marx and Engels, *Collected Works*, vol. 5, 59.

particular interpretation of the labor theory of value. For the most part, they accepted a more or less orthodox Marxist analysis of the economy and focused their attention elsewhere.[8]

The response of Marxists to innovations in economic theory and its abandonment of the labor theory of value were roughly of three sorts. First was simple rejection and dismissal of "vulgar" economics as mere ideological justification for capitalism.[9] Second was to enter into a debate with economists by attacking their arguments against the labor theory of value. The most extensive such debate was over the so-called "transformation problem"— that is, the problem of the relationship between value and prices and whether labor values could be transformed into prices. Third was to see what could usefully be drawn from innovations in economic theory for a revision of Marx's analysis. Such willingness to learn from the analysis of economists—exactly what Marx did with those whose work he respected—nevertheless had to confront their abandonment of the labor theory of value.[10]

The first two of these responses largely characterized the reaction of those Marxists who adhered to some variant of orthodoxy;

---

8   Two exceptions to this preoccupation with culture at the Frankfurt School were Henryk Grossmann (1881–1950) and Frederick Pollack (1894–1970). The former, a Polish economist, wrote extensively on Marxist crisis theory. The latter wrote on Marx's theory of money and on automation.

9   In this, they were echoing Marx's own dismissal of some economists of his day, those he juxtaposed to the more "scientific" work of Adam Smith and David Ricardo.

10   These different responses by Marxists to economics have long been paralleled by economists' responses to Marxism. Many, perhaps most, have simply dismissed it because it didn't meet their needs. Some have attacked it, as part of a more general attack on the idea of alternatives to capitalism, more particularly during the Cold War as part of the opposition to Soviet-style state capitalism. A few have taken Marx's analysis seriously, despite differences, and have drawn upon it to enrich their own pro-capitalist work. Among these last, perhaps the best known are Joseph Schumpeter (mentioned in the previous section), who drew upon Marx in his analysis of capitalist development, and Wassily Leontief (1906–99), whose development of input-output analysis—that utilized matrices delineating how the output of some industries constituted inputs for others and provided the basis for multisectoral planning models—was partly based on the reworking and generalizing of Marx's reproduction schemes in volume 2 of *Capital*.

thoughtfully or in simple reaction, they fiercely defended Marx's analysis—as they understood it—against its critics. That defense was usually coupled with their own critique of the neoclassical theories economists elaborated to replace the labor theory of value. At first they focused on a critique of utility theory, the earliest form of what, for a while, was called price theory (because it was focused on the determination of prices through an analysis of supply and demand) and later dubbed "microeconomics."[11] Later, it also involved a critique of the new "macroeconomics" heavily influenced by the work of John Maynard Keynes (1883–1946).[12]

The third of these responses sometimes led to at least some of the ideas of economics displacing some of those of Marx, even as the individuals who did this continued to retain and employ other Marxian ideas. The apparent reason for such displacement was a belief that some innovations in economic theory corresponded to real changes in the world that had to be taken into account. This seems to have been the case with the most influential post–World War II Marxists in the United States, those associated with the journal *Monthly Review* and its publishing house: Paul Sweezy (1910–2004), the journal's founder, and his coauthor Paul Baran (1909–64). Although their appeal to activists in the 1950s and 1960s probably derived mainly from their positive accounts of struggles in the Third World (e.g., in Cuba, Vietnam, and China), they also provided their own version of what appeared to be well-thought-out Marxist theory, a version in which the labor theory of value was abandoned.

The Monthly Review Abandonment

Sweezy's initial contribution was a book-length and largely positive summary of Marxist economics that sketched its development from Marx through his early twentieth-century interpreters: *The Theory of Capitalist Development.*[13] It was published the same

---

11   One early example is Nikolai Ivanovich Bukharin, *The Economic Theory of the Leisure Class*, written in 1914 and available since 1972 from Monthly Review Press in English translation with an introduction by Don Harris.

12   One example is council communist Paul Mattick's *Marx and Keynes: The Limits of the Mixed Economy* (Boston: Porter Sargent, 1969).

13   See Paul M. Sweezy, *The Theory of Capitalist Development: Principles of Marxian Political Economy* (1942, New York: Monthly Review Press, 1968). I find

year as Joan Robinson's *An Essay on Marxian Economics*, which was much less positive.[14] Sweezy's book contained a summary of one fairly orthodox interpretation of Marx's theory, some history of debate over a few key issues, and his own critiques (e.g., of the tendency of the rate of profit to fall).[15] Among those critiques, there was no rejection of the labor theory of value.

Five years later, with the financial backing of a friend, Sweezy founded *Monthly Review: An Independent Socialist Magazine*, and it has been in circulation ever since. Initially and for many years he edited the journal, at first with Leo Huberman (1903–68) and later Harry Magdoff (1913–2006).[16] *Monthly Review* was soon enjoying

---

the practice by Sweezy and many other Marxists—especially those few employed in departments of economics in universities—mistaken in understanding much of Marx's theory as "economics" and thus presenting their work as moments of "Marxist economics." Marx's primary work, presenting his most worked-out theory of capitalism, was *Capital*, and its subtitle is "Critique of Political Economy." His thinking on aspects of the capitalist economy, therefore, does not represent a "Marxist economics"—standing as an alternative to mainstream or bourgeois economics—but rather a critique of economics, just as it constituted a critique of political economy. It is, I think, a critique designed to achieve the exact opposite of the goals of economics; instead of being formulated to facilitate finding ways to promulgate capitalism, it is formulated in a way designed to find ways to transcend it. Therefore, in this essay my use of the terms "political economy" and "economics" always refers to the work of economists who seek to understand capitalism in ways that facilitate the identification of its problems and the finding of solutions to them.

14 Joan Robinson, *An Essay on Marxian Economics* (London: Macmillan, 1942). No Marxist, despite having studied with Maurice Dobb (1900–76), Robinson (1903–83) taught economics at Cambridge University in England. A contemporary and colleague of John Maynard Keynes, she became a major figure in "post-Keynesian" economics—whose proponents contested neoclassical microeconomics and who continue to contest neoliberal economics.

15 Sweezy, *The Theory of Capitalist Development*, 100–108. In this book, his argument against Marx's theory of "the tendency of the rate of profit to fall" was based on what Sweezy saw as a logical flaw. He argued that a rising organic composition of capital in the production of the means of production made the direction of change in the rate of profit ambiguous. Later he would offer other reasons for setting the theory aside. (See below.)

16 Wikipedia provides a brief history of *Monthly Review*, many links to sources,

input from the Russian-born Marxist economist Paul Baran, who
had emigrated from Russia to the United States via Germany and
obtained a tenured professorship at Stanford University. In 1957,
the Monthly Review Press published his book *The Political Economy of Growth*.[17] Sweezy and Baran became close collaborators,
and in 1966 the Monthly Review Press published their signature
work *Monopoly Capital*, whose theory of contemporary capitalism
provided the basis for all of their subsequent work and for that of
their followers.[18] The theory laid out in that book drew heavily on
economics and constituted a distinct departure from Marx's own
work—even more than Sweezy's critiques in his *Theory of Capitalist Development*. So different was their theory that it earned the
rubric "neo-Marxism" from many of its critics.

The primary basis for Baran and Sweezy's revision of Marx's
theory was their perception that capitalism had evolved from a
competitive system to one dominated by giant, multinational,
monopolistic or oligopolistic corporations. Much of Marx's own
theory, they argued, was based on, and only valid in the context
of, widespread competition among capitalist firms. The rapid concentration of capital in the twentieth century and the resultant increase in oligopoly or monopoly required the revision of his theory.
This centering of market structure was both in tune with developments in economic theories of the "imperfectly competitive" firm
and quite distinct from Marx's central focus on production (i.e.,
the imposition of work and resistance to it).[19] Indeed, they quite

and a list of its editors down through the years. Its current editor—since 2000—
is John Bellamy Foster. A much more detailed history is Foster's February 27,
2004, memorial for Paul Sweezy. See Monthly Review, http://monthlyreview.org/
commentary/memorial-service-for-paul-marlor-sweezy-1910-2004.

17   Paul Baran, *The Political Economy of Growth* (New York: Monthly Review
Press, 1957).

18   Paul Sweezy and Paul Baran, *Monopoly Capital: An Essay on the American
Economic and Social Order* (New York: Monthly Review Press, 1966).

19   See, for example, Joan Robinson, *The Economics of Imperfect Competition*
(London: Macmillan, 1933); Edward Chamberlin, *The Theory of Monopolistic
Competition: A Re-orientation of the Theory of Value* (Boston: Harvard University
Press, 1933); Chamberlin, "Monopolistic Competition Revisited," *Economica*, New
Series 18, no. 72 (November 1951), 343–62.

explicitly acknowledged their debts to economists—to John Maynard Keynes and his main American interpreter Alvin Hansen (1887–1975), to Michał Kalecki (1899–1970), and to Josef Steindl (1912–93), especially the latter's theory of secular stagnation.[20] To these perspectives they added a typical Frankfurt School preoccupation with the irrationality of capitalism.[21]

Among those aspects of Marx's theory they felt to be invalidated by the historical shift from a competitive phase of capitalism to a new monopoly phase was his theory of the tendency of the rate of profit to fall.[22] In its place, Baran and Sweezy substituted a theory of the *tendency for surplus to rise*. This shift involved the replacement of Marx's concept of surplus value with that of "surplus" *tout court*. Their notion of "surplus" differed more in tone than in concept from economists' notion of "savings"—whose reinvestment

---

20   Josef Steindl, *Maturity and Stagnation in American Capitalism* (Oxford: Basil Blackwell, 1952). Sweezy had studied economics at Harvard with both Joseph Schumpeter and Alvin Hansen.

21   Their theory of *real* surplus was akin to Keynes's concept of savings. Chapter 2 of Baran's *Political Economy of Growth* also contained concepts of *potential* and *planned* surplus, derived from the Frankfurt School's notions of the irrationality of capitalism and of surplus under a more rational socialism. (Before coming to the United States, Baran assisted Friedrich Pollock at the Institute for Social Research in Frankfort. See Paul Sweezy, "A Personal Memoir," *Monthly Review*, 16, no. 11 (March 1965), 32–33.) In Sweezy and Baran's collaboration on *Monopoly Capital*, the labor theory of value completely disappeared. When more orthodox Marxists critiqued this abandonment, Sweezy "assure[d] them that this is simply not so" and went on to argue against their position in terms of the labor theory of value. See Paul Sweezy, "Some Problems in the Theory of Capital Accumulation," *Monthly Review* 26, no. 1 (May 1974), 38–55. Despite this momentary reversion, Sweezy and pretty much the whole Monthly Review School continued to set forth their theory of monopoly capital with little or no reference to the labor theory of value. Their choice of "surplus" over "surplus value," most recently defended by John Bellamy Foster in his *The Theory of Monopoly Capitalism: An elaboration of Marxian Political Economy*, new edition, New York: Monthly Review Press, 2014, Chapter 2, while usefully focusing on the waste of human and natural resources under capitalism, also continues to avoid confronting Marx's detailed analysis of the substance, measure, and form of value in class terms.

22   This critique differed from Sweezy's earlier dismissal—based on a perceived logical flaw. (See above.)

played a key role in both Keynes's macroeconomics and in what became known as the theory of growth.[23]

As they developed their theory, not only did any discussion of the tendency of the rate of profit to fall disappear, but so did any discussion or use of Marx's basic theories of value and surplus value. The exception to their neglect of those theories in the 1950s and 1960s was the Monthly Review Press publication of an American edition of Ronald Meek's *Studies in the Labor Theory of Value* (1956), which included an interpretation similar to Sweezy's (and vulnerable to much the same critique).[24]

Let's look briefly at how Sweezy in 1942 and Meek in 1956 understood the value theory that Sweezy and Baran would set aside. Their understanding of the labor theory of value was based on the work of earlier orthodox Marxists, much of whose work was unavailable in English during most of the post–World War II period.[25] In Sweezy's 1942 book, the key moment of his analysis

---

23 The difference in tone was a function of emphasis on the source of savings or surplus. For macroeconomists, savings derive from all actors whose income exceeds their expenses—workers as well as capitalists "save." Indeed, the usual textbook treatment of savings usually attributes them to "households," with little or no mention of corporate undistributed net profits. Baran and Sweezy's preoccupation with surplus mostly evoked monopoly capitalist profits and carried the same aura of critique as Marx's concept of surplus value.

24 Two years after the publication of *Monopoly Capital*, Monthly Review Press published Ernest Mandel's two-volume *Marxist Economic Theory*. Despite being the foremost theoretician of the Trotskyist Fourth International, Mandel had virtually nothing to say about the key concepts of Marx's theory of value and passed quickly to reliance on an ill-defined "law of value" for most of his analysis. Of abstract labor, for instance, he wrote merely that it was a name for "general human labor" (vol. 1, 65). Much later, long after the period that interests me here, Monthly Review Press also published *Labor and Monopoly Capitalism* (1974) by Harry Braverman (1920–76). In that book Braverman closely examined the evolution of the organization of labor in the twentieth century. His analysis became widely discussed among those preoccupied by post-Fordist changes in the organization of production.

25 Among those earlier Marxists upon whom Sweezy drew were Franz Petry (1889–1915), Michael Tugan-Baranowsky (1865–1919), Rudolf Hilferding (1877–1941), Henryk Grossmann (1881–1950), Evgenii Preobrazhenskii (1886–1937), and Maurice Dobb.

of Marx's theory of value was his explanation of the reasonableness of the concept of "abstract labor"—the substance of value. Drawing on Marx's comments in the *Contribution to the Critique of Political Economy* (1859), he pointed out that it made sense to speak of labor in the abstract within the dynamics of capitalist industrialization, where rapid changes in job structures and the high mobility of workers from one kind of labor to another reduced the importance of particular skills. In such situations, he argued, quoting Marx, "the abstraction of the category 'labor,' 'labor in general,' labor *sans phrase*, the starting point of modern political economy, becomes realized in practice."[26] After a brief discussion of the measurement of value in terms of socially necessary labor time, and the problem of reducing skilled labor to simple labor, Sweezy then goes on to make an argument that will eventually allow him to abandon Marx's value theory, namely that the correspondence between values and prices in that theory depends on competition. Here Sweezy implicitly accepts economists' demands for a theory of relative prices and argues that Marx's labor theory only provides one when there is competition among firms.[27] Once he and Baran perceive that capitalism has passed from a *competitive* stage to a *monopoly* one, they argued that the correspondence was broken; from that point on, Marx's value concepts disappeared from their analysis—until they were challenged (see below).

Meek's treatment of abstract labor in 1956 paralleled Sweezy's. He drew on the same sources but made somewhat more use of volume 1 of *Capital*. His analysis of the problem of reducing skilled to simple labor was similar, as was his emphasis on the role of competition. His interpretation led him to equate abstract labor with simple labor, as can be seen when he writes, "Marx, then, defined

26 Sweezy, *The Theory of Capitalist Development*, 32.

27 Sweezy doesn't emulate neoclassical microeconomists by making his position depend upon conditions of "perfect competition," where there are so many firms, all producing the same product, that no single firm's decisions about output can affect prices. But he does make the relevance of Marx's theory contingent upon the existence of some un-modeled quantity of competition. He also takes up, and gives a critical account of, the debate over the question of whether values can be accurately transformed into prices.

the value of a commodity at any given time and place as the amount
of socially-necessary simple labor required to produce it."[28]

For me there are two striking things about both Sweezy's and
Meek's presentations of Marx's theory: first, the total absence of
class struggle in their discussion of abstract labor, and second, a
similar absence of any substantive discussion of section 3 of chapter 1 of *Capital*. Section 3 not only deals extensively with the *form*
of value but is by far the longest part of the chapter. The only explanation for ignoring this aspect of value was given by Meek: "There
is no need," he asserted, "for us to follow Marx's rather complex
analysis of the 'elementary', 'expanded' and 'money' forms of value
in any detail."[29] He then justified this neglect by quoting Engels,
who thought that all that detail was just about how the emergence
of money overcame the inefficiencies of barter exchange.[30] But
both Engels and Meek were wrong. Marx's dissection of the form of
value was an integral part of his analysis of fully developed capitalism. It is, therefore, essential to our understanding of the capitalist
imposition of work and the struggle against it.

A related problem can be found in Baran and Sweezy and their
followers' replacement of surplus value with surplus. Whereas for
Marx the central problem faced by capitalists was imposing enough
work to realize a surplus value, in Baran and Sweezy the generation
of surplus was no problem at all—the only problem lay in "absorbing
it," finding some use for it. For Marx, imposing work was a problem
because of the resistance and struggles of workers. But for Baran and
Sweezy there were no struggles to be overcome, only an endless flow
of surplus to be absorbed. In their understanding of the theory, workers' struggles disappeared completely.[31] In short, I found nothing in

28 Ronald Meek, *Studies in the Labor Theory of Value* (New York: Monthly Review Press, 1956), 177.

29 Ibid. 173.

30 Ibid., 173–74.

31 While workers' struggles disappeared completely in their *theory* of monopoly
capitalism, they reappeared consistently in their broader work on the evolution of
post–World War II American imperialism and resistance to it in the Third World.
Consistent with this theory, Baran and Sweezy basically wrote off the US working class as having sold out and could only find working-class struggle abroad,
first in the Cuban Revolution and then in many other places, including China and

either Sweezy's or Meek's treatment of the core concepts of Marx's labor theory of value that addressed the struggle against work.

No more illuminating were the various Marxist-Leninists (Stalinists, Trotskyists, and Maoists) who critiqued Baran and Sweezy's deviations from the perspective of orthodox Marxism.[32] Despite their dedication to revolution and the overthrow of capitalism, their interpretation of Marx's theory of capitalism amplified his own tendency to focus on the mechanisms of domination rather than on workers' struggles against that domination. Their resulting propensity to read *Capital* as a theory of *capitalist* development, rather than as one of a two-sided class struggle, justified their Leninist belief in the need for Communist Party leadership of workers' political struggle.[33] All those Marxists critical of Baran and Sweezy's abandonment of the labor theory of value who still embraced some version of it—whether they were members of some Marxist-Leninist party or not—tended to simply reject the premises and restate, or marginally reformulate, long-held orthodox

---

Vietnam. It was that focus that made their work appealing to a generation of activists who revered Che Guevara and opposed the US government's efforts to suppress the movement for national liberation in Vietnam.

32   Baran and Sweezy's *Monopoly Capital*, in particular, set off a whole series of critiques by various more-or-less orthodox Marxists such as Mario Cogoy, David Laibman, and David Yaffe, as well as various self-styled "radical economists" such as Samuel Bowles, Herbert Gintis, David Gordon, Thomas Weisskopf, Anwar Shaikh, and Richard Wolff. Spurred on by such controversies, by the middle of the 1970s the first major American "return to Marx" in the twentieth century was well underway within university courses being offered by veterans of the New Left who found positions in academia and within a proliferating number of outside study groups devoted to reading *Capital*.

33   This distinction between the economic and the political has haunted Marxism ever since. Leninists long argued that workers' day-to-day struggles (e.g., fighting for higher wages or shorter working days) are merely particular "economistic" battles. As such, they fail to rise to the level of the interests of the working class as a whole. Only an enlightened party leadership, thanks to Marx and Lenin's analysis, could grasp those interests and lead the struggle. Such reasoning justified Communist Party political hegemony not only during the struggle against capitalism but after the revolution, during the "dictatorship of the proletariat"—which, of course, became the dictatorship of the party.

interpretations. As will become apparent below, while I share their rejection of Baran and Sweezy's abandonment of the labor theory of value, I do not share their interpretations as to either the nature of that theory or the problems to which the abandonment gives rise.

The Analytical Marxist Abandonment

Whereas the Monthly Review school's abandonment of the labor theory of value grew out of the influence of perceptions and theories of imperfect competition and Keynesian preoccupations with the macroeconomics of growth and stagnation, the emergence of "analytical Marxism" blossomed in the 1980s as one variant of the "radical economics" that arose in the late 1960s in response to the struggles of that period. Radical economics as a self-defined subfield of economics can be roughly dated from the creation in the United States of the Union for Radical Political Economics (URPE) in 1968 and the publication of its journal *Review of Radical Political Economics* (*RRPE*), whose first issue appeared in May 1969.[34] This organization and the editors of its journal define "radical economics" broadly to include not only Marxist economics but pretty much any non-mainstream approaches that are critical of capitalism and supportive of activist efforts to change it. Issues of *RRPE*, therefore, can be found to contain a variety of evaluations and critiques of both economics and Marxism. So defined, radical economics includes "analytical Marxism" as one set of critical approaches to Marxism—a set that while embracing Marxism's critique of capitalism, reformulates and then sets aside the labor theory of value in favor of a variety of alternative theoretical formulations.

Although the work of Gerald Allan Cohen (1941–2009), a Canadian who did graduate work at Oxford and was then appointed professor at University College London and All Souls College, Oxford, is often credited with being the starting point of analytical

---

34   *RRPE* is similar to *Monthly Review* in not being associated with any particular political party or grouping but unlike it in defining itself as a "peer-reviewed" academic journal. Nevertheless, the second issue of *RRPE* contained an article by Paul Sweezy, "Toward the Critique of Economics," reprinted from the January 1970 issue of *Monthly Review*. The creation of URPE is generally seen as roughly paralleling that of the Conference of Socialist Economists (CSE) in England. The CSE soon published a *Bulletin of the CSE* that eventually became *Capital and Class* in 1977.

Marxism,[35] it was the work of the Japanese economist Michio Morishima (1923–2004) and later that of the American economist John Roemer (1945–) that seem to me to best illustrate the fate of Marx's labor theory of value among "analytical Marxists." Both economists saw Marx as an economist and as a mathematical economist, albeit a very weak one, and set out to bring modern mathematical methods to bear on what they saw as the important subjects Marx had identified but could only treat with the simplistic mathematics available to him.[36] Cohen's *Karl Marx's Theory of History: A Defense* (1978) established one trend of this school's work by reformulating historical materialism using the techniques of analytical philosophy. Morishima and Roemer completely reformulated Marx's core theories of capitalism in the language of modern mathematics and crafted precise models to provide new "microfoundations" for some of Marx's central concepts such as value, class, and exploitation.

As early as 1961, Morishima wrote on "Aggregation in Leontief Matrices and the Labor Theory of Value."[37] A few years later, he published a much elaborated exploration of Marx in *Marx's Economics: A Dual Theory of Value and Growth* (1973).[38] The next year, he spelled out his overall assessment of Marx as a mathematical economist in a succinct article, "Marx in the Light of Modern Economic Theory."[39] Thinking like an economist and reading Marx

---

35   See James Farmelant's obituary of Cohen in the *MRZine* of August 8, 2009, http://mrzine.monthlyreview.org/.

36   This bias of economists to read Marx as an economist is hardly surprising given that a great many non-economists have read him that way as well. More surprising was their willingness to take his "economics" seriously enough to try to modernize his mathematics.

37   Michio Morishima and F. Seton, "Aggregation in Leontief Matrices and the Labour Theory of Value," *Econometrica* 29, no. 2 (April 1961), 203–220. As mentioned earlier, Leontief was one economist who took Marx seriously enough to draw on his ideas (of "reproduction schemes" in part 3 of volume 2 of *Capital*) in the elaboration of his "matrices." Unlike Leontief, Morishima reworked Marx's analysis to evaluate its promise rather than simply appropriating and using his work for capitalist purposes.

38   Michio Morishima, *Marx's Economics: A Dual Theory of Value and Growth* (Cambridge: Cambridge University Press, 1978).

39   Michio Morishima, "Marx in the Light of Modern Economic Theory," *Econometrica* 42, no. 4 (July 1974), 611–32.

as one, Morishima characterized Marx's labor theory of value as a
"program for technocratic calculation of labor congealed in commodities," and he read Marx as having constructed a "two-stage
general equilibrium theory."[40] Because he found Marx's reasoning
"confused," he set out to "rescue" what he felt was Marx's main idea
from the man's incompetent treatment. Not surprisingly, when he
formulated what he called the "Fundamental Marxian Theorem"
(that profit and growth depend upon an excess of labor over subsistence), all "'mysterious' concepts such as 'value' or 'exploitation'"
disappeared.[41] In short, his rescue of Marx amounted to setting
aside the labor theory of value while appreciating the "essential
Marx" as a growth theorist who, had he been able to draw upon later mathematics could have formulated his position more precisely.
At the end of his 1973 book, Morishima quite explicitly recognized
his abandonment of Marx's key theory: "Our solution, a Marxian
economics without the labor theory of value, is unlikely to be accepted by Marxists, but I shall nevertheless strongly recommend it
to them at the end of this final chapter."[42]

Roemer, in turn, drew on Morishima's work in four books that
might be considered the theoretical core of analytical Marxism:
Analytical Foundations of Marxian Economic Theory (1981), *A
General Theory of Exploitation and Class* (1982), *Value, Exploitation and Class* (1986), and *Free to Lose: An Introduction to Marxist
Economic Philosophy* (1988), written for a general audience and
with the least math of the four.[43] This last book, echoing similar critiques by mainstream economists whose functional interest in "value" is always market prices, dismisses Marx's labor theory of value
as one-sided. "In fact, the labor theory of value is a supply-side theory, in which prices are thought to be determined entirely by their

---

40   Morishima, *Marx's Economics*, 2.

41   See Micho Morishima, "The Fundamental Marxian Theorem: A Reply to Samuelson," *Journal of Economic Literature* 12, no. 1 (March 1974), 71.

42   Morishima, *Marx's Economics*, 181.

43   John Roemer, *Analytical Foundations of Marxian Economic Theory* (Cambridge: Cambridge University Press, 1981); *A General Theory of Exploitation and
Class* (Cambridge, Mass.: Harvard University Press, 1982); *Value, Exploitation and
Class* (Reading: Harwood Academic Publishers, 1986); *Free to Lose: An Introduction
to Marxist Economic Philosophy* (Cambridge, Mass.: Harvard University Press, 1988).

labor costs; in contrast, emphasizing the importance of the degree to which a commodity fulfills desires or needs or welfare in determining its price is the demand side. The correct theory of market price must take both supply and demand into account."[44]

In reality, as I have indicated, Marx had no such theory, recognized that market prices were determined by supply and demand, and embraced the labor theory of value for a quite different purpose, namely to focus our attention on the social role of labor in capitalist domination and its results: exploitation, alienation, poverty, and the violence of enclosure, of protecting capitalist property, of colonialism, and of war.

Roemer's reformulations include his treatment of "labor value" in the third of these four books. There he presents what he calls "the modern theory of labor value" using linear input-output theory—an approach he attributes to several earlier authors.

Characteristically, Roemer's methodology is typical of neoclassical economics in constructing his theory on the basis of assumptions about individual behavior. So, for example, he deduces the structure of class from individual decisions about each person's decisions to either hire out or hire others according to the wealth available.[45] His "Class-Exploitation Correspondence Principle" derives from this and states "that every agent who is in a labor-hiring class is an exploiter, and every agent who is in a labor-selling class is exploited." Whether one is exploited or one exploits is basically defined as having to do more work or less work than the social average. He quite carefully builds models that result in exploitation even in the absence of labor markets. Although formulated in a precise mathematical way, this amounts to a restatement of the orthodox Marxist association of property ownership with class status: those who own the means of production can hire others, those who don't must hire out and are exploited. Thus, this analysis, as

44 Roemer, *Free to Lose*, 49.

45 Although the methodology is quite different, Roemer's neoclassical approach is reminiscent of Jean Paul Sartre's effort to generate Marxian classes starting from the existential situation of individuals in his *Critique de la raison dialectique: Tome I, Théorie des ensembles pratiques* (Paris: Gallimard, 1960) and *Tome II: L'intelligibilite de l'histoire* (Paris: Gallimard, 1985), published in English as *Critique of Dialectical Reason*, vol. 1 (New York: Verso, 1991) and vol. 2 (New York: Verso, 2006).

Roemer makes clear, founds the existence of exploitation on relations of property rather than on those of extracted surplus labor. In so doing, he critiques Marx and his followers as having "a misplaced emphasis on the labor process" and seeing exploitation at the point of production. They confuse alienation with exploitation, he argues—although his definition of alienation is quite different than Marx's, being limited to disgruntlement associated with narrowly defined tasks.[46]

The Post-*Operaismo* Abandonment[47]

Throughout its development in Italy in the years following World War II, *operaismo*—or workerism—centered, as the name suggests, both work and the self-activity of workers in its theory and politics. The *operaisti* critiqued the collaboration with capitalist rebuilding and modernization of the main left-wing parties and unions. They blasted their leadership for their willingness to subordinate workers' needs to capitalist development and their embrace of a social democratic participation in electoral politics. At the same time, they anchored their critique in a serious rereading of Marx and rethinking of his concepts within the context of growing worker resistance to that subordination.

As "modernization" proceeded, the progressive introduction of the latest production technologies undermined traditional forms of worker self-organization on the shop floor and led to more and more overt resistance. By the early 1960s, rank-and-file revolts were multiplying, against not only the leadership of the relatively conservative Unione Italiana del Lavoro (UIL) but also against the politics and strategies of the Partito Socialista Italiano (PSI), the Partito Comunista Italiano (PCI), and those of their affiliated unions—especially the Confederazione Generale Italiana del Lavoro (CGIL). Their collusion with capitalist development led

---

46   The disgruntlement that results from alienation was not the primary object of Marx's theory. Instead he focused on how the capitalist imposition and control of work alienates workers from their work, their products, each other, and their "species being" (the exercise of their individual and collective will).

47   The first part of what follows—the description of the development of *operaismo*—is adapted from an essay on the "Genesis of Zerowork #1" that can be found on the website www.zerowork.org.

growing numbers of working-class militants and radical intellectuals to rethink their politics and their theory.[48] Inspired by the revolts, by discovery of the writings of American and French workers describing similar developments in the United States and France,[49] and by the rediscovery of the detailed questions in Marx's *A Workers' Inquiry* (1880), radical Italian sociologists such as Raniero Panzieri (1921–64) and Romano Alquati (1935–2010) went into factories such as Olivetti and Fiat to talk with workers about their concrete job situations and their struggles, both day-to-day and periodic wildcat strikes.[50] Sociologists, yes, but sociologists of a new sort—conscious re-innovators of *conricerca*, or co-research, in which the "objectivity" of their investigations was co-produced by these outside researchers *and* the workers *with whom* they investigated the situation at hand.

These investigations were carried on, at least at first, in the hope of bringing new understanding and new politics to the unions and to the left-wing parties. Panzieri, for example, thought to influence the PSI despite past differences with it. Over time, however, such hopes faded, and even when this or that new concept, in one form or another, was assimilated by those faithful to those

---

48   The well-known turning point at which rank-and-file anger exploded was the July 1962 Piazza Statuto attack on the offices of the UIL in Turin. Fiat workers were furious that the union bureaucrats had signed an agreement with management without consulting them, thus undermining their strike.

49   The American sources were produced by the Johnson-Forest/Facing Reality group, the French ones by Socialisme ou Barbarie.

50   Marx's *A Workers' Inquiry* first appeared in France in 1880 and consisted of one hundred questions that he thought should be asked of workers to reveal their concrete situation. His purpose was to pressure the French state to follow the example set by the English government whose factory inspectors had done so much to reveal the shocking conditions in which workers lived in that country—and whose reports contributed to legislation that improved workers' lives. Only the workers, Marx wrote, "can describe with full knowledge the misfortunes from which they suffer, and . . . only they, and not saviors sent by Providence, can energetically apply the healing remedies for the social ills to which they are a prey." The inquiry was first published in the United States in the December 1938 *New International* (379–81). The bulk of the fifth issue of the workerist journal *Quaderni rossi* was devoted to contributions to a 1964 seminar on the "Socialist use of the Workers' Inquiry."

institutions, or when one of these innovators returned to the fold, the new concepts were sometimes wielded in support of the same old social democratic politics.

Nevertheless, their studies and theoretical reformulations led to the creation of a series of new concepts and new journals to disseminate and discuss them. At the heart of the new reformulations was the replacement of the traditional Marxist focus on capital and its "laws of motion" with an understanding of capital as a set of antagonistic social relations of class in which workers' struggles drove the development of the whole. Moreover, their concept of the working class—informed by the extensive empirical research mentioned above—recognized how divisions in the class were not merely those of labor but also constituted particular *compositions* of class power. That is to say, changes in the division of labor were not just evolving vehicles of capitalist control (pitting one group of workers against others in hierarchies of power) but also the result of historical cycles of workers' struggles that *recomposed* both the internal divisions of the working class and the balance of power between the classes. The concept of *cycles* undermined the linear notion of building a party organization that would grow and grow until it eventually overthrew capitalism. What they came to recognize was that struggles might grow and become more effective as workers found new ways to organize in a given situation and those new ways circulated, built momentum, and often succeeded in throwing capital into crisis. But again and again capital would find a response, a way to *decompose* those methods of struggle and restore the balance of class power. As they did, the struggles would ebb and subside, bringing the cycle to an end. Their analysis provided new theoretical foundations for the phenomenon some Marxists in America and France had postulated years earlier: that workers' struggles repeatedly generated new organizational forms. These Italians extended their studies backward in time and across space, examining not merely the history of Italian workers' struggles but also those of American workers. They discovered how past cycles of struggle not only generated new organizational forms and recomposed the balance of class power but also led, inevitably, to changes in the character of working-class interests and demands—changes that both required and produced new organizational forms.

Bringing these insights to bear on the contemporary situation in Italy, they argued that the post–World War II wave of capitalist rebuilding, especially in the industrial belt of the Po Valley, was not only based on the pitting of large numbers of young workers from southern Italy against northern workers but had gestated a new "mass worker" akin to those organized by the Wobblies in the United States in the early twentieth century and to that working class formed in the Fordist mass-production factories of the 1920s and 1930s. In other words, the pattern of capitalist development that Antonio Gramsci—patron saint of orthodox Italian commun-ism—had identified as being a uniquely American phenomenon was being imported into Italy and was being used against Italian workers just as it had been used against American ones.[51] Against this importation, the *operaisti* developed a whole new set of Marx-ist concepts to understand the class dynamics of that development, concepts offered to militants in several new journals.

The first of the new journals to have a substantial impact was *Quaderni Rossi* (Red Notebooks) whose first issue in 1961 included a collection of documents on class struggles in Fiat by Alquati and a path-breaking theoretical piece by Panzieri, "On the Capitalist Use of the Machine" that returned to Marx's analysis of "machinery and modern industry"—chapter 15 of volume 1 of *Capital*—to re-focus attention on how machinery was used by capitalists not just to raise productivity (part of the rationale of the leftist parties and their unions for collaborating with capitalist development) but also to undermine workers' self-organization and power. That analysis explained both rank-and-file wildcats against the efforts of corpo-rate bosses to introduce Fordist methods into the plants and their refusal to follow the dictates of union bureaucrats to cooperate with such changes.[52] This amounted to a renovated Marxist theory

51 For Gramsci's analysis, see "Americanism and Fordism" (1934) in Antonio Gram-sci, *Selections from the Prison Notebooks* (New York: International Publishers, 1971).
52 See Raniero Panzieri, "Sull'uso capitalistico delle macchine nel neocapital-ismo," *Quaderni rossi no. 1* (1961), 53–71 reprinted in R. Panzieri, *La ripresa del marxismo leninismo in Italia* (Milan: Sapere, 1975) and published in English as "The Capitalist Use of Machinery: Marx versus the 'Objectivists,'" in Phil Slater, ed., *Outlines of a Critique of Technology* (Atlantic Highlands, N.J.: Humanities Press, 1980), 44–68.

of technological change in class terms that identified opposed class interests and drew organizational conclusions.

In issue after issue of *Quaderni Rossi*, its pages were filled with both empirical work and theoretical innovations. Panzieri's piece on the capitalist use of the machine was soon followed in 1962 by Mario Tronti's "Factory and Society" that argued how "the pressure of labor-power is capable of forcing capital to modify its own internal composition, intervening within capital as essential component of capitalist development"—workers' struggles drive capitalist development. Moreover, that pressure forces capital to colonize "the whole of society" such that it comes to exist "as a function of the factory and the factory extends its exclusive domination over the whole of society."[53] This analysis Tronti deepened in the third issue of *Quaderni Rossi* with an essay on "capitalist planning" that argued that business was driven to ever more comprehensive planning by the resistance and struggles of workers.[54] The old orthodox dichotomy of capitalist "despotism" on the shop floor and capitalist "anarchy" in the social division of labor dissolved as planning was extended ever more widely—to the point where capitalist society becomes a gigantic "social factory." In the process, all traditional distinctions between economic and political power disappear. That article was complemented by Panzieri's "Surplus Value and Planning: Notes on the Reading of *Capital*" in the fourth issue of *Quaderni Rossi*.[55] In short, these Italian Marxists, drawing on their studies of actual workers' struggles and detailed rereadings of Marx in the light of those studies, were elaborating what amounted to a revolutionary theoretical grounding of workers' autonomy. Tronti would go on, in essays such as "The Strategy of Refusal" and "Struggle Against Labor," to identify and articulate how the dynamics of workers' struggles had led beyond the

---

53   Mario Tronti, "La fabbrica e la società," *Quaderni rossi* 2 (1962), 1–31.

54   Mario Tronti, "Il piano del capitale," *Quaderni rossi* 3 (1963), 44–73, reprinted in Mario Tronti, *Operai e Capitale* (Turin: Einaudi, 1966), 267–311, and published in English as "Social Capital," *Telos*, no. 17 (Fall 1973), 98–121.

55   Raniero Panzieri, "Plusvalore e pianificazione: Appunti di lettura del Capitale," *Quaderni rossi* 4 (196?), 257–88. In English: "Surplus Value and Planning: Notes on the Reading of Capital," *The Labour Process and Class Strategies*, CSE Pamphlet no. 1 (London: Stage 1, 1976), 4–25.

traditional skilled workers' demand to take control of their tools to contemporary demands of unskilled "mass workers" on assembly lines for less work, period (i.e., not just the refusal of capitalist-imposed work but of work as the only focus and preoccupation of life). This historical shift was also documented by Sergio Bologna in his "Class Composition and the Theory of the Workers' Party in the German Workers' Council Movement" (1967) and much later in "The Theory and History of the Mass Worker in Italy," (1987).[56] *Quaderni Rossi* (1961–66) was soon accompanied or followed by other organizational efforts and other publications—for example, *Quaderni Piacentini* (1962–84), *Classe Operaia* (1963–67), *La Classe* (1967–68), *Potere Operaio* (1969–74), and *Lotta Continua* (1969–76).

Throughout the key texts cited—such as Panzieri's "Surplus Value and Planning"—although many of Marx's concepts were reworked or given more explicit political interpretations, his labor theory of value was pretty much assumed. It was the fundamental tool wielded by Marx throughout *Capital*, and various sections of its three volumes were the main objects of reinterpretation. That began to change as workers' struggle in the late 1960s and early 1970s threw capitalism and its postwar Keynesian or Fordist organization into crisis.

For workerists, the crisis posed new problems for the capitalist organization of work and for the working class whose struggles had precipitated it. For many it also suggested a crisis for Marxist theory. Having learned to reinterpret that theory in the light of changing class conditions, a major crisis in the evolution of class relationships—which was certainly the way workerists understood the situation by the early 1970s—caused them to do some serious theoretical rethinking. That rethinking involved a reexamination of several key texts and concepts.

---

56 Sergio Bologna, "Composizione di classe e teoria del partito alle origini del movimento consiliare," in Sergio Bologna et al, *Operai e Stato: Lotte operaie e riforma dello stato capitalistico tra revoluzione d'ottobre e New Deal*, (Milano: Feltrinelli, 1972), 13–46. "The Theory and History of the Mass Worker in Italy" was translated from the German and published in abridged form in *Common Sense*, nos. 11 & 12. The original German was published over three issues of *1999–Zeitschrift für Sozialgeschichte* des 20 and 21 Jahrhunderts.

For one thing, a striking aspect of the crisis was a new capital-ist offensive on the terrain of money. Engineered inflation and the replacement of the Bretton Woods system of fixed exchange rates provided capitalist policy makers with new tools to wield against workers' successes at raising wages independently of productivity. As a result, Marx's analyses of money in volume 1 of *Capital*, of finance in volume 3, and his many articles on financial crises in the nineteenth century became objects of intense workerist scru-tiny.[57] (The results of that scrutiny are discussed below in part 2 of this book.)

For another thing, the emergence of historically high levels of persistent unemployment (high with respect to the Keynesian period) in the North raised questions—not only among workerists but among many social critics—about the ability of capitalists to overcome the crisis through the imposition of previous levels of waged work. The "Great Recession" of 1974–75, the slight and slow recovery in 1976–79, and then, the deep global depression of the early 1980s gave rise to an "end of work" literature that proliferat-ed in the 1980s and 1990s. That literature included Andrés Gorz's *Adieux au Prolétariat* (1980), *Les Chemins du paradis* (1983), and *Métamorphoses du travail* (1988), Jeremy Rifkin's *The End of Work* (1995), and Stanley Aronowitz's *Jobless Future* (1995). All of these works suggested that if capitalism could no longer impose enough work to guarantee most people income, then income should be in-creasingly divorced from jobs.

Whereas those books mainly sought to chart the increasing difficulty faced by capital in finding jobs to impose, Antonio Ne-gri—long an influential thinker among workerists—offered an in-terpretation of this difficulty grounded in a rereading of Marxian theory. Negri, who had already begun to critique the "law of val-ue" in the early 1970s, turned from *Capital* to the *Grundrisse* for inspiration.[58] Drawing on its "fragment on machines," he argued

---

57   See Steve Wright, "Revolution from Above? Money and Class Composition in Italian Operaismo," in Marcel van der Linden and Karl Heinz Roth, eds., *Beyond Marx: Theorizing the Global Labour Relations of the Twenty-First Century* (Chica-go: Haymarket Books, 2014), 369–94.

58   An example of that early critique is his article "Crisi dello Stato-Piano: co-munismo e organizzazione rivoluzionaria," *Potere Operaio*, no. 45 (September 25,

that these developments amounted to the historical realization of Marx's prediction that the progressive introduction of machines to raise productivity would eventually marginalize labor as the basis of wealth production and undermine it as measure of value.[59] Value based on labor, Marx predicted, would be replaced by "disposable time." Negri and Michael Hardt brought this interpretation to public notice with their book *Empire* (2000), which offered a comprehensive analysis of the crisis faced by capitalism at the global level.

Negri's reading of the "fragment on machines" focused on a passage where Marx argued that a logical outcome of the capitalist strategy of repeatedly substituting machines for living labor would lead to a situation in which the worker

> steps to the side of the production process instead of being its chief actor. In this transformation it is neither the direct human labor he himself performs, nor the time during which he works, but rather the appropriation of his own general productive power, his understanding of nature and his mastery over it by virtue of his presence as a social body—it is, in a word, the development of the social individual which appears as the great foundation-stone of production and of wealth. The theft of alien labor time, on which present wealth is based, appears as a miserable foundation in face of this new one, created by large-scale industry itself. As soon as labor in the direct form has ceased to be the great well-spring of wealth, labor time ceases and must

1971), translated into English as "Crisis of the Planner-State: Communism and Revolutionary Organization," in Toni Negri, *Revolution Retrieved: Selected Writings on Marx, Keynes, Capitalist Crisis and New Social Subjects*, 1967–1983 (London: Red Notes, 1989), 97–148.

59   The most referenced English version of the "Fragment on Machines" can be found on pp. 699–712 of Karl Marx, *Grundrisse*, Pelican Marx Library (Harmondsworth, UK: Penguin Books, 1973). Negri systematically laid out his rereading of the *Grundrisse* in a series of lectures at the Sorbonne in Paris. Those lectures were assembled in *Marx au-dela Marx: cahiers de travail sur les «Grundrisse»* (Paris: Christian Bourgois, 1979) and *Marx oltra Marx: Quaderno di lavoro sui Grundrisse* (Milan: Feltrinelli, 1979), translated into English as *Marx beyond Marx: Lessons of the Grundrisse* (South Hadley, Mass.: Bergin & Garvey, 1984) and available since 1991 from Autonomedia in the United States and Pluto Press in England.

cease to be its measure, and hence exchange value [must cease to be the measure] of use value.[60]

In Negri's interpretation, if the development of capitalism has actually reached this point, where "labor time" can no longer measure wealth or provide the foundation of exchange value, then the labor theory of value is no longer relevant. Ever since deciding that this has actually occurred—or at least is in the process of occurring throughout leading industrial sectors—Negri and his followers have been formulating alternative theories to interpret the emerging character of modern class relationships. Like the analytical Marxists who sought to rescue Marx from the errors of his labor value theory, Negri and others have sought to rescue Marx from what they have seen as that theory's historical obsolescence. In the process, they have drawn heavily on the work of Michel Foucault (1926–1984), Friedrich Nietzsche (1844–1900), Baruch Spinoza (1632–77), and Gilles Deleuze (1925–95)—especially the latter's own readings of Foucault, Nietzsche, and Spinoza. In this work, they have been joined by other post-*operaisti*, such as Paolo Virno (1952–). The results have been a series of highly controversial propositions—none of which draw upon the labor theory of value.[61] In Negri's view, work remains important but now no longer as a source of value, instead uniquely as a means of domination. Some of those propositions—especially those

---

60   Marx, *Grundrisse*, 705.

61   Early critiques of this line of argument concerned the way in which Negri's focus on the difficulties faced by capitalist efforts to impose traditional levels of waged employment ignored its much greater success in imposing unwaged work— as workers sought to compensate for falling real wages through more housework and subsistence production. See H. Cleaver, "Work, Value and Domination: On the Continuing Relevance of the Marxian Labor Theory of Value in the Crisis of the Keynesian Planner State," originally written June 1989, published in *Vis a Vis: Quaderni per l'autonomia di classe* (Bologna), no. 2 (Spring 1994, 73–90), as "Lavoro, Valore e Dominio: Sull'attuale rilevanza della teoria di Marx del laboro-valore nella crisi dello stato piano Keynesiano." George Caffentzis, "The End of Work or the Renaissance of Slavery? A Critique of Rifkin and Negri," *Common Sense: Journal of the Edinburgh Conference of Socialist Economists*, no. 24, December 1998, reprinted in George Caffentzis, *In Letters of Blood and Fire: Work, Machines and the Crisis of Capitalism* (Oakland: PM Press, 2013), 66–81.

that have reinforced the abandonment of the labor theory of value—will be discussed and critiqued in what follows.

An Alternative Interpretation

In my own notes on Marx's various presentations of the labor theory of value, both within *Capital* and elsewhere—eventually reworked into *Reading* Capital *Politically*—I set out the results of my research in the form of a reinterpretation of chapter 1 of volume 1 of *Capital*. The overall conclusion of my reading, and of the book, was that Marx's labor theory of value can be most usefully interpreted as embodying a working-class perspective on the capitalist imposition of work and the struggle against it. I have since come to reformulate that interpretation by characterizing the labor theory of value as *a theory of the value of labor to capital*—as its fundamental means for organizing and dominating society.

Another way of expressing this idea is by saying that the primary *social use-value* of labor to capital is its role in organizing capitalist society and maintaining control over it. This is an adaptation of the way Marx uses the term "use-value." He employs it in his analysis of commodities in an almost vernacular sense, denoting the various ways people find them useful—even if their usefulness for workers is quite different from their usefulness to capital. For example, food provides us the use-value of nutrition and energy for life; we also find it a source of pleasure, a focal point for social gatherings, a religious symbol, et cetera. But as Marx also shows, the use-values of food for capital—besides constituting a whole domain of commodity production and source of profits—are the power that its control gives to impose labor and its role in keeping us healthy enough to work.

When I say that the labor theory of value is a theory of the value of labor to capital, I am not arguing that capitalists necessarily see it that way. I am not making an argument about the conscious evaluation people make—in this case capitalists—about what is good and what is bad.[62] That argument is important when we turn to our own

---

62 My argument, therefore, differs from that made by Massimo de Angelis, who draws on anthropologist David Graeber's work and emphasizes this conscious evaluation. See de Angelis's discussion of "value systems" and "value practices" in his book *The Beginning of History: Value Struggles and Global Capital* (London: Pluto Press, 2007), 24–28.

values—ones we contrast and oppose to the value of labor to capital. Some capitalists *may* think putting people to work is a good thing to do—they may see themselves, as Irving Kristol suggests, in his *Two Cheers for Capitalism* (1978), as giving the gift of jobs (and income). Some others may think beyond that and see how providing employment is a social good in establishing order. But most capitalists, outside of policy circles, may simply see labor the way economists do—as just another input they must pay for in order to make profits. What they think, however, is entirely secondary to the social use-value of labor to capital. It provides capitalists, as a class, with their most fundamental means of organizing and controlling society.

In Marx's theory, unlike in economics, labor is not a commodity; the commodity we have to sell, and is sometimes bought by business, is *labor power*, our ability and willingness to work for, and under the direction of, a boss. The use-values for capital of the commodity labor power—discussed by Marx in chapter 6 of volume 1 of *Capital*—are twofold. The first essential use-value is the particular skill we employ in our concrete useful labors to produce commodities capital can then sell for profit. The second essential use-value is our ability to work more than is required to produce what is necessary for the maintenance and reproduction of our labor power, that is to say surplus labor or surplus value.[63] But the primary use of surplus value is the imposition on us of more labor, via investment. So the *social use-value* to capital of the *labor* it extracts from our labor power is the social control it gives over our lives in the present. And the *social use-value* of the *surplus value* it

---

63   The degree to which capital is able to realize these use-values by successfully imposing work is a separate issue from the selling and buying of labor power in the labor market. For many years, the models employed by neoclassical economists *assumed* that labor purchased served as an unproblematic input. Eventually, however, they were forced to recognize what capitalists had long known, namely that actually getting hired workers to work enough to generate surplus value is always an open struggle. Thus their inevitable use of overseers, productivity measures, and quality control. One moment of such recognition by economists concerned the analysis of "efficiency wages"—that is, wages higher than market-clearing rates that are paid in order to obtain workers' cooperation, higher productivity, and lower turnover. Such had been key motivations for Henry Ford's practice of paying some of the highest wages in American manufacturing.

extracts from us is the ability to impose more work on us and thus more social control over us in the future.

The usual readings of Marx—pretty much since Engels's *Origin of Family, Private Property and the State* (1884)—have interpreted him as celebrating labor as the defining trait of humankind. Therefore, those readings have also celebrated being working class as a good thing, with the goal of struggle being the *liberation of work* from being the vehicle for capitalist exploitation and cause of alienation. Instead, I argue that precisely because Marx did see work as the fundamental means of capitalist domination, he also saw workers' struggles as the only means of *liberating their own lives* from being defined solely (and poorly) by their work. Liberation from capitalism would involve *not just* the coming-into-being of a free *homo faber*, but also of human beings for whom work would be only one of many potentially fulfilling means of self-realization. This was the vision, I think, in Marx's oft-quoted evocation of a communism in which "nobody has one exclusive sphere of activity but each can become accomplished in any branch he wishes, society regulates the general production and thus makes it possible for me to do one thing today and another tomorrow, to hunt in the morning, fish in the afternoon, rear cattle in the evening, criticize after dinner, just as I have a mind, without ever becoming hunter, fisherman, herdsman or critic."[64]

My interpretation, while sharing some elements of more traditional Marxisms, refocuses our attention on struggles *against* work and *for* the liberation of time and energy for activities of individual and collective self-valorization—in a manner I find consistent with what I have experienced within various social struggles and have observed elsewhere.

---

64 "The German Ideology," in Marx and Engels, *Collected Works*, vol. 5 (New York: International Publishers, 1976), 47. Note especially: this well-known passage should make clear that it is wrong to interpret Marx and Engels as imagining a communism that completely abolishes labor in favor of an "indolent future," as Terry Eagleton and Steven Shaviro seem to think. Hunting, fishing, and rearing cattle all fit Marx's definition of labor. See Terry Eagleton, "Communism: Lear or Gonzalo?," in Costas Douzinas and Slavoj Žižek, eds., *The Idea of Communism* (New York: Verso 2010); Steven Shaviro, *No Speed Limit: Three Essays on Accelerationism* (Minneapolis: University of Minnesota Press, 2015), 49–50.

Understanding Marx's theory as a theory of the value of work
to capital, leads to the recognition of how each and every aspect of
value analyzed in sections 1–3 of chapter 1 of volume 1 of *Capital*
is an aspect of the work relationship that capital imposes and that
workers resist. Understanding this in turn reveals how rupturing
one or another or all of these aspects undermines the value of work
to capital. One result is to see how, within capitalism, *money em-*
bodies all aspects of those antagonistic relations of imposed work
and therefore becomes a terrain of struggle as capitalists try to use
money to manage and expand their social order while workers re-
sist that usage, often subverting money for their own purposes.[65]

Chapter 1, of course, is only the beginning of Marx's analysis
of the nature of money and its roles in the class struggle. Although
most of Marx's analysis in all three volumes of *Capital* is carried out
in terms of value, chapters 2 and 3 of volume 1 elaborate his exposition of the "money-form" of value, especially its role as universal equivalent and universal mediator. Chapters 19–22 of volume 1
deal with how capital seeks to use the money wage to both hide
and increase exploitation. Chapter 31 of volume 1 briefly treats the
role of the state in the capitalist manipulation of money. Volume 2
situates money within more detailed circuits of capital. Volume 3
discusses the money-form of surplus value—profit—while providing the beginnings of an analysis of one domain specializing in the
capitalist manipulation of money, and through money of the class
relation: the financial sector.[66] Beyond *Capital*, of course, there are

---

65 Such a reading, I think, achieves precisely the necessary de-fetishization that
Marx calls to our attention in section 4 of chapter 1. He begins that process in
chapter 2 by resituating commodities in the hands of their owners and continues
through the next few chapters. My reading simply shows how the kinds of class relationships that he slowly reveals are more concrete embodiments of those already
present in his analysis of the substance, measure, and form of value.

66 Before proceeding, it is important, I think, to be clear about Marx's notion of the
relationship between profit—a familiar monetary phenomenon—and surplus value.
The first part of volume 3 of *Capital* deals with this relationship, the gist of which
can be stated as follows. "Monetary profit is generally understood as the excess of
revenue over costs," but that understanding hides the antagonistic social relationships involved and makes profit appear as a relation of capital to itself. The labor
theory of value, however, reveals those relationships—especially the exploitation of

the many other places—especially his journalism—where Marx recorded his own extensive tracking of the capitalist use of money and his analysis of its class role in the various crises of his time. Here I will focus briefly on some aspects of his analysis in chapter 1 of *Capital* that I think are particularly important for understanding "financialization" within the class struggle of our times.

Before I lay out what I think are some of the most important ways in which the relations being analyzed in chapter 1 are characteristics of the class relations of money, I want to make two preliminary comments. First, although I refer to my reading of Marx as an "interpretation," I do not pretend that this interpretation tells us what Marx really meant. I am no Marxologist; a great many of Marx's texts—either available in the *Marx-Engels-Gesamtausgabe (MEGA)* or still in archives—are inaccessible to me because I do not read German. Moreover, I have come to agree with those who argue that there are no such things as definitive interpretations. I merely offer an interpretation that I find useful. Second, unlike those who read chapter 1 as an analysis of any and all commodity exchange throughout history, from that recorded on the cuneiform tablets of ancient Sumer to the present, I understand it to contain an analysis of value within the context of a fully developed system of commodity exchange—something that has only existed within capitalism.

---

labor that results in those put to work by capital working more than is necessary for the reproduction of their labor power. "Profit is," Marx writes, "a transformed form of surplus-value, a form in which its origin and the secret of its existence are veiled and obliterated. In point of fact, profit is the form of appearance of surplus-value, and the latter can be sifted out from the former only by analysis. In surplus-value, the relationship between capital and labour is laid bare." Karl Marx, *Capital*, vol. 3 (New York: Penguin, 1990) 139.

THE SUBSTANCE OF VALUE:
ABSTRACT LABOR OR WORK AS SOCIAL CONTROL

As has often been noted, Marx organized chapter 1 of volume 1 of *Capital* in the manner of Hegel's *Science of Logic*—proceeding from the more abstract to the less abstract or to the more concrete. Less abstract means fewer aspects of the phenomenon analyzed are left out; more concrete means more aspects are taken into account. In other words, as his presentation progresses, as he brings in more and more aspects, his analysis becomes richer and a closer approximation of the real world phenomena that interest him. However, whereas in the beginning of his *Logic*, Hegel the philosopher strips down *being* to discover *nothingness* and then reconciles the two in the dialectical moment of *becoming*, Marx the revolutionary begins, instead, with *commodities*—concrete use-values produced for exchange by various kinds of labor commanded by capital—and strips them down not to nothingness but to *labor in the abstract,* or *abstract labor.*

Before taking up Marx's analysis of abstract labor, let's look at why he used Hegel's *Logic* as a template for his own presentation in *Capital.* He appears to have done so for two reasons. First, Hegel's very schoolbook-like, step-by-step, methodical exposition of his theory appealed to Marx because he wanted his own presentation to be accessible to "young people, etc., who are thirsting for knowledge."[1] Second, he agreed with Hegel that the dynamics of capitalist

---

1   Marx to Engels, June 22, 1867, in Marx and Engels, *Collected Works*, vol. 42, 384. While this motive is understandable, it is also true that several generations of readers have disagreed with his judgment about the accessibility of this approach. They have repeatedly found the highly abstract presentation in the first few chapters of *Capital* every bit as difficult to penetrate as those in Hegel's *Logic*. It is for this reason that during the forty-odd years that I taught volume 1 of *Capital*, I always had students start with part 8, on primitive accumulation. That section analyzes the historical rise of capitalism and illustrates how capital has imposed work—creating a "working" class—and in so doing made the imposition of work central to its organization of society. Once that is recognized, then the appropriateness of a theory of value centered on labor becomes clear, and the first chapter of the book can be read not just as an analysis of commodities but of aspects of the class relationship.

development were "dialectical." But what did they mean by dialectical? Clarifying this obscure term, warrants, I think, a parentheti-
cal, preparatory pause in this discussion of abstract labor.

*****

The term "dialectical" derives from the Greek *diálogos* and *dialek-
tikē* that originally referred to back-and-forth conversations between persons of opposing views, such as the Socratic dialogues
related by Plato. However, with Hegel and Marx—the two main
nineteenth-century analysts of capitalism who saw its development
as proceeding in a dialectical manner—their analysis of that dialectic was much more complex than an interaction between competing views. Hegel, a philosopher, saw dialectical relationships in
everything and knit virtually every kind of relationship previously
identified by philosophers and scientists into one comprehensive
dialectical system. That system included, but was not limited to,
the dynamics of capitalism. Marx's work, in contrast, focused almost exclusively on capitalism and consisted of discovering how
it reproduces its conflicted social relations on an ever-expanding
scale.[2] In doing so, he drew upon Hegel's analysis of the dialectical
character of various social relationships but elaborated a theory of
those relationships aimed at undermining them.

His elaboration involved first identifying how the most fundamental social relationships within capitalism are those of work
and then formulating theoretical categories denoting essential
aspects of those work relationships. Because he also recognized
and pointed out how capital had to *impose* work against the resistance of people to having their lives subordinated to work, his
categories also grasped the inherently antagonistic character of
capitalism. Where Socrates and Plato illustrated the dialectical
character of debate and Hegel found it throughout the cosmos,
Marx focused on the dialectical character of struggle within capitalism between those who seek to impose work and those who
resist—while often seeking to elaborate alternative ways of being

---

2   This was not the case with his best friend and collaborator Friedrich Engels—
who tried to correct Hegel's dialectic by reworking it on what he considered a more
materialist basis. In so doing, he laid the groundwork upon which later, orthodox
Marxists built their theories of historical and materialist dialectics.

and kinds of relationships. His theoretical categories are those of his labor theory of value.

But, in providing an analysis of how capitalists try to organize the world, his theory also provides a useful weapon against that organization, against the endless subordination of our lives to work. The theory provides a weapon by identifying both the dialectical chains that bind us and the possibilities for us to rupture them, progressively and then definitively.[3]

In Hegel's philosophy, every ruptured relationship is always superseded by a new one—but one still trapped within his dialectic. The new one always incorporates something of the one superseded and something of whatever force created the rupture—for example, *nothingness* may negate *being*, but both are preserved in *becoming*. This dialectic of *aufheben* (of both transcending but also preserving) is inevitable and eternal. Hegel's dialectic goes on forever.[4]

In Marx's theory, on the contrary, the dialectical relationships of capitalism are not eternal but were imposed in recent history and are repeatedly threatened with rupture, or actually ruptured, by our struggles. To reproduce those relationships, capitalists must constantly re-create and manage a complex set of conflicts, each one of which constitutes a moment of antagonistic class struggle and possible rupture. They must force us to come to them for jobs, wages, and livelihood. With those of us they hire, they must actually succeed at getting us to work producing commodities at costs low enough to guarantee profits. But to realize those profits, they must also convince us to buy those commodities at high enough

---

3 Something similar can be discovered in economics if one studies it not merely as ideological justification but as part of the strategic thought of capital. Because economics studies how to promulgate capitalism and how to solve problems that arise in its development, and because the most fundamental source of problems is the resistance of people and their efforts to escape, the policies developed by economists invariably involve strategies and tactics aimed at combating that resistance and frustrating those efforts. Understanding those strategies and tactics are essential in figuring out how to defeat them.

4 A common English translation of "*aufheben*" among Hegel scholars is another unfamiliar word: "sublation." Inasmuch as Hegel himself felt compelled to write quite a few words explaining what he meant by *aufheben*, I see no reason to substitute an English word that also requires an explanation.

prices. We have ruptured each of these relationships, again and again, each time adding stories to our own history of struggle. We have fled being put to work; this is the story of immigration, of escaped slaves, and of Maroon colonies. It is the story of the American frontier where our immigrant ancestors went West in search of land and freedom from capitalist jobs. It is also the story of our Native American ancestors who fought back, generally preferring death-in-armed-resistance or flight to being forced to work for those stealing their land and trying to destroy their way of life. Those of us who have not escaped but have entered the labor market and obtained jobs have often laid down our tools and walked away from those jobs, bringing the assembly lines and the production of commodities to a halt. Those are stories of strikes and insurrections. Even when we have continued to work, we have often refused to buy commodities produced by others of us in struggle. These are stories of shoplifting, consumer boycotts—such as the famous grape boycott in the 1960s that forced California growers to negotiate with the United Farm Workers—and urban "commodity riots," uprisings in which a primary activity is direct appropriation.

So far, capitalists have succeeded in overcoming many ruptures and reestablishing the original or new relationships of imposed work. Sometimes that overcoming has been quick: our strikes have been broken, our rebellions crushed. Sometimes it has taken long years: the closing of the frontier and the replacement of family farms by agribusiness corporations and factory farming. In some cases, capital has even been able to use the ruptures we have caused for its own development. Such is the essence of "instrumentalization," a concept akin to *aufheben* and dear to the hearts of critical theorists who have identified and analyzed many ways in which capital has sought to internalize our struggles.

Our struggles off the job, say in schools, have sometimes provoked new forms of schooling, new ways of socializing us into the acceptance of a life of work.[5] Similarly, while struggles by women to

---

5   In the 1960s and 1970s, in response to the widespread student protests on campuses across the country, not only was the architecture of campuses often reconfigured to render protests more difficult (large open spaces broken up by walls and plantings), the concept of breaking up and dispersing campus facilities was also toyed with. The objective was to reduce the facility with which students could

escape the burden of endless housework have forced capital to offer pay for such work through "family allocations" or Aid to Families with Dependent Children (1935–1996) and then Temporary Assistance for Needy Families (1997–), the primary welfare programs in the United States, such programs have been structured to provide ways to manage the reproduction of the labor force.[6]

Our struggles on the job, for fewer hours and higher wages and benefits, have often goaded business into mechanization and automation—substituting passive machines and robots for troublesome workers. But higher wages have also produced another kind of adaptation: soliciting—through advertising and the ideology of consumerism—the expenditure of our increased income on ever more commodities, whether they improve our lives or not. The more commodities they succeed in convincing us that we want, the more work we must do to obtain the money necessary to buy them.[7] Both the growth of the advertising industry itself and the increased industrial output that results from expanded markets create ever more opportunities for putting us to work. Of course, faced with the daily onslaught of advertising, we resist, either developing sharp critical theories of their attempted manipulation or

---

organize and protest within single-site campuses. It is arguable that the recent rise of online education and Massive Open Online Courses (MOOCs) is a long-term, technological effort to achieve the longed-for dispersal of college students. The strategy of workplace-dispersal by business predated such efforts in schools and had the same aim: to reduce the ability of their workers to organize—most notably in Italy, where such scattered production facilities are called *la fabbrica diffusa* or diffused factory. The scattering of production facilities across the face of the earth by multinational corporations also serves the same purpose.

6   See Mariarosa Dalla Costa, *Famiglia, welfare e stato tra Progressismo e New Deal* (Milan: FrancoAngeli, 1983), just recently available in English translation as *Family, Welfare and the State: Between Progressivism and the New Deal* (Brooklyn: Common Notions, 2015). Dalla Costa shows how at the same time workers won various kinds of income for the unwaged, the state was able to structure those programs as essential parts of the new Keynesian productivity deal that would seek to frame class struggle over the next three decades.

7   It is because buying more stuff requires more work that consumerism merely complements the imposition of work rather than replacing it as capital's fundamental means of domination.

simply mocking and condemning their efforts. For some, rebellion against the seduction of the "newest thing" and the endless work required to purchase it takes the form of minimizing work and shopping, in favor of various forms of self-valorization in the time and energy set free by those refusals.[8]

Recently I saw a news report on *femvertising*, a business response to years of protests against advertising that demeans women. The response involves a reorientation away from images and stories of women in traditional, stereotypical gender roles, to those that emphasize women's power to shape their own lives. Thus, femvertizing provides an excellent example of attempted instrumentalization, or the internalization of our struggles for capitalist purposes. Instead of ignoring or opposing feminism, business tries to use it to convince women to buy commodities. The transition from the use of demeaning images to the use of "empowering" images of women measures both our power to critique and resist as well as capital's efforts to harness that power. At the same time, this case reminds me of the old adage "a capitalist will sell you the rope to hang him with, if he can make a profit in the process." Advertising that demeans women serves to keep them in their subordinate places in a gendered hierarchy. Advertising that actually empowers them can only lead to further struggles against such subordination and thus further threats to the capitalist order. Where critical theorists have seen only instrumentalization, the perspective offered here recognizes it but also forecasts new struggles within a still antagonistic composition of class relationships.[9]

More generally, the unsurpassably antagonistic character of capitalist social relationships means that each supersession of rupture only leads to new vulnerabilities. Future supersession is never guaranteed. Ruptures may expand; the number of people

---

8   Although such resistance might seem to exist only among the relatively affluent, this is not the case. In Tepito, a Mexico City barrio known for its fierce political independence, families often distribute necessary tasks so as to minimize the time each must spend working in order to free up time and energy for political engagement (and communal festivities). See H. Cleaver, "The Uses of an Earthquake," *Midnight Notes*, no. 9 (May 1988), 10–14.

9   See Nina Bahadur, "'Femvertising' Ads Are Empowering Women—and Making Money for Brands," *Huffington Post*, October 3, 1014.

involved in a strike or rebellion may grow.[10] Ruptures may circulate and spread; an uprising in one place may lead to others elsewhere. Ruptures of one sort may lead to ruptures of other sorts. Strikes shutting down production, if prolonged, may lead to inventory depletion and the inability of struck corporations to sell. Those strikes or broader uprisings may reduce investment and increase layoffs and unemployment, resulting in a collapse of demand. Ruptures in demand can spread, creating a commercial crisis. Commercial crises may lead to the collapse of credit and financial crises. The collapse of credit may bankrupt some corporations and many consumers, producing greater unemployment, reductions in income, housing foreclosures, and so on. As ruptures expand and catalyze others, the crisis facing capital spreads and deepens, increasing the possibility of complete rupture—of the revolutionary overthrow and transcendence of the system as a whole. This understanding of the ever-renewed possibilities of rupturing and overthrowing capital's dialectic justifies the optimism of Marxism—an optimism repeatedly frustrated but forever renewed.

As I will illustrate in the body of this text, Hegel's integration of previously identified types of relationships into his overall philosophy mirrored capital's own conversion of many preexisting relationships into moments of its own command, its own way of organizing society. The rupture of that command, therefore, often involves the destruction of existing relationships only in the sense of freeing them from capital's grip and of reorganizing them in healthier, more appealing ways.

*****

Returning to the concept of abstract labor, Marx argues, as Sweezy, Meek, and many others have noted, that we can meaningfully abstract from the concrete forms of labor and see abstract labor as the *substance* of value. He then goes on to analyze, in section 2 of chapter 1, the *measure* of value and in section 3, the *form* of value. Although most Marxists have been content to accept the logic of

---

10   There is a wonderful scene in Elia Kazan's 1952 film *Viva Zapata!* that vividly illustrates such phenomena. In that scene, protesting peasants marching along a road are joined by more and more of their fellows, who put down their tools and leave their fields.

Marx's argument, *the key question for me has been what seman-tic sense does it make to abstract labor from its various, concrete forms?*[11] The traditional answer, in those passages of Marx cited by Sweezy and Meek, points to the malleability of labor under capitalism, to the ever-changing array of labor tasks and associat-ed redistribution of workers among them. It suggests that if, over time, the particular content of labor is increasingly secondary, then it makes sense to speak of labor abstracted from that chang-ing content. But in what sense is it *secondary?*[12] Clearly, there are some important passages in *Capital* where the particular content of labor is vitally important to Marx's analysis. For example, in chapters 12–15 of volume 1 of *Capital*, repeated alterations in the technical composition (e.g., the shop floor arrangement of work-ers, tools, machines, and raw materials) are shown to have been historically essential in maintaining or regaining control over the working class.

But, in capitalism, "control" means, above all, the ability to keep people working at producing commodities—including the com-modity labor power.[13] Although the capitalist class has historically exercised many other kinds of control, many violently coercive (e.g., wars of conquest, slavery, beating, rape, gassing or shooting work-ers on strike or people just for being black and walking or standing

---

11   This question emerged from a conversation with Joan Robinson in December 1971 while strolling through the French Quarter of New Orleans one evening of the annual conference of the American Economic Association. We were discussing Marx's theory, and she asked, "What is value?" At the time, I could only repeat what I had read in Marx. But I realized she wanted an answer that explained—in the vernacular—the meaning of value. With no ready answer, I returned to her simple question many times, as I sought an interpretation of Marx's theory that made some kind of everyday sense to me.

12   Marx will also refer to the labor that qualifies as abstract labor as "undiffer-entiated human labor." But, again, what justifies *not* differentiating among various kinds of concrete labor?

13   An interesting challenge has been repeatedly raised to limiting Marx's analysis of such control to *human* workers. See Jason Hribal, "Animals Are Part of the Work-ing Class: A Challenge to Labor History," *Labor History* 44, no. 4 (2003), 435–53, and his *Fear of the Animal Planet: The Hidden History of Animal Resistance* (Oak-land: AK Press, 2010).

in the street, and torture in police stations, prisons, and mental hospitals) and some more subtle (e.g., the mechanisms of cultural and political hegemony that preoccupied Gramsci, the Frankfurt School theorists, the Situationists and many others), the overwhelmingly dominant form of control, around which all the others are organized, *the form of control that eats up the bulk of most people's time and energy, is work.* Both *how* people are forced to give up most of their time and energy to working for capital and the *particular kinds* of work people have been forced to do have been extremely important, but the *how* and the *kinds* have been means to an end. From the point of view of capitalist control, *the particular kinds of work have been secondary to the mere fact of working.*

On the job, all forms of concrete labor—skilled or unskilled, complex or simple, waged or salaried—serve the same basic purpose within capitalism: they provide the fundamental means by which capitalists organize, control, and dominate our time, our energy, and thus society. Waged or salaried work on the job also dominates our lives beyond the formal working day—turning so-called leisure or spare time into unwaged work. In Marxian jargon, this is the work of producing the most fundamental commodity of all: labor power, or the ability and willingness to work for capital.

Before illustrating the kinds of unwaged activities that produce and reproduce labor power, I want to address an obvious question: do those activities qualify as "labor" (or work) according to the definition Marx provided in *Capital* that I pointed to in my discussion of Thesis #2 above (i.e., people using tools on raw materials to produce commodities)? People rearing and taking care of other people would seem to be a case of interacting wills, rather than one will acting on will-less, passive objects. However, because what is being produced is labor power—not only the ability but the willingness to work for capital—I think that we can see that human beings (babies, then children and adults themselves) are being treated as raw materials in the production of labor power. The creation of the willingness to work for capital involves shaping people to subordinate their own wills to that of capital—both of direct employers and of capitalist-constructed laws and "norms." Doing so is not easy; people resist. It takes years of conditioning. It also takes threats and penalties to cope with rebellion that escapes such subordination. All this requires specialized tools, indeed, a wide variety of instruments, starting with human bodies that procreate and provide milk and later other forms of nourishment, including psychological care, and in the process are annexed as bio-capital. Other tools include those only available as commodities (e.g., in vitro-fertilization, surrogate bodies, breast-pumps, milk bottles, raw food, cooking equipment, clothing, and housing), as well as institutions such as single-family dwellings, factory-like schools, homelessness, immigration, police forces, jails, armies, and a plethora of cultural practices designed to manufacture consent. All these and more are required to achieve and maintain this warping of human being into elements of capital.

However much *we* might want having children, rearing them, and taking care of each other to be purely expressions of our mutual love and affection, examining the history of pro-capitalist understandings reveals how well Marx's definition of labor (work) fits capital's successes in turning acts based on affection into the work of producing labor power.[14] Early political economists such as Adam Smith were quite aware of the need to shape people into beings both able and willing to do the work required of them by capitalists.[15] More recently, economists formulated such shaping as the forming of "human capital"—that, like physical capital, must be produced and reproduced.[16] Based on such formulations, they have designed policies of "manpower" planning that include programs of immigration, education, and welfare to achieve that result.

Therefore, as Dolly Parton recognized, work is not just "9 to 5." Dressing for the job is work. Preparing our faces for the

---

14 I highlight affection as a best-case scenario. Clearly capital has also reshaped other modes of domination into forms suitable to the production and reproduction of labor power (e.g., patriarchy, caste-based systems, and ethnic and racial hierarchies).

15 See Adam Smith, *An Inquiry into the Nature and Causes of the Wealth of Nations* (1776), book 5, article 2 (*"Of the Expense of the Institution for the Education of Youth"*).

16 See Theodore W. Schultz, "Investment in Human Capital," *American Economic Review* 51, no. 1 (March 1961), 1–17; Gary S. Becker, *Human Capital: A Theoretical and Empirical Analysis, with Special Reference to Education* (National Bureau of Economic Research, 1964).

job by shaving them or decorating them with makeup, dressing with uniforms and drugging ourselves with caffeine are all work. Commuting to the job is work. Getting home from the job and recuperating—both physically and psychologically—is work.[17] Even such mundane activities as washing clothes, preparing food, eating food, and sleeping—to the degree they are necessary for our jobs—become just more hours of work subordinated to the requirements of our bosses. Added to these everyday activities of waged or salaried workers, we must also count the endless hours of procreating, rearing, and educating children. Although much of the effort we expend in maintaining our homes and caring for our children is motivated by affection, to the degree that those activities involve shaping them as the next generation of workers they constitute one more kind of work. Think, for example, of the state laws that require parents to do the work of truant officers, making sure their children attend school.[18] Think, also, of the very real work, increasingly expected of parents, of forcing their children to do homework mandated by their teachers. Where schools are primarily geared to preparing children for future labor markets or housework—instead of helping them learn what they need to struggle against exploitation and alienation or to realize their creative talents—both homework and its enforcement is work-for-capital. Marx's labor theory of value provides tools for understanding the value of all these different kinds of work to capital. The value of work lies in its appropriation of people's time and energy. It eats up people's lives, or, as Marx liked

---

17 Recognition of the derivative nature of all these activities can also be found in the Kinks' concept-album *Soap Opera* (1975). It contains a whole series of songs, each of which deals with a different moment of a day subordinated to work. It predated Parton's 1980 movie and song about working "9 to 5."

18 In Texas, until just recently, truancy was a criminal offense—a misdemeanor offense but tried in adult courts. According to one source, in fiscal year 2014, nearly 100,000 Texas students received misdemeanor charges for too many unexcused absences. Fines—generally paid for by parents—were up to $500. "Parents Contributing to Nonattendance" was also a misdemeanor offense. See *Class, Not Court: Reconsidering Texas' Criminalization of Truancy* (Texas Appleseed, 2015), http:// blogs.edweek.org/edweek/rulesforengagement/TruancyReport_All_FINAL_ SinglePages.pdf.

to damn it in Gothic terms, capital, "vampire-like, lives only by sucking living labor."[19]

Moreover, capital does not just suck *some* living labor; it sucks as much as it has the power to suck and in the process sucks the grounds of life itself: time and energy. During periods when it has succeeded in expanding its power, it has imposed more and more work—see Marx's detailed history in chapter 10 of *Capital* on the working day or his analysis of the expansion of colonialism. As Bram Stoker's Dracula set sail for England, so did England's capitalist vampires cross oceans to build an empire, "sucking living labor" wherever they had the power to impose work. Today the thirst rages on as measured by the successes of multinational capital in imposing longer and more intense working hours, on the job and off, reversing decades of worker-won *reductions* in work.[20] It is also manifested in contemporary campaigns at the elementary and secondary school level to extend the hours of the school day and the length of the school year and at the college and university level to increase degree requirements and accelerate their completion.

Many Marxists often argue that the value of labor to capital is simply profit-making—that is, they put us to work producing commodities they can sell at such prices as to realize a surplus value or profit. Capital operates, they assert, "for the sole purpose of the endless growth and reproduction of its monetary value."[21] To this I respond as follows. "Yes, but as some capitalist ideologists (e.g., Irving Kristol and many socially and politically aware capitalists) have recognized, the primary *social* role of profit is maintaining and creating jobs." Kristol the apologist sees creating jobs as a gift capitalists give workers, allowing them to live. Marx shows us how the "gift" is actually a theft, how the imposition and expanded imposition of work steals our time, our energy, our lives. Or, in the terms he uses in chapter 25 of volume I of *Capital*, the expanded

---

19   This famous passage—only one of several such Gothic metaphors—can be found in section 5 of chapter 10 of volume 1 of *Capital*.

20   Between roughly 1880 and 1940, workers succeeded in chopping the working week down from an average of eighty hours to only forty. Thereafter, their efforts won paid holidays, unpaid vacation time, and earlier retirement—not as much in the United States as in Europe but still significant gains.

21   De Angelis, *The Beginning of History*, 6.

imposition of work is *accumulation*, or the expanded reproduction of the class relation. Therefore, socially and politically speaking, profit-making is merely the capitalist means to its social end of controlling us by forcing us to work.

Clearly the realization of *surplus* value is a necessary condition for the continued imposition of any concrete labor (or set of concrete labors) and thus for the continued realization of value *tout court* (i.e., of labor as social control). But as Marx wrote at the beginning of section 2 of chapter 10 of *Capital*, "Capitalism did not invent surplus labor." Obviously, earlier dominant classes imposed work on subservient classes (slaves, serfs, etc.) that went beyond what they had to do for their own survival. What then did capitalism invent? His answer: the *endless* imposition of labor. In earlier class societies, the amount of surplus labor was limited by the particular concrete work requirements of the masters (e.g., a pyramid for a pharaoh, a temple for a Greek religious cult, a castle for a feudal lord). But in capitalism the imposition of work and the realization of value and surplus value goes on endlessly, as long as the system manages to survive. Capital progressively commodifies more and more of life by converting more and more human activities into commodity-producing, value-producing, and surplus-value-producing labor. It commodifies chunks of nonhuman nature by converting them into mere resources for processing by more labor. It turns even unwaged activities (e.g., home life and school life) into the work of producing and reproducing the commodity labor power. And that unwaged work, by holding down the value of labor power, increases surplus value and through it the imposition of ever more work.[22] In all of this, it turns society—first local and re-

---

22   The seminal discussion of the relationship between housework, the value of labor power, and surplus value is Mariarosa Dalla Costa, "Donne e sovversione sociale" (usually translated as "Women and the Subversion of the Community"), originally written as a discussion piece for a gathering of feminists in Padua, Italy, in 1971. Her analysis was widely interpreted and critiqued as arguing that housework produces surplus value in the same manner as commodity-producing factory labor. However, I argue that a better interpretation sees her pointing out how housework contributes to increasing surplus value by lowering the value of labor power, by reducing the amount of commodity-producing labor that must be allocated to those consumer goods necessary for the production and reproduction of labor power. See H. Cleaver,

gional, then national and continental, and finally global—into one giant work machine, organized according to its own logic.

However, thanks to the diligent work of several generations of bottom-up and subaltern historians, we also know that the entire history of the construction of this global work machine has simultaneously been a history of resistance to the imposition of work and to the logic of its organization. It has been a history of revolt against the exploitation it requires and against the alienations it produces. It has been a history of invisible covert and barely visible overt resistance. From time to time, it has also been a history of quite visible rebellion and revolutionary struggles to free life from the endless subordination to work in order to gain space, time, and energy to elaborate alternatives. The class relations of capitalism have always been *antagonistic* relations, and, because work has been the fundamental form of domination, the struggle against work has always been at the heart of resistance, rebellion, and the search for autonomy—no matter the particular content of the autonomy sought in particular struggles or the consciousness of those in struggle. For example, the struggle against racism has opposed both racist attitudes and how racial prejudice has been used by capitalism to relegate racial minorities to the worst jobs and most difficult living conditions. The civil rights movement sought the vote as a means to end such discrimination. Women's struggles against patriarchy have not only opposed male dominance but how that dominance has been used by capitalism to keep so many women working without wages, producing and reproducing labor power. The welfare rights movement—led overwhelmingly by women—sought changes that would lighten the workload of mothers imposed by welfare agencies and low levels of income support. Those struggles have also attacked the capitalist tendency to confine women who have succeeded in getting jobs to lower paid ones.

The labor theory of value, interpreted as a theory of the value of labor to capital, captures labor as the substance of capitalist domination and provides many of the characteristics of the antagonistic class relations it imposes and seeks to maintain. In chapter 1 of volume 1 of *Capital*, Marx's exposition assumes capital's dialectical

---

"Domestic Labor and Value in Mariarosa Dalla Costa's 'Women and the Subversion of the Community' (1971)," Caring Labor, https://caringlabor.wordpress.com/.

relationships are well-managed and stable. But, as he soon points out in chapter 3, these relationships can be ruptured. In the case of the dialectic of *abstract labor*, rupture involves stripping various kinds of human activity of their common usefulness to capital as a means of social control.[23]

Piecemeal, ruptures occur every time people engage in activities, either on the job or off, that do *not* contribute to the expanded reproduction of the social relationships of capital. So, when carpenters in eighteenth-century London shipyards diverted their woodworking skills to scraps of lumber appropriated on the job in order to make things they could use at home or sell, or when machinists in the twentieth-century Red Star Tractor Factory in Budapest used their machines to make "homers" for similar purposes, those activities ruptured the capitalist appropriation of their skills, energy, and time as means of social control.[24] When office workers use their computers to browse the Internet instead of processing their spreadsheets, they steal time from their bosses, momentarily rupturing the process of production. When students sitting in classrooms ignore their professors while texting their friends, or shirk their homework in favor of pursuing their real intellectual agendas, they are rupturing the production of labor power and capitalist control over their lives. When women limit the number of children they are willing to bear and rear, or reduce the amount of other forms of housework they are willing to perform, they too are undermining the production of labor power.

---

23 In the process, the concept of abstract labor and the associated notion of a generic concept of labor (or work)—as laid out by Marx in section 1 of chapter 7 of volume 1 of *Capital*—both become irrelevant. See H. Cleaver, "Work Is Still the Central Issue!"

24 On the shipyard carpenters, see "Ships and Chips: Technological Repression and the Origins of the Wage," in Peter Linebaugh, *The London Hanged: Crime and Civil Society in the Eighteenth Century* (London: Verso, 2006), 371–401. On the Budapest machinists, see Miklos Haraszti, *A Worker in a Worker's State* (London: Penguin, 1977). Haraszti wrote the original manuscript in 1972 and titled it *Darab-bér* (Piece-rates); it was suppressed by the Hungarian state but was eventually published in Germany (1975) and in England and France (1977). By detailing workers' struggles, it makes a fine complement to chapter 21 (on "piece-wages") of volume 1 of *Capital*, where the emphasis is on methods of exploitation.

Collectively, when workers put down tools and go on strike, they obviously rupture production—whether they occupy their factories or offices or simply leave them. Students do the same to the production of labor power when they down pencils, close their laptops, and walk out of schools. Instead of reproducing their labor power, they engage in entirely different kinds of activity. When they occupy university buildings, they also often rupture ongoing research and whatever role it plays in capitalist reproduction—or they appropriate the space for self-organized, autonomous learning through teach-ins and discussion. When women get together and organize movements for their liberation from patriarchal institutions that burden them with the bulk of unwaged housework, they undermine their role in the reproduction of labor power.

Insurrections involve all kinds of people, rupturing all kinds of work for capital. Every time some concrete form of labor for capital is stopped, its quality as "abstract labor," as a means of social control, is ruptured. The revolutionary overthrow of capitalism can and will only be achieved with the end of work as a means of social control—the abolition of the material grounds of the concept of abstract labor. As the memory of capitalism fades, the meaning of the word "work" will likely be reduced to its vernacular sense of exerting a lot of effort or one of its scientific senses (e.g., of exerted force causing a displacement).[25] Human activities would continue to exist in all their variety, but there would no longer be any reason to lump those activities (that currently fit Marx's definition of "labor/work" within capitalism) under a single rubric.[26]

---

25 If you look into the concept of "work" in physics, you will find several different ways in which work is defined in relation to such associated concepts as force, energy, entropy, and so on. The most interesting connections between such scientific definitions of work and human work within capitalism that I have come across can be found in the Midnight Notes essay on *The Work/Energy Crisis and the Apocalypse* (1981), reprinted in George Caffentzis, *In Letters of Blood and Fire: Work, Machines, and the Crisis of Capitalism* (Oakland: PM Press, 2013), 11–57.

26 Cleaver, "Work Is Still the Central Issue!"

CAN VALUE BE MEASURED?

If imposed work is the fundamental means for organizing and controlling capitalist society, then clearly *measuring the amount of work imposed* is vital both to those who want to impose lots of it and those of us who want to minimize or escape it. An obvious, simple measure of the amount of work capitalists succeed in imposing in its global work machine is the number of us it is able to put to work. Another measure of their success might be the *percentage* of the world's population brought under their sway and put to work. As capitalism spread across the face of the globe, colonizing ever-greater numbers of people and seizing and enclosing ever greater swaths of land, that percentage grew steadily from the sixteenth century on. The result, of course, was resistance and rebellion. Unfortunately, sometimes when people thought they had broken free, as in the great revolutions in Russia and China, they soon found themselves once again commanded by a government hell-bent on putting them back to work.[1] Even the post–World War II tide of anticolonial, independence movements failed to exorcise the capitalist hold on people everywhere. Management of the imposition of work merely passed from foreign to local hands.

However, given the almost universal resistance to imposed work, whether in European factories, colonial plantations and mines, or postcolonial workplaces, it is not merely the number of people who are put to work, but just *how much work* capitalists actually succeed in imposing on individuals that matters. Getting ex-peasants and farmers, habituated to the daily rhythms of rural life, to accept machine time in urban factories has been a constant problem from early industrialization to current projects of outsourcing in the Global South.[2] Getting alienated factory workers to show up on time, work steadily, and not leave early, continues

---

1   One of the first demands of Russian workers after the revolution was a shortening of their hours of working. Lenin immediately started figuring out how to curb that vice and impose more work rather than less.

2   See the discussion in Herbert Gutman, "Work, Culture, and Society in Industrializing America, 1815–1919," in Herbert Gutman, ed., *Work, Culture, and Society in Industrializing America* (New York: Knopf), 1976, 3–78.

to be a problem for capitalists everywhere. Therefore, measuring the work done by individuals has always been as important as the number of them employed.

The most obvious measures of the amount of work of individuals are time and intensity; the longer and more intensely people can be made to work, the more work is actually done—and the greater the degree to which their lives' time and energy are drained by capital. Conversely, the fewer the hours and the more relaxed the pace of work, the more time and energy are left over for folks to utilize for autonomous purposes. Under these circumstances, it is not surprising that in volume 1 of *Capital*, after presenting his analysis of work as the substance of value, Marx devoted one of the longest chapters in the book, chapter 10, to "The Working Day," which was the conventional unit when discussing work time in the mid-nineteenth century.[3] There he traced capitalist success in imposing more and more hours of labor, working-class resistance to such lengthening of the workday, and then their success in forcing a reduction of working hours. Edward Thompson later added to this analysis by examining the imposition of mechanical clock time and how capitalists manipulated it to squeeze the maximum number of minutes of labor out of each working day.[4] In chapter 15, on "Machinery and Modern Industry," Marx took up the struggle over intensity, as capitalists removed control over the rhythm of work from the hands of workers by subordinating it to the speed of machines under managerial control.[5]

---

3 Keep in mind that vast numbers of workers worked seven days a week—until their own struggles (with support from religious Sabbatarians) freed first one day and then two, creating the weekend and making it common to speak of a "working week" of five days.

4 Edward Thompson, "Time, Work-Discipline and Industrial Capitalism," *Past and Present* 38, no. 1 (1963), 56–97.

5 One classical—must watch—critique of this method is portrayed during the opening twenty minutes of *Modern Times*. One of the better known contemporary battles over line speed concerns slaughterhouses. Faster speeds endanger workers wielding knives and prevents effective control over the spread of infectious disease from animal feces. In these cases, workers' resistance and self-defense are joined by animal rights activists and environmentalists. Little has changed, it seems, since Upton Sinclair wrote his devastating novel *The Jungle* in 1906 based on

Marx analyzed these struggles over time and intensity using his labor theory of value. The longer and more intensely capitalists succeed in making people work, the greater the value to capital of the labor embodied in the commodities they are producing, and—when the value of labor power is held steady—the greater the surplus value they earn upon the successful sale of those commodities. His analysis of this struggle over the time and intensity of labor is based on his analysis of value in chapter 1 of volume I of *Capital*.

There, in section 2, he argues that the proper measure of the value of a commodity is the *socially necessary labor time* required to produce it. This socially necessary labor time he carefully differentiates from the actual, concrete labor time used to produce particular commodities by particular sets of workers employing particular sets of skills. Clearly, this differentiation requires justification. To simply say that socially necessary labor time is the measure of abstract labor, rather than of concrete or useful labor, is insufficient. For Sweezy and Meek—as with many of their orthodox predecessors—getting from actual concrete labor, that is always a heterogeneous mix of skilled and unskilled, simple and complex labor, to a homogenous socially necessary labor was a major problem. They believed that the difficulty of measuring value lay in the varying levels of skill among different workers and of varying levels of complexity in different kinds of work. More skillful workers, they thought, would produce more value in a given time period than less skilled workers. Workers employed on complex production tasks might also produce more value—perhaps because more complex tasks require more skill.

There are two problems with this way of thinking. First, the notion that workers "produce" value suggests that value is some kind of thing. "To produce" is a transitive verb, so "value" appears as a direct object. This unfortunate formulation—utilized, all too

---

investigative reporting in Chicago's stockyards and slaughterhouses. Now, as then, a great many workers are immigrants with less ability to defend themselves. See Richard Linklater's 2006 film version of Eric Schlosser's *Fast Food Nation* (2001) for a vivid portrayal. So many guerrilla, whistle-blowing videos of the outrageous conditions in factory farming have been made—and posted on YouTube—that agribusiness corporations have promulgated Ag-Gag laws in several states to criminalize the exposure of their own lawbreaking.

often, by Marx himself—evokes a vague, mystical notion of value as a phlogiston-like substance exuded from workers' fingertips.[6] Second, as a corollary, the notion that skilled workers produce more value than unskilled workers implies that more of that mystical substance flows from skilled fingertips than from unskilled ones. But, if we set aside the notion that value is a thing, and that it is produced, there is nothing mystical about the notion of socially necessary labor time. Once we recognize that the concept of abstract labor, which Marx calls the substance of value, denotes one particular attribute of labor—its role as the primary vehicle of capitalist social control—the worrisome measurement problem as formulated by Sweezy and Meek disappears. If abstract labor is the mere quality of working for capital and thereby being under its control, then an hour of socially necessary labor, simple or complex, skilled or unskilled, serves the same social and political purpose. Why "socially necessary"? Because *when the value of labor to capital is its value as a vehicle of social control and domination, then the value of any particular product to capital as a whole is the average amount of control via labor it can impose in its production.* Concretely, that amount varies from production unit to production unit, from firm to firm, according to varying levels of labor skill and productivity. But for capital *at the social level of the class relation* (as opposed to mere local worker-capitalist ones), it is the *average* time labor can be imposed in producing some commodity that measures its value to capital as a whole.

This remains true even when we take the *intensity* of work into account—assuming that by increased (or decreased) intensity we mean working harder (or less hard), and by "harder" I mean exerting more effort, whether that means working more intently, working faster, or working more strenuously. A familiar twentieth-century example of the use of machinery in modern industry to speed up—and thus intensify—production is the infamous Fordist assembly line.

Ford introduced the assembly line to improve labor productivity—output per hour of work—in order to lower the costs of

---

6   There is a longer discussion of this problem in my online study guide's commentary on chapter 8 of volume 1 of *Capital*. In that chapter, Marx repeatedly uses transitive verbs in writing about "creating," "transferring" and "preserving" value.

production and increase profits.[7] This was achieved by imposing a fine division of labor in which workers assembling automobiles worked sequentially—each worker undertaking one narrowly defined task—at a rhythm imposed by the speed of the line.[8] Such lines not only involve a new division of unskilled labor that raises productivity, but they also provide a mechanical means to speed up work. As management speeds up the line itself, work tasks are presented to each worker more quickly, requiring them to work faster. In such cases, we need merely reformulate the concept of "social average" from "the average *time* labor can be imposed" to "the average *amount* of labor that can be imposed" in producing a unit of some commodity. The more labor (whether measured by time or by amount of effort) that can be imposed on us in producing a unit, the more of our lives are being subordinated to capitalist control in the production of that unit and thus the more valuable that unit is to capital.[9] Clearly, as Marx understood, the harder we can be forced to work, the more of our life energy is being drained. So the

---

7   Increased productivity also made it possible for Ford to pay higher than average wages—and thus reduce the notoriously high turnover in his plants—and still increase profits.

8   Discovering how complex work processes could be broken down into narrowly defined tasks was the work of "scientific management" developed by Frederick Taylor (1856–1915). Imposing this new division of labor on workers not only increased productivity but also benefited their bosses by reducing workers' control over production. This was understood early on by Adam Smith who discussed the advantages in *The Wealth of Nations* (1776). Marx offered his own analysis of sequential tasking in chapter 14 in volume 1 of *Capital*, on the division of labor. The twentieth-century assembly line helped undermine forms of working-class organization based on skilled workers' control over the labor process in the existing division of labor (e.g., the kind of craft unions formed by skilled workers that made up the American Federation of Labor).

9   Such increased imposition of work must be taken into account when judging the degree to which a rise in productivity (measured in terms of output per hour) actually reduces the amount of work required per unit and thus the usefulness of the production of those units for imposing work. If, for example, a change in production technique results not only in a 100 percent increase in productivity (doubling output in a given period), but also in a 100 percent increase in the amount of work imposed in that same period, there would be *no* reduction in the amount of work required per unit.

more intense our working days, even if the hours remain the same, the more valuable to capital than less intense ones—the more living labor is sucked, the more the vampire's hunger is sated, the more control over our lives is achieved.

The implications of this strategy of speedup are far-reaching, both on the job and off.

For one thing, the more successful capital is in forcing us to work harder on the job, the less energy we have off the job; more of our time and energy must be given over to recuperation—in evenings, on weekends, and on vacations. In other words, the work of reproducing labor power, our ability and willingness to work, also gets harder and more time-consuming. This is true both for the waged workers who arrive home beaten down during arduous workdays, and for unwaged spouses and children who must exert more time and energy helping the wage-earner recuperate. The same is true for schools. As those edu-factories increasingly subject students to speedup in their classrooms, in their homework, and in their progress toward completing their studies, the less and less time and energy is available for unrelated activities.

For another thing, in volume 3 of *Capital*, Marx argues that this strategy of raising productivity with new machinery and, in the process, reducing the amount of work that can be imposed to produce each unit of output undermines the class relationship itself, by undermining the imposition of work. That argument can be found in the chapters on "the tendency of the rate of profit to fall." Most Marxists interpret that tendency literally and often look for data to demonstrate that the rate of monetary profit actually has had an historical tendency to fall. What I am arguing here is that "the tendency" concerns how it becomes harder and harder to impose work as the rise in productivity reduces the amount of work (including surplus work) that can be imposed in the production of each unit of output. As this strategy comes to be applied in production process after production process, in industry after industry, the problem of finding the means to impose work, and the social control it provides, becomes greater and greater. Solving that problem requires all kinds of offsetting innovations such as the creation of new products (and new production processes) that provide new opportunities to impose labor. It matters not if the new products contribute only very marginal advantages over existing ones, or even if they are downright detrimental to the general welfare; as long as they provide profitable new opportunities to impose work, their production helps keep people busy and the system growing.

This contradiction—between the way capital organizes society and the way this strategy undermines its ability to impose that organization—has not been merely theoretical but has become manifest at several different moments in the history of capitalism.

One such moment in the United States was in the late 1950s and early 1960s, when the rapid spread of automation in manufacturing led economists and other policy makers to worry about where the jobs could be found to maintain the full employment mandated by the working class at the end of World War II and judged necessary by capitalist policy makers to avoid the kind of social upheaval prompted by the high unemployment of the 1930s.[10] The solution that emerged in the 1960s was the rise of the service sector, where low levels of productivity provided great opportunities for imposing work. Inevitably, of course, the same dynamic has been developing in the service sector (e.g., computerization in the financial sector) and undermining the usefulness of *that* sector as a domain in which lots of work can be imposed.

A second set of such moments in the 1960s that raised the same question arose in the Global South, where the importation of capital-intensive technologies in production were failing to provide enough jobs to absorb rapid increases in urban populations brought on by rural enclosures and by the increased mechanization of agricultural production. These phenomena and their dangers were familiar from US experience in the 1940s, where the mechanization of cotton picking in southern states had led to massive out-migration from rural areas—first to big cities in the South and then to big cities in the North. That influx of largely African-American labor was channeled into urban ghettos, eventually providing recruits to the civil rights movement and then

---

10   The Full Employment Act of 1946 codified that mandate, charging the federal government with the responsibility to so manage the economy as to avoid socially costly and disruptive levels of unemployment. It was one important parameter framing the overall Keynesian strategy with which capital sought, and was largely able for a time, to limit and harness workers' struggles (more on this below).

exploding in the uprisings of the mid-1960s. The dangers of such parallel phenomena in the Global South haunted a generation of development economists as well as policy makers fearful that the absence of jobs would lead to political upheavals and further mass migrations—northbound migrations, across borders and into the United States and northern Europe, that would far outstrip the need for immigrant labor.[11] The solution in those cases, if it can be called a solution, was provided, for a while, mainly from below: the rise of the so-called *informal sector*, in which people have found myriad ways of surviving in cities without waged jobs—ways varying from begging and peddling through small-scale production to organized crime. In other words, those unable or unwilling to find waged or salaried jobs have found or created various kinds of activities, outside the formal economy, enabling them to survive.[12] To what degree such activities keep people busy and are thus valuable to capital is an interesting question. Some have celebrated the entrepreneurial character of such bottom-up initiatives and paint images of hardworking go-getters; others have pointed out how

11 Although the immediate sources are different, the current influxes of refugees from Syria into western Europe and from Central America into the United States are precisely the kind of uncontrolled movement feared by those policy makers. The keyword is "uncontrolled" because importing and pitting cheap foreign workers against local, more expensive workers has been a capitalist strategy since Marx's time. He saw it in the way British capital pitted Irish workers against English ones and in the way slavery in the United States undercut the struggles of waged workers. See Marx to Sigfrid Meyer and August Vogt, April 9, 1870, in Marx and Engels, *Collected Works*, vol. 43, 471–76.

12 It should never be assumed that those without waged jobs want them. They may, or they may not, depending on circumstances, especially the availability of alternative sources of income and social support—whether formal, as in welfare, or informal, as in participation in personal, community-based, off-the-books production and commerce. In research on women's struggles in the *favelas* of Brazil, Karen Palazzini discovered that women who were selling cooked food out of their homes—a typical informal sector occupation—preferred that source of income to waged labor, even when it was available. Their reasons included the ability to stay in their neighborhood, with their children and friends and all the mutual aid that situation provided. See Karen L. Palazzini, *Women's Work in Lauro de Freitas, Bahia, Brazil: Marginalization or Autonomous Development*, PhD diss., University of Texas at Austin, 1997.

such activities have both provided the means for struggle against capitalist plans and been intentionally limited in order to free up time and energy for such struggle.[13]

A third such moment came with the high and persistent unemployment in the North that characterized the Carter-Volcker-Reagan depression of the early 1980s and in turn triggered the international debt crisis. The failure of the subsequent upturn in production to generate enough jobs to dramatically reduce unemployment resulted in much debate among policy makers about "jobless recoveries" and the possible disruptive consequences of being unable to provide enough jobs.

More recently Antonio Negri and his collaborators have argued that the undermining of labor as the basis and measure of value has occurred not because rising productivity has reduced labor to a secondary factor of production, but because the changing nature of work makes it impossible to differentiate between work and nonwork, and thus to measure the former. This argument has evolved through the elaboration of two concepts, one, the *general intellect*, plucked from the above-mentioned "fragment on machines," and another, *immaterial labor*, designed to capture what are viewed as increasingly hegemonic forms of labor. This elaboration first unfolded in various issues of the French journal *Futur Antérieur* in 1991–92 and then became central to a whole research agenda whose results have been published in subsequent issues of *Futur Antérieur*, then in the journals *Multitudes* (2000–), *Luogo Comune* (1990–93), and *Derive Approdi* (1993–), and in a whole series of books, including Christian Marazzi's *Il posto dei calzini* (1994), Michael Hardt and Toni Negri's trilogy: *Empire* (2000), *Multitudes* (2004), and *Commonwealth* (2009), Paolo Virno's *Gramatica della moltitudine* (2001), Yann Moulier-Boutang's *Le capitalisme cognitive* (2007), Virno's *Multitude: Between*

---

13 The primary celebrant who has argued that informal sector initiatives amount to proto-capitalism that should be encouraged and freed of state regulation is Hernando de Soto, who has written several books on this theme, beginning with *The Other Path: The Invisible Revolution in the Third World* (1986). An influential interpreter of the opposite view—that valorizes the anti-capitalist struggles of those in the informal sector—is Gustavo Esteva. See his "Regenerating People's Space," *Alternatives* 12 (1987), 125–52. For a case study, see H. Cleaver, "The Uses of an Earthquake."

Innovation and Negation (2008), and Franco (Bifo) Berardi in essays collected in *After the Future* (2011).

In the "fragment on machines," Marx used the term "general intellect" to evoke all of the accumulated mental labor, scientific and technological, that was embodied in those machines that capital was increasingly using as part of its strategy to limit and control workers' power.[14] In the literature cited in the previous paragraph, this *general intellect* became a concept that denotes not only scientific and technological mental labor but other kinds of *immaterial labor* as well, such as affective labor, communicative labor, creative labor—pretty much all kinds of labor other than the manual sort said to have preoccupied Marx in the mid-nineteenth century. As these kinds of labor have become ever more central to the production of wealth in capitalist society—most obviously in the computer industry, in the production and commodification of information, in the various entertainment industries (television, film, computer games), in medical and financial services—*immaterial labor*, it is argued, has not only become hegemonic but also virtually omnipresent in society. In this view, most clearly expressed by Negri in adapting yet another concept from Marx, capital has been achieving not only the "real subsumption of *production*" (i.e., the reshaping of production according to its own needs), but has also been achieving the "real subsumption of *society*" (i.e., reshaping of all of human activities as work that contributes to its expanded reproduction). This vision of totalization evokes that of Hegel's all-embracing dialectic; but whereas Hegel's vision bespoke bourgeois optimism, Negri's reeks of workerist despair that the "refusal of [Fordist] work" merely drove capital to an even more thorough imposition of labor.

As all human activities are being subsumed by capital as work, Negri and others argue, it becomes impossible to distinguish work from nonwork, "the division between work time and non-work time" breaks down. Under such conditions, he argues,

---

14 Marx made the centrality of mental labor quite explicit in chapter 7 of volume 1 of *Capital*, where he famously noted that the worst of human architects was better than the best of bees—who craft precise arrays of hexagonal chambers for larvae and honey—because humans think out their projects in advance.

appropriating a concept from Foucault, life becomes "biopolitical labor," and it becomes impossible to quantify and *measure* labor that produces value (abstract labor) as something distinct from other human activity. Therefore, Negri has written, "When the time of life has entirely become the time of production . . . when exploitation has reached such dimensions, its measure becomes impossible."[15] Of course, Negri goes on to argue that under these conditions exploitation has not disappeared, it has simply been "thrown out of all economic measures; its economic reality becomes fixed in purely political terms."[16]

A similar line of argument has been developed by some working on the consequences of new communication technologies, especially the rise of so-called social media such as Facebook, Twitter, and YouTube. Despite their call for a "return to Marx" and "taking a Marxist approach for studying media," their interpretation of the dynamics of social media parallels that of Negri and others, namely that the ability of capital to turn consumption into productive "digital" labor—not just the production of labor power, but also of profitable commodities—makes the measurement of labor value impossible. This interpretation, it appears, dates back to the argument by Dallas Smythe that not only is workers' leisure time organized for the reproduction of labor power, but also as media consumers they also work, performing "essential marketing functions for the producers of consumers' goods." He rephrases, audiences "work to market . . . things to themselves."[17] Ultimately, he concluded, "for the great majority of the population . . . 24 hours a day is work time."[18] The subsequent defense, appropriation, and elaboration of Smythe's formulations by those engaged in "the digital labor debate" have been spelled out in great detail by Christian Fuchs (2012) and critiqued by, among others, Brett Caraway (2011,

---

15 "Quand le temps de la vie est devenu entièrement temps de production, qui mesure quoi? . . . quand l'exploitation atteint de telles dimensions, sa mesure devient impossible." Toni Negri, "Valeur-travail: crise et problèmes de reconstruction dans le post-moderne," *Futur antérieur*, no. 10 (1992), 34.

16 Ibid., 35.

17 Dallas Smythe, "Communications: Blindspot of Western Marxism," *Canadian Journal of Political and Social Theory* 1, no. 3, (Fall 1977), 3–4.

18 Dallas Smythe, *Dependency Road* (Norwood, N.J.: Ablex, 1981), 47.

2015).[19] One of the striking things that emerges in this literature, despite Smythe and his followers' view that essentially all participation in corporate media—whether consuming or producing—amounts to work for capital, is the extreme preoccupation of capitalists with *measuring* participation. The much lamented—and increasingly outflanked—surveillance of social media users has always been aimed at identifying and quantifying forms of participation that lend themselves to commodification. Neither the surveillance industry nor those to whom it sells its quantified results assume, as Smythe and others do, that all participation is automatically of value to capital. They are well aware of the possibilities for people to utilize social media in ways that fail to generate profits and can even contribute to the rupture of capitalist relationships.

These lines of argument about how capital successfully converts everything we do into value and surplus value producing work are clearly premised on an *economic* concept of labor value quite distinct from the kind of understanding I have laid out above, in which the substance of labor value (abstract labor) is precisely its very *political* usefulness in providing the most fundamental vehicle of capitalist domination and control. From this point of view, the capitalist process of subsuming not only what we normally think of as production but also of all kinds of other social activities has certainly involved an extension of capitalist power and control but hardly an immeasurable one. Moreover, this process has been going on throughout the history of capitalism, but especially since workers began to succeed in forcing down the length of the official working day. Marx analyzed the success of English workers forcing their bosses to accept shorter hours in section 6 of chapter 10 of volume 1 of *Capital*. David Roediger and Philip Foner laid out a parallel history of such struggle in the United States in *Our Own*

19   Christian Fuchs, "Dallas Smythe Today—The Audience Commodity, the Digital Labour Debate, Marxist Political Economy and Critical Theory: Prolegomena to a Digital Labour Theory of Value," *Triple C: Open Access Journal for a Global Sustainable Information Society*, 10, no. 2 (2012), 692–740; Brett Caraway, "Audience Labor in the New Media Environment: A Marxian Revisiting of the Audience Commodity," *Media, Culture and Society* 33, no. 5 (2011), 693–708; Brett Caraway, "Crisis of Command: Theorizing Value in New Media," *Communication Theory* 26, no. 1, February 2015, 64–81.

Time: A History of American Labor and the Working Day (1989). Marx went on to argue, in chapter 15, that those successes in reducing the length of the working day *forced* capital to shift the emphasis in its strategies of social control from imposing more hours of work to raising productivity and intensifying work during reduced hours. What he failed to explore, but later generations of Marxists have explored, is how those successes also *forced* capital to colonize the time workers liberated from waged labor.

Such colonization has been so studied by such a wide array of scholars, including Marxists, that it is a bit surprising to read Negri and Hardt present the "subsumption of society" as essentially a post-Fordist phenomenon of the age of empire. To study the history of such colonization—and I prefer "colonization" to "subsumption" because colonization has always been resisted, has never been complete, and has frequently been overthrown—is to see, among other things, that because capital has always been well aware of its own limits, it has always sought to *measure* the degree of subsumption or colonization achieved, and it continues to do so. Those hired to conduct such measurement, from the managers of waged workers to academics and government bureaucrats, are well aware that such measurement is neither easy nor very accurate. It is harder, for example, to measure the productivity of service labor than it is to measure the productivity of manufacturing labor.[20] It is also harder to measure just how much time and energy are actually devoted to the reproduction of labor power in the home than it is to measure official working hours in factories, offices, and fields. But even the latter has never been easy, given the heterogeneity of both labor and products, given the ambiguities involved in defining the use-values of commodities (e.g., to what degree does the use-value of a Mercedes lie in its ability to transport one reliably from here to there, or in the status its mere possession accords its owner or licensee) and given the endless, covert ways waged workers shirk on the job.

---

20   The problems here include both the measurement of the amount of work and the measurement of the product being produced by that work. For instance, what exactly is the product of psychiatric services? Economists often dodge the problem by measuring the monetary value of output, however it is defined, but they know that by so doing they are forced to assume that the market actually provides a reasonable proxy measure of the products themselves.

My interpretation of the concept of abstract labor short-circuits these problems by seeing that regardless of the productivity of an hour of work time, that hour is an hour of life absorbed in the self-reproduction of capital and turned against workers as a vehicle of capital's control over them. From this point of view, the capitalist preoccupation with measuring productivity lies in determining, as best it can, just how much control over people can be achieved through the imposition of various labor processes. This is true whether the labor processes involved are those of the factory, field, or office, or those of the kitchen, bedroom, school, or social media. In the former, the capitalist preoccupation with measure is currently signaled by the pervasive spread of what are called "metrics" (i.e., this or that measure of work accomplished in a given period). But this preoccupation has also long haunted capital outside the domains of waged work and led to, among other things, efforts to gather data on and measure hours of work in "household production" and to use surveillance to measure online activities.[21]

Let me take an example from the terrain of unwaged work: schools. Ever since workers began to succeed in shortening the hours of waged work and extracting their children from mines and mills and factories, capital has succeeded all too well in *incarcerating* children in schools, to use Foucault's term, in order reduce their humanity to the willingness and ability to work for future employers.[22] The school thus became a new terrain of class struggle, where battles have been fought over what goes on there. Workers have demanded that their children have the time and freedom to learn—in order to improve their lives and exceed, to some degree,

---

21   This preoccupation has derived partly from capitalists' concern with the production and reproduction of what economists call "human capital" (i.e., labor power) and partly from women's struggles against such work and their demands that it be shared by men.

22   Foucault's analysis of incarceration includes the prison—in his book *Surveiller et punir: Naissance de la Prison* (Discipline and Punish) (1975)—but also the insane asylum—in his book *Folie et deraison: Historire de la folie a l'age classique* (Madness and Civilization) (1960s) and the hospital—in *Naissance de la Clinique* (Birth of the Clinic: An Archaeology of Medical Perception) (1963). All these analyses basically revealed the type of incarceration characteristic of the factory (that Marx had analyzed) as a fundamental method of capitalist social control.

their parents' achievements. That demand has been confronted and largely instrumentalized by capitalists who have sought to 1) define "achievement" purely in terms of one's job and position in the wage/salary hierarchy, and 2) structure schools in the same hierarchical manner that they have shaped their businesses. Already in the nineteenth century, observers such as Freidrich Nietzsche and Thorstein Veblen were critiquing this "subsumption" of learning by capital.[23]

As the twentieth century unfolded, capitalists sought to incorporate the latest developments in industrial management into the administration of schools. Nowhere has this been demonstrated more clearly than by Raymond Callahan in his *Education and the Cult of Efficiency* (1962).[24] Moreover, as Callahan discovered, while exploring a largely ignored history of school administration, those efforts to transfer the methods of "scientific management" from the factory to the school involved extensive efforts to *measure* success (i.e., measure the degree to which work was being successfully imposed in the schools). Today, while Hardt and Negri are pronouncing measure to be impossible, state committees and school administrators are devising and imposing new methods of measure to determine just how much actual work is going on, by both students and teachers—and they are doing this at every level of the school system right up through the university. Contra Negri and others, Massimo De Angelis and David Harvie have tracked these efforts in the United Kingdom.[25]

---

23 See Friedrich Nietzsche's 1872 lectures "On the Future of Our Educational Institutions" and Chapter 14 on "The Higher Learning as an Expression of the Pecuniary Culture" in Thorstein Veblen's *The Theory of the Leisure Class* (1899) as well as his later book *The Higher Learning in America: A Memorandum on the Conduct of Universities by Businessmen* (1918). Similar perceptions motivated students in the 1960s to turn against what they called "universities as factories." In recent years, as business has been increasing its influence on the structure of schooling, a whole new body of literature has emerged critiquing the "corporatization" of education.

24 Raymond E. Callahan, *Education and the Cult of Efficiency: A Study of the Social Forces that have Shaped the Administration of the Public Schools* (Chicago: University of Chicago Press, 1962).

25 See Massimo De Angelis and David Harvie, "Cognitive Capitalism and the Rat Race: How Capital Measures Ideas and Affects in UK Higher Education," *Historical Materialism* 17 (2009) 3–30.

What subverts or undermines capital's measurement of work, its estimation of socially necessary labor time, of just how much labor it can impose in the production of any particular commodity? There would seem to be various ways in which this occurs. One way involves the subversion of the very processes of measurement. Another involves the contingent nature of workers' resistance and the way in which fluctuations in intensity cause such fluctuations in socially necessary labor time as to make measurement unreliable.

The subversion of measurement is often achieved by workers who succeed in hiding the details of their work (and nonwork) from those managers or industrial engineers tasked with measuring what they do and the results. Details of such subversion can be found in many accounts of struggles at the point of production. Let me give just two illustrations, one from waged labor and one from unwaged labor.

In the case of waged labor, an ex-manager of an East Coast plant producing telephones told me the story of how his workers hid what they actually did from the company for whom they worked. They were paid on a piecework basis—the more units they produced the more they got paid. To maximize their income, they developed work methods more efficient than those designed by the company engineers. As a result, the level of productivity in this particular plant exceeded that of other plants, and the workers earned more than workers at other plants. Discovering this, the company dispatched engineers to discover how this was being achieved. If they could generalize whatever had changed, they could attribute the increased productivity to technical changes and lower piece rates, cutting wage costs and raising profits. However, when the engineers came to study the situation, the workers (with the tacit approval of the amused manager; he liked his workers to be happy and disliked being an overseer) reverted to following the original instructions given to them by the company. As a result, the engineers could find no explanation for the higher productivity, and after they departed, the workers went back to using their own methods for generating higher productivity and higher pay. Unlike the workers in the Hungarian factory mentioned above, the organization of a union and negotiated contract made it impossible for the company to reduce piece rates solely at that one plant, so the workers continued to earn their higher pay, and the company's ability to accurately measure the amount of work required to produce a unit of output was subverted.

In the case of unwaged labor, let me take, once again, the example of students. In resisting the imposition of schoolwork, students often cheat. Now cheating takes many forms, but many methods are clearly designed to dramatically reduce the amount of time students have to spend studying (i.e., doing work teachers impose upon them). Because cheating is expressly banned in schools, they must hide their actions from their teachers (and school administrators). Such motivations have clearly been behind long-standing practices of smuggling answers into tests, or copying answers from other students' answer sheets.[26] They have also been behind the contemporary surge in students using the Internet to seek out, download, and turn in (often with very little modification) papers written by someone else. In both cases, the amount of time and energy students find it necessary to divert from the rest of their lives into schoolwork is reduced. As a result, individual teachers have very little ability to measure the amount of work students actually do. As a result, grades, and ultimately diplomas, turn out to be poor measures of the amount of work students are actually willing and able to do for either teachers or future employers. Not only has measurement been subverted here, but so has the production of labor power.[27]

---

26 Cheating has, it seems, always been a way of subverting the imposition of standardized testing. A study of cheating in China, where such tests were used for millennia to choose government bureaucrats, has made this quite clear. Only in capitalism, however, has forced schooling become widespread and therefore cheating such an omnipresent form of struggle against imposed work. See Hoi K. Suen and Lan Yu, "Chronic Consequences of High-Stakes Testing? Lessons from the Chinese Civil Service Exam," *Comparative Education Review* 50, no. 1 (February 2006), 46–65.

27 The well-known concern with "grade inflation" is motivated by the way it is perceived to undermine the ability to distinguish hard workers from slackers and degrees of competence. A lead article in the October 14, 2012, *Chronicle of Higher Education*, "Grades Out, Badges In," proclaimed, "Grades are broken . . . college grades are inflated to the point of meaninglessness—especially to employers who want to know which diploma-holder is best qualified for their jobs." The article then goes on to discuss current experiments with the substitution of "badges" for grades and suggests that "one key benefit of education badges could simply be communicating what happens in the classroom in a more employer-friendly form."

The measurement of socially necessary labor time (SNLT) is also undermined by the irregular withdrawal of time and energy—individual or collective—from work. In the waged workplace, such withdrawals may be momentary or chronic, partial or total. Total withdrawal (e.g., strikes) obviously makes any measurement impossible. Less than total withdrawal (e.g., momentary work stoppages that increase the time necessary to produce some commodity or sabotage that results in work having to be done over again) has the effect of lengthening SNLT. Because both kinds of disruptions are, over time, highly contingent upon changing intensities in worker resistance, measurements at one point in time give poor approximations for the next period. If measurement is done during a period of disruption, it will overestimate SNLT, and if done during a period of no disruption, it will underestimate SNLT. For measurement to be meaningful, capital needs regularity and continuity in work so that measurement estimates continue to be accurate—thus its repeated efforts to achieve regularity by subordinating workers' activities to controllable machinery. But, because workers' self-activity is the one element of production that cannot be planned, complete control over the rhythm of work on the shop floor has forever eluded managers—and undermined their efforts to measure work.

This kind of problem in measuring the SNLT required for the production of commodities for sale is also present in efforts to measure the work involved in the production of labor power. Although the number of hours teachers and students spend in school may be easily measured, the amount of work that is actually getting done during those hours is not. Nor is the amount of work done after hours (e.g., grading and class preparation by teachers or homework by students). Discovering whether students have divided up homework, shared their results, and by so doing reduced their work is difficult. Discovering whether teachers have assiduously and carefully graded tests or papers or tossed them on a flight of stairs and randomly assigned grades according to where each paper landed would require far more effort than any administration is likely to undertake. The same is true for efforts to measure housework. Most studies have had to rely on voluntary responses from survey participants where there is no way to verify the accuracy of what is reported, and the infrequency of the surveys makes it hard to determine patterns of irregularity in the amount of effort put into various tasks and thus of the representativeness of the data gathered. Moreover, many aspects of work are not even measured (e.g., travel time to and from schools, shopping, doctors' offices, welfare agencies, or unemployment offices) because they are not recognized as work. As a result of all these problems, neither capitalists nor the rest of us can have much confidence in what few measures exist.

Nevertheless, from all this it seems obvious to me that measuring work time continues to be both essential to capitalists and difficult because of our struggles to work less. Every reduction in the hours and effort we are forced to concede to capital is an expansion in those we have available for self-valorization and for developing alternatives. On this point, I agree wholeheartedly with Maurizio Lazzarato, who concludes—despite being in general agreement with the views of Negri and others that capitalism has become biopolitical and all-invasive—that just because "capital exploits life," it "does not mean that life coincides with capital. It is always possible to distinguish life from work."[28] If we can distinguish the two, we can also measure our success in withholding our lifeblood (time and energy) from the vampire and in retaining it for our own autonomous purposes.

---

28 Maurizio Lazzarato, *Governing by Debt* (South Pasadena, Calif.: Semiotext(e), 2013), 252, in the final chapter, "Conclusions for a Beginning: The Refusal of Work."

EXCHANGE AND MONEY AS THE FORM OF VALUE

Marx follows his analysis of *abstract labor as the substance of value* and of *socially necessary labor time as the measure of value* with a dense examination of *exchange value as the form of value*. Exchange value, he explains, is the form through which the purely social equivalence of commodities becomes perceptible, despite their differences as distinct, useful things (or services). The social equivalence that interests him we have already seen to be the labor that can be imposed in their production. His frequently ignored analysis of the *form* assumed by value turns out to be very useful in understanding both the class struggle in general, and the class dynamics of such phenomena as money, credit, debt, and the present repressive period of financialization, the imposition of austerity, and the widespread resistance that has exploded in response. The analysis is useful not only because it reveals aspects of the class relation but because it does so in a way that helps us to see the possibilities of rupturing those aspects through struggle.

Perceiving that usefulness, however, requires not only understanding the abstract concepts of chapter 1, but also seeing how they apply to more concrete moments of everyday class dynamics. Methodologically, analogies come easily to mind. Understanding chemical and biological concepts of food as nutrition, as something our bodies need, is not the same as figuring out which items in our environment can be eaten with good nutritional results. We must study what's available and discover which contain nutritional elements—by taking a bite and experiencing the results or by using more scientific methods. Once we understand the various abstract relationships embodied in exchange value—revealed by the analysis in chapter 1—we must then discover those abstractions as moments of the class relationships that trap us, in order to discover how we might rupture and escape them.

Let me be clear. In section 3 of chapter 1, Marx spells out his analysis of the form of value (exchange value) entirely in terms of the relationships among commodities—just as he has done in analyzing its substance and its measure. He does this in four steps, examining what he calls: 1) the simple form of value, 2) the expanded form of value, 3) the general form of value, and, finally, 4) the money form of value. Each step reveals and examines specific determinations or attributes of exchange value. Later, in chapters 2 and 3, we discover that the fourth and final step, analyzing the money form, was just the first step in presenting his explicit analysis of money. As his presentation proceeds from step one through two and three to four, we discover his analysis becoming more and more concrete, identifying and analyzing first one, then another, then still another aspect of exchange and of money.

Another way of grasping the logic of the presentation is to read this section on the form of value backward, from the money form to the simplest form of value (or the whole chapter, all the way back to abstract labor). Because the analysis is cumulative and ends with the money form, we know that each and every moment of that analysis treats an aspect of the money form. Reading backward would then provide an *analytical dissection* of the money form, a picking apart and examining its components. As we worked our way backward, we would discover more and more aspects until we reached its simplest form. (Or, if we kept moving back through the chapter, we would discover socially necessary labor time as the measure within the quantitative dimension of exchange value and then abstract labor as the substance of the value measured.)

Marx's exposition, however, advances in the other direction, gradually moving from relations among commodities to relations among their owners to relations among classes. But what is true of the relationship between the money form and what precedes it is also true for the class relationship. My project, therefore, has been to discover each aspect of value revealed in Marx's analysis of its form and to examine them within the current dynamics of class struggle. Although we can do this with all of the material in *Capital*—a broader project I have undertaken in teaching—in this book I want to show only how these oft-neglected sections on the form of value while elaborating his labor theory of value also illuminate the nature of the antagonistic class relations of capitalism, including those of financialization. That elaboration includes fundamental elements of a theory of money in those relations—a theory further developed in the second and third chapters and in many other parts of the three volumes of *Capital*. Showing this requires repeatedly mapping important abstract concepts in his analysis of the world of commodity exchange to the more concrete world of the class relation.

The Simple Form and Reflexive Mediation

The first step of his analysis in *the passages on the simple form* focuses on one random exchange between two commodities, **A** and **B**, within the capitalist world of commodities. There are both qualitative and quantitative dimensions in the exchange of some amount **x** of commodity **A** for some amount **y** of commodity **B** (which Marx represents as **xA** = **yB**). However, his primary emphasis is on the qualitative characteristics, especially the way in which **B** expresses the value, or worth, of **A**.[1] The importance of this simple form was spelled out by Marx in a letter to Engels in 1867. "The economists have hitherto overlooked . . . that the *simplest form of the commodity*, in which its value is not yet expressed in its relation to all other commodities but only as something *differentiated* from its own natural form, embodies the *whole secret of the money form* and thereby, *in nuce* [in embryo], *of all bourgeois forms of the products of labor*."[2]

In other words, because the "bourgeois forms of the products of labor" are commodities and money, essential aspects of the money form, the final step of his presentation, are present in the very first step. Marx illustrates his analysis in terms of the exchange of commodities important in his time (e.g., cloth, clothes, and iron). The textile industry was, for a long time, the heart of British industrialization. Iron, and steel made from it, was essential to the ships, guns, and cannons necessary to impose that cloth on the rest of the world. Beyond such particular commodities, however well chosen, we can see how the analysis also applies to the class relation by examining the exchange between the commodity labor power (**LP**)—that workers are forced to sell—and money (**M**, or the wage) that capitalists use to buy that labor power.[3] By examining

---

1   Marx's focus on the qualitative aspects of the relationship is facilitated, in part, by *assuming equality in exchange*—an assumption that he later uses to differentiate his theory of exploitation from cheating in exchange. In other words, **y** is assumed to be whatever quantity is necessary for **yB** to accurately express the value of **xA**.

2   Marx to Engels, June 22, 1867, in Marx and Engels, *Collected Works*, vol. 42, 384.

3   In terms of Marx's exposition, the analysis of this exchange is not reached until chapter 6 on "Sale and Purchase of Labor Power"—a discussion that necessarily includes the wage (the money form of the value of labor power), which hasn't been introduced in the first chapter.

the exchange of labor power for the wage as a concrete example of the simple form of value, we already begin to see an important aspect of money within capitalism: its role in buying labor power is simultaneously its use in bringing people under control as workers.

Outside of capital's labor market, individuals' abilities and activities are diverse and autonomous. People are not workers per se; they are perhaps subsistence farmers or coopers or shipwrights or gypsies or traveling players or highway robbers, but they are *not* part of capital's active army of waged laborers.[4] In his *Phenomenology of Spirit* (1807), Hegel pointed out how masters require slaves to be masters, indeed require slaves to recognize themselves as slaves for the masters to recognize themselves as masters.[5] So too, no matter how much money people have, they can only be capitalists—and can only recognize themselves as such—when they can force us into the labor market, into begging for jobs and into thinking of ourselves as workers and of them as our bosses.

In the language of Hegel's *Science of Logic*, a language adopted by Marx, this is a relationship of *reflexive mediation*—where the relationship of a thing to itself is mediated by a second that reflects some aspect of the thing back to itself, as a mirror reflects an image back to the person looking into it. Dialogue, for example, only exists through such mediation; without some reaction from a mediating interlocutor, one is merely talking to one's self. In any social setting, where people interact with each other, such mediation is part of what builds and shapes relationships.

Capitalists, unfortunately, try to organize this kind of relationship in ways that give them power over us. They seek to impose our relationship to them to such a degree that we come to define

4 Capital may see them as part of an unwaged latent "reserve army of labor," but whether they will eventually be forced into the labor market always remains to be seen and will depend on the dynamics of their struggles.

5 There is an interesting discussion of "recognition" that differentiates between the kind of *contradicted, unequal,* and *alienated* recognition revealed both by Hegel's analysis of master-slave relationships and by Marx's dissection of capitalist-worker ones, and equal and un-alienated *mutual* recognition, in Richard Gunn and Adrian Wilding, "Revolutionary or Less-than-Revolutionary Recognition?" Heathwood Institute and Press, July 24, 2013, http://www.heathwoodpress.com/revolutionary-less-than-revolutionary-recognition/.

ourselves, and are defined by others, primarily in terms of our jobs. "Hello, I don't believe we have met. What do you do?" "Nice to meet you; I design semiconductors." Or, "I teach economics." The wage or salary we receive certifies us as workers, to ourselves, to capital, and to others. In actuality, of course, we may *do* and *be* a great many things, but within capitalism the expectation is that we will identify with our work.[6]

Alongside this primary identification, capitalists also seek to manage the relationship of reflexive mediation among those of us they have hired by pitting us against each other. To the degree that they are successful, we see ourselves, and are seen by our fellow workers, as competitors—whether we desire to compete or not. Those of us higher up the wage or salary hierarchy—whether because of our higher income, our color, our gender, or our ethnicity—are conditioned to look down upon those below as threatening potential replacements. Those below, imposed on by those above, are conditioned to both resent and seek to replace those above.

A corollary of this very capitalist way of subordinating personal relationships to the wage is how the *absence of a wage*, for a housewife or a student, *hides* their status as worker-for-capital from themselves and from others.[7] The centrality of jobs and wages means that those who don't have them are defined, and often define themselves, negatively by what they lack rather than by positive aspects of their lives. They are "unemployed" even though they may be engaged in all kinds of unwaged work.

---

6   At one point, I found it amusing to respond to the question "What do you do?" by recounting something I was doing besides the work required by my job. Unfortunately, so pervasive is the expectation that one will respond about one's job, that if I answered "I carve wood," the quick response was, "Oh, you're a professional woodcarver?" Sigh.

7   It does not, however, hide the character of their work from capitalists. From the teaching of home economics through laws regulating childhood, parenting, and medicine to the neoclassical theory of human capital, the managers and theorists of capitalism have demonstrated their understanding and desire to shape private life to their own ends—namely the reduction of life to work and the reproduction of labor power. For early examples of such intervention, see Michel Foucault, "The Politics of Health in the Eighteenth Century," *Foucault Studies*, no. 18 (October 2014), 113–27. Today they are omnipresent.

They are "jobless," "wageless," dependent upon either others or on illegal activities for income and branded with disparaging descriptions. "And what do *you* do?" "Oh, I'm just a housewife." Or "I'm still in school, just a student." The "just" in these responses reflects the hierarchy capital imposes in the relationship between the waged and the unwaged. The former are not only treated as superior, but their command over money gives them both status and power over those who lack it. In this hierarchy, all participants are conditioned to feel and accept the inferior status and power of those without a wage.

The traditional orthodox Marxist definition of the working class as those receiving a wage, coupled with the belief that work differentiates human being from other kinds of being, reinforces this capitalist hierarchy. It results in the celebration of the struggles of waged workers because they are thought to be only one revolutionary step away from finding complete fulfillment in un-alienated work, freed from capitalist domination and exploitation.[8] Inevitably this celebration has been accompanied by a parallel disparagement of those without a wage, who have not been considered part of the working class nor their resistance and demands an integral part of working-class struggle. Unwaged housewives and students have often been told that if they want to join the class struggle they needed to get a job and a wage.[9]

---

8   Nowhere has this been more obvious than where orthodoxy has ruled—for example, the Soviet bloc, with its socialist work ethic, its celebration of Stakhanovism, its financing of heroic statues of workers, and its cultivation of "socialist realism" in literature and the arts. Stakhanovism was the practice of rewarding those workers who worked the hardest. The name comes from Aleksei G. Stakhanov (1906–77), a Soviet coal miner—a Soviet counterpart to the American, steel-driving John Henry, celebrated in legend and song.

9   Despite the central role of peasant struggles throughout the twentieth century (Mexico, Russia, China, etc.) and the indigenous renaissance of the late twentieth and early twenty-first centuries (often based in rural communities), Marxists have had similar attitudes toward peasants. Assuming, a priori, that virtually all peasants are destined to meet the same fate as English farmers—proletarianization, by being driven from the land or reduced to waged agricultural laborers—all too many Marxists have been dismissive of peasant struggles or desirous only of subordinating them to those of waged workers.

  Missing in *Capital*—and for a long time in the work of Marxists who came later—is any detailed analysis of how capitalist success at organizing the activities of the *unwaged* has reorganized relations of reflexive mediation throughout society. As we know from his analysis of primitive accumulation in part 8 of *Capital*, Marx was well aware of how business and the state have created and renewed a "reserve army" of the jobless (and therefore unwaged) through enclosures and tried to manage it via "bloody legislation," poor laws, workhouses, prisons, and the military (e.g., impressment). In his analysis of ongoing accumulation—especially in section 3 of chapter 25 of volume 1 of *Capital*—he also discussed how capitalists' substitution of machinery for labor, and downturns of the business cycle, repeatedly throw workers out of waged jobs and into the reserve army. In section 4, his analysis of that army, however, was limited to dividing it into three sections: the *floating reserve* (those looking for waged work), the *latent reserve* (those who might, at some point, enter the labor market—e.g., unwaged wives or children, hard-pressed subsistence farmers) and the *stagnant reserve* (those stuck in domestic production, adult paupers able to work, orphans and pauper children who might be able to work). Beyond these "reserves," he also evoked a "surplus population," cast off in the process of capital's development that includes those unable to work due to injuries, disease, or old age and those that he classified as lumpenproletariat, e.g., "vagabonds, criminals, prostitutes" who were, he judged, unlikely to ever go looking for a wage from a capitalist employer.[10] But nowhere, that I have found, did he explicitly

---

10 Although providing points of departure, these categories have required serious rethinking and modification. Analysis of unwaged housework, schoolwork, and subsistence production has demonstrated that those Marx classified as part of the latent reserve army are "in reserve" only in the sense of being potentially available for waged labor. See Dalla Costa, "Women and the Subversion of the Community," and similar work by Marxist-feminists. Historical research on the working class and crime in the eighteenth century has also forced a reassessment of Marx's view of the lumpenproletariat. See Peter Linebaugh, *The London Hanged*, and similar work by Marxist historians. Recent confused discussions of the capitalist genesis of a "surplus population" via an accelerated substitution of cybernetic machines for human workers demands clearer thinking about the conditions under which people are truly surplus to a capitalist system based on the imposition of work both waged and

discuss *reflexive mediation* as an aspect of the various relationships between capital and the unwaged.

In Marx's time, those with little income, "the poor," only became "paupers" when so defined by capital's poor laws and workhouses. Those who lived off the land only became "poachers" and "thieves" when enclosures made hunting and gathering illegal and those who did so anyway were caught and prosecuted by the courts.[11] The same was true with beggars, gypsies, or freed slaves who only became "vagrants" or "vagabonds" when begging and wandering were outlawed. Free Africans lived all sorts of lives until capital seized them in the slave trade and colonialism enclosed their lands, impressing them into various ranks of its labor force, both active and "reserve."[12] Capitalists affirm their identity partly by imposing work directly and partly by so reducing people's income as to drive them into the labor market—where they may or may not find a job and a wage. In each case, the wageless are induced by want and oppression to redefine themselves vis-à-vis their new overlords—either as jobless and in need of income or supportive of those with wages.

unwaged. See Nick Dyer-Witheford, *Cyber-proletariat: Global Labor in the Digital Vortex* (London: Pluto Press, 2015).

11 Interestingly, Marx's original interest in workers' struggles concerned the criminalization of the gathering of wood in German forests. See Karl Marx, "Proceedings of the Sixth Rhine Province Assembly. Third Article. Debates on the Law of the Theft of Wood," in Marx and Engels, *Collected Works*, vol. 1 (New York: International Publishers, 1975), 224–31; Peter Linebaugh, "Karl Marx, the Theft of Wood, and Working Class Composition: A Contribution to the Current Debate," *Crime and Social Justice*, 6 (Fall/Winter 1976), 5–16.

12 Slaves employed in capitalist industry—whether producing raw materials or processing them—must certainly be recognized as part of the "active" workforce even though they are unwaged. Marx echoed views dating back to ancient times when he highlighted the kinship of waged workers and slaves by referring to the former as "wage slaves"—while also pointing out how the existence of out-and-out slavery undermined the struggles of waged workers. It was for that reason that in 1864 he wrote a letter to Abraham Lincoln, thanking him for freeing slaves in the United States. See Karl Marx (on behalf of the International Working Men's Association), "To Abraham Lincoln, President of the United States of America," first published in the *Daily News*, December 23, 1864, in Marx and Engels, *Collected Works*, vol. 20 (New York: International Publishers), 19–21.

All of these kinds of unwaged relationships continue in our time (including slavery, albeit mostly hidden in covert factories, isolated farms, homes, boats, and the dens of sexual traffickers).

In the late nineteenth and early twentieth centuries, as workers were successful in fighting for shorter working hours, as adult workers succeeded in imposing child labor laws, and as male workers succeeded in marginalizing female waged labor, the *latent* reserve army was substantially expanded by the increased numbers of children in schools and women in homes.[13] In the former, children suffer from years of imposed unwaged labor and in the latter women find themselves condemned to life sentences of unwaged and often isolated domestic labor. In both cases we can find relations of reflexive mediation of the sort Marx analyzes in his section on the simple form of value. In both cases we also find resistance that ruptures those relations.

Repeated business intervention has shaped "education" into a hierarchy of work and power that includes both the waged work of administrators, staff, and teachers, and the unwaged work of students. Within that hierarchy, the basic work of one and all is the producing and reproducing of labor power. Administrators impose work on teachers (or professors) and they, in turn, impose it on students. In the relationship between teachers and students, we see how the power of waged teachers to impose work and discipline on unwaged students creates the same kind of reflexive mediation characteristic of the labor power–capital relationship elsewhere. Teachers can only be teachers if their students do the work the teachers seek to impose, accept their authority, and see themselves as students.

Teachers (and administrators) want young people to think of themselves as students and to accept grades as legitimate

---

13 Throughout most of the eighteenth and nineteenth centuries, with a few exceptions—such as the schools for working-class children created near his textile factory by the capitalist reformer Robert Owens—most capitalists were doing their best either to incorporate children into factory labor or to confine them in workhouses. Schools were for the children of capitalists, not workers. By the time Marx was writing *Capital*, Owen's efforts to spread his practices had come to naught, and the driving of women and children into factories had proceeded so far that Marx thought it was undermining the very reproduction of the working class.

quantitative measures of their quality as students (i.e., of their abilities and knowledge). For those students who accept their assigned role and these measures, high grades become ego-boosting; low grades cause anxiety and depression. The latter is a chronic and rampant problem because only a few are awarded high grades and everyone else gets something less, down to and including failure. Most notorious, perhaps, are those fixed distributions imposed by either administrators or by teachers themselves, in which, for example, only 5 percent are allowed to receive "A's," 5 percent are automatically failed, and everyone else falls in the mediocre no man's land in between. As standardized testing has become more and more omnipresent these last decades, these problems are replicated in one setting after another.

Some teachers embrace this power they have been given over students and have no problem ranking them quantitatively with grades, rewarding hard work, and punishing the refusal to work. Others may judge themselves all too readily in terms of the degree to which they have succeeded in getting students to do the work they have sought to impose and of the degree to which students have succeeded in meeting or exceeding the goals set for them. Where student evaluations of teachers are mandated, poor evaluations not only give administrators another tool to discipline teachers, but also undermine some teachers' sense of their ability.

However, as I have argued, for every dialectical relationship that capital imposes, for every moment of the dialectic, there also exists the possibility of its rupture. In these cases of reflexive mediation, ruptures occur when we cease to work for capital, when we replace capital with other people as the mirrors through whom we see and understand ourselves in other terms. Reflexive mediation doesn't disappear, we reshape it as part of redefining ourselves autonomously from capital. This can happen both in our role as workers and when we step out of that role.

For those of us who are waged, this is sometimes achieved through the kind of self-organization that occurs in the covert formation of networks of resistance or in the overt formation of unions. In both cases, self-redefinition occurs through the formation of new relationships of reflexive mediation with our fellow workers. Ceasing to compete and collaborating in struggle changes both our relationships among ourselves and our relationships with our bosses. When we engage in collective sabotage or strikes, we redefine ourselves as not just part of the working class in-itself, but as part of the class-for-itself.[14] In the process, we affirm our antagonism but also, in the process, often seek entirely new ways of relating to each other, beyond those of mutual recognition as workers.[15] Such self-redefinition is also sometimes achieved in time set free by absenteeism, when we seize time and energy to build new relationships with others (e.g., lovers, friends, family members, and neighbors), autonomous from our jobs and our waged work.

Salaried teachers and professors (like other waged workers) can, and sometimes do, refuse capitalist command and subvert or withdraw from the relationship. They may subvert by actually helping students learn in domains other than those of required schoolwork; they may withdraw, either temporarily and collectively in

---

14   This was a distinction made by Marx in his analysis of the French peasantry after the 1848 revolution. See note 1 of my Preface.

15   Despite often being arduous and time-consuming, the search for and creation of new forms of reflexive mediation is an essential element of struggle. Self-organizing, when it begins, sometimes simply replicates capital's typical and familiar forms of hierarchy (e.g., adherence to Robert's Rules of Order). But when that happens, intra-class struggle often forces changes. In the 1960s, within "the movement," a great deal of time and energy were devoted to exploring more participatory forms of democratic discussion and decision-making. Women, for example, demanded the replacement of any gender hierarchy that emerged with real equality—no more expecting only women to make the coffee and clean up after meetings. No more ceding the floor to the loudest and most articulate speakers. Those of us who created the Pacific Studies Center in East Palo Alto and published "underground" newsletters and newspapers often spent every bit as much time trying to find better forms of reflexive mediation among ourselves as we did attending to the planning and preparation of those publications. During the Zapatista rebellion in Chiapas, Mexico, women within the EZLN formulated and imposed a Revolutionary Women's Law on the traditionally male-only community leadership councils. In many cases, persistent resistance to such abandonment of traditional hierarchies has led those challenging them to simply go their own way and form autonomous organizations. Many struggles of the 1960s and 1970s by women and by people of color wound up taking this form. Such autonomy, however, did not eliminate the need to work out new kinds of interactions, it merely reframed the context within which such efforts unfolded.

strikes, or permanently, fleeing their long, intense working hours and low pay. Collective struggle has been difficult because school administrators have long used the power of faculty over students to argue that the former qualify as "management" and should not be allowed to organize and bargain collectively. However, as those administrators have progressively undercut what little power faculty have by replacing tenured faculty with untenured adjuncts, they have inadvertently undercut their argument against faculty unionization. This struggle has been unfolding at the level of the National Labor Relations Board and the Supreme Court as well as within particular schools.

For those of us without a wage, such struggles involve both the identification and rejection of no longer acceptable roles *and* the creation of new relationships of reflexive mediation with others.

Unwaged housewives may refuse to continue to be defined solely as homemakers and mothers, escape the family, either partially or completely, and craft new kinds of relationships with family members and with those outside. Feminists have generally embraced such refusals, explored alternative roles, and redefined themselves, in action and in the minds of others and of themselves. Sometimes they have accomplished this through the refusal to procreate or to perform other kinds of housework, through the demand for a wage and through the crafting of, and struggle for social and legal acceptance of entirely new kinds of relationships between and among individuals, including gender roles. Similarly, the "coming out" of lesbian, gay, bisexual, and transgender (LGBT) individuals, the increasingly overt self-organization of LGBT communities, and the struggle for legal rights (e.g., the right to marry and be free from discrimination), have involved the affirmation of kinds of reflexive mediation quite different from those of workers and bosses.

Unwaged children are so inclined to forming and reforming their identities in relation to others that strict discipline is usually required to curb their spontaneous exploration of life, to condition them into "being a student" and to gain acceptance of their subordination to teachers. It takes years to further constrain their efforts to learn within the framework of preparing for the job market (i.e., reducing their lives to labor power). Despite overall success in imposing these relationships—through decades of shaping schooling with these aims—young people have often broken free, refusing to accept the subordination of their learning to job training. Individually they have often refused to "follow the rules," by cheating, skipping school, or leaving entirely. Collectively they have organized protests ranging from walkouts to occupations shutting down schools and universities. Student *movements* have fought to change the content and structure of education, to refuse higher costs (tuition and fees), and to reduce or eliminate the taking on of heavy debt. Graduate teaching assistants, caught between their status as students and that of teachers, have been moving, like faculty, to unionize—against great resistance from school administrators.

In all these cases, the refusal to do the work their teachers or professors would impose has liberated time and energy for autonomous learning. As many of us have discovered, we have often *learned* far more during such withdrawals than we ever did in the classroom or bent over homework outside of it. In short, reflexive mediation as a moment of capital's dialectic can be, and has been, ruptured by the unwaged, just as it can be, and has been, ruptured by the waged. In its place, students have substituted a multiplicity of mutual interactions—reshaping and making use of reflexive mediation to redefine themselves independently of capital. Individual rebels are often dismissed as deviants, delinquents, and dropouts. When they act collectively, dismissal is more difficult, and students who have taken such actions have sometimes achieved their goals. Such withdrawals, refusals, and ruptures may be short-lived or long-lasting, depending upon circumstances.

Throughout his active political life, Marx observed, noted, and often analyzed and wrote about workers' struggles that brought about such ruptures, especially when they happened on a large scale—for example, strikes and insurrections such as the 1848 revolutions or the Paris Commune. He paid less attention to the molecular withdrawals of individuals or small groups that have repeatedly ruptured capital's ability to define people as workers, but several generations of Marxists have largely filled that gap with detailed examinations of how on-the-job struggles often result in the

partial rupture of production and sometimes lead to walkouts and
strikes that rupture it completely.[16]

The Expanded Form, Totalization, and Infinity

In the second step of Marx's analysis of the form of value, *the passages on the expanded form*, the primary emphasis is again on
qualitative relationships, but one of them has a very quantitative
dimension. Because the value of any commodity—for example, a
bolt of linen (xA)—can be expressed, in exchange, by a random
and particular equivalent—for example, a coat (yB), that value
could also be expressed or mirrored *by any other commodity*
($zC, \ldots nN$) throughout the entire world of commodities. This
includes the subworld of the labor market. In the class relationships of capitalism, ideally people have the possibility not just of
selling their labor power to one capitalist but to any capitalist.[17]
Capitalists, on the other hand, strive to create a world where they
can hire laborers anywhere and everywhere by forcing people into
the labor market all over. As Marx pointed out in chapter 31 of
volume 1 of *Capital*, toward the end of his discussion of "primitive
accumulation," colonialism was essentially the extension of the

---

16   The work in the 1950s of the American Johnson-Forest Tendency and that of
the French Socialisme ou Barbarie group marked a turning point in Marxist attention to day-to-day struggles. In their wake came a great many detailed studies of
the dynamics of on-the-job struggles. As mentioned above, the work of Romano
Alquati and Raniero Panzieri in Italy is particularly notable. Both researched factory conditions and published articles in the early 1960s in *Quaderni Rossi* that were
subsequently collected in Alquati, *Sulla Fiat* (1975) and Panzieri, *La ripresa del
marxismo leninismo in Italia* (1975). The term "molecular" is from Felix Guattari's
analysis of everyday resistance and how it adds up. See Felix Guattari, *La revolution moleculaire* (Fontenay-Sous-Bois: Recherches, 1977). Mainstream sociologists,
of course, with their research largely financed by capitalist institutions, have long
studied such struggles. Economists, on the other hand, having shuffled off such
concrete worries about work, largely ignored such struggles until forced—by a new
generation of young radical economists in the late 1960s—to confront labor market
segmentation and the concept of efficiency wages.

17   Economists call a labor market where there is only one possible employer a
monopsony. Such labor market conditions—that give undue power to the unique
employer—are found in one-company towns.

enclosure of the commons and the imposition of labor markets throughout the world.[18]

In other words, capitalists seek *totalization*, the imposition of their way of organizing society everywhere. They seek to convert all elements of human life—both things and relationships into commodities and, in the process, to convert all human activities into commodity-producing work. Making things becomes waged factory labor and salaried engineering labor. Growing things becomes hired field labor. Cooking for and feeding each other becomes waged labor in the processed food industry and that of cooks, dishwashers, and waitpersons in restaurants. Taking care of each other becomes the paid work of nurses, doctors, psychiatrists, day-care monitors, and prostitutes working for brothel owners. Helping our children learn becomes teaching jobs in schools, colleges, and universities. Figuring out how to live together with all our differences is reserved to professional politicians. Defending ourselves becomes the specialized labor of police and military forces. Understanding our place in the universe becomes the specialized labor of scientists and, for some, salaried priests and theologians. And so on.[19] With no theoretical limit to the variety of human activities, or

---

18 In retrospect, this was the most important social and political aspect not only of colonialism but also of postcolonial counterinsurgency campaigns—aimed at pacifying insurgent populations of the Global South—and anti-nationalist, nation-building efforts to limit obstacles to international trade and investment. Although the antiwar movement may have limited the butchery of efforts in Indochina, it failed to prevent the subsequent induction, after the wars ended, of the war-weary populations into the global labor market and their use by capital against higher waged workers elsewhere. See Philip Mattera, "National Liberation, Socialism and the Struggle against Work: The Case of Vietnam," *Zerowork*, no. 2, 1977, 71–89. We can say something similar about how covert, then overt struggles in the Soviet Union and eastern Europe ended Communist Party rule. When those populations were unable to elaborate alternatives to capitalism, they were delivered into the hands of local or foreign capitalists.

19 Writing in the period of rapid industrialization, Marx's emphasis in his writings was mostly on the capitalist transformation of making into manufacturing and machine production. Decades later, Ivan Illich would trace and critique the capitalist transformation of human relationships into jobs in the "service sector" and the associated dependency of individuals on the buying of those services. See his

to the variety of elements that play roles in those activities, there is no theoretical limit to capitalist expansion. Capitalist totalization is, therefore, at least potentially, *infinite*. This tendency has for a long time been nicely captured by many science fiction novels and movies that have portrayed capitalism expanding off-planet.[20]

Marx's recognition of this tendency of capitalism was misinterpreted by many post-modernists and post-structuralists in the 1980s and 1990s as an attempt by him to impose his own "master narrative" of class and class struggle on the world. They correctly identified a diverse array of relationships that involved discrimination and exploitation—many that predated the rise of capitalism as a social system (e.g., sexism and racism)—but analyzed them as distinct forms of domination separate from, albeit often parallel to, relationships of class. Marx and his followers were wrong, they judged, to dissolve these distinct forms of domination into those of class. Their confusion resulted from two mistakes. First, their critiques were only effective against orthodox Marxism. Second, they failed to differentiate between the tendency of capital to subordinate all existing forms of discrimination, exploitation, and domination to its own particular uses and Marx's analysis of that tendency. The orthodox variety, by clinging to a narrow definition of working class as the waged factory proletariat, privileging its role in social change and failing to take other kinds of struggle seriously, was indeed vulnerable to their critique; but Marx's own analysis was not.

Marx fully recognized, for example, how nineteenth-century, race-based cotton slavery differed from British factory labor—although he sometimes emphasized the parallels by calling the latter wage-slavery. He also recognized the existence of ethnic discrimination—such as that of the British in their treatment of the Irish, both in Ireland and within England, and, of course, the treatment of the diverse peoples in British colonies in Africa and Asia. However, recognizing these differences and consequent different patterns of discrimination, modes of exploitation, and domination did not

---

Medical Nemesis (London: Calder & Boyars, 1974) and *Toward a History of Needs* (New York: Pantheon Books, 1978).

20   The recent decision of the US National Aeronautics and Space Administration to hand off the development of the next generation of orbital shuttle craft to the private sector is one depressing step in this direction.

blind Marx, nor should it blind us, to how capitalists have sought to incorporate and utilize them within its own forms of exploitation and domination. Differences in race, ethnicity, nationality, gender, and age have all been used by capital to divide those it has put to work. They have been used to divide in order to conquer, to pit one group of workers against other groups of workers, in changing combinations designed to achieve, maintain, or restore control over them all. The "master narrative" was not Marx's but capital's, as it has sought to integrate everything, including differences, into its mode of social domination.

Those who have failed to see how these differences have been used by capital have also interpreted the inevitable struggles against them as constituting separate *social movements*—distinct from working-class struggle. In so doing, losing sight of the constraints imposed by capitalist institutions on those movements has crippled their ability to evaluate existing struggles and design more effective ones. However, those I have called "autonomist" Marxists have long recognized 1) how capital has instrumentalized differences such as race and gender in its organization of the working class, and 2) how the diverse situations of the people so organized have generated diverse forms of organization. They have recognized this complexity in their readings of history and theorized it with the concept of "class composition"—a recasting of Marx's concepts of the composition of capital in terms of the relationships of power both among different kinds of workers and between workers and capital.[21]

Against the capitalist project of infinite totalization and expansion, people have resisted commodification, defended the commons, and refused work. Every successful resistance, every rupture of existing capital-labor dialectics, whether in the factory, office, school, or home, has limited or set back capitalist expansion.

Despite providing a useful expression of these tendencies of capitalism, Marx pointed out how the expanded form of value is still an inadequate *representation* of value. The inadequacy, he argued, lies in its character as a patchwork or motley mosaic of

---

21   On the development of the concept of "class composition," see Steve Wright, *Storming Heaven: Class Composition and Struggle in Italian Autonomist Marxism* (New York: Pluto Press, 2002).

multiplying, but still distinct, relationships. In $xA = yB$ and $xA = zC$, et cetera, **B** and **C** are distinct equivalents and expressions of the value of **A**, no matter how long the list, even if extended to the entire world of commodities and even if theoretically extendable to infinity. The expanded form is, in Hegel's terms, "a bad infinity" because while value is unitary (with its common substance of abstract labor and its unique measure of socially necessary labor time) the potentially infinitely expandable list of equivalents is not.

We can illustrate this situation within the class relationship by recognizing how wages have often been paid not with money but in kind. For example, agrarian capitalists who have hired people to work in their fields to harvest crops have frequently paid those workers a small share of what they have harvested. Marx's analysis of the criminalization of the gathering of wood in forests, a traditional right, revealed how it was aimed at reducing peasant income and increasing their exploitation by capital.[22] Even manufacturers, early on, partly paid their workers in kind, by allowing shoemakers to retain scraps of leather, silk workers to keep scraps of silk, shipwrights to take home scraps of wood, and so on. In each case, these parts of the wage were particular use-values that could be worked up and consumed directly or transformed into something that could be sold.[23] Each of these particular use-values—leather, silk, and wood—constituted an equivalent for at least part of the value of those workers' labor power, but they were all distinct. We could speak of the leather-value of the leatherworker's labor power, or the silk-value of the silk worker's labor power, but not of the value of their labor power. Just as Marx writes that "any expression of value common to all commodities is directly excluded" in this form, so too is any expression of the common value of labor power to capital.[24] Unlike such particular use-values, and the particular kinds

---

22 See Karl Marx, "Proceedings of the Sixth Rhine Province Assembly"; Peter Linebaugh, "Karl Marx, the Theft of Wood and Working Class Composition."

23 Peter Linebaugh in his *London Hanged* (2006) has traced how the money form was progressively imposed on just such workers during the eighteenth century, replacing payments in kind.

24 Karl Marx, *Capital*, vol. 1 (New York: Penguin, 1990), chapter 1, section 3 on the value-form; subsection C on the general form of value; part 1 on the changed character of the form of value.

of labor they embody, an adequate representation of value must be, Marx argues, as unitary as the value of those different kinds of labor to capital—their common character of providing the means of social control. The unitary representation that he suggests offers a solution to this problem is the general form of value.

The General Form and Syllogistic Mediation

In the third step of Marx's analysis of the form of value, *the passages on the general form of value*, the overcoming of the "bad infinity" is easily achieved. A unitary representation of value immediately appears when we recognize that if any commodity can be exchanged for any other—for example, **xA** can be exchanged for either **yB** or **zC**—then some particular commodity, let's say **A**, can serve as a *universal equivalent* that expresses the value of each and every commodity being sold (e.g., of **B** and **C**). This obviously includes the case of the commodity labor power. If each person, or group of people, can sell their labor power to any capitalist or corporation in exchange for a wage—that takes the common form of money—then the wage amounts to a universal equivalent that expresses the value of everyone's labor power in the same manner. While each person's labor power is unique, that they all receive common wages expresses the common value of their labor to capital; no matter what kind of work they do, their work serves to keep them busy and under control.

As Marx elaborates his analysis of this general form of value, once again his emphasis is on the particular *quality* of the relationships involved. Most importantly, the universal equivalent plays the role of *universal mediator*. In the case of most commodities, be they things or services, they come to be exchanged for each other only via the mediation of the general equivalent. For example, in order for **yB** to be exchanged for **zC**, it must first be exchanged for **xA** that can then be used to obtain **zC**. So the universal equivalent **A** mediates the relationship (of exchange) between **B** and **C**. Whereas in the simple form we discovered Hegel's dialectical relation of reflexive mediation—where a thing is related to itself through a second—here in the general form of value we find his dialectic relation of *syllogistic mediation*—where the relationship between two things is mediated by a third. Marx's familiarity with Hegel's treatment of this kind of mediation in his *Science of Logic* undoubtedly informed his analysis of value in the capitalist world of commodity exchange.[25]

When we focus on that subset of commodity exchange that constitutes the labor market and its antagonistic class relationships, as Marx does in chapter 6 of volume 1 of *Capital*, we find the same kind of syllogistic mediations. The most obvious, and most widely recognized mediator of this kind, besides the labor market itself, is the wage, through which capital seeks to mediate among all members of the working class and between groups of workers. Some are hired and paid, others are not and remain wageless.

Although the wage has been a central vehicle of mediation, it has been complemented by many others. Rates of waged or salaried employment and unwaged unemployment differ by race, gender, age, and ethnicity. Legal labor contracts are used to mediate the exchange between workers and their bosses. Contracts impose conditions of wage and benefit negotiation, restrict conflict to specific, planned periods just prior to contract renewal, and require union officials, from shop stewards to top union bosses, to get rank-and-file workers to adhere to the terms of the contract—even when their employers are not doing so. Labor market segmentation separates workers, undermining their ability to collaborate. In outsourcing, employment agencies replace the mediation of personnel officers, sorting and sifting job applicants to find those most willing and able to work. Differences in modes of hiring may be structured along racial, ethnic, gender, or age lines. For example, it is common in the United States for employers to hire more expensive, skilled local labor directly while obtaining cheap, unskilled immigrant labor through formal or informal labor contractors. Schools and independent testing companies mediate between employers and potential hires when jobs are contingent on various forms of certification. Where some family members are waged and others are not, the needs of the latter are used to pressure those looking for work to accept offered wages and working conditions. Ideology, mass media, and racial, ethnic, and gender divisions of the labor force are all used as mediations to manage the class relationship.

---

25 Hegel's discussion of syllogistic mediation in *Science of Logic* can be found in the section on the Doctrine of the Notion (or "Concept" in Giovanni's translation).

Beyond the labor market, both in the domain of waged production labor and in that of the unwaged labor of reproduction, we can find capital seeking to impose these kinds of mediation again and again. On the job, capital has traditionally insisted upon its authority—what Marx called its despotism and in the United States is called "managerial prerogative"—to organize every last detail of production and thus to mediate and manage the relationships between workers and their tools and machines and other workers. Some are paid more, others less, to create a hierarchy that divides and pits some against others in what it pretends is a zero sum game. But these relations of greater or lesser pay are also mediated by race, gender, and age. Whites are generally paid more than nonwhites, men more than women, adults more than teenagers, and so on. Job tasks are also often allocated with similar mediations (e.g., locals get the easier, safer, less boring jobs, immigrants get the harder, more dangerous, monotonous jobs). In such job hierarchies, capital seeks to use each level to mediate—that is, help control and absorb the anger of those below it—while also using competitive pressure from those below to keep those above working hard.[26]

Beyond waged workplaces, in schools and homes, capital has also sought to organize things so that it can regulate/mediate the relations of reproduction. I have already pointed out the systematic intervention of business in schooling; part of that intervention has involved mediating the relationship between teachers and students by shaping curriculum and testing and by setting administrators over both teachers and students with the power to impose rules on both that pit them against each other. Forcing teachers to impose work uses teachers as mediators and pits them against students; using student evaluations against teachers pits

---

26 In the 1960s, in the midst of the civil rights movement, Bob Dylan wrote a song—in response to the assassination of activist Medgar Evers by Byron De La Beckwith, a member of the Ku Klux Klan and a White Citizens' Council—to make people aware of how such divisions were used to pit poor whites against protesting blacks. That song was "Only a Pawn in Their Game." The "game," of course, was capitalist control of the entire working class through the cultivation of racism. There are at least two videos on YouTube of Dylan singing the song at civil rights rallies in 1963. The song was released on his album *The Times They Are a-Changin'* (1964).

students against teachers. Teachers are also supposed to absorb the anger of students, deflecting it from administrators—who are one step removed from the direct imposition of work. As Hegel pointed out, in complete syllogistic mediation in any triadic set, each moment mediates the relationships of the other two. In the case of administrators-teachers-students, capital has sought to organize schools in precisely such a manner.[27]

In the home, capital has done much the same through the state, by shaping laws to define marriage and family and laws to regulate intra-family relationships and the distribution of wages so as to divide the family between waged and unwaged and pit them against each other—thus poisoning the relationship between spouses and between parents and children. Systemic sexism in which more husbands than wives have been able to obtain waged jobs has given men more power within the family, and they have often been expected to control their unwaged wives. Similarly, both parents have been expected to control their children. Controlling unwaged wives has meant making sure they do the domestic work of producing (procreating) and reproducing labor power—that of their husbands, themselves, and their children. Controlling unwaged children has meant bringing them up to accept the capitalist way of life, in part by playing truant officers and study hall monitors, making sure that their kids actually go to school and do their homework. Failure to do the former can be punishable by law.[28] At the same time, the needs of unwaged spouses and children—for which the waged spouse is deemed responsible—have been used to keep the latter working hard.

Once again, for every imposed mediation, there is the possibility of its rupture through struggle that either bypasses or destroys the existing mechanisms of mediation. *In the labor market*, the most obvious rupture is the out-and-out refusal to participate—refusal to search for a job. In the United States, travel to the frontier was one mode of escape that lasted hundreds of years. More recently, since workers were successful in obtaining unemployment compensation

---

27   A more detailed discussion of the various forms of mediation can be found in my evolving essay "On Schoolwork and the Struggle Against It" (2006), http://www.libcom.org/.

28   See note 18, page 81 on the criminalization of truancy in Texas.

from the state, through their struggles in, and since, the 1930s, *pretending* to look for work after being laid off from waged jobs has become, for some, a veritable art form.[29] Similarly, victories by the welfare rights movement and urban insurgencies have won non-wage income that has supported avoidance of the labor market—especially by mothers, already engaged in the unwaged work of rearing their children, and by those children themselves. It was those victories that were targeted by the so-called welfare reforms passed by the joint efforts of a Republican-dominated Congress and the Democratic administration of Bill Clinton. Those reforms imposed "workfare"—that is, the requirement that those receiving welfare be engaged in some kind of labor outside the home as well as doing the work of reproducing labor power.[30]

On the job, complicity between managers and workers (as in the telephone plant mentioned above), lateral collaboration across job categories in the organization of play instead of work, and the direct appropriation of things and time, including the use of capitalist-owned equipment for nonwork purposes, all rupture capital's attempts to mediate and control the waged workplace.[31] Wildcat strikes refuse the mediation of union officials when they act more like the labor-relations arm of management than representatives of worker interests.

Similar struggles arise in schools when adjunct teachers and graduate teaching assistants fight for the right to organize and bargain collectively. Collective action may reduce the ability of administrators to pit tenured teacher against adjunct teacher, or teachers against graduate students, but success in creating a union creates a new form of mediation in union representatives, which may come

---

29 Within the United States, unemployment compensation is usually managed by each state—and each state puts locally defined conditions on its payment, conditions that usually include the submission of evidence of having looked for a job.

30 The legislation mandating this change was the Personal Responsibility and Work Opportunity Reconciliation Act of 1996, which instituted Temporary Assistance for Needy Families, replacing Aid to Families with Dependent Children, which had been in effect since 1935.

31 See the description of rod-blowing contests and other play in an auto plant in Bill Watson, "Counter-Planning on the Shopfloor," *Radical America*, May/June 1971, 77–85.

to require refusal—just like in industry. Student walkouts refuse the mediation of teachers, of representatives in student governments, of curriculum, and of official administrators. In the United States in the 1960s, students repeatedly bypassed the mediation of professors and administrators to directly confront boards of trustees (or regents), whose role in overseeing universities is roughly equivalent to that of boards of directors in overtly for-profit corporations. In the 1999 strike at UNAM, the Autonomous National University of Mexico (the largest in Latin America), which lasted almost a year, students and parents bypassed professors and university administrators and aimed their struggle against the imposition of tuition directly at the state. As so often happens, they developed new organizational methods—loosely adapted from those used within the indigenous Zapatista rebellion.[32] In the Arab Spring and Occupy movements we have seen this same bypassing, and thus rupturing, of virtually all the traditional forms of capitalist mediation.

The women's movement has repeatedly refused the mediation of men, of marriage laws, and of commercial definitions of beauty—all shaped by capital to maintain a gender hierarchy to women's detriment. Civil rights movements, which in the United States began with blacks but soon spread to Hispanic Americans, Native Americans, and Asian Americans, have all refused and ruptured both legal and extralegal mediations that have organized racial and ethnic hierarchies. Older workers and retired people have organized to resist capitalist efforts to demonize them among younger workers (e.g., to blame them for capitalist-engineered economic problems and by so doing use the latter against the former).[33]

The Money Form

In the fourth and final step of his analysis of the form of value, in *the passages on the money form*, Marx argues that the essential universal equivalent that comes to express the value of all commodities is

32   See Alan Eladio Gómez, "People's Power, Educational Democracy and Low Intensity War: The UNAM Student Srike, 1999–2000," master's thesis, University of Texas at Austin, 2002.

33   See Lynne Segal, *Out of Time: The Pleasures and Perils of Ageing* (London: Verso, 2014), chapter 2 ("Generational Warfare").

money. In his time, the primary money, which itself embodied value, was some commodity, selected historically because of its high value, durability, and divisibility—most often gold in the Western world and silver in much of Asia. Despite such commodity money having already been largely replaced in commerce and finance by paper money and credit, Marx assumed in his exposition that the various roles of money were played by gold. Because he carried out his analysis of money in terms of gold, the implications of the replacement of such money by paper and credit has been much debated by Marxists. Today, when precious metals such as gold and silver have been largely demonetized (i.e., no longer serve as money) and have been almost entirely replaced by credit money, the debate continues. Within that debate, I side with those who think that despite fiat and credit money being representations of value rather than embodiments of it, they still serve the same purposes as commodity money (e.g., measures of value, standards of price, means of circulation, and means of commanding labor).[34]

What is true of the relationship between all commodities and money is also true of the relationship between the commodity labor power and money. Its value has come to be expressed primarily by its monetary value, its price (e.g., the wage or a salary).[35]

---

34 A recent contribution to the debate is George Caffentzis, "Marxism after the Death of Gold," in Marcel van der Linden and Karl Heinz Roth, eds., *Beyond Marx*, 395–415. Caffentzis addresses the issue of whether non-commodity monies can provide valid expressions of "the measure of value immanent in commodities, namely labor-time." Setting aside Marx's reliance on Hegel's analysis of immanence and appearance and drawing on the insights of modern science and philosophy, Caffentzis points out that all kinds of things can have indirect measures (e.g., heat of a gas, understood as the average kinetic energy of its atoms, can be measured by several different kinds of thermometers). True for heat, true for value—via monies that we can assume to have been produced with negligible socially necessary labor time—as long as we keep in mind the substance being measured (i.e., abstract labor or the quality of labor as social control).

35 As already mentioned, money has not always been the sole equivalent of the value of labor power. Payments in kind still exist in some rural areas where, for example, agricultural laborers are still paid with part of the harvest. Not only is the wage only one particular form of the price of labor power—other examples include salaries, commissions, and tips—but the wage itself takes many forms. In volume 1

Of all the mediators that capital uses to manage the relationships among things and people, money has become the most pervasive. In search of profit, capitalists tend to turn almost everything (including every relationship) into a commodity, sold and bought in some market. As commodities with prices, each forms one moment of the money form of value. Qualitatively, all individuals who sell their labor power to capital in return for money are in a similar situation. Quantitatively, the amount of their wage or salary measures the value of their labor power, while situating them within an elaborate money income hierarchy designed to pit them against each other so that they can all be controlled—that is, kept at work.

As Marx argues in chapter 6 of volume 1 of *Capital*, the value of labor power is determined by the amount of socially necessary labor that must be allocated to produce everything necessary for its reproduction. In his day, Marx, like the classical political economists before him, could comfortably call the means of reproduction required by the vast majority of workers the "means of subsistence" and speak of a "subsistence wage." In that period, a great many workers, slaving away in the infamous "satanic mills" of British industry, lived close to mere biological subsistence, with their income rising a little above it when labor markets were tight, but all too often falling below it when the demand for labor lessened. Obviously, even the notion of "biological subsistence" is fuzzy because between full health and immediate death lies a whole range of degrees of wellness and illness, strength and weakness, and consequently of life expectancy. With little or no savings, and very little material wealth that could be pawned when laid off and unwaged, workers suffered from malnutrition, starvation, and disease.[36]

---

of *Capital* Marx analyzes two of these forms—time wages and piece wages—where he shows not only how these forms of a form hide exploitation but also how capital seeks to manipulate them to impose more work.

36 Chapter 6 of Elizabeth Gaskell's novel *Mary Barton* (1848)—based on Gaskell's own experiences in Manchester—vividly illustrates such dire straits. An unemployed worker, ill with typhoid fever, and his family, having already pawned their few worldly goods, are starving and sleeping on straw in a fetid cellar. Despite a friend pawning his coat and handkerchief to buy some bread, candles, and coal, the man dies, leaving behind a wife and children who only survive thanks to neighbors and a pittance from the local Poor Law Board.

Yet, as Marx recognized, the value of labor power is also determined historically and socially. Some workers have been successful at raising their standard of living over time. This is the result of two factors. First, the evolution of capitalist industry has necessitated the diversion of more resources to insure the reproduction of some workers. Partly this has been due to such phenomena as the need for more schooling. Skilled workers, technicians, engineers, or scientists require more schooling, which in turn implies a greater diversion of work to the production of everything required for such schooling and thus a higher value of labor power. To the degree that such workers must pay for such expanded schooling, they must receive higher income.[37] Second, changes in the value of labor power over time, and across sectors of the working class, have also been a function of variable success in workers' struggles for higher wages and benefits. *Some* workers have become well enough organized to fight successfully for higher wages and more benefits—just as they have fought successfully for shorter working hours. In the process, they raised the value of *their* labor power. This effectively forced capital to allocate more of the work it imposes to producing things and services those workers have achieved the power to make necessary for their continued willingness and ability to work.[38]

Please note: worker success in forcing a diversion of value from surplus value to the value of labor power, or, in money terms, from profits to wages, while it may reduce the rate at which capital can expand, nevertheless increases the amount of work it can impose producing the things workers are able to buy with their increased wages. Thus higher-waged workers are more "valuable" to capital, not just in the sense that it must spend more money on them, but

---

37   This is true even when much of schooling is financed through the state—when the necessary monies are raised through all forms of taxation that lower workers' real income.

38   Worker success in raising wages—like that in reducing working hours—has often spurred capitalist investment in productivity-raising innovations, such as new, more efficient machines. Such innovations, by lowering the per unit value of consumption goods, have offset the effect of rising wages on the value of labor power. Indeed, if productivity increases enough, increasing wages can be associated with *reductions* in the value of labor power. Thus the seeming paradox that reductions in the value of labor power can be accompanied by higher standards of living.

because the production of the consumer goods they purchase with higher wages provide expanded opportunities to impose work. In macroeconomics, such consumption expenditure is recognized as the largest source of "effective demand" and thus the major source of employment. Other workers, less well organized for whatever reasons, have been less capable of imposing higher wages, raising the value of their labor power, and improving their standards of living. It has been partly in response to such differential success that capital has shaped its wage hierarchy—a hierarchy that has come to extend upward from bare subsistence through what we now call the middle class to high salaried managers.[39]

Throughout this history of antagonistic class struggle, there have always been the unwaged, those who do not earn a money wage or salary in exchange for selling their labor power but who play vital roles in the reproduction of capital. Whether generated through 1) enclosures forcing indigenous peoples or farmers off their land, 2) the laying-off of once-waged workers, 3) population growth, or 4) immigration, the unwaged constitute—in the language of chapter 25 of volume 1 of *Capital*—a "reserve army" that must still receive some kind of income or die. That income may be money derived from someone else's wage or salary (e.g., the income of stay-at-home spouses or children). It may be accorded by the state in either money or in kind, (e.g., family allocations, unemployment compensation, welfare payments, public services, or school lunches). It may be made available by nongovernmental organizations, more often in kind than in direct money payments (e.g., charity-organized soup kitchens or shelters for the homeless). Or unwaged income may be gained through autonomous

39 The resulting wide range of waged and salaried incomes, coupled with the varying degrees to which individuals have work imposed on them versus the degree to which they are responsible for imposing work on others has contributed to considerable debate over how to define the working class and who should be considered a part of it. Capital and its sociologists generally prefer to eschew the category of class altogether and simply speak of income "strata." Marxists, on the other hand, wedded to the concept of class, have struggled with the implications of the emergence of the "middle class" and upper-income managers who still work long hours while imposing work on those below them. For my opposition to "classification," see the preface to this book.

action—direct appropriation (e.g., "theft") or self-organized production (e.g., peasant subsistence production or family or community gardening). Direct appropriation from other individuals
merely redistributes income within the working class. Appropriation from business (e.g., bank robbery), redistributes income from
capital to workers.[40] Subsistence production generates income in
the form of use-values that can be consumed directly or sold in
markets for money, which is then spent on consumer goods impossible to produce at home. Such participation in markets is
non-capitalist to the degree that it merely supports consumption
and doesn't generate investable profit. Examples include the sale of
surplus domestic production and the peddling of homemade goods
or services in the urban informal sector.

Into all these activities, capital seeks to intervene with a variety
of mediating institutions, laws, and policing with the objective of
organizing and gaining enough control to shape them as forms of
its own reproduction. The money form is clearly present in many
of these situations as a central form of mediation despite not taking
the form of the wage. One recently popular form of mediation has
involved efforts, both private and public, to peddle micro loans designed to tie people into the formal economy via debt. Such access
to credit has not been won from below through successful struggle
in raising wages and wealth collateral but has been designed from
on high by those trying to gain leverage over autonomous social
activities that have hitherto escaped their control.[41]

The money form also plays a role in various institutions that
we normally think of as separate from the sphere of waged labor.
One of those is schools. To what I have already discussed about
how capital has sought to organize unwaged students in schools,
let me just add two points. First, while at lower levels the vast majority of students are clearly unwaged, at higher levels, in what are
often called graduate studies, where students are working toward

---

40 Capital, of course, tries to pass on the costs of such direct appropriation to
other workers through price increases—not only to protect its profits but to gain
support for laws that protect property. It tries the same dual ploy with taxes, seeking
working-class support for tax reductions on business.

41 See the discussion of micro debt and the role of the World Bank in George
Caffentzis, "Against the Debt Economy," *Red Pepper*, February/March 2014.

advanced degrees, some students are paid money and are effectively waged (e.g., teaching and research assistants), while others
are not—a situation that, *ceteris paribus*, divides and weakens the
ability of such graduate students to organize collectively. Thus, the
according or withholding of such wages provides another form of
mediation to manage students. Second, money mediates the relationship between capital and students not only in the payment
of wages to faculty, administrators, and some students, but also in
the size and patterns of both the state and private sectors' expenditures on schools. In periods such as the late 1950s and 1960s, US
government investment in "human capital" development involved
spending a great deal of money to enhance the production of labor
power in order to improve productivity and spur accumulation.
Such investment included the sharing of federal tax revenue to finance school expansion, the subsidizing of university research, and
grants of fellowship aid to students. As such expenditures grew,
money played a larger and larger role as mediator between capital
and students. In more recent years, as the imposition of austerity
has included reducing public expenditures on schools, subsidies
have been reduced, and grants have been replaced by loans. Such
disinvestment in schools and students has been partly a response to
the student movements of the 1960s and early 1970s. Those movements not only attacked university complicity in the Vietnam War
(and other counterinsurgency efforts around the world) but also
challenged the subordination of schools to corporate needs. Those
linked attacks and challenges seriously reduced the legitimacy of
business influence in schools—a reduction corporations have been
trying hard to reverse ever since. So, as the state has disinvested
in schooling, the private sector has stepped up its expenditures as
part of a long-term strategy to strengthen its influence and ensure
the subordination of schools and of the work of their students and
researchers to its needs.

Beyond the educational system, capitalist efforts to mediate the struggles of the largely urban unwaged who have either
dropped out of school or finished school has also often involved the
manipulation of money, through state welfare programs. Originally conceived in the 1930s as a socialization of the costs of economic
change, later designed in the 1950s as investments (like those in
education) to improve the quality of the labor force, such programs

were dramatically expanded in response to urban uprisings of the 1960s with the aim of staving off further rebellions. At the time, I was a student with a temporary job in the federal Office of Economic Opportunity. In those days between the uprising in Watts, and before those in Newark, Baltimore, and Washington DC, I listened to government economists discuss how to structure income support high enough to ward off future uprisings but low enough to induce the unwaged to look for waged work.[42] Much of the discussion was over how money could best be spent to achieve these aims. Some supported a "negative income tax" in which those whose income was judged to be too low would simply receive a check in the mail. Others supported a variety of programs with tighter controls over the beneficiaries—for example, Aid to Families with Dependent Children where parents could be closely monitored by local welfare officials, or community action programs designed to channel the energies of struggle into forms easier to manage.

In all of this, we can see how the capitalist organization of the entire society into a global work machine involves a complex array of carefully structured syllogistic mediations—in which a wide variety of institutions have been carefully organized to manage money flows so as to keep everyone in society working, on the job and off.

However, once again, just because capital pays wages to hire labor power directly, or shapes its formation indirectly through the structuring of consumption (or through private or public expenditures of money on schools, welfare, etc.), such uses of money by no means guarantee the intended results. We can use, and elaborate, Marx's analysis of what capital tries to achieve to see how it often fails and how that failure is often due to our own subversive efforts. As a prelude to examining those efforts, let's look at one of the symbolic representations Marx offered of what capitalists try to achieve and what is required for them to succeed.

From the Money Form to the Circuits of Capital

Let us begin with Marx's analysis in chapters 2 and 3 of *Capital*. The former draws on Hegel's analysis of property and the contract in the *Philosophy of Right*, to bring humans into the picture as

---

42 While the economists discussed, of course, other parts of the government were preparing police and military troops to quell future uprisings.

the owners and exchangers of commodities. The latter introduces simple commodity exchange (**C—M—C**), that is to say, exchanges in which commodities (**C**) are sold with the objective of obtaining money (**M**) in order to buy other commodities (**C**). Such a sequence is typical of family farmers or subsistence peasants who sell some of their produce on the market to obtain goods they cannot produce at home. These exchanges form a circuit in the sense that they begin with commodities, end with commodities, and are repeatedly renewed (e.g., every time a family farmer or subsistence peasant has a surplus to sell, these exchanges are repeated).[43] Marx's representation of such situations also provides us with a schematic of the kind of exchange characteristic of our participation in the labor market—to which he turns in chapter 6. There we find what is for us the most important form of **C—M—C**, namely **LP—M—C(MS)**, where **LP** equals our labor power that we sell to capitalists, for money (**M**) that we use to buy the means of subsistence **C(MS)**, or consumer goods and services. As with the case of family farmers and subsistence peasants, we engage in market exchange in order to buy what we need to live and what we think will enrich our lives. The flipside of our participation in the market, however, the purchase of our labor power (**M—LP**) by our bosses, is an expenditure undertaken with objectives quite different from our own. Our bosses hire us and put us to work to make money profits for them. But profits for what? Although capitalists may use part of their profits in the same way we do—to live—Marx was uninterested in such personal motivations. What interested him was how profits were reinvested in expanding the scale of capitalist production and the imposition of work.

The expenditure of money on hiring us, however, is only one

---

43 Traditionally, variation in growing conditions was the main determinant of whether harvests brought a surplus or were barely sufficient for subsistence. Bad weather or floods and lowered crop yields often meant no surplus, no sales **C—M** and no ability to buy items in wider markets, **M—C**. Surpluses might also be reduced or eliminated by such things as increased taxes in kind or the devastations of war. In modern times, reductions in the availability of inputs (e.g., irrigation water) or of credit necessary to their purchase can also wipe out surpluses and sometimes even reduce production below subsistence, forcing those working the land to look for jobs elsewhere.

part of the expenditure by business of money as capital. Other monies are spent on the means of production (e.g., factories, tools, machines, and raw materials). In chapters 4 and 5 of volume 1 of *Capital*, Marx begins to discuss the overall logic of such investment expenditures and their purpose (profits), representing the capitalist project symbolically as $M—C—M'$. In the case of merchant or commercial capital, M represents the money merchants expend to buy commodities that are then resold at higher prices. In the case of industrial capital, the purchased commodities (one of which is usually labor power) are transformed into new commodities that are then sold. In both cases, if capitalists are successful, M' is greater than their previously invested M, and the difference constitutes a profit.

Writing in a period of rapid industrialization, in which agricultural and manufacturing industries were displacing commerce as the most important generators of social wealth and as the primary employers, Marx was mainly interested in industrial capital. Therefore, most of volume 1 of *Capital* is devoted to laying out an analysis of how the capitalist imposition of commodity-producing work is achieved and repeatedly reproduced on an ever larger scale. In the course of working out that analysis, Marx elaborated the circuit of capital in greater detail. That detail can be found in part 1 of volume 2 of *Capital*, where the circuit $M—C—M'$ is expanded in a way that presents expenditures on labor power (LP) and various means of production (MP) as constituting but the first step in a sequence of steps that industrial capitalists must successfully manage to generate the profits necessary to the expanded reproduction of its social order. In his more detailed representations, Marx points out how the purchase of labor power and means of production must be followed by industrial production (P_I), where workers are successfully put to work using tools and machines to transform raw (or intermediary) materials into new commodities. These new commodities (C') are of a higher value because their production has afforded the opportunity to impose more labor, but they must be sold in order to obtain more money (M') than initially invested. Thus $M—C—M'$ is expanded to $M—C\,(LP, MP)\dots P_I \dots C'—M'$.

If all these steps are completed—unruptured by our struggles—M' will be realized, and its investment will start the whole process over again, on a larger scale. The investment of M' will

generate **M"** (>**M'**), et cetera, in an ever-expanding process of reproduction or accumulation. This circuit can represent either the
necessary activities of a single industrial firm or of industrial production as a whole.

At the level of the whole, because **C'** includes **MP**, the only
element whose expanded reproduction is unaccounted for in his
representation is labor power. Capitalists count on our wages or
salaries providing us with the means of purchasing sufficient consumer goods to reproduce our willingness and ability to work. As I
have argued elsewhere, if things go according to their plans, then
our consumption is reduced from the enrichment of our lives to the
work (P_c) of reproducing our labor power so that it will be available
to them in the next period. Therefore, we can add to Marx's exposition (in volume 2 of *Capital*) of the "circuits" of capital, a *circuit
of the reproduction of labor power*: **LP—M—C(MS) . . . P$_c$ . . . LP***.

This new circuit portrays how things unfold when capitalists
are successful in their manipulations.[44] If we juxtapose the two circuits, **LP—M—C(MS)** and **LP—M—C(MS) . . . P$_c$ . . . LP***, we can
see the former not as just an incomplete version of the latter, but as
representing our own (a working class) point of view as opposed to
the latter, which represents capital's objective.

Those of us who sell our labor power for a money wage or salary do so to finance the elaboration of our lives. But that elaboration need not be in line with our bosses' desires that we merely
reproduce our ability and willingness to work for them. The ends
to which we put our wages or salaries may be quite different from
what they want and need. As a class, through both public (state)
and private (corporate) efforts to structure our lives, capitalists
have certainly tried to shape our consumption. But they do not always succeed. Sometimes we are able to subvert their purpose by
spending our wages in ways that do *not* reproduce labor power.
There are endless examples of such subversion. Some are dramatic, say when we spend our wages to buy guns that we then use in
revolutionary uprisings.[45] Other uses are far less violent but no less

---

44 I first set out this circuit in an appendix to H. Cleaver, "Malaria, the Politics of
Public Health, and the International Crisis," *Review of Radical Political Economics*
9, no. 1 (April 1997) 97–99.

45 Some of this happened in the United States during the central city insurgencies

subversive. We may buy cell phones, instead of guns, and use them to organize mass protests—as illustrated vividly during the Occupy movement in the United States and the Arab Spring in North Africa and the Middle East.[46] When our wages are high enough to enable savings, we have repeatedly used them to avoid work, individually by quitting jobs and taking vacations, collectively through strike funds used to support us during prolonged strikes and union pension funds that permit retirement before death from overwork. Pretty much all uses of money wages that finance the diversion of time and energy from work and the reproduction of labor power subvert the employer's expenditure of such money as capital.

The same has been true for monies expended for the purpose of reproducing labor power through channels other than wages (e.g., state spending on education and welfare as investments in "human capital"). As already mentioned, much of the money spent on education for this purpose in the 1960s in the United States was subverted by those of us who used it to finance our struggles against schools and schoolwork, against the wars in Southeast Asia, and against racial, gender, and ethnic discrimination. In that period, more or less similar struggles emerged in many other countries throughout the world. The same was true with regard to welfare state expenditures; such programs were progressively subverted by "poor people's movements" and turned into vehicles of their struggles.[47]

Beyond such negative subversion of money wages, we have also used money to pay for our own creative forms of self-activity,

---

of the mid-1960s. It also happened when the Zapatista communities of Chiapas in southern Mexico sold cattle and pooled their money to buy guns for their army— the Ejército Zapatista de Liberación National (Zapatista Army of National Liberation)—that came out of the jungle and took over six towns in the early hours of January 1, 1994.

46 Sometimes one such use may be exchanged for the other, as in Chiapas where the Zapatistas switched from armed uprising to political struggle, or Syria, where the failure of peaceful protest led to armed insurgency.

47 On such efforts to "unionize the ghettos," see Paolo Carpignano, "US Class Composition in the Sixties," *Zerowork*, no. 1 (1975). See also the classic work by Frances Fox Piven and Richard A. Cloward, *Poor People's Movements: Why They Succeed and How They Fail* (New York: Pantheon, 1977).

or self-valorization, in which we have elaborated ways of being that constitute alternatives to those characteristic of capitalist society. In the United States, "the movement" of the 1960s included a "cultural revolution"—that challenged existing institutions, such as schools, ghetto poverty, welfare programs, or systematic discrimination. Millions of us, both those of us who were young and many of our elders, participated in the discovery, invention, and experimentation with all kinds of ways of being that provided alternatives to working for capitalists and reproducing life as labor power. From Woodstock on the East Coast to Haight-Ashbury on the West Coast, we diverted our scholarships, wages, time, and energy into the exploration of alternatives to practices we had come to despise and oppose. Although, with time, "the movement" as an identifiable mass activity disappeared, such invention and experimentation did not. Any serious investigation of the existing manifold separate struggles through which we continue to challenge this or that aspect of the ways capitalism organizes society will also reveal how we have complemented our protests of what we don't like with the creation of alternatives and efforts to circulate and elaborate them.

All of this, I maintain, demonstrates how Marx's theory of money helps us to situate money within the antagonistic class relations of capitalism and to recognize it as a highly contested terrain of struggle.

PART II

Decoding Finance, Financial Crisis, and Financialization

For the most part, both economists and Marxists understand and analyze the current crisis, and the histories of finance and financialization that led up to it, in almost purely economic terms. Neoliberal apologists for free markets celebrate financial deregulation and innovation, dismissing crises as only temporary disruptions in an otherwise well-functioning system. Neo-Keynesian critics of that deregulation—and of many aspects of the resulting innovations—lament the high unemployment, falling wages, growing homelessness, and widespread suffering brought on by crisis and austerity. Marxists add to the critiques of the neo-Keynesians, condemnations of capitalism in general and various theories of its inevitable tendency to crisis.

People and the social relationships among them enter into these celebrations, lamentations, and condemnations in very limited ways. Neoliberals applaud the inventiveness of those who have innovated new financial instruments and blame the crisis on reckless government leaders and imprudent corporate and family borrowing. Neo-Keynesians also condemn government recklessness but mainly for deregulating finance and imposing austerity instead of countering private sector collapse with expansionary fiscal policies. They also point to how both deregulation and innovation contributed to the risky, and often fraudulent, lending by financial institutions that contributed to the buildup of both public and private debt. Marxists, of course, condemn capitalists of all sorts, including governments that act in their interests, while lamenting the ways in which the working class has been made to

pay the price of capitalist folly. Class struggle, completely absent
in the narratives of neoliberals and neo-Keynesians, rarely enters
Marxist analysis except in calls for resistance to the imposition of
austerity and support for systemic reforms.

Instead, I propose that every element of finance, financial crisis, and financialization can be decoded in class terms and that
by doing so we can re-center our own struggles, both those that
contributed to these phenomena and those that have responded
to them. Doing so, I think, offers a more useful analysis of the current situation and facilitates imagining ways out that are in the
interests of both those of us who have contributed to rupturing accumulation and those who are suffering the ways in which capital
has counterattacked. In part 1 of this book, I argued that Marx's
labor theory of value reveals how money in capitalism is far more
than the means of exchange and store of value it has played for
millennia. As one of many moments in the organization of the class
relations of capitalism, it embodies those relations in all their antagonistic complexity, in their dialectical unity when things go as
capitalists plan, while remaining one of many moments vulnerable
to subversion and rupture by our struggles. Allow me now to sug-
gest how we can apply that class analysis of money to the worlds of
finance, financial crisis, and financialization.

The burgeoning literature on financialization and how it has
contributed to crisis focuses on the ever more prominent role
of finance in the organization of society. Therefore, I will begin
with finance—a phenomenon that predated capitalism but was
soon integrated into it. Marx's analysis of finance is primarily of
finance-among-capitalists—of the methods existing financial institutions evolved to turn money into capital and to profit from its
manipulation. Understanding those methods makes it easier to
understand the increasingly central role of finance in recent years,
the return of financial crisis, and to interpret both in class terms.
Finally, because financialization has indeed been a widespread and
significant process, understanding it is vital to decoding the class
meaning of financial crisis in the current period.

DECODING FINANCE AND FINANCIAL CRISIS

In the most general sense, the term "finance" refers to all kinds of money management—by individuals, businesses, and government. As long as there have been various kinds of monies—in the generic sense of widely recognized tokens that facilitate exchange—managing their stocks, flows, and interchangeability has been both necessary and often handled by specialists in both the private and public sectors. The history of finance, therefore, has been a history of the evolution of the methods and institutions through which money has been managed, sometimes mismanaged, and its intended uses thwarted. As long as there has been finance, there have also been financial crises. My interest in understanding both has been in situating them within the specific dynamics of class struggle within capitalism. It is easy to bog down in the often esoteric details of finance; it is harder to keep in mind how money embodies the antagonistic relations of class and therefore how its management must as well.

Over time, the heart of finance became the extension of *credit*—the deferment of payment, either for goods and services or for money borrowed. By Hegel and Marx's time, finance had already evolved to include the extension of credit to individuals, governments, and businesses, both commercial and industrial. Those who borrowed, accrued *debt*—an obligation to repay the money borrowed from their creditors. Those with enough money to extend such credit have also often been involved in other kinds of financial operations as well, including insuring merchants against losses in trade, and the exchange of one kind of money for another. In all such transactions, there is the possibility of cheating, of fraud, and, in the case of credit and debt, of the failure to repay. The overwhelming sources of credit today, for individuals, for governments, and for business, are capitalist financial institutions, ranging from payday loan sharks through private multinational banks and public central banks to supranational institutions such as the International Monetary Fund and the World Bank.

Not surprisingly, the social relations of finance and their frequent dramas have been repeatedly portrayed in classical literature. In the New Testament, Jesus throws the money-changers out of the temple in Jerusalem. In Dante Alighieri's *Inferno* (1314), usurers are condemned to the Seventh Circle of Hell, where flames lick their feet and fall upon their heads. In Boccaccio's *Decameron* (1353), set in early Renaissance Italy, the money-lender Melchizedek proves his wisdom to would-be borrower, the Sultan Saladin. In François Rabelais's *Le tiers livre des faicts et dicts héroïques du bon Pantagruel* (1546), Panurge argues eloquently of the virtues of lending, borrowing, and debt, while Pantagruel abhors them all and would free his friend from the "thralldom of debt." In William Shakespeare's *Merchant of Venice* (1596–98), also set in Renaissance Italy, the moneylender Shylock demands his literal "pound of flesh" as forfeited collateral when a failed commercial venture leaves his debtor unable to repay a loan. In Sir Walter Scott's *Ivanhoe* (1820), set in the twelfth century, the trials and tribulations of the moneylender Isaac of York and his daughter figure prominently. In Honore de Balzac's grand collection of stories and novels *La Comédie humaine*, written in a nineteenth-century France in the midst of a financial transition to the subordination of finance to capitalism, crises of credit, both economic and moral, play recurrent roles—for example, in *La Peau de chagrin* (1831) and *Père Goriot* (1835). In Charles Dickens's novel *Little Dorrit* (1855–57), set in nineteenth-century England, the title character grows up in a debtor's prison—a repressive state institution created to punish the failure of individuals to repay their debts. In more recent years, perhaps Tom Wolfe's novel *The Bonfire of the Vanities* (1987), set in the 1980s and featuring a wealthy, Wall Street bond trader, should be added to the list.

Although first Engels and then Marx began to pay attention to finance and financial crisis in the 1840s and throughout the 1850s and 1860s, with the latter publishing many newspaper articles on contemporary developments, I want to begin my decoding of Marx's analysis with his technical exposition in *Capital*.[1] There, in

---

1   Marx closely studied the development of finance and its function in the economy. He kept extensive notes, and his many newspaper articles traced the various roles of the financial sector and of state monetary policies in the crises of accumulation of that period. Long available only in extremely hard-to-read microfilms of those newspapers, those articles are now more readily available in Karl Marx and Frederick Engels, *Collective Works* and some special collections—for example, Karl Marx, *Dispatches for the New York Tribune: Selected Journalism of Karl Marx* (New York: Penguin Classics, 2008).

volume I, chapter 3, Marx first takes up credit in his discussion of the role of money in the circulation of commodities. Credit, he points out, allows commodities to be sold (and purchased) with delayed payment, such that money serves as "means of payment." This is the kind of credit with which we, as individuals, are most intimately familiar. Although consumer credit was quite limited in Marx's day, when workers had little or no collateral, today we visit various businesses (from grocery stores to doctors' offices) with credit card in hand, acquire goods or services, and only pay for them later. Although Marx's "little circuit," $LP-M-C(MS)$, assumes that after selling our labor power (LP), we receive our wages (M) and then buy stuff $C(MS)$, with access to credit we are often able to obtain consumer goods *before* we are paid money for our labor power; once we are paid, we can then pay for the goods previously acquired. Frequently, if we pay off our debt immediately, there is no interest charge. If, however, we pay over time, the credit card companies charge interest—often quite substantial interest. A similar situation obtains for mortgages—those bank loans that permit us to buy houses. In that case, we borrow from a bank—putting up the house we are buying as collateral—pay the seller, obtain the house, move in, and then spend the next two or three decades repaying the bank out of our current income. Or, if we lose our jobs—as so many did in the recent crisis—we find ourselves unable to pay, suffer foreclosure on our homes, and are turned out into the street.[2] For most of us, buying a car entails the same sequence: borrow, pay over time, and if we are unable to meet our repayment obligations, find our car being repossessed. Finally, yet another example of such credit is the availability of loans to students. Students borrow to pay tuition, fees, and living expenses and then repay their debt over time. In some cases, repayment is delayed until graduation, but then repayment must be made—usually with interest.

---

2   Although most of us associate mortgages with house-buying, such bank loans are made for many purposes (e.g., refinancing or improvement of an existing home or covering farm costs in seasons of failed crops). Bank foreclosures on farms— where homes, farm equipment, and land have served as collateral—has long been one of the primary financial vehicles of enclosure and the expropriation of families from the land. I have always found John Cougar Mellencamp's 1985 song "Rain on the Scarecrow" a particularly poignant expression of such loss.

At first Marx discusses credit in chapter 3 in purely economic terms. But then, almost immediately, he brings in class struggle.

> The same characteristics can emerge independently of the circulation of commodities. The class struggle in the ancient world, for instance, took the form mainly of a contest between debtors and creditors, and ended in Rome with the ruin of the plebeian debtors, who were replaced by slaves. In the Middle Ages, the contest ended with the ruin of the feudal debtors, who lost their political power together with its economic basis. Here, indeed, the money-form—and the relation between creditor and debtor does have the form of a money-relation—was only the reflection of an antagonism, which lay deeper, at the level of the economic conditions of existence.

Those "economic conditions of existence" were, of course, the antagonistic class relationships in each of those two periods. Marx's reminders of these historical dramas of class struggle between debtors and creditors should evoke, for us, an immediate resonance with the current crisis, which all too often has resulted in the ruin of working-class debtors, as creditors have foreclosed on homes, family farms, automobiles, and other forms of personal collateral.

It remains to be seen to what degree contemporary working-class debtors will, like the plebeians of ancient Rome, be replaced by slaves. Lest you dismiss the very idea of such a threat, please note that not only is the imprisonment of debtors making a comeback in the United States, but also forced labor or slavery is widespread in contemporary capitalism.[3] It is found not only in brothels, agriculture, construction, domestic work, and manufacturing, but also in government-chartered prisons, where thousands of once-waged workers are being forced into laboring for private-sector businesses for negligible pay.[4] The International Labor Organization estimates

3   On US debtor prisons, see Jessica Silver-Greenberg, "Debtor Arrests Criticized," *Wall Street Journal*, November 22, 2011. See also the efforts of the American Civil Liberties Union since 2009 to fight imprisonment for debt.

4   See George Caffentzis, *From Capitalist Crisis to Proletarian Slavery: An Introduction to Class Struggle in the US, 1973–1998* (Jamaica Plain, Mass.: Midnight Notes, 1999); Mike Elk and Bob Sloan, "The Hidden History of ALEC and Prison

that globally over twenty million people suffer coercion, of which almost eighteen million are exploited in the private economy. The Walk Free Foundation's estimate is substantially higher. It counts some 45.8 million individuals living in slavery—of which some 58 percent are in India, China, Pakistan, Uzbekistan, and Russia.[5]

In all these cases, there has been resistance and struggle. In the case of home foreclosures, there have been both physical community resistance to evictions and the formation of tent cities where such resistance failed. In the case of farm foreclosures, small farmers and peasants have been fighting back for over a century throughout the world. Individual families have fought to retain their farms and have also organized collectively to recoup lost land through legal means, or, when that path has been frustrated, through militant seizure and reoccupation. Throughout the world, decolonization included struggles to retake lands stolen by colonial powers—lands that were rarely restored to their original owners by the new independent governments. In North America, Native Americans in the United States and First Peoples in Canada have long fought for the restoration of at least some of their lands, stolen by European invaders. In the 1960s, Chicanos waged a fierce struggle in New Mexico to recuperate stolen lands.[6] More recently, as part of the 1994 indigenous Zapatista rebellion in Chiapas, Mexico, dispossessed peasants took back land they had previously lost.[7] Opposition to forced prison labor has been an

Labor," *Nation*, August 1, 2011. For a caution as to the still-limited extent of prison slavery, see James Kilgore, "The Myth of Prison Slave Labor Camps in the U.S.," *Counterpunch*, August 9–11, 2013.

5 See *ILO Global Estimate of Forced Labor: Results and Methodology* (Geneva, Switzerland: International Labour Office, 2012); *The Global Slavery Index, 2016* (Dalkeith, Australia: Walk-Free Foundation, 2016). Among the many struggles dedicated to fighting this scourge, see http://www.anti-slavery.org.

6 See Reies Lopez Tijerina, *They Called Me "King Tiger": My Struggle for the Land and Our Rights* (Houston: Arte Publico Press, 2000); Richard Gardner, *Grito! Tijerina and the New Mexico Land Grant War of 1967* (Indianapolis: Bobbs-Merrill, 1970).

7 See John Ross, *Rebellion from the Roots: Indian Uprising in Chiapas* (Monroe, Maine: Common Courage Press, 1995); Aaron Bobrow-Strain, *Intimate Enemies: Landowners, Power and Violence in Chiapas* (Durham: Duke University Press, 2007).

integral part of the more general struggle against outrageous prison practices in the United States.[8] In the case of imprisonment for debt, there is an active movement to fight the re-emergence of this practice—denounced by Dickens in *Little Dorrit* and later overthrown by judicial reformers.[9] Another struggle against capitalist creditors has finally coalesced in opposition to the burden of debt incurred by students forced to finance their education by borrowing. With that burden often so high as to cripple graduates' ability to live decently and save for the future, a growing movement is demanding the radical writing-off of all student debt.[10] At the most general level, the return of financial crisis has prompted collective efforts to force financial institutions to bear the costs of their risky and even fraudulent lending, instead of letting them seize debtor assets and asking taxpayers to bail them out.

Although Marx does not discuss it until the third volume of *Capital*, similar credit is used by capitalists to finance industrial investment, $M—C$ **(LP, MP) . . . P**, or commercial operations **C'—M'**. In both cases, credit has played a vital role in overcoming periodic difficulties associated with business shortages of money. His emphasis was, therefore, on identifying the functionality of finance in facilitating accumulation (i.e., the expanded reproduction of the antagonistic class relations of capitalism). With respect to investment, capitalists can borrow to start up a new business or to supplement the use of in-house profits to finance an expansion. Sometimes employers need to borrow money to mediate their relationship with workers (e.g., to pay wages). Sometimes they need money to deal with each other (e.g., to buy new supplies of raw materials or to cover short-term debt obligations). With respect

---

8   See, among others, ACLU National Prison Project, https://www.aclu.org/aclu-national-prison-project.

9   Outrage over the incarceration of individuals unable to pay fines on trumped-up charges has been one factor among many motivating mass protests against local racist actions of both police and local judiciary in Ferguson, Missouri, in the wake of the killing of Michael Brown.

10   See *Reclamations*, no. 4 (August/September 2011), special issue on debt, especially the article by George Caffentzis, "The Student Loan Debt Abolition Movement in the United States"; Strike Debt movement (strikedebt.org) and its *Debt Resisters' Operations Manual*.

to commerce, money can be borrowed, as it has long been, to finance trade, whether by producers or commercial intermediaries. Most of this borrowing in Marx's time was through banks and securities markets. Such "financial intermediaries," in the language of economics, facilitate the collection and transfer of money from those who have no current need for it—and who have deposited it in banks or bought interest-bearing paper assets like stocks or bonds—to those who do need it and are willing and able to pay the costs of borrowing it.

Successful investment in both production and trade results in sales revenue equal to the original invested value plus a surplus value or profit. For Marx, interest paid to banks and interest or dividends paid to bond or stock purchasers—all usually lumped into the category of interest—were portions of the surplus value realized by the borrowing capitalist.

His analysis of the use of credit in investment and trade, by identifying the specific relationships that must be realized for everything to proceed smoothly, also reveals the many possibilities of rupture that can bring on crisis in the reproduction of the class relationship. Failure in any phase of the circuit of capital would undermine the ability of the debtor to repay and the ability of the creditor to recoup the money lent at interest.

Obviously, investment cannot even begin if a would-be capitalist, or group of capitalists, does not have and cannot borrow the money needed for investment.[11] But even if the required money is

---

11 Innovating workers, who would like to directly manage the sharing of their creations with the world but do not have the money, must become entrepreneurs. They must turn to sources of financing—banks and other investors—borrow and become capitalists (i.e., impose enough labor on their workers to earn sufficient profit to be able to repay their debts). Marx's analysis in volume 3 of *Capital* of the situation of many farmers foreshadowed that of many of today's entrepreneurs. Farmers often find themselves acting simultaneously as workers and capitalists—imposing enough work on themselves and on farmhands to be able to pay themselves and their hired hands wages, plus rent to landlords and principle and interest to any creditors. In the case of peasants in the Global South, the situation is often even more complex, with individuals hiring in during their own harvests but hiring out during those of others—or even looking for off-farm waged employment when necessary. Although for some purposes (e.g., taxes) small farmers in the United

available—on terms and at an interest rate that can foreseeably be met, given current estimates of future profitability—workers, tools, raw materials, and such must first be obtained and then successfully combined in a production process. Every one of these elements of production can break down. Tools can break, literally; raw materials can prove to be of such inferior quality as to be unusable. But most importantly, workers, even once hired and set to work, can bring the production process to a halt through sabotage, strike, or rebellion and by so doing subvert investment and rupture that part of the planned circuit of capital. Such rupture would mean a reduction or termination in the production of **C'** and therefore the impossibility of realizing **M'**. The inability to achieve **M'** > **M** means both the failure to turn money into capital and a difficulty or complete impossibility of repaying the initially borrowed money and whatever interest was owed. Thus the significance of our struggles within production: our potential ability to rupture capitalist plans and throw them into crisis.

Where those plans depend on borrowed funds, such actions on our part can rupture not only production but financial arrangements as well. Beyond such initial effects, the failure to repay reduces the value of the loan-assets of banks or the value of stock held by shareholders, thereby causing a rupture in the plans of those actors in this story of capitalist finance. Because of such interconnections among debtors and creditors, a rupture at one point can ripple through a chain of connections, causing a cascade of ruptures through a whole series of relationships. Just as credit helps capitalists interweave their mutual connections, so too can a failure at one point circulate, causing further failures, unraveling the fabric of relationships and bringing on wider crisis.

Even if all goes well, and capitalists are able to turn **M** into **C'**, there remains the need to market **C'** and successfully realize **M'**. The accomplishment of this denouement of the circuit of money capital often requires financing through credit, just as much

---

States generally claim the status as businesses, sometimes they are quite clear about their dual situation. In one case, during a miners' strike to build solidarity, farmers arrived with food to support the miners with an argument that when their "profits" were calculated in terms of income per hour of labor, their "wages" were far lower than those of the miners.

as production. Either the producing capitalist firm must borrow money to finance shipping, advertising, and marketing, or a commercial intermediary must do so, in order to finance the purchasing of output to be sold later at a (hopefully) sufficiently higher price to realize an average rate of profit. In such cases, the risk of financial crisis lies in the possible failure of such shipping or in the failure to find or create markets where goods can be sold at profitable prices. Both phases are susceptible to rupture by workers' struggles.

In the case of the *Merchant of Venice*, the ability of the merchant Antonio to repay is dependent upon the completion of a voyage at sea and the sale of his cargo. The play's drama begins when the ship carrying his cargo wrecks on the treacherous Goodwin Sands in the English Channel and sinks. The sinking causes the loss of **C'**, thus rupturing **C'—M'** and causing the loss of **M'**. As a result, Antonio realizes no value, no surplus value, no profit, and no ability to repay his loan.[12] The same loss could have occurred due to a working-class mutiny on the part of the ship's sailors. It could also have been occasioned by piracy—sometimes on the part of one-time, working-class sailors who had previously mutinied, seized their ship, and proceeded to use it to live independently of their former masters. To the degree that pirates subsequently sold the ship's cargo, it would be they, rather than Antonio (and Shylock) who would realize the value of the cargo (**C'—M'**).[13] In the mid-nineteenth century, when Marx was writing, all of these phenomena were common obstacles for merchants from countries, such as Britain and the Netherlands, with far-flung trading empires. Fear of mutiny was a constant motivation for the imposition

---

12   In Marx's analysis, independent merchants, such as Antonio, would have bought the goods from producers at a price that allowed the producers to realize immediately part of the surplus value embodied in them. The ability of those merchants to subsequently recoup their investment and realize profits themselves would depend upon their ability to find markets in which they could sell the goods at their full value.

13   It is a peculiarity of the drama in Shakespeare's play that Shylock, although a moneylender who normally charges interest on money lent, does not charge Antonio interest and thus would not, had the ship not sunk, have realized any profit when Antonio repaid his loan.

of strict discipline and harsh punishment on ships.[14] Fear of piracy prompted merchants to form convoys at sea—protected by national naval forces—as they sought to sell their goods abroad and build empires.[15] Today piracy is back in the news with the seizure of ships off the Somali coast in the Gulf of Aden—where, once more, government gunships have been made available, at taxpayer expense, to guard commercial vessels.[16]

Generally less dramatic, but no less important, are other difficulties capitalists—industrial or commercial—face in realizing the sale of their goods and services in foreign markets. In Marx's time, it was not unusual, given long delays in communication, for ships to sail to foreign ports, be unable to sell any or all of their cargo, and be forced to sail on to other shores in search of markets. The formal colonization of foreign places, as is well known, was partly the result of efforts to find or create markets for goods that could

---

14 A history of mutinies, such as that on the HMS *Bounty* in 1789 motivated the strict discipline and harsh punishment on both government and commercial ships. The severity of discipline and punishment was, in turn, the cause of mutinies. Herman Melville's novella *Billy Budd* (1888) and Peter Ustinov's movie (1962) based on it dramatically illustrate, and effectively critique, such harsh punishment.

15 Although pirates have long been viewed simply as criminals on the high seas, a revisionist history has emerged in recent years examining the relationship between the struggles of working-class sailors and piracy. See Marcus Rediker, *Between the Devil and the Deep Blue Sea: Merchant Seamen, Pirates and the Anglo-American Maritime World, 1700-1750* (New York: Cambridge University Press, 1987); Peter Linebaugh and Marcus Rediker, *The Many-Headed Hydra: Sailors, Slaves, Commoners and the Hidden History of the Revolutionary Atlantic* (Boston: Beacon Press, 2001); Marcus Rediker, *Villains of All Nations: Atlantic Pirates in the Golden Age* (Boston: Beacon Press, 2004); Marcus Rediker, *Outlaws of the Atlantic: Sailors, Pirates and Motley Crews in the Age of Sail* (Boston: Beacon Press, 2015).

16 This modern piracy and military intervention has provided story lines for several films in recent years. *The Highjacking* (2012), by Tobias Lindholm, *Stolen Seas* (2012), by Thymaya Payne, and *Captain Philips* (2013), by Paul Greengrass, all portray the conflicts between pirates and commercial capitalists. Two others try to show the Somali side of the story: *The Pirates of Somalia: The Untold Story* (2011), by Neil Bell, and *Fishing without Nets* (2014), by Cutter Hodierne. Both provide a deeper examination of the situation of the poor Somali fisherfolk whose circumstances led to their turn to piracy.

not be sold at home. Supplying new kinds of goods (e.g., British opium to China), might create new markets (and would require two wars to open them), but supplying common goods—such as textiles—often prompted the destruction of local production in order to create markets for imperial goods (e.g., the East India Company undermining of Indian cotton textile producers).[17]

Beside the simple need for markets to realize $C'-M'$, such exports were also essential to keeping English textile mill workers employed. Some unemployment has always been necessary in capitalism—to pit unwaged workers against waged ones and thereby limit wage increases and maintain order among the employed population. However, too much unemployment has often led to uprisings and rebellion. Marxists, as well as some economists, have tended to focus on the inability of the workers to buy back the goods they produce (i.e., under-consumption or inadequate consumption demand), as one cause of colonization and empire, but too often ignore its essential role in limiting workers' struggles at home.[18] The greater those struggles, the more urgent the need for foreign markets.

Although financial institutions are often useful to capitalists, there are also inherent conflicts. In the first place, repaying borrowed money requires borrowing firms to pay interest. So there is a natural tussle between creditors—who charge interest as high as they can—and debtors—who want to pay as little as possible. Second, when borrowing firms are weak and financial institutions are strong, the latter are not only able to extract higher rates of interest, but they may also seek to exercise control over firms that are

---

17 Already in the *Communist Manifesto* (1848) Marx and Engels argued: "The cheap prices of its commodities are the heavy artillery with which it batters down all Chinese walls, with which it forces the barbarians' intensely obstinate hatred of foreigners to capitulate."

18 One economist who based his theories of both economic crisis and imperialism on this inability of workers to buy back the goods they produced was John A. Hobson (1858–1940). See his collaboration with A. F. Mummery, *The Physiology of Industry* (1889) and his own *Imperialism: A Study* (1902), a book drawn on by Lenin in his work on the subject, *Imperialism: The Highest Stage of Capitalism* (1917). Hobson's work was influential enough for Keynes to take the trouble to rebut it in his *General Theory of Employment, Interest and Money* (1936).

dependent upon them. The economist Rudolph Hilferding (1877–1941) observed just this kind of relationship in Germany early in the twentieth century. The title of his major work, *Finance Capital* (1910), evoked this ascendance of concentrated financial over industrial capital. Decades later, in the post–World War II period, Paul Baran and Paul Sweezy argued that while Hilferding was correct about the tendency of capital toward concentration and monopoly, the rapid growth and spread of multinational industrial corporations, with vast profits, enabled them to internalize most of their financing, marginalizing the power of purely financial institutions.

Independently of the issue of corporate control, all credit that involves the creation of paper claims or assets—bills of credit, stocks, bonds, mortgages, et cetera—leads to the emergence of secondary markets, where those assets can be traded quite independently of their origins. Unregulated, such markets quickly become domains of speculation in which the value of paper claims can rise far above, or fall far below, the actual value of the real assets they represent. And rise and fall they have, in recurrent waves of speculative booms and busts that contributed to the instability and recurrent crises of accumulation throughout the nineteenth and well into the twentieth century. Throughout that period there were also recurrent efforts by the state, especially by central banks (e.g., the Bank of England), to counteract such phenomena but with little success. Indeed, Marx took repeated pleasure in commenting on their failures.

At this point, just as we recognize how access to credit and the relationships between debtor and creditor are *formally similar* for both capitalists and workers, so too should we pay attention to the *differences* in the roles played by such financial operations for the two classes. For capitalists the availability of credit to industrial investors permits access to the means of production and insures the ability to hire, impose work on, and extract surplus labor from workers ($\mathbf{M-C}$ $\mathbf{[MP, LP]} \ldots \mathbf{P} \ldots \mathbf{C'}$). In the case of commercial operations, borrowing buys the resources, labor, time, and opportunity to realize surplus labor as surplus value and profit through the sale ($\mathbf{C'-M'}$) of commodities produced. In both cases, Marx is adamant that what the capitalist borrower is obtaining is the use-value of the borrowed money as capital; it becomes capital only when actually invested in such a manner as to realize a profit (surplus value). Assuming the investment of the borrowed money is successful, interest is paid out of the surplus value realized by the investment.

In the case of workers, on the other hand, access to credit—whether borrowing from pawnshops in Marx's time or the extensive use of consumer credit today—facilitates the immediate acquisition of the means of life. What workers are borrowing in the case of consumer credit is not money as potential capital but money for its use-value as means of purchase or as means of payment. This is true whether credit provides access to mortgages that enable the purchase of houses or to bank credit and plastic cards that enable the purchase of both consumer durables and items of immediate consumption. In this case, the interest that must be rendered to creditors is not paid out of surplus value but out of incomes—wages or salaries. Given that such borrowing eventually provides our creditors with a share of our income, the obvious question is whether this borrowing and the payment of interest is another vehicle of exploitation, beyond that utilized by our immediate employer. Does capital—first in the form of our employers and then in the form of our creditors—exploit us twice?

For the most part, Marxists have tended to answer "Yes!" and emphasize the negative side of consumer credit. This remains the bias of even some of the most interesting and recent Marxist treatments of the implications of the spread of financial services. For example, Midnight Notes' *Promissory Notes: From Crisis to Commons* (2009), Christian Marazzi's *The Violence of Financial Capitalism* (2010), and Maurizio Lazzarato's *The Making of the Indebted Man* (2012) emphasize the capitalist use of debt as a form of domination—while perpetuating the lamentably all too common Marxist habit of largely ignoring what borrowing makes possible for workers—and thus why they often struggle to obtain credit, even if later they may struggle to escape the burden of debt.[19] Even

---

19 Midnight Notes Collective and Friends, *Promissory Notes: From Crisis to Commons* (Jamaica Plain, Mass.: Midnight Notes, 2009); originally published and circulated as a pamphlet; it is now available online. Despite its emphasis on the capitalist use of credit against the working class, *Promissory Notes* does concede that "it is an important achievement for workers to be able to 'use someone else's money' in order to have a home . . . to have the desire (real or fancied) evoked by a commodity satisfied today, to have access to education . . . and to have an automobile." Christian Marazzi,

when the desire for access to credit is recognized, however, it is more often than not treated as a mere trap laid by capital to catch those made desperate by low or falling wages. This one-sidedness is typical of the tendency of many Marxists to focus more on capitalist mechanisms of domination than on our struggles—for example, critical theorists who have carefully analyzed mechanisms of cultural domination but who failed to study or theorize how workers' struggles rupture or move beyond capitalism. As discussed below, what we get, when we obtain access to credit, is the ability to purchase a service whose use-value to us is the access it gives to all kinds of other use-values and to the possibilities opened by that access.[20] Understanding the dynamics of consumer credit, therefore, requires paying attention to how such access may strengthen our ability to struggle as well as undermine it.

Whether credit is made available to us through our employers, such as credit in a company store, or from an external financial institution, such as a bank or credit union, repayment over time—deducted from wages or salaries—generally includes interest. This interest we pay out of our income just as we pay for other consumption goods. We borrow today, rather than saving up to pay cash on the barrelhead tomorrow, in order to obtain what we need immediately. Whether interest amounts to one form of surplus value or constitutes a payment for a service will be taken up in the next section on the source of financial profit.

In the meantime, looking back at the history of this aspect of class struggle, it is easy to understand why we have sought access to credit despite its costs and risks. No access to credit, especially for those of us with income too low to have made savings possible, means that any shortage of ready cash means going without. Such has been the fate of millions who, for one reason or another, have been unable to buy food and so starved, have been unable to buy adequate clothing or shelter and taken sick, have been unable to buy medicine and died. Credit has made it possible to meet immediate

The Violence of Financial Capitalism (Los Angeles: Semiotext(e), 2010); Maurizio Lazzarato, *The Making of the Indebted Man* (Los Angeles: Semiotext(e), 2012).

20   When Marxists neglect the value of this service, they leave struggles around credit open to reformist demands that may fail to insist on changes that will constrain capitalists in ways that strengthen future efforts.

needs in the absence of money income (e.g., while waiting for wages to be paid or a crop to be harvested or during illness or strikes).

For many years in mining and mill towns, the only credit available to workers was in stores owned by their employers. Credit available in such stores was often manipulated to keep workers in perpetual debt, or what economists and historians call "debt peonage." This has been more extensively studied in the case of sharecroppers in the US, but the phenomenon has been recorded in places such as mining camps where exclusive control over the only credit available made such practices possible. In one illustrative scene in the film *Coal Miner's Daughter* (1980), set in the 1930s, Loretta Lynn's father, having just received his wages, says to his little girl, as they head for the company store, "Let's go give the company back its money." The inability to repay credit—for whatever reason—also has led to the exploitation of workers' wives and children in non-monetary ways. The latter included substituting a family's child for a sick or injured miner or forcing a wife to cover credit-due by submitting to rape.[21]

Over time, workers have sought to escape such isolation and the monopoly power it confers on local capitalists. Certainly, flight to cities has been at least partially motivated by the desire for better paying jobs, but also moving from a mining camp to a city gives access to a wider variety of jobs, stores, and sources of credit.[22] Although, for decades, workers' access to credit was limited to pawnshops and loan sharks, success in winning higher income also opened doors to more diverse, competitive, and cheaper credit. Rising working-class income in the Keynesian period led to company-specific and then general credit cards. Access to credit from banks and savings and loan institutions has made it possible for many middle-income, as well as upper-income workers, to buy homes. In the same period, ostensibly non-financial companies developed the same kind of consumer credit operations carried on by banks and credit unions. Perhaps the best known example is automobile producers—such as

---

21 Evidence of these practices, including miner testimony, has been collected in Wess Harris, ed., *Truth be Told: Perspectives on The Great West Virginia Mine War, 1890 to Present* (Gay, W. Va.: Appalachian Community Services, 2015).

22 Even in big cities, however, the high costs of isolation have persisted for those unable to easily leave their neighborhoods to access cheaper goods and credit in other areas.

General Motors—who will loan you the money to buy their cars and trucks—loans that you then repay over time, with interest. Under such circumstances, access to consumer credit, allowing us to obtain our own homes and consumer durables outside the control of our employers has clearly improved our bargaining power. Indeed, such credit has often been vital during strikes when it has complemented whatever strike funds workers have been able to accumulate collectively to replace wages lost during their time off the job.

Over time, there has been an enormous diversification in the forms and vehicles of credit for both capitalists and workers. Probably the most important innovation for capitalists was the issuance of stocks and bonds—pieces of paper giving the purchasers a share of ownership in a business and/or claims on future income (dividends) in exchange for money the issuers can turn into capital. The sale of such financial assets gave capitalists—both industrial and financial—an important new source of money to finance their operations, investing it in the startup or expansion of an enterprise. Such assets could be purchased by banks, just as they could be by individuals with enough money or by other non-financial businesses, but it made industrial capitalists less dependent on borrowing from banks. Among the best known of such early stock-issuing companies were the English East India Company, chartered in 1600, and the Dutch East India Company, which first issued shares in 1602 and quickly created the Amsterdam Stock Exchange to facilitate the selling and trading of its stocks and bonds. Both capitalist entities operated under charter from and with the protection of their respective governments and served to dramatically expand and manage the British and Dutch Empires in South, East, and Southeast Asia.

The increasingly widespread distribution of stock—of "shares" of ownership—led to Marx perceiving a differentiation of managers (whom he called "functionaries" of capital) from mere owners and eventually to some economists embracing the concept of "managerial capitalism."[23] Both perspectives recognized a shift from the centrali-

---

23   See, for example, Adolf Berle and Gardiner Means, *The Modern Corporation and Private Property* (New York: Macmillan, 1932); Robin Marris, *The Economic Theory of 'Managerial' Capitalism* (London: Macmillan, 1964); Alfred D. Chandler, *The Visible Hand: The Managerial Revolution in American Business* (Cambridge, Mass.: Belknap Press, 1993).

ty of ownership to that of control. Diversified sales of stock (shares) to a wide variety of purchasers not only permitted such "joint-stock" companies, as they were known in Marx's day, to amass sizable sums for investment but also made it easy for managers to retain control despite the formal sharing of ownership. True then, it is even truer today—when ownership is even more broadly distributed.

Early on, Marx studied how the absence of any regulation of the information made available to the purchasers of shares opened the door to fraud on the part of the managers who could raise money by withholding information about their actual business situation and risks. Such asymmetrical information—whether due to the issuers simply withholding it or releasing cooked-up, fraudulent information—encouraged speculation. While the lack of accurate information on the part of purchasers sometimes led to overoptimistic speculative spurts in stock purchases, driving up their prices, the availability of more accurate inside information could also allow managers responsible for issuing stock to buy their own shares, driving up the price, then to sell them off before any fall in their value. Such speculative booms and the resulting inevitable collapses in stock prices led to numerous business failures, financial crises, and the demand for more regulation.[24] The most extensive of Marx's studies of such activity were those of the Crédit Mobilier—an early French investment bank.[25] Such conflicts continue to this day, as non-manager shareholders have repeatedly demanded—in self-defense—more detailed information about corporate operations and financial health. Experience with corporations' dishonesty in their reporting has also led to demands for closer regulation (e.g., in the United States by the Security and Exchange Commission).

---

24 Some classics on these recurrent financial crises include Walter Bagehot, *Lombard Street: A Description of the Money Market* (New York: Charles Scribner's Sons, 1873); Charles Kindleberger, *Manias, Panics, and Crashes: A History of Financial Crises* (London: Macmillan, 1978), a work that synthesized existing economic analysis of financial crises.

25 See Marx's many articles on the Crédit Mobilier and its scandals, published in the *New York Daily Tribune* in 1856, available in volume 15 of Karl Marx and Frederick Engels, *Collected Works*. Also João Antonio de Paula, et al., *Marx in 1869: Notebook B113, the Economist and the Money Market Review* (Belo Horizonte, Brazil: UFMG/CEDEPLAR, 2011).

While this sketch of the emergence, uses, and risks of stock and bond issuances as a form of corporate finance focuses, as is usually the case, only on intra-capitalist relations, there are three ways in which this form of finance is closely connected to the working class and its struggles. First, and most obviously, the value of securities depends, at least in part, on the profitability of the issuing corporations. That profitability, in both the short and longer term, depends upon the degree of managerial control over the labor force. All forms of workers' struggles that undermine control, raising costs or lowering productivity or both, also undermine corporate profits, the tradable value of their securities, and their possibilities of raising more money by new issuances.

Second, because the market price of such tradable securities depends, at least in part, on the risk perceptions of both stock and bond holders and potential buyers, any substantial upswing in workers' struggles—either against an individual company or more generally—can augment the perception of risk and result in a drop in the market value of the security. This kind of sensitivity is akin to that discussed in part 1 about how such an upswing can affect foreign exchange markets (e.g., the Zapatista uprising's contribution to the crisis of Mexican peso in 1994). Also troublesome for managerial control and shareholder perceptions of risk has been the collusion of small shareholders to challenge existing methods or goals through (usually) non-binding resolutions presented at annual meetings. Although such resolutions are commonly defeated, even when backed by well-known nonprofits and labor union pension funds, they have provided one more form of collective working-class struggle—contributing to the public critique of more pernicious corporate activities.

Third, today's extremely broad distribution of corporate stocks in the hands of a multitude of shareholders has partly been a by-product of workers' successful struggles to raise wages and salaries sufficiently beyond subsistence to permit savings that can be held in interest-bearing or dividend-yielding assets. Very short-term savings that used to be held as cash are now commonly held in *checking accounts* (often issuing debit or credit cards). When savings exceed expected expenditures, they are also held in bank or credit union *savings accounts*. Both such accounts, however, earn very little interest. Therefore, where their income has been high enough, workers have joined those much higher up the income hierarchy in buying interest-bearing assets such as certificates of deposit or bonds and stocks whose value they hope will rise, or which will pay dividends to maintain or augment the real value of their existing income. Capitalists have been happy to retrieve, for their own purposes, those portions of wages and salaries expended in this manner. They are well aware that owning a few shares of stock or a handful of bonds gives individual workers no control and little leverage over their business operations. Nevertheless, access to such assets, as with higher wages and access to credit, strengthens workers' abilities to both live and struggle.

After setting aside the issue of credit for most of volume 1 of *Capital*, Marx finally returns to money and credit, toward the end, in part 8, chapter 31. There, his focus is on one aspect of "public finance," namely the provision of credit to government by banks.[26] Formally, loans made to governments are similar to those made to individuals and businesses; money is loaned and paid back later with interest. This has been one way financial institutions have long enriched themselves at taxpayer expense. Their loans finance government borrowing to cover fiscal deficits (i.e., expenditures in excess of immediately available tax revenue), and because the debt is sovereign debt, backed by the power of the government to tax, the banks are assured of repayment and profit. Such bank lending to governments preceded the rise of industrial capitalism and was a source of government funds for everything from building palaces to armies and war-making.[27] The resulting debt (plus interest) is repaid with money drawn from taxpayers (or from further "rollover" loans from creditors).

Marx's interest in part 8, however, was not just in banker enrichment or the financing of government per se but in the way

---

26 As a subfield of economics, public finance includes all of the ways governments raise money and spend it. Borrowing to cover fiscal deficits complements other money-raising methods such as taxation of all kinds and drawing on the revenues of state enterprises—especially important for countries such as those in OPEC who rely on income from state-owned oil production and exports.

27 Probably the most recent spectacular such use of government borrowing was by the George W. Bush administration that borrowed huge sums to finance the invasion of Iraq—and the subsequent prolonged effort to squash resistance—even as it cut taxes to those best able to pay.

in which this was (and continues to be) one mechanism through which huge amounts of money are amassed that can then be made available as loans to capitalists. In other words, public finance is one vehicle for transferring income from taxpayers to those who would borrow to put people to work. True in the 1860s, true today.

What is missing from Marx's exposition of these relationships in chapter 31, which he discusses elsewhere, are three essential elements in this mediation. First is the degree to which taxes are deductions from working-class income (e.g., customs taxes, whose costs are passed on to working-class consumers through increased prices, as opposed to deductions from, say, business profits). Second is the degree to which government expenditures serve to manage the antagonistic class relationships of capitalism. Such expenses include domestic infrastructure to subsidize business (including roads, canals, railroads, hydroelectric projects), domestic judiciaries, police forces and prisons to control the working class at home, and military forces to build an empire (i.e., to colonize and impose work on the peoples of foreign lands and to protect the resulting commerce on the high seas).[28] Third is the degree to which the holders of public debt (e.g., banks) actually make their amassed sums available for capitalist investment. One of the reasons for Marx's intense interest in the early behavior of the Crédit Mobilier, established in 1852, was its role as one of the first French joint-stock investment banks. To the degree that it made the money invested with it—mainly from the well-to-do bourgeoisie—available for investments, such as railroads, mines, and steamship lines, it acted as a classical financial intermediary, concentrating small sums of money and making large ones available for investment. Marx was

---

28 The Marxist analysis of imperialism has long focused on the actions of governments in support of capitalist interests based in this or that nation-state. It has only been recently that the development of multinational corporations, whose interests often conflict with those of the nations within which they are legally constituted and the creation of supranational institutions (such as the IMF) that oversee and seek to enforce generally agreed upon rules of investment and trade, that some Marxists have developed a critique of the traditional analyses of imperialism and sought to replace them with one of empire, in which the interests of capital and those of nation-states are no longer equated. The prime example of such a critique is that of Michael Hardt and Antonio Negri's *Empire* (2000).

also interested in how its actual operations often proved to be a vehicle of speculation and swindling. It was to limit the possibilities of such bank speculation that federal regulations were designed and implemented during the Great Depression of the 1930s to separate investment from commercial banking (e.g., the Glass-Steagall Act) and to protect the modest savings of lower- and middle-income workers (e.g., the Federal Deposit Insurance Corporation).

The Source of Financial Profit—Revising Marx

In all of these connections between debtors and creditors—be they between individuals, between individuals and financial institutions, between non-financial corporations and financial corporations, among financial institutions, or between them and governments—the realization of profit by creditors comes from the payment of interest by borrowers. In economics, interest is just the price of borrowing, and the primary concern is its quantitative determination. Thus, in classical political economy interest was mostly thought to be determined by the supply and demand for loanable funds and in Keynesian macroeconomics by the supply and demand for money.[29] Microeconomics often conflates interest with profits and treats it as the marginal product of capital (with wages or salaries attributed to the marginal product of labor). In Marx's analysis, while supply and demand determine interest rates in the short term, interest tends to equal average profit due to the entry and exit of capitals. As in other sectors, when financial capitalists are unable to earn a rate of profit equal to that of industrial or commercial capital, they shift their investments from their less lucrative specialization in managing money to other domains of investment. When, on the other hand, financial deregulation increases the profitability of finance, investment money pours in from other sectors—as has happened in recent decades.

However determined quantitatively, when viewed in its qualitative dimension we must recognize that *interest is the payment for a service*: the temporary use of someone else's money. Just as

---

29 There have been other explanations and justifications for interest, such as economist Nassau William Senior's argument that interest was payment for the risk taken by creditors—an argument that Marx mocked, noting that the real risk takers in capitalism were workers.

you might pay to rent a trailer for hauling or an apartment for living or lease an automobile for transportation—in order to enjoy the use-values of your temporary control of those items—so too do debtors pay to enjoy the use-value of the money they borrow. This is true whether the borrower is a capitalist, a worker, or a government agency. For the capitalist the use-value of borrowed money is its potential as capital; for the individual its use-value is means of purchase or payment; for government its use-value may be of either sort—borrowed money may be spent funding state programs or it may be invested in state enterprises that function just like other capitalist firms.[30]

But in all these cases, the mere existence of automobiles, trailers, apartments, or money in someone's hands do not make them available as service commodities. All these things, including money, must be organized and managed. Car dealerships and rental agencies organize the availability, upkeep, and paperwork of leasing. U-Haul and such businesses organize the availability, upkeep, and paperwork of renting. Apartment rental agencies organize the availability, upkeep, and paperwork of apartments. In the case of money, financial institutions have to organize both the obtaining of money (e.g., deposits, investments, and borrowing) and the preparation of various forms of credit (e.g., mortgages, credit and debit cards, and cash loans). All of these activities involve work—generally accomplished by employees—that gives the services value, especially the value to capital of the production of these services in providing opportunities to put people to work producing service commodities for profitable sale. It is work that is exploited and generates surplus value for the businesses providing these services.

---

30 Given the vast array of government programs, there can be no unique characterization. Money spent on education, research, or welfare can be seen as an investment in human capital. But that spent on research also often subsidizes private enterprise. That spent on police, prisons, and military personnel, equipment, and bases can all be seen as both expenditures on the management of human capital (i.e., control of the working class) or as a vast wasteful subsidy to the police-military-industrial complex. And so on. Although state enterprises are few in number in many countries (e.g., the United States, France, and Germany), in others (e.g., Mexico, Brazil, and Argentina,) they have been numerous—and their privatization a major objective of neoliberal policies.

Unfortunately, in Marx's work, there is little recognition or discussion of interest as payment for a service. While fully grasping the use-value of credit to capital (i.e., its potential to become "the means to the appropriation of the labor of others" via investment), he does not associate that use-value with being a produced service commodity for which interest is a payment and therefore one cost of production.[31] As a result, in his treatment, interest paid by industrial capital is a deduction from the surplus value realized through its investment. Reasoning analogically—given that he had little occasion to analyze such situations—the interest paid by individual borrowers must be paid out of wages and salaries and amounts to a deduction from the value of their labor power. Thus the inclination of Marxists to answer "Yes!" to the question of whether financial capital exploits workers through consumer credit. For both business and workers, the payment of interest involves both a transfer of money and a *redistribution* of value—from capitalist to capitalist and from workers to capitalists. Recognizing how interest can be the price of a service commodity necessitates a revision in Marx's analysis.

Much of the material from Marx's notes that Engels assembled to form volume 3 of *Capital* is concerned with analyzing the redistribution of surplus value—in the forms of commercial profit, interest, and rent.[32] Clearly, those engaged in commerce, finance, and the renting out of land require profits—or they would disengage from those activities and invest elsewhere. But they can only obtain those profits, according to Marx, via redistribution of surplus value from industry. This was because he believed value and surplus value (or profit) could only be obtained by putting people to work in industries producing commodities for sale—the primary business, in his day, of agricultural, mining, and manufacturing capitalists.[33] Marx reasoned that mere buying and selling (charac-

---

31 Marx, *Capital*, vol. 3, chapter 21 ("Interest-Bearing Capital").

32 See, in particular, ibid., part 5 ("The Division of Profit into Interest and Profit of Enterprise").

33 Agriculture here includes fishing—a domain of human interaction with nature that capitalists seek to subordinate to their control in order to earn profits from the work of those who harvest from water instead of from land. In his discussion of primitive accumulation, Marx excoriates the duchess of Sutherland for driving her

teristic of commerce) or the mere collecting of interest (characteristic of the financial sector) or the mere collecting of rents (the
"business" of landlords) could not generate either value or surplus
value. Therefore, commercial capitalists (merchants), financial
capitalists (bankers and such), and landlords could only get their
hands on surplus value by obtaining a share of that generated in
industry. The basis of this analysis lies in the argument that only
those workers in industry are "productive" who generate an excess
or surplus beyond the costs of their own reproduction.

This distinction between "productive" and "unproductive"
workers predated Marx; it was elaborated contra the mercantilists who had long argued that trade was the key to wealth production.[34] The Physiocrats, such as François Quesnay (1694–1774),
reasoned that only farmers who worked fertile land could produce
a true surplus—a surplus that others (merchants, landlords, and
manufacturers) might seek to share but could not produce. Adam
Smith argued that while Quesnay was right about the labor of
farmers, he was mistaken to think that workers producing manufacturing products were not productive. Smith shared the Physiocrats' critique of mercantilists, whom he rather harshly accused
of offering self-serving theories, but also condemned the landed
gentry for surrounding themselves with legions of servants who
could be productively employed elsewhere. Servants, he argued,

---

clansmen first from their fields and then from the seashore when she discovered
there were profits to be made from fishing. After the conquest of Ireland, those
who had long fished for eels were driven from Loch Neagh and a monopoly was
handed to the Toome Eel Fishery. Conflicts over fishing rights between indigenous
fishermen and capitalist corporations have continued ever since. They have been
joined by ecologically minded working-class consumers who contest the methods
used in corporate fishing operations (e.g., overfishing and the use of gill-nets that
harm whales, dolphins, and sea turtles while gathering vast quantities of unwanted
fish that are simply killed and discarded wastefully). A recent insightful analysis of
the ongoing resistance to capitalist takeover of fishing is Mariarosa Dalla Costa and
Monica Chilese, *Our Mother Ocean: Enclosure, Commons, and the Global Fishermen's Movement* (Brooklyn: Common Notions, 2014).

34 In all fairness, while focused on the acquisition of gold-as-wealth through trade,
some of the Physiocrats also saw the importance of domestic production and supported its development to provide trade goods. So they were not all gold fetishists.

provide only immediate services, whereas workers hired in agriculture, mining, or manufacturing to produce commodities, also produced, at least potentially, profits. So, although both those who hired servants and those who hired commodity-producing workers provided employment, only the latter generated a surplus for expanded investment to fuel growth in the overall economy. Marx adopted Smith's distinction, privileging industry over commerce and rent-producing land ownership, but he also used it to critique financial capital as another rapidly proliferating set of institutions dependent for profits on the surplus value produced by workers in industry. In other words, he argued that the money constituting commercial profit, rent, and interest only embodied the substance (abstract labor) and measure (socially necessary labor time) of value and surplus value because that money was originally realized through the sale of commodities produced by workers in industry.

In the case of financial capital, Marx highlighted what he saw as the unproductive character of work in financial institutions by simply excluding it from his symbolic representation of the circuit of financial investment. In the place of the circuit of industrial capital that I have discussed above, he offered simply:

$$\mathbf{M_F} - \mathbf{M_I} - \mathbf{M'_I} - \mathbf{M'_F}$$

In other words, financial capitalists begin with money ($\mathbf{M_F}$), loan it out, charging interest for the loan, to industrial capitalists who invest it ($\mathbf{M_I}$) and realize a surplus ($\mathbf{M'_I}$); the industrial capitalists then repay their creditors (principle plus interest), who wind up with more money ($\mathbf{M'_F}$) than they started with. The interest they receive (total repayment $\mathbf{M'_F}$ minus the amount loaned $\mathbf{M_F}$), or their portion of surplus value ($\mathbf{S_F}$) is only one part of the total surplus value ($\mathbf{S}$) generated in industry. The total surplus value, for Marx, is $\mathbf{S} = \mathbf{S_I} + \mathbf{S_C} + \mathbf{S_F} + \mathbf{S_R}$, where surplus value is shared among industrial capitalists, commercial capitalists, financial capitalists, and landlords (who receive rent).

One result of this analysis has been the propensity of Marxists analyzing finance—both past and present—to see nothing but a set of parasitic practices, an intra-class division and a source of conflict among capitalists that can be treated independently of struggles between workers and capitalists. In this view, the real class conflict is between commodity-producing workers and their would-be industrial masters. Both financial capitalists and those who work for them are parasites whose activities absorb resources and contribute little beyond facilitating the circulation of money and trade while creating myriad opportunities for unproductive speculation—itself but another, particularly unstable form of redistribution.

In Marx's writings, however, there are important caveats to his argument that only the labor of industrial workers counts as value and can therefore be considered productive in the sense of contributing to the creation of surplus value—caveats that have generally been ignored by those drawing on his work to analyze recent financial crises. Those caveats can be found in his recognition of how labor employed in producing *services as commodities* can count as value and generate surplus value and profits for capitalists. He defined services as including products either "separable" or "not separable from the act of producing."[35] In both cases, he argued, workers producing services were potentially productive, as long as they were working for a capitalist who sold their products for profit and in the process realized a surplus value from their labor. In the first category, he recognized such labor as that of writers, artists, or sculptors. Although he saw that a writer "who turns out work for his publisher in factory style is a productive worker," he clearly had a hard time imagining any large-scale harnessing of such labor: "these people [writers, artists] mainly work for merchant's capital, e.g., booksellers."[36] In the second category, he includes such labor as that of teachers, musicians, dancers, or other performers. "A schoolmaster who instructs others is not a productive worker. But a schoolmaster who works for wages in an institution along

---

35 Marx, *Capital*, vol. 1, 1048. This analysis appears in the unpublished "sixth chapter," included in the Penguin edition as an appendix, titled "Results of the Immediate Process of Production." The same material, translated somewhat differently, can be found in Karl Marx and Frederick Engels, *Collected Works*, vol. 34 (New York: International Publishers), 442–452. See note 237 in that volume, on page 496, for references to Marx's earlier treatments of the distinction between productive and unproductive labor in the notebooks that make up the Economic Manuscripts of 1861–1863.

36 Ibid.

with others, using his own labor to increase the money of the entrepreneur who owns the knowledge-mongering institution, is a productive worker."[37]

Such service labor, however, Marx also considered of marginal importance at the time because of the small size of the service sector. "On the whole, types of work that are consumed as services and not in products separable from the workers and hence not capable of existing as commodities independently of him, but which are yet capable of being directly exploited in capitalist terms, are of microscopic significance when compared with the mass of capitalist production. They may be entirely neglected."[38]

Virno rightly draws attention to such passages but misreads them.[39] He interprets Marx as dismissing work that does not produce "a finished work that lives on beyond the activity of the performance" as unproductive labor. But the example of the schoolmaster "who works for wages" and produces surplus value directly contradicts such a reading. The only dismissal here is of the quantitative relevance of historically undeveloped spheres of work, spheres that would later become whole industries.

Had Marx recognized the work of schoolmasters as productive not only of profits for their employers but also of the commodity labor power, he would have had to classify their work as service labor producing a quite separable commodity. The sale of that commodity would not realize a profit, but labor power is a separable commodity nevertheless, in a dual sense—an acquired attribute of students, and one those students could, in due time, sell to capitalists.

A clear exception to "microscopic significance" he did *not* neglect, an exception that was already a large-scale industry, was *transportation*. By the mid-nineteenth century, transportation was an absolutely essential element of commerce that Marx explicitly argued went beyond mere buying and selling to employ labor constitutive of value and surplus value. With respect to the

---

37 Ibid., 1044.

38 Ibid., 1044–45.

39 Paolo Virno, "Virtuosity and Revolution: The Political Theory of Exodus," in Paolo Virno and Michael Hardt, *Radical Thought in Italy: A Potential Politics* (Minneapolis: University of Minnesota Press, 1996), 190–92.

transportation of people, commodities, and information, Marx argued that "what the transport industry sells is the actual change of place itself. The useful effect produced is inseparably connected with the transport process. . . . People and commodities travel together with the means of transport, and this journeying, the spatial movement of the means of transport, is precisely the production process accomplished by the transportation industry."[40]

Therefore, Marx judged that the labor involved in transportation created use-value and, like labor in industrial production, could, if properly managed, contribute to surplus value and profits. In modern parlance, transportation provides a service, and the labor involved in transportation counts as labor in the service sector.

That labor, employed on the wooden, deep-sea sailing vessels of his era, was vast and operated what Marcus Rediker calls "the most sophisticated machine of their day," a verdict with which Herman Melville would undoubtedly agree.[41] Hundreds, sometimes more than a thousand, sailors were employed on each of these complex machines that formed ever larger fleets of commercial ships—protected by similar but more heavily armed military ones—that formed the sinew holding empires together.

In more recent decades, the service sector has been steadily displacing agricultural, mining, and manufacturing industry as the primary sector in which workers are employed with the goal of making profits. Not only have the small-scale and ignorable book publishing, commercial art, and education businesses of Marx's day expanded to become large-scale, profitable industries, but the service sector has expanded dramatically to include radio, television,

---

40 Marx, *Capital*, vol. 2, 135.

41 Rediker, *Outlaws of the Atlantic*, 1. Melville's *Moby Dick* (1851), of course, is undoubtedly the clearest rendering in literature of the labor employed on what was the most obvious sailing vessel-qua-factory of the time: the whaling ship that killed, processed, and transported the remains of the sea's greatest creatures. In contemporary nautical fiction, such as C. S. Forester's Horatio Hornblower novels (1937–67) or those of Patrick O'Brian (1970–2004), although the focus is generally on the captains (Hornblower and Jack Aubrey) rather than the seamen, both the commands given and the descriptions of their implementation give some idea of the complexity of those "sophisticated machines" and of the difficulties and dangers of working on them.

film, health care, education, telecommunications, legal services, entertainment, waste disposal—*and the financial industry.*[42]

The case of individuals who are not engaged in the business of finance, loaning money to other individuals, with or without interest, can be seen as an example of those unproductive personal services Adam Smith deplored. The loan redistributes value from the individual creditor to the debtor; the repayment of that loan merely redistributes value from the debtor back to individual creditor. But, to the degree that financial institutions provide services, their workers must be seen as generating value and, at least potentially, surplus value and profit, just like those in agriculture, mining, manufacturing, and transportation.

What are these services? Banks are generally thought to have originated in providing the service of storing and safeguarding money and items of high value, such as precious metals, jewelry, et cetera. This service is still provided in the form of safety deposit boxes located in what most believe to be impressively secured vaults. *Finance,* on the other hand, whether engaged in by individuals, banks, or other financial institutions, we have already seen to provide a different kind of service: either creditors loaning out money on hand or extending credit (allowing immediate purchase without money), in exchange for (usually legal) promises by the borrowers (debtors) to repay their debt with interest.

The loaning of money and the extension of credit is a service that allows borrowers to *immediately acquire commodities and their use-values* even though they do not have enough present income. Borrowers get their commodities in exchange for legal obligations to repay the money plus interest over time; the creditor loans money for a debt that constitutes an asset that will, in principle, provide a stream of income as repayment proceeds. Borrowing allows individuals to acquire the means of consumption, businesses to acquire labor power or means of production, and government to meet any excess of its money needs beyond what it raises through taxation. In all cases, commodities are obtained, their use-values

---

42   There are many different classification systems for defining and subdividing the service sector, sometimes called the tertiary sector, and they often differ from country to country or region to region (e.g., the United States system differs from that of the European community).

can be realized, and payment is deferred. The additional interest (and sometimes various fees) constitute the price of such borrowing. Not surprisingly, because creditors negotiate each loan, they are able to differentiate the demand for this service, charging some more and others less—according to the value of the debt and estimation of risk of non-repayment. Thus, governments are charged less to borrow because they have the power to tax (or create money) to cover sovereign debt. Stable, well-established businesses also get lower "prime" rates while startup enterprises and individuals are usually charged more. The denunciation of the charging of interest (and fees) as usury by churches that have seen it as a usurpation of God's power of creation,[43] and by Marxists who have seen it as mere redistribution of value, ignores the way creditors are providing debtors with a concrete service—the use of someone else's money to make otherwise impossible purchases and realize whatever use-values or benefits those purchases bestow.

Another long-standing and highly developed financial service is insurance against risk. A ship sinks, a factory explodes, a home burns down, a car crashes, a container (or container ship) is hijacked, or a home burglarized, and those who have paid for the service are reimbursed some percentage of the value lost. (Apparently, Antonio in Shakespeare's *Merchant of Venice* failed to purchase insurance for his cargo, or he would have had the wherewithal to repay Shylock.) This service is usually paid for through a one-time or regular transfers of income from the buyer to the seller. As with interest charged borrowers, the cost of insurance depends on estimations of risk. So, for example, in modern times, with the advent of piracy off the coast of Somalia, the cost of insurance for shipping in the Gulf of Aden and the Indian Ocean has risen.[44] More familiar are how insurance companies differentiate the cost of insurance according to accumulated statistical estimates of risk

---

43 See Jacques Le Goff, *Your Money or Your Life: Economy and Religion in the Middle Ages* (New York: Zone Books, 1988).

44 "Today, ship owners are forking over some $400 million a year to cover themselves against a roughly 1% chance that their vessel will be attacked (200 attacks out of 20,000 annual voyages through the region). That comes to an average $20,000 in extra insurance costs per voyage." Christopher Helman, "The Profits of Piracy," *Forbes*, April 15, 2010.

(e.g., between teenage and adult drivers) as well as to actual experience. Individual involvement in automobile accidents results in an increase in insurance premiums; having one's home burglarized results in an increase in the cost of home insurance; installation of security systems reduces it; repeated crop failures result in rising premiums for farmers; and so on.

Adding to such familiar examples of insurance as a service, the financial industry has, over time, developed a wide range of less familiar forms of insurance against risks involved in commerce and finance itself (futures contracts, for example, in which buyers make contracts in the present to guarantee the availability of the commodities they need in the future, or sellers make contracts today to guarantee buyers tomorrow). Such contracts, however, have long provided not only insurance but vehicles for speculation. Speculation in commodity trading, for example, is as well known as speculating in stock and bond markets; all involve gambling against fluctuations in market values. With financial deregulation this kind of financial service has proliferated, the most notorious being those associated with insuring against losses on paper assets—such as derivatives contracts designed, in principle, as services to diversify and reduce risks of all kinds. Especially since the beginning of financial deregulation in the early 1980s, innovations in such "insurance services" in finance have proliferated, facilitating speculation on future changes in the value of paper assets just as deregulation has facilitated speculation in real estate.

It is worth noting, however, that most financial services—even before deregulation—always involve speculation about the future—in the general sense of basing today's decisions on one's expectations about tomorrow. When money is borrowed, the creditor who loans, and debtor who borrows, generally anticipate sufficient future debtor income to cover repayment, whether that income be from future profits, future wages or salary, or future taxes.[45] Whether one buys insurance and how much one is willing to pay (or an insurance company will charge) depends on one's

---

45 I say "generally" because, as the recent crisis in sub-prime mortgages has revealed, when creditors can pawn off their assets onto others, they need not worry about whether the debt will actually be repaid. (See below.)

estimates of, or speculation about, future probabilities concerning the likelihood of losses. Effectively, virtually every activity involves some degree of speculation about an uncertain future, susceptible to all kinds of crises. Every capitalist investment involves speculation against estimated future profits. All workers who take jobs speculate that they will be paid for the work they perform.[46] Uncertainty about the future is inherent in life, and that uncertainty necessitates speculation and prompts efforts to insure or hedge against loss. Within capitalism, such efforts have become opportunities for the marketing of services to provide that insurance and those hedges.

It is also important to note that, as with other commodities, it is entirely unimportant to capitalists, who put some of us to work producing service commodities, whether the products they have to sell benefit us or not. Just as capitalists regularly have some of us produce myriad things that undermine our and other people's well-being—bad drugs, food that poisons, industrial operations that pollute our world, toys that explode, bombs and other police and military equipment—so too have they put many of us to work producing services that undermine our lives. The word "service" evokes the notion of someone or some institution doing something or providing something that "serves" (i.e., benefits) someone. Servants have long been hired to make their masters' lives more comfortable and easy. But the services that capitalists sell may or may not contribute to our well-being. In the domain of money and finance, clearly some services are of use to us—even if we can imagine better ways to obtain what we need. But a great many are detrimental. Tracking and evaluating our purchases and our use

---

46 Hard as it may be for some to believe, because as a general rule people work first and are only paid later, sometimes they are laid off without being paid for work already performed. Such rip-offs are so common that a web search will quickly reveal any number of such cases—involving a variety of employer methods—along with links to legal help in fighting back against such abuses. Increasing the probability of payment is one reason workers have been willing to sign legal contracts specifying what work they will perform and what their payment will be. They have not always done so. Most famously, early in the twentieth century, members of the Industrial Workers of the World refused to sign contracts, preferring the threat of strikes and work stoppages to guarantee payment of their wages.

of credit makes it possible for some capitalists to compile lists of potential customers or credit ratings that they then sell to other capitalists. The result is endless harassment by advertisers and, all too often, the denial of actually useful services such as affordable credit for those of us trying to buy homes, automobiles, or other things that we can only pay for over time.

Recognizing that financial institutions actually provide services—some useful and some detrimental to our well-being—and are not merely unproductive receivers of redistributed surplus value, has two implications. First, as suggested above, those services should be subjected to evaluation as to their use-values, and so too should the useful labor that produces them. With respect to their evaluation, as indicated above, some allow people benefits that would otherwise be denied them. On the other hand, the degree to which they lend themselves to speculation has been their primary characteristic that has drawn condemnation. Labor employed in providing the former might be considered socially worthwhile (at least within the framework of capitalism), whereas labor employed in the latter is widely condemned. To take just one example, the labor of making money available to workers for buying homes or of providing insurance on those homes are services without which most could never afford to buy or protect a home—or acquire the benefits many associate with homeownership. On the contrary, the labor involved in diverting money to speculation in real estate (i.e., buying at one price in the expectation of later selling at a higher one—as was done en masse by deregulated savings and loan institutions in the 1980s) have not only deprived potential homebuyers of funds but also led directly to the collapse of the industry, the loss of jobs, wages, and a huge further rip-off of workers' money, qua taxpayers, to bail out the speculators. Such diversion of money from consumption and productive investment to speculative activity has naturally been condemned both by workers who are harmed by it and by those capitalists who understand that their primary social responsibility as managers of the system is investment that puts people to work producing profits that can be used to put more people to work. Thus the September 16, 1985, *Business-Week* cover story during the Reagan administration condemning the rise of the "Casino Society," Susan Strange's 1986 book *Casino*

Capitalism, and endless calls by pro-capitalist neo-Keynesians for re-regulation to limit the possibilities of such diversions.[47]

Second, with respect to the labor involved in the financial industry, while we can theoretically differentiate between labor that contributes to the production of useful services and labor dedicated solely to speculation, it is not immediately obvious how to accomplish such differentiation empirically. In the case of mortgage loans, much the same work is required to evaluate the value of properties and the credit-worthiness of borrowers in the case of prospective homeowners and in that of prospective real estate speculators. Close examination, however, might well reveal relative changes in the distribution of labor. For example, in the run-up to the 2007 collapse of the housing bubble that set off the most recent financial crisis, it seems that much of the labor that usually goes into careful evaluation of property values, borrower income, and risk was dispensed with through the fraudulent filling out of applications by loan officers.[48] Instead they spent their time drumming up new, risky sub-prime mortgages with little regard to whether the borrowers would have income streams adequate for repayment. They could do this because financial deregulation made it possible to bundle up mortgages, sell securities based on the bundles, and thus pass on the risk of default to buyers of those securities who had no direct way of evaluating the likely income stream they would generate.[49] In the midst of the housing boom, those buyers were simply gambling on its continuation, on the steady

47   Anthony Bianco, "The Casino Society: Playing with Fire," *BusinessWeek*, September 16, 1985; Susan Strange, *Casino Capitalism* (New York: Basil Blackwell, 1986).

48   Similarly, retrospective evaluations of the international debt crisis of the 1980s and 1990s revealed that such evaluations of credit-worthiness and risk were either not performed or ignored in the 1970s rush to loan as many petrodollars as possible to governments and private investors reeling under the shock of high oil prices and resistance to austerity at home.

49   Their only recourse was to the judgment of so-called rating agencies, such as Moody's, Standard & Poor's, and Fitch Ratings—agencies that many consider to operate dishonestly, often giving much higher ratings than much debt deserves (e.g., securitized sub-prime mortgages), to the benefit of debt sellers and the losses of debt purchasers.

rise in the value of the securities they were purchasing with the intent to sell them at a higher price than they had paid. Such "mere buying and selling" was precisely the kind of labor Marx judged "unproductive" because it redistributed value rather than generating it. During that bubble, and in others like it, as the prices of assets were bid up beyond their underlying ability to generate value streams, the money invested certainly deserved his condemnation as "fictitious capital"—and its fictitious character was dramatically revealed when the bubble collapsed.

Given the myriad forms of financial activities existing both before and after the onset of deregulation, an examination and evaluation of the degree to which the labor involved in each actually contributes to the production of a service or only facilitates exchange is a task beyond the scope of my concerns here. I desire only to argue how the examples cited above illustrate the need for such research to thoroughly ground our understanding of the role of labor—and the forms of worker struggle—in the financial industry. Marx undertook such research with respect to manufacturing factories in his day; we need to do the same today with respect to the offices of the financial industry—and with respect to workplaces in the service sector more broadly.[50]

Such research is essential in order to move from the abstract economic categories of "industry," "commerce," and "finance" to the gritty concrete world of the class relationships of work, exploitation, alienation, and struggle in each of those domains. That gritty and frequently bloody world is one economists often prefer to avoid completely, content with abstract theory or policy recommendations for others to implement. But for those of us who work and suffer exploitation and alienation and are trying to understand in order to explore kinds and forms of struggle

---

50 One kind of service-producing labor that has been recognized and subjected to analysis recently is "caring labor"—one kind of work performed by nurses and attendants employed in for-profit hospitals, hospices, senior care facilities, and so on. See the special issue of *The Commoner*, no. 15 (Winter 2012). Another to which considerable attention has also been paid is the labor at call centers—those phone banks of more or less skilled technicians who provide support to purchasers of computers and communication services (e.g., cable TV, Internet, and phones). See the various issues of *Processed World* (1981–2005) now archived online.

that might help us transcend them, such investigation is essential. Only through it can we craft a trajectory for our struggles that begins with our suffering, copes with the constraints and violence inflicted upon us, explores our strengths and our weaknesses, and helps us to build upon the former, overcome the latter, and find ways out of both constraints and violence.

To conclude this discussion of finance and financial crisis, let me summarize. 1) Finance in modern times—in its many forms and through most of its permutations—evolved as a functional adjunct to capitalist domination of society. As a network of institutions devoted to the specialized task of managing money—that rarified and fetishized embodiment of the value of labor to capital—it has provided services that have facilitated the ability of capital to impose work. In so doing, it has become a capitalist industry in its own right—putting people to work providing those services, exploiting them, and, where successful, adding to whatever value it manages to extract from other industries. 2) Despite this fundamental role, the working class's ability—our ability—to raise average wages and benefits beyond the needs of immediate consumption has not only added our savings to the pool of monetary resources available to financial institutions but has also won us access to what had heretofore been a kind of monetary "commons" to which only capitalists had access. As a result, by winning access to credit we have enlarged both our ability to live and our ability to struggle. Therefore, as with every other moment or aspect of capitalism, credit and finance have become terrains of class struggle.

DECODING FINANCIALIZATION

Although definitions and evaluations of its extent, sources, and character differ, virtually all interpretations of financialization consist of assessments of more or less profound transformations in the structures of contemporary capitalism, involving the *increasing importance and centrality of financial operations in relation to non-financial enterprise, government, and households*. A common measure of the significance of such changes is the rising percentage of corporate profits earned by financial institutions—from roughly 12 percent in 1965 to 29 percent in 2013.[1]

Everywhere what we find are lengthy dissections of the celebrated (or condemned) financial mechanisms involved in the growing dominance of finance in the economy, its role in crisis, and recommendations for future economic policy. Let's look at the narratives of financialization currently on offer—first those of economists and then those of a few of their Marxist critics.

The Stories Economists Tell[2]

Like Panurge in Rabelais's great masterwork, economists have generally celebrated lending, borrowing, and debt as essential sinews holding together not only the economy but also society. Where they have found institutions of modern finance missing or under-developed, as in the Global South, they have argued for their introduction. Economists see profit-making in the financial sector the same way they see it everywhere else—as the generation of greater revenue than the costs of investment. The rapid growth of financial profits as a percentage of total corporate profits is thus attributed to the better performance of financial corporations as opposed to non-financial ones, although neo-Keynesians generally recognize

---

1 *Economic Report of the President for 2015* (Washington, D.C.: GPO, 2015), appendix B, table B-6 (Corporate profits by industry, 1965–2014), 391.

2 The stories that economists have told about finance have been manifold, based on many different and incompatible theoretical constructs. The extremely brief summary of current positions provided here ignores that long history of storytelling as economists have sought both to justify the roles of finance and to find solutions to its crises.

that the better performance has been facilitated by deregulation, a dramatic expansion of speculation and government bailouts.

As for the relationship between the expanding role of finance and crisis, economists generally understand the latter as rooted in debt-repayment difficulties. Of particular significance, they report, have been difficulties associated with the expansion of financial activity from its traditional roles in financing production and trade to the financing of a wide variety of individual expenditures (e.g., consumer durables, housing, and education). Thus, the rapid expansion and subsequent collapse of the US housing bubble—fueled by speculation—is generally understood to be the key factor in the onset of the financial crisis of 2007–2008 and the subsequent dramatic recession. Governments are also recognized as having played important roles in the onset of crisis by a) borrowing heavily themselves, b) deregulating the financial sector, c) subsidizing housing and student loans, and d) demonstrating a willingness to bail out those banks "too big to let fail," thus reducing the risks of speculative losses. Heavy state borrowing, as neo-Keynesians have repeatedly pointed out, has covered fiscal deficits, themselves the result of conservative governments cutting taxes on the wealthy or on corporations, and inflating the profits of creditors that lend to the state. Government deregulation of the financial sector has made possible the invention and introduction of a wide variety of innovative financial instruments whose proliferation facilitated new forms of speculation rendering the system, as a whole, more vulnerable to crisis. Government subsidies to the financing of home buying and student loans drew more borrowers into the market and increased the opportunities for fraudulent and risky "sub-prime" lending. By engineering a punitive change in the financing of individual schooling from grants to loans—under conditions of rapid cost increases—the state dramatically accelerated the piling up of student debt.[3] Gov-

---

3   This change has been a striking one. From the late 1950s, throughout the 1960s, governments, both local and national, invested heavily in "human capital" development through expenditures on education from K–12 through universities. Those expenditures included both individual grants and support for research that included funds for research assistantships. But in the wake of the student movements of the 1960s and early 1970s, that funding was not only cut back but progressively converted from grants to loans—sowing the seeds of the current vast burden

ernment bailouts have transferred prodigious sums from working-class taxpayers to financial institutions faced with bankruptcy and collapse. The refusal of the obvious alternative—taking over or breaking up those institutions and prosecuting those responsible—created an additional incentive to risky behavior.

With respect to policy, neoliberal economists recommend further deregulation, privatization of state enterprises, and, to the degree that government debt to financial institutions is perceived as a source of crisis, they enthusiastically embrace debt reduction via austerity measures—mainly cutbacks in government spending, usually on social services and public employee wages and benefits (in other words, a direct assault on working-class income and welfare). Neo-Keynesians recommend a restoration of regulation to eliminate the most egregiously risky financial practices contributing to instability, expansionary fiscal policies to reduce unemployment and raise wages, as well as new measures such as debt restructuring to bail out homeowners and consumer, student, and national debtors.

One Marxist Counter-narrative

The recurrence of one kind of financial crisis or another throughout the past forty years has resulted in virtually all Marxists developing some kind of theoretical perspective on finance, financial crisis, and financialization. The number of those addressing these issues is large, and the number of their writings even larger. Anything approaching a comprehensive exposition and critique of those efforts would require far more space than this elaboration of a conference essay. Therefore, for the most part I will focus on a single thread of analysis, one associated with the Monthly Review school of Marxism, or neo-Marxism. I choose this thread partly because the influence of those associated with it is substantial; the theories and historical analyses set forth by its authors have had a widespread impact around the world. Few, if any, Marxists have failed to either cite them with approval or to feel it necessary to critique them—precisely because of that influence.[4]

---

of student debt that continues to haunt its recipients long after graduation.

4 On a personal note, in the fall of 1971 I gratefully accepted an invitation from Paul Sweezy to participate in a session of the annual meetings of the American Economic Association. At the time, I was still working on finishing my dissertation for

Within the United States during the 1960s, analyses in *Monthly Review*, along with some articles in a few other radical publications, were vital sources of insight into the social forces underlying the struggles that preoccupied student activists, especially conflicts in Southeast Asia and Latin America. Baran and Sweezy's *Monopoly Capital* was one of the writings, along with those of Herbert Marcuse, C. W. Mills, William Domhoff, and revisionist historians, that provided an alternative analysis of capitalism and imperialism for those of us in the New Left (e.g., Students for a Democratic Society) who embraced notions of participatory democracy rather than the democratic centralism of Old Left groups. The influence of their ideas was evident in articles published in New Left magazines such as *Ramparts* (1962–75) and in numerous "underground" newspapers, such as the *Berkeley Barb* (1965–80), the *East Village Other* (1965–72), the *Midpeninsula Observer* (1967–69), and the *Los Angeles Free Press* (1964–78) as well as in more focused journals such as *Viet Report* (1965–68), the *Bulletin of Concerned Asian Scholars* (1969–2000) and the *NACLA Newsletter* (1967–71).[5]

I have also chosen to focus on the Monthly Review school's treatment of financialization because I believe my main critiques of the way they have dealt with this phenomenon are frequently applicable to the writings of other Marxists. Because the volume of writings of those associated with this one school down through the years is too great to treat in detail here, I examine and critique only a few examples, ones I take to be representative of both the continuities and changes in their thinking about capitalist development and the role of finance. I think of these examples as cairns made of piles of paper and digital essays instead of stones, marking the trail crafted by the contributors to the development of this particular counter-narrative of capitalist development and financialization.

Stanford while teaching at the Université de Sherbrooke in Quebec. As a result, I had the pleasure of meeting Paul Sweezy and Harry Magdoff. Subsequently, they published my paper "The Contradictions of the Green Revolution" in the June 1972 *Monthly Review*, along with the other essays presented at that session.

5   NACLA is an acronym for the North American Congress on Latin America. In November 1971, the *NACLA Newsletter* was renamed *NACLA's Latin America & Empire Report*, which later became *NACLA Report on the Americas* (still published).

Like other Marxists who generally recognize the existence of all those phenomena associated with the increasing role of finance, the Monthly Review folks have offered a counter-narrative arguing that lurking beneath, and ultimately responsible, is a fundamental, unsurpassable contradiction inherent in capitalism. No matter how many fixes economists come up with, they maintain, the underlying contradictory force causing both financialization and crisis is endemic and inescapable.

Early on, two fundamental referents for them were Hilferding's theory of finance capital—of a structural change in early twentieth-century capitalism that involved the ascendency of banking control over industry—and Lenin's theory of imperialism as "the highest stage" of capitalism that built on a variation of that theory. They did not embrace those theories without modification, but the notion that the internal dynamics of capitalism had undergone such fundamental structural changes as to necessitate revising Marx's theory left a clear imprint on their thinking.

Cairn #1: Paul Sweezy's *Theory of Capitalist Development* (1942)

In his first book, *The Theory of Capitalist Development*, Sweezy repeatedly drew on Hilferding's *Das Finanzkapital* (1910)—in those years only available in the German original—to sketch a historical-stages theory of capitalist development.[6] He appropriated Hilferding's two stages, a competitive stage and a finance-capital stage, reduced the latter to a transitional one, and added a final monopoly-capital stage. Eventually his followers, in the light of the expanding role of finance in the last thirty years, added a fourth stage: monopoly-finance capital. Sweezy based his reduction of Hilferding's finance-capital stage to a transitional one on the argument that the domination of banks over industrial capital had already—in the 1940s—been transcended by a continued concentration and centralization of industrial capital under the control of giant and increasingly multinational corporations. That change, he

---

6   For roughly seventy years, the only English versions of *Das Finanzkapital: Eine Studie über die jüngste Entwicklung des Kapitalismus* (Vienna: Wiener Volksbuchhandlung, 1910) were two largely inaccessible, unpublished typescripts. Eventually, when rights were acquired from Hilferding's son, Tom Bottomore drew on the two translations to form a new one that was published by Routledge & Kegan Paul in 1981.

argued, rendered them largely independent of banks because they were able to generate enough surplus value internally to largely free themselves from need to borrow to finance new investment. An inevitable by-product of this view was a relative neglect by Sweezy of finance. It would not be until he and Paul Baran were crafting *Monopoly Capital* that he would once again take up the issue of the importance of finance, and even then it would still be relegated to a subsidiary preoccupation of industrial firms.

Sweezy concluded his critique of Hilferding's theory by commenting on its use by Vladimir Ilyich Lenin (1870–1924) in his *Imperialism: The Highest Stage of Capitalism* (1917).[7] At that point, his main concern was to argue that Lenin's "highest stage" was conceptually closer to his own "monopoly capitalist stage" than Hilferding's and that, therefore, the former's use of the term "finance capital" was not subject to the same critique that he made of Hilferding's.[8] When Sweezy took up the theory of imperialism at length, in chapter 17 of *The Theory of Capitalist Development*, he began by embracing Lenin's theory with the "minor qualification" of replacing Lenin's use of "finance capital" with his own "monopoly capital." Otherwise, his analysis proceeded along the same lines as Lenin—in terms of the dynamics of relationships among capitalists and between national blocs of capitalists. Among capitalists he saw increasing concentration and monopoly. Between national blocs of capitalists he saw increasing competition—"rivalry in the world market," "territorial division" (colonies and spheres of influence)—and inevitable wars.

Already in these early treatments of the financial and imperial dimensions of capitalism—in any of the stages identified by Hilferding, Lenin, and Sweezy—we can see a recurrence of the problem pointed out in part 1 of this book with respect to Sweezy and Meek's

---

7   Lenin drew not only on Hilferding's work but also on that of the English economist and reformer John A. Hobson, whose *Imperialism: A Study* was published in 1902, and fellow Bolshevik Nikolai Bukharin's *Imperialism and the World Economy* (1917). Hobson attributed imperialism to under-consumptionism—the inability of workers to buy back the goods they had produced because of low wages. Unlike Lenin and Bukharin, Hobson thought both poverty and imperialism could be overcome by simply paying workers high enough wages.

8   Sweezy, *The Theory of Capitalist Development*, 269.

interpretation of Marx's value theory. Here too we find a failure to grasp the phenomena in question as internal to the antagonistic class relationships of capitalism. Throughout we find a one-sided analysis that either ignores the working class or only examines the consequences for it of the various changes wrought by capitalists.

At the beginning of his main treatment of Hilferding's theory of finance capital, Sweezy reads it as a "Marxian theory of the corporation."[9] Unlike Marx's extensive analysis in *Capital*, Sweezy completely ignores any historically identifiable or even possible roles that workers' struggles might have played in the changing structures of industrial corporations or in the relationships between those corporations and banks, at any stage. Instead he focuses on the role of the "growth of a reliable market for corporate securities" in the rise of Hilferding's finance capital and on that of the growing centralization of industrial capital in the rise of his monopoly capital. Both issues were clearly of importance, but neither are analyzed in class terms. Instead of analyzing, say, the relationship between the impact of workers' struggles on industrial profits and increasing corporate recourse to bank loans, he sees only Hilferding's "promoter's profit," gained through the manipulation of share prices.

The same phenomenon is even more glaring in Sweezy's adaptation of Lenin's theory of imperialism. While financial relationships among a diminishing number of giant corporations may be so hidden from public view that ignoring the ways in which they reflect workers' struggles is not noticeable, those of imperialism— from wars of conquest and colonization to wars between imperial powers for redivision of the world—are highly visible and clearly involve millions of workers. So clear are the diverse forms of involvement that neither Lenin nor Sweezy can ignore them. However, instead of identifying and analyzing how workers' struggles may play determining roles in the birth and spread of imperialism, both men focus instead on the impact of imperialism on workers. Instead of analyzing, say, the relationship between differentials in the strength of workers' struggles in various countries as an explanation for increasing foreign investment, they see only corporate investment decisions divorced from such considerations. For them, causality runs only one way, from the actions of capitalists to the impact on

---

9   Ibid., 258.

workers. For example, both emphasize the traditional importance of imperialists' quests for new, profitable market outlets for goods overproduced at home and the increasingly prominent quest for new investment opportunities—involving what they both call "capital export."[10] However, their only conception of how the need for such markets was related to the relationships between workers and capital lay in the inadequacy of the former's wages to buy up all the consumer goods being produced (under-consumption).

The failure to examine the roles workers' struggles may have played was perhaps most striking in the case of Lenin, because he actually quotes the famous British imperialist Cecil Rhodes, who was quite conscious of how export markets could help control workers at home. "My cherished idea is a solution for the social problem, i.e., in order to save the 40,000,000 inhabitants of the United Kingdom from a bloody civil war, we colonial statesmen must acquire new lands to settle the surplus population, to provide new markets for the goods produced in the factories and mines. The Empire, as I have always said, is a bread and butter question. If you want to avoid civil war, you must become imperialists."[11] Astonishingly, Lenin's only purpose in quoting this extraordinary statement was to use it as evidence of the self-consciousness of imperialists. He labels Rhodes's statement "crude and cynical," yet this particular statement is striking evidence of a sharp consciousness of how the settling of new lands and the opening of foreign markets can be weapons in the class war, a means of maintaining control over one's domestic working class.[12]

---

10   "Capital export," Sweezy writes, "is correctly defined by Hilferding as 'export of value which is destined to breed surplus value abroad.'" Sweezy, *The Theory of Capitalist Development*, 289n. In the language of contemporary economics, "capital export" usually refers to either portfolio or direct investment abroad, where portfolio investment involves buying foreign stocks and bonds, and direct investment involves taking control over foreign operations. Both may result in more surplus value, or they may merely redistribute it from local to foreign investors.

11   Lenin, *Imperialism: The Highest Stage of Capitalism*, chapter 6 ("Division of the World among the Great Powers").

12   Lenin repeats this failure to see workers' struggles as a driving force in imperialism a little later in the same chapter when he quotes a French ex-colonial administrator on how imperialism can channel working-class and middle-class "impatience, irritation and hatred" into "employment abroad in order to avert

The use of newly acquired lands to "settle the surplus population" included penal transportation to the colonies, a prime method of getting rid of militant workers in seventeenth- and eighteenth-century England and France. The finding or creating of more markets allows more sales, more revenue, and thus more resources to make concessions to workers while imposing ever more work.

Elsewhere, Lenin—following Engels—and Sweezy do recognize how imperialism provides capitalists with the ability to make concessions to workers' struggles. But instead of highlighting how those struggles have driven imperialist expansion, they condemn those workers as constituting a "labor aristocracy" whose high wages, they claim, have been gained at the expense of lower waged workers abroad. Unlike Rhodes, who clearly saw that such a strategy was driven by such dangerous workers' struggles at home as to threaten "bloody civil war," Lenin and Sweezy present it as merely a successful ploy by capitalists to buy off opportunistic workers.[13]

---

an explosion at home." Maurice Wahl, *La France aux colonies* (Paris: Librairies-Imprimeries Réunies, 1896), 91–92. (Wahl's title was "Ancien Inspecteur général de l'Instruction publique aux Colonies.") Although Lenin doesn't mention it, Wahl also described how, in the wake of the revolution of 1848, the French government spent fifty million francs resettling unemployed workers from Paris as part of the colonization of Algeria (p. 30) and attempted, in the same period, to replace freed slaves in French Guiana with political prisoners condemned to forced labor (pp. 85–86).

13 Certainly one source of Lenin's disdain for labor's "aristocracy" was the complicity of the bureaucratic leaders of many unions with social democratic party politics—especially those who abandoned international solidarity, sold out to nationalism in the run-up to World War I, and destroyed the hopes of the Second International. In the 1940s and early 1950s, Sweezy was also aware of how leftists were being purged from the US labor movement as its leadership was reshaped to transform it from a vehicle of workers' struggle into "business unionism" (i.e., union leaders willing to cut deals with employers while eschewing any challenge to capitalism per se). By all evidence, largely ignorant of rank-and-file resistance to such subservience, Sweezy—like Lenin—dismissed not only union leadership but all those workers whose struggles had won them higher wages and benefits. Contrast his work, and that of *Monthly Review* more generally in the 1950s and 1960s, with, say, that of Facing Reality—a militant Marxist group closely attuned to rank-and-file struggles. See Paul Romano (Paul Singer) and Ria Stone (Grace Lee—later Grace Lee Boggs), *The American Worker* (1947) (Detroit: Bewick Editions, 1974).

Lenin, Hilferding, and Sweezy could each have made a parallel argument for "capital export"—had they conceived of "capital" in terms of antagonistic class struggle. Any of them might have pointed out how the annexing of less powerful workers abroad provided leverage for dealing with workers at home. Instead these Marxists see only an extension of capitalist exploitation. Lenin recognized, for example, how finance capital added the search for "sources of raw materials" to the other motives of colonial policy. He might have pointed out how the reduction in costs occasioned by cheap raw materials would make it easier to make concessions to workers' increasingly strident and well-organized demands for higher wages, shorter working hours, and better working conditions at home (i.e., made it possible to pay those higher wages of his "labor aristocracy"). Instead, for Hilferding, Lenin, and Sweezy, the objective of "capital export" is merely the investment of a "surplus of capital" to earn greater profits abroad, where, as Lenin points out, "wages are low, raw materials are cheap." But, of course, raw materials are cheap because wages are low and wages are low because workers—having been conquered during colonial takeovers—are less well-organized and less able to resist exploitation. Without explaining how and why they are less able to resist, we are left with no understanding of capital export or of how those "impoverished masses" will ever be able to become the revolutionary force that Sweezy counted on.[14] At any rate, in Sweezy's case, the driving force is the tendency of monopoly capital to produce ever larger quantities of surplus, and one possible outlet is investment abroad.

When they do consider the relationship between workers and imperialism, it is mainly to discuss the impact of the latter on the former. Sweezy, for example, examines both positive and negative effects—where imperialism might result in rising wages or how it could lead to unemployment. While he sees the impetus for imperial adventures as deriving from the internal dynamics of capitalist accumulation, he does recognize the need to avoid resistance to imperialism and war on the part of workers in the imperial

---

14   The reasons for lower wages vary across time and space—from the aftermath of colonial conquest and the repression of colonial rule to the results of devastating wars (e.g., the post–World War II weakness of the European working class, whose low wages drew massive US corporate investment in the postwar period).

countries—by cultivating nationalist and racist sentiments.[15] Both Lenin and Sweezy also argue that ultimately the real limitation to imperialism lies in workers' struggles—in both the imperialist and colonized countries. But because their theories of capitalist development are centered on the internal dynamics among capitalists— independent of workers' struggles—what they predict as inevitable revolts of workers at home and abroad appear as mere unexplained by-products of those dynamics (e.g., the Russian Revolution). There, Sweezy wrote, "the chain of world imperialism" broke at its weakest link.[16] In truth, the chain didn't just break, it *was broken* by peasant and worker struggles, but because we are offered no analysis or theory of those struggles, the breaking remains unexplained.

Cairn #2: Paul Baran and Paul Sweezy's *Monopoly Capital* (1966)

In *Monopoly Capital*, Baran and Sweezy sharpened and fleshed out their theory of how, in its monopoly stage, capitalism generates such surplus, and such difficulties in finding uses for it, as to generate tendencies toward stagnation and imperialism. The primary differences between their work here and their (and Lenin's) earlier work is twofold. First, they asserted that rather than stagnation being a recurrent interruption in the basic tendency of capitalism to grow, monopoly capitalism reverses the relationship, with stagnation becoming the new normal, offset only by various contrived methods of employing the ever growing surplus. Second, they amplified, to a much greater degree than ever before, their analysis by devoting whole chapters to each method that they judged significant: capitalist consumption and investment, the sales effort (that includes finance), civilian government, militarism, and imperialism.

In terms of fundamental theoretical concepts, Baran and Sweezy quite explicitly abandoned Marx's concepts of value and surplus value—the object of study in Sweezy's earlier book—in favor of Baran's concept of "economic surplus." This they defined— following Baran's earlier exposition in chapter 2 of his *Political Economy of Growth*—as "the difference between what a society

---

15 Sweezy includes, in an appendix, a translated passage from Hilferding on this cultivation. Sweezy, *Theory of Capitalist Development*, 375–78.
16 Ibid., 325.

produces and the costs of producing it."[17] That they were not just proposing a change in terminology becomes obvious when they asked Joseph Phillips to calculate the magnitude of economic surplus in the US and changes in it over time. As Phillips explained in detail in an attached appendix, he used national income accounting statistics—adjusted in various ways—for his calculations. The unit of measure of all such statistics, of course, are dollars. They pass from Marx's analysis in terms of value to one uniquely in terms of money. What Baran and Sweezy were asking us to abandon was not one word for another but an analysis in terms of antagonistic class relationships for one in purely economic terms. Evidence that they were at least partially conscious of this appears when they protested, in their introduction, that although they neglected the social relations of work, they were still concerned with class struggle. As they immediately made clear, however, the class struggles that concerned them were those of "the impoverished masses in the underdeveloped countries."[18] They proceeded throughout the rest of the book to discuss, quite one-sidedly, both the generation of surplus and its utilization, or absorption, purely in terms of the activities and problems of capitalist enterprises and of the states that support them. Capitalist consumption and investment, the sales effort, civilian government, militarism, and imperialism were all analyzed purely in terms of methods employed by capitalists and governments to utilize or absorb or dispose of an encumbering surplus in order to ward off stagnation and crisis. A systematic critique of each of these phenomena, designed to show how they can be analyzed using Marx's concepts of value and surplus value instead of Baran and Sweezy's economic surplus, is both possible and necessary—because they are all important—but, once again, requires a much lengthier exposition than I am willing to offer here. Instead, let me just point out one obvious example of how the application of their theoretical perspective ignores worker's struggles.

The example is "civilian government" spending.[19] Baran and Sweezy couched their analysis, from the beginning of the chapter devoted to that spending, in macroeconomic terms of effective

---

17 Baran and Sweezy, *Monopoly Capital*, 9–10.

18 Ibid., 9.

19 Ibid., chapter 6 ("Civilian Government").

demand. How big is the spending? How much does it add to effective demand, once we take its flip side—taxation—into account? How much surplus does it absorb? What are its effects? To what degree does it stimulate investment, employment, and wages? The framework, in other words, was the one designed by Lord Keynes to help solve the problems of stagnation in consumption and investment demand. Because sizable chunks of government spending directly benefit workers (e.g., unemployment benefits, retirement pensions, veterans' allowances, public education, health and sanitation, conservation and recreation, public housing, fire protection, etc.), Baran and Sweezy had to recognize both the expenditures and the benefits. But how did they account for them—given their extended analysis of how capitalists control government and wield it primarily in their own interests? They did not account for it—other than as a useful but very minor means of absorbing surplus. Nowhere was there either recognition or analysis of how workers had fought and won much of this spending—usually against stiff capitalist resistance.

This combination of an awareness of capitalist problems and a blindness to the role of workers' struggles appears to be a legacy of their experiences in the Great Depression. Both men studied economics, and both worked within government organizations trying to find solutions to high unemployment and economic stagnation.[20] Years later, Sweezy and Harry Magdoff explained

---

20 As John Bellamy Foster points out in his memorial to Sweezy, in the late 1930s, Sweezy worked at "various New Deal agencies," including the National Resources Committee, the Security and Exchange Commission, and the Temporary National Economic Committee. Then, during World War II, he worked for the Office of Strategic Services (OSS, predecessor agency of the CIA)—mostly in London keeping "an eye on British economic policy for the U.S. Government." Baran too had formative experience with the US government. During World War II he worked for the Office of Price Administration and then, both during and after the war, for the OSS. After leaving the OSS, he worked for the US Department of Commerce and the Federal Reserve Bank of New York. When Baran took a job at Stanford in 1949, the announcement in the *Stanford Daily* was titled "New York Banker to Join Faculty." "Paul A. Baran," the story explained, "a top executive in the research division of the Federal Reserve Bank of New York and former U.S. Commerce Department official, will teach courses on comparative economic systems as an associate professor next

how their experience—largely shared by Baran—shaped their perspective: "We both reached adulthood during the 1930s, and it was then that we received our initiation into the realities of capitalist economics and politics. For us economic stagnation in its most agonizing and pervasive form, including its far-reaching ramifications in every aspect of social life, was an over-whelming personal experience."[21]

But among the most important reasons for the drama, depth, and length of the Great Depression of the 1930s were the intense working-class struggles of those years; millions mobilized to force the creation of industrial labor unions, of social security, of unemployment compensation. Sweezy and Baran's blindness to those struggles, and their failure to recognize their role in undermining business investment, was perhaps attributable to their remoteness from them. They were trained in elite universities in a field—economics—dedicated to solving capitalism's problems and went to work for those trying to find solutions.[22]

Moreover, after they left government and began to work together both on theory and on putting together a socialist journal, they continued to be surrounded by workers' struggles. The productivity deals, that made concessions to those struggles while seeking to harness and contain them, took years to implement in major industries. Growing rank-and-file resistance to increasingly reactionary trade union bureaucracies raised costs at home and undermined those very investment opportunities whose dearth

---

fall." In short, formative experiences for both men unfolded within institutions preoccupied with solving the problems of capitalism and among policy makers dedicated to doing so. *Stanford Daily*, April 1, 1949, 1.

21   See the introduction to Paul M. Sweezy and Harry Magdoff, *Economic History as It Happened*, vol. 4 *Stagnation and Financial Explosion* (New York: Monthly Review Press, 2009), 11.

22   Sweezy could not have been totally unaware of workers' struggles. Not only were newspapers full of stories of factory occupations, marches by the unemployed, et cetera, he was also, at least briefly, a member of the National Student League—a radical student group at least partially interested is such working-class actions as a coal miners' strike in Harlan County, Kentucky. While his involvement probably contributed to his interest in Marxism, it apparently did not make enough of an impression to be seen as a determining factor in his theory of stagnation.

Baran and Sweezy saw as a source of stagnation and as an impetus to imperial expansion. Indeed, in that period, those struggles were prompting US corporations to seek out more profitable opportunities abroad—where foreign working classes, devastated by war, could be put to work more cheaply. Yet despite the intensity of conflict surrounding them, Baran and Sweezy saw only the *limits* to the gains that were won. They could only emphasize how, in domain after domain, capitalists had been successful at preventing spending from matching demonstrable need. This blindness certainly contributed to their emphasis on imperialism and militarism and their embrace of the struggles of "the impoverished masses" in the Third World as the only revolutionary solution to overcoming capitalism. Baran and Sweezy were foremost among those soon to be labeled "Third Worldists" by Marxists more attuned to all those struggles they dismissed as participating in the spoils of imperialism.[23]

With regard to finance, they had very little to say, lumping it in with insurance and real estate as related modes of "utilizing surplus." In this case, at least, their neglect is understandable. During the period in which they were writing the book, domestic finance was fairly strictly regulated by the limitations imposed in response to the Great Depression and contributed very little instability to the US economy. Similarly, international finance had also been stabilized by the Bretton Woods system of fixed exchange rates. Worries about international financial issues would not come to the fore in the United States until growing pressures on the dollar in the late 1960s began to throw its role and the fixity of exchange rates into question. Worries about domestic finance would not materialize until the onset of fiscal crisis, first in

---

23   These included orthodox groups traditionally focused on the industrial working class, such as the Socialist and Communist Parties in France and Italy—whose political work in the post–World War II period was the social democratic binding of workers' struggles within capitalist development. The juxtaposition that I find more interesting is between Baran and Sweezy's neglect of workers' struggles in the United States and Europe and the preoccupation with those struggles of such groups as the Johnson-Forest Tendency (later Facing Reality and News & Letters), Socialisme ou Barbarie in France, and early workerists in Italy. See my brief online history of the genesis of the journal *Zerowork*: http://www.zerowork.org.

New York City in the mid-1970s, then elsewhere, as accelerating inflation and negative real interest rates led to financial deregulation. Nevertheless, it is notable that in this book Sweezy's earlier concern with correcting Hilferding's views on financial capital completely disappeared. Moreover, the two authors felt little need to examine, in any detail, the internal mechanisms of corporate finance that they continued to consider dominant—other than the way in which it was manipulated by corporate managers in their own personal interests.[24]

Cairn #3: Paul Sweezy and Harry Magdoff's "The Financial Explosion" (1985)

By the early 1980s, a sequence of financial crises drove the *Monthly Review* folks to attempt a serious examination of finance, its expansion, and its relationship to what they continued to see as a deepening crisis of stagnation in the capitalist economy. The abandonment of the Bretton Woods system of fixed exchange rates had given way to a hodgepodge of floating and fixed rates that opened the door to widespread speculation. Accelerating inflation in the 1970s had led to negative real interest rates and the removal of many of the constraints on financial institutions that had been in place since the 1930s. The Carter-Volcker-Reagan strategy of fighting inflation (wages) by driving up interest rates produced both a world depression and an international debt crisis that threatened the collapse of a vulnerable banking system. Basic to the analysis of the *Monthly Review* contributors was their understanding of the relationship between finance and what they viewed as productive enterprise.

That understanding was spelled out clearly in an article, "Production and Finance," published in the May 1983 *Monthly Review*.[25] While rejecting a common economist distinction between "the real and the monetary," they nevertheless insisted that "the appropriate analytical separation" is between "productive and financial." As their analysis unfolded, they revealed why they felt this to be significant; they clung to the Marxian tradition of

---

24 Sweezy and Paul Baran, *Monopoly Capital*, chapter 2 ("The Giant Corporation").

25 Paul M. Sweezy and Harry Magdoff, "Production and Finance," *Monthly Review* 35, no. 1 (May 1983), 1–13.

viewing finance and the financial sector as functional for capitalism but parasitic in the sense of not producing either use-values or surplus value. "Clearly," they wrote, "the financial sector does not itself produce anything with significant use value."[26] With no use-value, whatever the sector does produce cannot be a commodity and cannot embody value, and its sale cannot result in new surplus value. As with Marx, and for so many Marxists before them, whatever surplus value the sector realizes must be derived from the "productive" sectors where commodities, values, and surplus value are generated. The rapid expansion of the financial sector creates a situation where "a large and growing part of money capital (i.e., money invested with a view to earning more money) is not directly transformed into productive capital serving as the means by which surplus value is extracted from the productive utilization of labor power."[27]

Two years later, in reaction to a cover story in *BusinessWeek*, "The Casino Society: Playing with Fire," Sweezy and Magdoff offered their interpretation of the "explosion" of this unproductive, parasitic sector and its potential for compensating for stagnation in truly productive enterprise.[28] In the first place, they argued, this was no end-of-upswing speculative boom but a more secular trend resulting from the eternal return of stagnation in the 1970s. From their point of view, that stagnation was merely a return to normal after abnormal stimuli following World War II had run their course (e.g., pent-up consumption demand, postwar rebuilding, and US wars in Korea and Indochina).

The absolute absence of any recognition of working-class struggle in *any* of these "stimuli" is quite remarkable. They did not even recognize how the stimulus resulting from the war on Vietnam—a long-standing concern of both *Monthly Review* and its readers— was the result of the anticolonial struggles of the "impoverished

26   Ibid., 10.

27   Ibid., 4. By the time this article was written, probably as a result of earlier challenges from other Marxists, the utilization of Marxian concepts such as surplus value (rather than surplus) and labor power had become fairly frequent in the pages of *Monthly Review*.

28   Bianco, "The Casino Society," *BusinessWeek*; Paul M. Sweezy and Harry Magdoff, "The Financial Explosion," *Monthly Review* 37, no. 7 (December 1985), 1–10.

masses" in that area. Despite the postwar consumption demand
being the obvious result of workers' successful struggles to raise
wages and benefits, and later to gain access to various lines of
credit, no mention was made of either those struggles or those
gains, only their effects on aggregate demand. Similarly, Sweezy
and Magdoff made no connection between the supposed end of
such stimuli and workers' struggles, neither those at home and in
Vietnam that defeated the US war effort nor those that ruptured
the Keynesian productivity deals and undermined corporate profit
in what Sweezy and Magdoff considered the "productive" sector of
the economy and pushed the "business climate" into pessimism.
So their answer to the question of why "a stagnant economy [be-
came] the breeding ground for a financial explosion," was simply
that, when growing stagnation reduced the ability of financial institutions to make profits lending to industry, they simply began
conjuring up new markets in which to peddle money; they became
"money pushers" at home and abroad.[29] The "debt-creation process," they wrote, "took on the character of a self-contained operation, with financial institutions (and wealthy individuals) playing
leading roles on both sides of the market, i.e., as both suppliers
and demanders."[30] Throughout their sketch of the proliferation of
financial instruments and mechanisms that followed, the working
class remained noticeably absent. They provided neither an analysis of why capital investment fled workers' struggles in the "productive" sector, nor one of how those struggles contributed to the
rapid expansion of financial markets catering to "households" (e.g.,
consumer and mortgage credit).

Cairn #4: Paul Sweezy's "The Triumph of Financial Capital" (1994)

By the summer of 1994, Sweezy was ready to pronounce the "triumph" of financial capital complete. At a June conference in Istan-
bul, Turkey, he gave his usual account of the rise of monopoly capital and the inevitable return of stagnation after the dwindling of
the external stimuli of the post–World War II era. He then argued

---

29   This metaphor of drug pushing was also used by Sandy Darity and Bobbie
Horn, *The Loan Pushers: The Role of Commercial Banks in the International Debt
Crisis* (New York: Ballinger, 1988).

30   Sweezy and Magdoff, "The Financial Explosion," 6.

not only that a "financial superstructure" had arisen but also that by feeding on the stagnating flesh of industry (profits with nowhere to go) it had become dominant in the spheres of both the economy and politics.[31]

On the side of the economy, he said, the "tiny minority of oligopolists" who control the real economy, unable to make conventional profits by "expanding the capacity to produce the goods that enter into mass consumption," channeled their profits into financial assets. Financial capitalists, always greedy for more money to play with, were happy to take over control of those profits and use them to add new bricks to their rapidly expanding financial superstructure. The results? A whiff of Hilferding is detectable in Sweezy's conclusion that "the occupants of these [industrial] boardrooms are themselves to an increasing extent constrained and controlled by financial capital . . . the real power is not so much in corporate boardrooms as in the financial markets."[32]

On the side of political power, governments are also "controlled in what they can and cannot do by the financial markets."[33] Sweezy illustrated this control with three examples: 1) the power of the IMF and World Bank to impose policies in the Third World, 2) the subordination of US fiscal policy to "acceptability to the financial markets," and 3) reversals of policies by the socialist government in France in response to the disapproval of finance, evidenced by capital flight from "mild social reforms and fiscal expansionism."

As in previous writings, nowhere in Sweezy's analysis, either in his history of financial capital or his treatment of its current domination, do we find workers and their struggles playing a determining role in the evolving character of capital accumulation. Only at the end, when he poses the classic Marxist question of "What is to be done?" does he suggest that, eventually, the "great majority of the people in the world . . . have no choice but to challenge the structure itself."[34] In this case, his inability to connect people's struggles

31 Paul Sweezy, "The Triumph of Finance Capital," *Monthly Review* 46, no. 2 (June 1994), 1–11.
32 Ibid., 10.
33 Ibid.
34 Ibid., 11.

with his financial superstructure is perhaps most notable because of the way he ends his presentation by saying how impressed he was by the Zapatista uprising in Chiapas. In that summer of 1994, his theoretical perspective made him perfectly incapable of foreseeing how that uprising would contribute to the peso crisis a few months later, when the efforts of the Mexican government to defend the value of the peso—as frightened money fled the rising demands for democracy—proved futile.

The efforts by the Carlos Salinas government to defend the peso proved futile because the government ran out of foreign exchange reserves it had been using to buy up the pesos being dumped by nervous capitalists. The exiting Salinas then dropped the problem in the lap of his successor, Ernesto Zedillo, who, unable to do anything else, devalued the peso, which then suffered a precipitous drop in value. "Hot" money capital fled the peso— much as it had fled the French franc in one of Sweezy's examples. Unlike Sweezy, one of those giant, multinational financial corporations that he claimed had come to power, Chase Manhattan Bank, did see the Zapatista threat and demanded that the Mexican government "eliminate" them to stabilize the political and economic situation in Mexico.[35] Financial capital saw clearly what Paul Sweezy could not—how workers' struggles were determining the course of events both economic and political. Furious at the spreading pro-democracy movement that supported the Zapatistas, Zedillo, urged on by Chase Manhattan's admonition, dispatched fifty thousand troops into Chiapas in February 1995. That effort too proved futile, as protests across Mexico and around the world forced the Zedillo administration back to the negotiating table. The Zapatistas and their pro-democracy supporters quite

---

35 This demand for the elimination of the Zapatistas was spelled out explicitly in a newsletter written for Chase Manhattan Bank investors in "emerging markets" by Riordan Roett, a professor from the Johns Hopkins School of Advanced International Studies, then working for Chase. When those of us in the Zapatista solidarity movement made the newsletter public and spread it around the world, it caused such a stink and such widespread protests—including occupations of Chase branches—that the company fired Roett. He is now head of Latin American Studies at Johns Hopkins and a member of the boards of directors of "a number of closed-end mutual funds." See his page on the Johns Hopkins website.

thoroughly demonstrated their power to limit that of Sweezy's "triumphant" financial capital.[36]

Cairn #5: Foster and Magdoff's *Great Financial Crisis* (2006–2008)

In the twenty years following Sweezy's proclamation of the triumph of financial capital, little changed in the analysis of financialization being put forward by the editors and contributors to *Monthly Review*. Paul Sweezy died in February 2004, and Harry Magdoff died in January 2006, but their theory and practice has lived on in the work of their followers. This is abundantly clear in writings of Fred Magdoff—Harry Magdoff's son—and John Bellamy Foster, the new editor of the review. A collection of their articles in *Monthly Review* from the period 2006 (the beginning of the collapse of the housing bubble) to 2008 (the onset of general depression in the wake of financial collapse) was published by the press in 2009 under the title *The Great Financial Crisis*.[37]

Foster and Magdoff suggested a new title for contemporary capitalism—monopoly-*finance* capital—to highlight the centrality of finance in contemporary capitalist efforts to solve their perennial problem of surplus disposal. "The crucial problem of modern monopoly-finance capital," they wrote, is "the stagnation of production and the growth of financial bubbles in response."[38] Financial bubbles, of course, were the inevitable consequence of financial speculation, which is where, they believed, like Paul Sweezy and Harry Magdoff before them, more and more surplus was being dumped. Unfortunately for capitalism and the rest of us, they argued, this method of absorption, just like all the others, did little to solve the underlying problem. While "the financial expansion has helped to absorb surplus, it has not been able to lift the productive economy out of stagnation to any appreciable degree."[39] So, in

---

36 For a brief sketch of the determining role of the Zapatista rebellion in the Mexican peso crisis, see the "Historical Overview" chapter in Subcomandante Marcos, *Conversations with Durito: Stories of the Zapatistas and Neoliberalism* (New York: Autonomedia, 2005).

37 John Bellamy Foster and Fred Magdoff, *The Great Financial Crisis: Causes and Consequences* (New York: Monthly Review Press, 2009).

38 Ibid., 7.

39 Ibid., 74.

the place of Hilferding's according of primacy to financial capital
because of its domination of industry (productive economy), they
accorded financialization primacy because of the way it has come to
constitute "the largest of the countervailing forces [to stagnation]
during the last three decades."

Inasmuch as they continued to embrace the story that "creep-
ing stagnation" in the productive sector continues to provide the
flesh on which financialization feeds, one might have expected
Foster and Magdoff to deepen the analysis of the sources of that
stagnation. Instead, in the final article (from 2008), when they got
"back to the real economy," they merely pointed to the decline in
decennial growth rates of GNP.[40] They provided no analysis whatsoever of how the changes in class struggles within the productive
sector might be contributing to the failure of industrial capital to
develop new, profitable avenues of investment instead of handing
its net revenues over to the financial sector.

Nor did they apparently feel the need to examine the impact
of workers' struggles in other domains on the swelling and subsequent bursting of various financial bubbles. For example, in their
chapter "The Household Debt Bubble," originally published in May
2006, the emphasis was totally on how working-class recourse to
borrowing was purely the desperate by-product of falling real wages. There was no examination of the long and ultimately successful
struggle by a great many workers to gain access to credit as a complement to winning higher wages in the Keynesian period. Nor did
they examine such collective struggles as those that finally forced
local financial institutions to make savings collected in a community available as loans to those in the same community—as opposed
to earlier practices of draining off money for use elsewhere.[41] Nor,
finally, did they examine the concrete uses (including housing) to
which workers have put the monies they have been able to borrow, either before or after the "bubble." As a result, we were offered
no basis for evaluating the particular roles of credit in workers'

40   Ibid., 129.
41   In contrast, conservatives have pointed to that success and blamed it for undermining the stability of the financial sector by forcing investment in inherently
risky undertakings—just as they have blamed workers for borrowing money they
proved unable to pay back.

struggles or the degree to which those roles have contributed to or undermined the power of workers to fight for the means to meet their needs. Instead, they began their historical account with the period of a decline in real wages—the end of the 1970s and beginning of the 1980s—when workers' use of credit to compensate for successful capitalist attacks on real wages fit their analysis. But with no recognition or accounting for the success of earlier struggles, they were unable to see the attack on real wages or the fraudulent manipulation of credit as responses to those struggles, as counterattacks in a class war. We were left, as usual, with a one-sided history of the internal contradictions of capital, productive and financial, that left the working class—us—entirely out of account, except as frequent victims.

Continuing their long-standing concern with imperialism—both capitalist depredations and resistance abroad—these contributors to the ongoing development of the *Monthly Review* thesis of stagnation tried to grasp these dynamics at the level of the world as a whole. However, despite couching their whole analysis of the rise of financialization in terms of the urgent need to dispose of a burdensome surplus, they also argued that today "monopoly-finance capital requires enhanced intrusion into the economic and social life of the poor countries for the purpose of extracting ever greater surplus from the periphery."[42] Given that such extraction would merely exacerbate the quantity of surplus to be disposed of, and contribute to the difficulties of doing so, some explanation of that "requirement" would seem to have been called for. Yet there is none. Rather, the need was assumed, and they passed on to discuss its achievement through the imposition of neoliberal economic restructuring, overseen by the IMF, the World Bank, and the World Trade Organization. "Third World countries have long experienced an enormous net outflow of surplus in the form of net payments to foreign investors and lenders located in the center of the world system."[43] While it is true that financialization has accentuated that outflow, as neoliberal restructuring has opened local capital markets to foreign speculators and subordinated those countries ever more thoroughly to foreign creditors, what was missing, once

---

42   Foster and Magdoff, *The Great Financial Crisis*, 75.
43   Ibid.

again, was any account of the enormous resistance raised by local struggles against that restructuring and against that bleeding off of income and wealth.[44]

Cairn #6: Fred Magdoff and Foster's "Stagnation and Financialization" (2014)

I want to conclude my commentary and critique of this whole line of argumentation with a few words on what I think is Foster and Magdoff's most recent formulation, another editorial "Review of the Month" published in *Monthly Review* in May 2014.[45] In that review the two authors noted, with satisfaction, that even economists such as Larry Summers and Paul Krugman have come to ponder the relevance of theories of secular stagnation. They then proceeded to offer their usual "deeper explanation" in the form of Sweezy's testimony in 1980 that capitalism in the twentieth century suffered from "overaccumulation" (i.e., "a strong, persistent, and growing tendency for more surplus value to be produced than can find profitable investment outlets").[46] They went on to reiterate the argument that they themselves have repeatedly put forward. "Faced with a shortage of investment outlets, the surplus capital available to corporations and the wealthy increasingly flowed into the financial sector looking for speculative opportunities unrelated to the production of use values."[47] In other words, they reiterated the position long held within the Monthly Review orbit that the financial sector is nothing more than one of those domains where economic resources are wasted in the financial bubbles of a desperate capitalist effort to keep the system going, and financialization is nothing more than the growth of that wasteland. They then employed this renewed statement of their long-standing analysis to account for the settling in of what they called the "stagnation-financialization

---

44 For quite different accounts of this history that *do* center workers' struggles see my "Close the IMF, Abolish Debt and End Development: A Class Analysis of the International Debt Crisis," *Capital and Class*, no. 39 (Winter 1989), 17–50; Midnight Notes Collective, *Promissory Notes*.

45 Fred Magdoff and John Bellamy Foster, "Stagnation and Financialization: The Nature of the Contradiction," *Monthly Review* 66, no. 1 (May 2014), 1–24.

46 Ibid., 3.

47 Ibid., 6.

trap" at the heart of all of the financial crises of the last thirty years. In the end, they questioned whether capitalism can ever escape an endless oscillation "between outright stagnation and periods of financial exuberance associated with rampant speculation."[48] Their conclusion echoed that of Paul Sweezy, Paul Baran, and Harry Magdoff before them: the only way out is through "revolutionary social transformations arising from mass action driven by the force of common necessity."

The source of such mass action? As has long been the response of Monthly Review's authors: "Such radical revolts against the system are likely to emanate initially from the global South"—although they do admit that "popular upsurges in the center are also essential."[49] In other words, we are left with the long-standing Marxist promise that somehow, somewhere, when things get bad enough, there will be revolt that will change the system. What is frustrating in this particular variation of the promise is the absolute lack of any analysis of existing struggles that might, could, or will constitute those "radical revolts" and "popular upsurges." This lack has been present from the beginning, from Sweezy's *Theory of Capitalist Development* to the present. Despite the repeated enthusiastic embrace of various Third World struggles, from Cuba through Vietnam and China to the Zapatistas, neither those struggles nor others in the center have ever been incorporated as determining factors in their theory of the evolution of capitalist development and crisis. They have remained external to the theory and mostly interpreted in terms of the resistance of victims. Thus, they have rarely seen whatever positive, creative alternatives those struggles have come up with as potentially generating either enough power to overthrow capitalism or the foundations of new worlds.[50] They

---

48 Ibid. 17.

49 Ibid., 22.

50 Because of their enthusiasm for various Third World struggles, they have, at various points, celebrated such creativity. Examples are their embrace of Che Guevara's calls for the genesis of new "socialist" men and the Chinese mobilization of "barefoot" doctors to confront health problems in that country. Unfortunately, such celebrations have never been integral parts of an analysis of workers' struggles as determining forces in capitalist development and crisis and therefore of little significance in evaluating the possibilities of transcending capitalism.

leave us with a promise and a hope but no analysis of what strength
we do have, upon which we might build to realize that promise and
fulfill that hope.

Taking Class Struggle into Account

The most striking thing about the Marxist counter-narrative
that I have sketched above has been its one-sided theorization
of accumulation and financialization almost purely in terms of
the actions, problems, and solutions of capitalists. That narrative excludes the rest of us almost entirely. From time to time,
we are allocated roles as victims or urged to some future role as
the victorious gravediggers of a regime whose logic we will ultimately be unable to tolerate. The problem I have with this exclu-
sion is not the economist's lament that a variable has been left
out, but that without the recognition and analysis of the roles our
struggles have played in determining the dynamics of accumulation and the emergence of financialization, we have no point of
departure—based on an evaluation of our current strengths and
weaknesses—of what to do next. However, we can do better. We
can analyze capitalism in terms of our struggles—*against* what
its functionaries try to impose on us and *for* alternatives—in ways
that re-center our agency and struggles. We can analyze accumulation and financialization in terms of the class struggles in which
we have been, and will continue to be, engaged. Let me begin
with "accumulation"—a word I too have used but with only limited definition.

For the most part, economists do not employ a concept or theory of *accumulation*; they reason instead on terms of investment
and the consequent growth of output, or of development—usually
defined as growth with qualitative change. Although Marxists do
employ Marx's term "accumulation," they too often tend to con-
ceptualize it in terms of investment and growth—even if, in this
period of financialization, they include financial or money capital alongside physical capital and labor power as an increasingly
significant element of growth. Such a concept of accumulation,
however, differs from that of Marx by failing to explicitly recognize how accumulation involves more than expanding quantities
of labor power (**LP**), factories, machines and raw materials (**MP**),
commodities (**C**), and money (**M**). Creating and reproducing

conditions that force people to prostitute themselves in the labor market and put more people to work in factories (or fields, offices, etc.) are fundamental elements of the antagonistic class relationships that constitute the social content of the capitalist organization of society. This is the basic point that Marx highlights when he takes up accumulation in chapter 25 of volume 1 of *Capital*. He immediately follows up a brief discussion of the accumulation of physical capital and labor power by pointing out that accumulation is, above all, the accumulation of the two classes. "Accumulation reproduces the capital-relation on an expanded scale, with more capitalists, or bigger capitalists, at one pole, and more wage-laborers at the other pole. . . . Accumulation of capital is therefore multiplication of the proletariat."

As his analysis in the chapters *leading up to* chapter 25 makes quite plain, the "multiplication of the proletariat" is inevitably the multiplication of antagonistic class relations of struggle. As his analysis in the chapters *following* chapter 25—those on "primitive accumulation"—shows, such accumulation and multiplication can only occur to the degree that capital is able to subordinate people to its organization of their lives around endless work. As he points out, and several generations of bottom-up and subaltern historians have amplified, such subordination has always been resisted and has never been fully successful.[51] Not only have some people avoided being driven into the proletariat, but even those who have been unable to avoid becoming wage-laborers, or becoming members of the unwaged reserve army of labor, also discussed in chapter 25, have repeatedly subverted the imposition of work, both waged and unwaged.

From this perspective, as I have suggested in part 1, every element of the circuits of capital within which capitalists try to confine us is an element of accumulation, understood as accumulation of class struggle. As such, the point is to identify and analyze the contested character of each of those elements. For example, in **LP—M** and **M—LP**, the wage deal, capital pays out

51   One introduction to bottom-up history can be found in Harvey Kaye, *The British Marxist Historians*, new ed. (London: Palgrave Macmillan, 1995); another can be found in the work of subaltern historians in Ranajit Guha and Gayatri Spivak, eds., *Selected Subaltern Studies* (Delhi: Oxford University Press, 1988).

wages to bind us to it; it tries to make sure wages only serve to buy what we need to reproduce ourselves as workers. But we take the money and often use it for our own purposes, both fighting against capital (e.g., strike funds or paying for campaigns against various of its policies) and elaborating alternatives to it. In . . . **P** . . . —whether in the circuit of industrial capital or in that of the reproduction of labor power—capitalists seek to impose work. In the one case, the work of creating commodities (**C'**), the sale of which (**C'—M'**) will bring them profits and the ability to impose more work in the future, or, in the other case, the work of creating the most essential commodity of all, our willingness and ability to work for them (**LP***). But we repeatedly contest the degree to which we actually work for those who have hired us, or the degree to which we work at shaping our lives as labor power. We show up late, leave early, play instead of working or studying, go on strike together, collectively invent ways of meeting our needs outside of their system, et cetera.

So, instead of simply asserting, as the Marxist narrative discussed above does, that stagnation in accumulation is the result of dwindling investment opportunities brought on by the inherent capitalist tendency toward centralization, oligopoly, and monopoly, we must examine the relationship between our struggles and those phenomena.

To begin with, the usual analysis of the processes of competition that drive toward centralization, oligopoly, and monopoly (and later imperialism and war) focuses only on the sordid family drama of capitalist versus capitalist (or capitalist bloc versus capitalist bloc). In that drama, some win and some lose, some take over others, by driving them out of business, by absorbing them in mergers, by subordinating them in networks, or by conquering violently. What that analysis leaves out is how the victors among the capitalists are almost always those who have proved themselves best able to limit or harness the struggles of their workers. This becomes obvious when we examine the most common mechanisms of competition in terms of the dynamics of struggle. Winning through so-called "price competition" requires being the most successful at holding wages and benefits down, while getting workers to accept productivity-augmenting changes in technology. Winning through "product differentiation" requires being the most successful at drawing out workers' creativity and inventiveness. A key strategy in both of those efforts has long been pitting workers against each other, unwaged against waged, high-wage against low-waged, white against black, men against women, ethnicity against ethnicity, national identity against national identity. Winning the contests of imperialism requires being the most successful not only in those ways but also in finding ways to convince or compel workers to join armies and navies and to fight or compete against other workers in other regions or countries. Competition among capitalists, therefore, in class terms, comes down to a Darwinian mechanism for selecting the capitalists most capable of manipulating workers (i.e., at managing their kind of society).[52]

That said, for those capitalists who win their competitive battles and succeed at replacing competition with oligopoly or monopoly in various markets—whether domestic, colonial, or foreign—the antagonisms at the heart of class struggle don't end. The antagonisms continue within new structures because the imposition of exploitation, alienation, and division and the pitting of some against others are essential to continued capitalist control. The emergence, therefore, of a "monopoly-capital" stage of capitalism—such as the one heralded by adherents to the Monthly Review school of Marxist theory—still requires detailed examination of how workers' struggles determine patterns of development under those conditions.

The Monthly Review folks were certainly correct that one of the characteristics of the crisis of Keynesianism in the late 1960s and early 1970s was a dwindling of sufficiently profitable investment opportunities. That dwindling could have been the result of fewer investment opportunities or of reductions in the profitability of existing opportunities. In both cases, the reduction can be seen to be due to our struggles. In part I, I pointed out how an international cycle of struggle undermined the Keynesian productivity deals of the post-World War II era. By succeeding in raising wages and benefits while reducing productivity in the industrial North, those struggles undermined profits, capitalist investment,

---

52   For more on the relationship between competition and class struggle, see my "Competition or Cooperation?," *Common Sense*, no. 9 (April 1990), 20–22.

and growth.[53] In the same period, guerrilla resistance to being accumulated and exploited in many parts of the Global South closed innumerable investment opportunities—limiting growth in those zones. The ferocity of the military efforts to crush such rebellion measured the intensity of capitalist anger over those limits and the fervor of their desires to regain access to potential investment opportunities estimated to be profitable by the eventual availability of cheap labor and plentiful raw materials.

In the same vein, we must examine the relationship between our struggles and the accelerating inflation of the 1970s that reached the point of so undermining real interest rates as to provide a rationale for financial deregulation. There is no doubt that accommodating monetary policies, in response to engineered increases in food prices and the quadrupling of oil prices by OPEC, played a role in allowing prices to rise. But in each case we can discover our struggles driving each of these phenomena. Prices were rising quite independently of loose money and OPEC as capitalists responded to the rupturing of productivity deals and rising wages at home by raising domestic prices to avoid falling profits. Moreover, the Johnson administration chose an accommodating monetary policy and more national debt because of its fear that raising taxes would exacerbate the widespread revolts against the War on Poverty at home and against the Vietnam War abroad. With

---

53 This analysis differed from two other Marxist "schools" of thought that also recognized declining rates of profit. One simply argued that it was the "tendency of the rate of profit to fall" finally manifesting itself; the other argued for a "profit squeeze," wherein rising wages undermined profits. Only the latter formulated their analysis in terms of class struggle. Unfortunately, they largely neglected the struggle against work of the period that was at the heart of the decline in productivity (first in its growth and then absolutely) that was the other side of the rupture of the productivity deals. An example of the former is Anwar Shaikh, "Political Economy and Capitalism: Notes on Dobb's Theory of Crisis," *Cambridge Journal of Economics* 2, no. 2 (June 1978), 233–51. An example of the latter is Raford Boddy and James Crotty, "Class Conflict and Macro-Policy: The Political Business Cycle," *Review of Radical Political Economics* 7, no. 1 (April 1975), 1–10. "We believe," they wrote, "that the key to understanding both current macroeconomic policy and the business cycles of the post–World War II era is still to be found in Marx's theory of the conflict between classes over income shares."

respect to the quadrupling of oil prices by OPEC, we must also recognize how US policy makers readily accepted OPEC's price increases because they thought they could use them against us. First, rising oil prices accelerated inflation, tending to undermine our real wages. Second, US policy makers recognized how the OPEC governments were charging higher prices because they needed the money to manage the growing demands of their own people—and the stability of OPEC oil supplies was vital to the global capitalist economy. Third, they foresaw how OPEC would inevitably deposit the bulk of its petrodollar surpluses in Western banks, making them available to finance corporate investments to undercut our struggles. In other words, the whole stagflation phenomenon of the 1970s was rooted in people's struggles in both the Global North and the Global South. Therein lie the roots of stagnation and financial deregulation that laid the basis for financialization.

Turning directly to financialization, instead of seeing the growing role of finance as merely another recent, clever capitalist strategy—however ultimately limited—let us recognize how it has been a response to our struggles and continues to be constrained by them. As I noted in the section on finance, for a long time after the ascendance of capitalism as the dominant form of social organization, credit and money-as-means-of-payment primarily developed in service to capitalist industry and commerce. However, the success of our struggles for better wages and benefits resulted in more and more of us not only having savings to contribute to the monetary commons—the collective pool of money organized by financial institutions—but also gaining access to it through various forms of credit. As we did, "consumer credit," and finance more generally, became an expanding theater of struggle—one in which the dramas of exploitation and bursting bubbles of financialization have played out.

What we need to discover, in order to find our best strategies and tactics of struggle, are the roles we have played and are playing in each domain of financialization. What are those domains? They are roughly three. First are all those financial mechanisms to which we have direct connections as individuals. This includes such things as credit cards, auto finance, installment loans, mortgage loans, insurance, and securities. The degree of our access, of course, depends on our position in the income hierarchy; those with higher incomes have more access, those with lower incomes have less access. Success in struggling for better and more secure wages gives more access to credit. The second domain, corporate finance, includes access to banks, to securities markets (including government debt), to foreign exchange markets, and to internal financial arrangements—with customers and between subsidiaries. The third domain is government or "public" finance—federal, state, and local. Governments at all levels collect taxes and issue debt, from national treasury bills to municipal bonds. They finance a wide variety of economic activities—for example, from schools and student loans through trade to state enterprises. Central banks determine, as best they can, interest rates (in the United States by setting reserve requirements and open market operations, buying and selling debt) and serve as lenders of last resort.

Today most of these financial relationships are organized to operate internationally. All of the largest financial and non-financial corporations are multinational in their operations—in their financial relations with people as workers and as consumers and in their financial relationships with each other and with governments. Government finance is also international. Tariffs are collected on trade; foreign aid is made available to other countries; government debt is sold to buyers both domestic and foreign. All kinds of corporate and government debt and securities are bought and sold in international markets. Governments collude to form supranational institutions such as the International Monetary Fund that, under certain conditions, makes loans to member states out of their pooled resources. The IMF and similar institutions—such as the European Central Bank—also act as mediators for financial conflicts between creditor and debtor governments and between debtor governments and private financial creditors. We have seen this during the international debt crisis of the 1980s and 1990s and during the current crises in Europe between debtor governments such as those of Greece, Spain, and Portugal and creditor banks and governments.

So where are *we* in this array of financial relationships, whose rapid recent expansion is called financialization?

To begin with, some of us, indeed millions of us, are employed by financial institutions. Those so employed do the work involved in the operations of those institutions. To the degree that such work provides services whose sales generate profits, those of us performing that work are exploited in the same general manner as workers in non-financial industries. We are put to work generating not only value but surplus value that can be reinvested to impose more work. To what degree and in what ways do those of us so employed struggle against our exploitation, the inevitable alienation and the way our work is used to exploit others? How have those struggles shaped finance and affected the expansion of financialization?

Unfortunately, because many Marxists have written off both finance and workers in finance as non-productive parasites that produce no use-values and hence no value or surplus value, they have produced few studies of such struggles. How this theoretical perspective has limited analysis is amply illustrated by *Monthly Review* author Harry Braverman's *Labor and Monopoly Capital*.[54]

That book filled a yawning gap in *Monthly Review*'s long-standing neglect of work. Indeed, it marked something of a turning point inasmuch as in its wake others associated with the *Review* would adopt its methodology and undertake further studies along the same lines. The book provided a wealth of illustrations of both the evolution of work within modern capitalism and why the changing ways in which work has been organized merely continued and deepened its exploitative and alienating nature. Those illustrations included a whole chapter devoted to "clerical workers," defined by Braverman in a way that explicitly included most of the work done by employees of financial institutions. His work was thorough and influential. In some ways, it paralleled work that had been done earlier in Italy by Marxist sociologists—although there is no evidence in his book of familiarity with their work.[55]

---

54   Harry Braverman, *Labor and Monopoly Capital: The Degradation of Work in the Twentieth Century* (New York: Monthly Review Press, 1974).

55   Because of that earlier work and continuing workerist interest, Braverman's book was quickly translated and published in Italy as *Lavoro e capitale monopolistico. La degradazione del lavoro nel XX secolo* (Turin: Einaudi Editore, 1978). Although authors associated with *Monthly Review* frequently portray the book as originating contemporary Marxist research on work (as opposed to that by earlier, mainstream sociologists), this was mainly true in the United States. Thanks to the work of John Merrington and Ed Emery (Red Notes) in England, translations of the earlier Italian materials were being circulated there while Braverman was still

However, despite demonstrating at length how the conditions of work of clerical workers have come to resemble those of workers in manufacturing, Braverman continued Baran and Sweezy's insistence on the "unproductive" character of their work.[56] He also chose not to analyze their struggles—neither those against their work nor those for higher wages, better benefits, fewer hours, or against speed-up. This is particularly remarkable because his descriptions of the imposition of manufacturing-like methods of control make it quite obvious that those methods have been aimed precisely against such struggles. He was quite explicit about his choice. In the introduction he explained, "This is a book about the working class as a class *in itself*, not as a class *for itself*.... [W]hat is needed first of all is a picture of the working class as it exists, as the shape given to the working population by the capital accumulation process."[57] But, as I have pointed out, accumulation includes class antagonism and conflict; the working class "as it exists" is an active, heterogeneous subject whose struggles shape accumulation. As a result of his choice, Braverman's analysis remains limited to "the degradation of work in the twentieth century"—the subtitle of the book—and never tries to systematically analyze workers' struggles against that increasingly degraded work. With no analysis of their struggles, there can be no analysis of how those struggles have ruptured the circuits of financial capital and therefore no analysis of the relationship between those struggles and either financialization or the financial crises associated with it.

Five years after Braverman's book appeared, Monthly Review Press followed up with a collection of fourteen *Case Studies on*

---

researching and writing. Among those Italian Marxist sociologists who had been studying the changing organization of work in Italy since the early 1960s—and the struggles against those changes that contributed to the rise of the Italian New Left—were Raniero Panzieri and Romano Alquati. See Panzieri's work collected in *La Ripresa del Marxismo Leninismo in Italia* (Milan: Sapere, 1975) and Alquati's writings collected in *Sulla FIAT e Altri Scritti* (Milan: Feltrinelli Editore, 1975).

56 Although his insistence shows up in the chapter on "clerical workers," Braverman later devotes a whole chapter to revisiting the tradition of differentiating between productive and unproductive labor and using it to justify the continuing application of the label "unproductive."

57 Braverman, *Labor and Monopoly Capital*, 27.

the Labor Process, edited by Andrew Zimbalist.[58] The articles in that collection were less interested in theoretical issues—such as whether workers were "productive" or "unproductive"—but were still mostly preoccupied with the effects of work organization on workers. Two of the fourteen studies dealt with clerical work, one of which looked at such work in insurance—a branch of the financial industry, primarily, although not uniquely, concerned with producing a service.[59] The article on clerical work in the insurance industry contributed a bit of what was missing in Braverman's treatment—some accounting of how workers in those years resisted and sometimes undermined the methods of control used against them. For example, pressured by supervisors who counted the number of standardized tasks performed, some workers figured out ways to increase the count without doing more work. Such illustrations suggest both rupture and how workers' struggles shape the evolution of control methods.[60] They give at least an inkling of the kind of further research that ought to follow from these studies' detailed accounts of evolving methods of control. Every new method is likely a response and an attempt to overcome some form of struggle.

---

58 Andrew Zimbalist, ed., *Case Studies on the Labor Process* (New York: Monthly Review Press, 1979). Both Braverman's book and Zimbalist's collection can be compared with the collection published by the British Conference of Socialist Economists, *The Labor Process and Class Strategies*, CSE Pamphlet no. 1, published in 1976 in preparation for the annual meeting of the CSE of that year. The pamphlet contained translated articles by Panzieri as well as ones by Sergio Bologna and Mario Tronti—two other theorists of Italian workerism.

59 The two articles on clerical work in Zimbalist, ed., *Case Studies on the Labor Process* were Evelyn Nakano Glenn and Roslyn L. Feldberg, "Proletarianizing Clerical Work: Technology and Organizational Control in the Office," 51–72, and Maarten de Kadt, "Insurance: A Clerical Work Factory," 242–56.

60 Not surprisingly, the only two articles in Zimbalist's *Case Studies on the Labor Process* where workers' struggles are front and center analyzed industries producing material commodities: Louise Lamphere, "Fighting the Piece-Rate System: New Dimensions of an Old Struggle in the Apparel Industry," 257–76; Nina Shapiro-Perl, "The Piece Rate: Class Struggle on the Shop Floor: Evidence from the Costume Jewelry Industry in Providence, Rhode Island," 277–98. These articles are akin to Miklos Haraszti, *A Worker in a Worker's State*.

In 1999, the twenty-fifth anniversary of the publication of *La-bor and Monopoly Capital*, Michael Yates defended Braverman against charges that he had neglected class struggle.[61] Pointing to his analysis of the capitalist control of work, Yates argued, "Far from ignoring the class struggle, Harry Braverman in *Labor and Monopoly Capital* has provided us with an invaluable weapon in that struggle; for how can we struggle effectively unless we know exactly what it is we are struggling against?" There is no doubt that Braverman's book is useful for understanding "what it is we are struggling against." The problem that Yates didn't recognize is that Braverman's investigation of the class struggle was one-sided. He gave us a great deal of information and insight into capital's meth-ods of controlling us but nothing about our struggles that those methods sought to control—and therefore no real understanding of the evolution of those methods. So when Yates then turns to sug-gest "the kinds of struggles which might derive from Braverman's analysis," his suggestions are based on "hope," not on any concrete analysis of actual struggles within and against production or of those seeking to craft alternatives. Hope, while desirable, is obvi-ously not enough. What we need are studies of the sort touched on in the examination of the insurance industry in Zimbalist's collec-tion: studies of workers' resistance, of how individual resistances coalesce to become collective and of how collective resistance plays out, whether covert or overt. Only then can we understand the particular methods capitalists are using to limit and control those struggles, the strengths on which we can build, and the weaknesses we need to overcome to defeat them.

Fortunately, recent work on "call centers," a proliferating phe-nomenon in the service sector, has begun to meet this need in our understanding of class struggle in the financial sector. Call centers have been properly described as communication factories—con-centrated or diffused, in-house or outsourced—teeming with often underpaid workers whose high pressure subjection to computer scheduling and surveillance has been provoking more and more self-organization and revolt. Some have been examining the char-acter of such labor, à la Braverman, but also studying the revolt

---

61   Michael D. Yates, "Braverman and the Class Struggle," *Monthly Review* 50, no. 8 (January 1999), 2–11.

against it. See, for example, the survey of such studies and a description of a bottom-up international research project on class struggle in such factories by Enda Brophy.[62]

Since the onset of the most recent financial crisis in 2007–2008 and the subsequent economic depression, financial corporations have responded to increased pressure for re-regulation and lawsuits against their illegal practices by attempting to roll back previous gains by their workers and by the communities in which they have operated. Banks have been cutting wages, reducing benefits, imposing more part-time labor, and increasing pressure on workers to speed up their work, accept unpaid overtime, and constantly increase sales regardless of the needs of customers. They have also continued to replace bank tellers with ATMs and online banking, have been closing outlets in communities that fought for local reinvestment, and have shifted thousands of jobs to lower-waged areas of the United States and overseas.

In response to such corporate efforts to increase profits at worker and community expense, there has been an expansion of collective efforts to expose their methods and fight back against them. Examples of the former are 1) UNI Finance Global Union, *Banking: The Human Crisis, Job Losses and the Restructuring Process in the Financial Sector* (2013), 2) the Committee for Better Banks, *The State of the Bank Employee on Wall Street* (2015), and 3) the Center for Popular Democracy, *Big Banks Are Dismantling the Middle Class* (2015). Beyond such exposition of the exploitation and alienation of bank workers, these groups are actively involved in supporting their struggles. The UNI Global Union, for example, claims to represent three million employees in 237 trade unions worldwide, fights for union recognition in financial institutions, demands a seat at the table in discussions of financial regulation, and supports typical union struggles for better wages and benefits, less work, and so on. According to their self-description, members of the Committee for Better

---

62 Enda Brophy, "The Subterranean Stream: Communicative Capitalism and Call Centre Labour," *Ephemera: Theory & Politics in Organization* 10, no. 3 & 4, 2010, 470–83; Enda Brophy, "Language Put to Work: Cognitive Capitalism, Call Center Labor and Worker Inquiry," *Journal of Communication Inquiry* 34, no. 4, 2011, 410–16.

Banks "organize together to make change in their workplaces. We have conference calls where bank employees from around the country discuss the challenges we face on the job and support each other. We meet with our coworkers, create petitions and join in days of action." The Center for Popular Democracy has supported the struggles of bank workers as well as those who have suffered from the practices that have been forced on those workers—for example, the Campaign for a Fair Settlement (CFS) and the Home Defenders League (against foreclosures)—and works with coalitions such as Americans for Financial Reform for financial re-regulation. While the deployment of Marxian concepts can deepen the evaluation of the potential benefits and limits of all such efforts, it is also true that the development of those concepts can benefit from the study of such struggles.

Whether we work within the financial industry or not, most of us *directly* engage with that industry when we give it our money or when we borrow from it and take on debt.[63] We are engaged *indirectly* through all of its activities that have an impact on our lives. Let's begin with our direct engagements.

If we have savings, odds are that we place our money somewhere it can "earn" interest. Those of us who can only save a little may put some in checking accounts. If we have more, we may shift some money into savings accounts. With interest rates on both checking and savings accounts very low, those who can afford to save for longer periods of time may buy certificates of deposit. Those with significantly higher income may buy stocks and bonds (either public or corporate). In each case, when we hand over part of our money to some financial institution, our hope and expectation is that the interest or dividends we receive will either preserve

---

63 I say "most of us" because even those with no bank accounts generally use some kind of financial service. According to an FDIC report, only 7.7 percent of US households are "unbanked," (i.e., have not placed money into any kind of an account at an "insured institution"). Such households, unfortunately, may well be engaged with some uninsured "alternative financial services" (AFS). Types of AFS include non-bank money orders, non-bank check cashing and non-bank remittances, pawn shops, payday loans, rent-to-own services, auto title loans, and "pre-paid debit cards." See FDIC, *2013 FDIC National Survey of Unbanked and Underbanked Households*, October 2014.

the value of our money—threatened by inflation—or increase our income in the future.

If we have little or no savings, we either live off cash income—as many working-class folks have been doing since the onset of capitalism—or we borrow. Those of us with little or no savings can only borrow at high cost (e.g., from payday loan sharks). Those of us who can access a wider variety of consumer credit can borrow more, often much more. Access to credit cards, consumer lines of credit, auto finance, or mortgages makes it possible for us to borrow enough to buy consumer durables, vehicles, and homes—be they single-family dwellings or condominiums. In all these cases, we take on a greater or lesser amount of debt—legal promises to repay the borrowed money, usually over time with interest.

The rapid expansion of such debt, often lumped together under the category "household debt," has been a major element of financialization that has preoccupied both economists and Marxists. Economists have tended to emphasize the way expanding household debt has stimulated output and growth in both commodity production and housing, although they have also recognized how deregulation has made possible the rapid expansion of debt bubbles—especially housing bubbles—whose collapse has rendered the economy more vulnerable to crises in both finance and production. Marxists have tended to emphasize the increased danger of crisis and the way our recourse to credit has often been, in recent years, a defensive response to stagnant or falling wages and benefits as many of us have tried to maintain the standard of living gained through earlier victories in raising wages and benefits. Inasmuch as capital has been on the offensive and effective since the early 1980s in attacking our income, our working conditions, our jobs, our unions, our access to welfare and social security, and our environmental protections, this preoccupation by Marxists with the capitalist use of crisis is hardly surprising. Yet, because of our resistance, those attacks have not been as effective as their perpetrators have hoped—which is one reason why those attacks continue.[64]

---

64 Early on, not long after the dramatic increase in the distribution of food stamps, the Nixon administration tried to cut back the program. It failed. A decade later, the Reagan administration sought not only to cut food stamps but to wipe out social security. It too failed. Because it did succeed in many of its other attacks,

In other words, whenever we enter into contractual relationships with financial capital, each contract adds a new terrain of struggle. Depositing our savings, borrowing money, or buying on credit adds a new element of antagonism to our class situation. As I discussed in the section on decoding finance, such connections provide capital with new ways to exploit us. They also provide us with more flexibility in our struggles. So, alongside the terrains of struggle over wages and benefits, over conditions of production and over those of consumption, we acquire those of our encounters with financial capital. As we multiply such connections and such conflicts, we multiply both the dangers of exploitation and the opportunities available to us. I will take up in the next section how such struggles have unfolded and their potential importance.

When we turn from our individual engagements with financial capital to corporate and government finance, our relationships become more distant and abstract. Unless you are employed in the relevant agencies or read business newspapers and magazines on a regular basis, you are unlikely to keep up with the latest twists and turns of corporate or government finance. From time to time, corporate shenanigans come to light—as in the infamous case of Enron—but mostly they proceed out of public view. The same is true for government financial operations. For the most part, government publications keep track of policy changes and statistics but are often understandable only to those directly involved and intimately familiar with the jargon. Mainstream corporate media reports on a few significant changes in financial matters—such as the latest Federal Reserve statement on interest rates, inflation, or monetary policy. Unfortunately, few outside the worlds of corporate finance and government policy circles are well enough informed to interpret the implications of such information for their own lives.

So, when the deregulation of corporate finance began at the end of the 1970s and continued into the 1980s, few of us noticed.

---

memories of such victories get lost in the shadows of defeats. The same is true in the class war over other social and environmental policies. Here again we need to remember how, over and over, efforts to beat back gains by women and by those fighting for greater ecological protections have failed. It is the reason those efforts are still being renewed.

Its complexities were obscure, and for many these have remained
so ever since. It was easier to see deregulation in other fields—for
example, the removal of regulations protecting workers on the job
or the effective deregulation of environmental protections as the
Reagan administration refused to fund the enforcement wing of
the Environmental Protection Agency. Financial deregulation concerned changes in unfamiliar and esoteric laws, changes many of
us either ignored or accepted passively merely because of the claim
that they would make finance more efficient and counteract economic recession. But a series of financial crises that have caused
millions to lose savings, homes, and jobs have, like the prospect of
being hanged, sharpened the attention of far more of us than ever
before. The collapse of the stock market and of the savings and loan
industry in 1987 and the bursting of the dot.com bubble in 2000
forced many to sit up and take notice. The bursting of the housing
bubble after 2004, which resulted in the financial crisis of 2007–
2008 and a deep economic depression, forced us to start paying
close attention. Despite a wee bit of re-regulation—causing the financial industry and its apologists to protest hysterically—nothing
fundamental has changed, and similar crises are inevitable in the
future. Today, even if most of us, as individuals, have neither the
time nor energy to delve into the esoteric mechanisms of finance,
we have become aware of the high cost to us of their dynamics. We
have seen how those dynamics have hurt millions while creating a
small handful of billionaires—dramatically increasing income and
wealth inequality to the point of creating a new Gilded Age.[65]

Once we started paying attention, we realized how financial deregulation amounted to capitalists freeing themselves from previous constraints by getting legislators to change the laws regulating

---

[65] The original Gilded Age in the United States unfolded in the late nineteenth and
early twentieth century, bringing dramatic increases in income inequality. During
that time, capitalist profits soared, making possible a huge surge in conspicuous consumption (e.g., vast estates such as the Rockefeller's Kykuit in the Hudson Valley, New
York, or the Vanderbilt's Breakers in Newport, Rhode Island), creating in the United States the kind of ostentatious consumption familiar these days in the TV show
Downton Abbey. Today only the forms of conspicuous consumption have changed,
with large high-tech homes (e.g., Bill Gates's 66,000-square-foot Xanadu in Medina,
Washington) and private jets replacing Highclere Castle and fancy carriages.

what they could and could not do with their, and our, money. Those legal changes opened up previously barred channels of speculation, and they substantially increased the leverage of the wealthy in shaping politics and policies. In the United States, the one virtue of the Supreme Court's decision in favor of Citizens United and against the Federal Elections Commission (and the rest of us) was to make the power of money to subvert democracy clear to anyone who bothered to look. Before, most politicians hid their corruption in the shadows; today more and more "dark money" is out in the open and easy to see as it reshapes the class war on the terrains of formal electoral politics and legislative action. The reshaping, of course, has been aimed against workers and their unions, against women and their independence, against those of us with the least income and the greatest need for a "social safety net," and against young people and their hopes and aspirations.

While the class war has often been fought around such fiscal policy issues as domestic taxation and expenditures—how much from whom, how much to whom—changes in monetary and debt policies have been much more remote. Indeed, in the post–World War II period, financial regulations relegated financial crises to something that happened far away in other lands. At home, economists were adamant that marginal changes in the money supply were useful tools in fine-tuning the economy and increases in the national debt were nothing to worry about because it was just a question of the left pocket owing money to the right pocket. At the international level, while the Bretton Woods agreements held, the fixity of exchange rates among major currencies made changes in them rare and mostly newsworthy only in business magazines and newspapers.

All that began to change when an international cycle of our struggles forced President Richard Nixon to unhook the dollar from gold and abandon the Bretton Woods fixed-rate regime. That was not the aim of those struggles, but it was their result. Suddenly changes in exchange rates were front-page news, and more of us were paying attention than just those who were traveling abroad. As exchange rates among major currencies devolved into volatile fluctuations—both in response to our struggles and aimed at countering them—we became much more aware of how those fluctuations affected us. For example, if our struggles provoked capitalists to move their money into other countries, the resulting depreciation of our money—or an explicit decision by central banks to devalue it—increased the cost of imports and undermined our real wages. Associated appreciations, or revaluations, elsewhere increased the cost of exports, and by so doing tended to decrease them, costing lost jobs and wages. The shift to flexible exchange rates was supposed to solve the problem of adjustment by shifting it from more visible government policies to less visible changes in exchange rates. But the effects of fluctuations were dramatic enough to keep them visible, and our refusal to accept the consequences (e.g., lower real wages or higher unemployment) was loud and strong enough to force central banks into intervening in exchange rate markets—"dirtying the float"—to dampen the effects, both in rate changes and in our opposition to their consequences.

Accelerating inflation, negative real interest rates, and exchange rate volatility led President Jimmy Carter to begin financial deregulation and to appoint Paul Volcker as chairman of the Federal Reserve. Volcker's dramatic tightening of monetary policy drove both nominal and real interest rates into the double digits—first in the United States and then abroad—and plunged the world into a global depression and an international debt crisis. The crisis was international because the primary creditors—the giant multinational banks—were threatened by possible default by creditors. Government after government—mainly in the Global South—found themselves unable to meet their contractual repayment schedules at the new, much higher interest rates.[66] The playing out of the crisis has been prolonged. It has continued through the 1980s and 1990s and into the new century, primarily because of the resistance of workers everywhere to accepting

---

66   The international debt crisis is usually discussed in terms of a fictitious conflict between debtor and creditor *countries*. In reality, the debtors have usually been governments that have not only borrowed but frequently nationalized the debts of local capitalists to save them from ruin. The creditors have included multinational banks, governments that have extended loans (in the guise of "bilateral foreign aid"), and supranational state institutions such as the IMF and World Bank that have also extended loans—at market or below-market rates. The fictitious character of this representation has been revealed, time and time again, as millions have mobilized against the deals with creditors signed by their governments.

the austerity, open capital markets, and privatization of state enterprises demanded by the international banks and the International Monetary Fund as a condition for the rolling over of artificially inflated and impossible-to-repay debt. As that austerity has taken its toll on workers' standards of living, they have revolted in country after country. As the opening of capital markets has facilitated rapid capital mobility, resulting in repeated financial crises as capitalists have moved money into and out of local markets according to their volatile estimations of risk (due, in part, to our struggles) and of profitability (also partly determined by our struggles), workers have naturally rebelled against their real wages and standards of living being subject to the whims of capitalist investors. They have also resisted the privatization of state enterprises where that process has ruptured previous contracts and worsened their situation.

The failure to use flexible exchange rates to finesse adjustment in Europe drove policy makers—acting, as usual, in the interests of capitalists—to seek socio-economic and political stability through the formation of a monetary union. In such a union, everyone would have the same currency—the euro—and there would be no more destabilizing fluctuations among exchange rates. But doing so required the subordination not only of monetary but also of fiscal policy to central European authorities—a move that has so undermined national sovereignty as to lay the basis for both local and collective resistance. As folks have discovered how the subordination of local interests to those authorities' dictates have been used against their initiatives, they have fought back across the political spectrum. On the left, there have been debates about whether workers' interests are best served within the European Community—through collective resistance—or by leaving it to regain more direct leverage against national governments. On the right, its traditional extreme nationalism has been wielded to recruit disaffected workers, suffering from austerity, to xenophobic, neo-fascist groups. The recent massive influx of refugees from Syria and elsewhere in the Middle East has provided new weapons for recruitment: fears of 1) a further loss of income support due to a diversion of already reduced social services to refugees, 2) a further loss of jobs due to their eventual entrance into the labor market, and 3) a loss of cultural identity due to the majority

Decoding Financialization 225

of the refugees being Muslim.[67] At the same time, the existence of a common enemy—the European capitalist policy makers—has led to collective mobilization across Europe, so far mostly on the left, in support of those who have resisted the imposition of unjust policies. Widespread resistance has come close to sabotaging the Eurozone several times—including the present, when it remains an open question as to whether popular resistance in Greece and beyond will so undermine the imposition of austerity as to lead to a collapse of this long-standing effort to subordinate workers to joint capitalist policy making.

---

67 These fears are the same nativist and racist ones that have been cultivated by conservatives in the United States. Their playing on the fears of Tea Party adherents and right-wing militia members has contributed to the strengthening of neo-fascist groups and the splits in the Republican Party that played out in the 2016 electoral campaigns and contributed to the election of Donald Trump.

PART III

Potential Strategies and Tactics for Rupturing the Dialectics of Money

This is the hard part. It's easy to say, "Let's get rid of capitalism and money along with it, free ourselves from both the chains of work imposed to control us and the accompanying imposition of an oppressive measure of value. And while we're at it, let's craft new, better, and diverse ways to live." It's also easy, and an old Marxist habit, to call for revolution: "Let's all unite and fight, overthrow the bastards, and get on with building a new society!" Unfortunately, we've been struggling to accomplish such goals for a long time now, and despite localized revolutionary upheavals—both large and small— we have achieved only partial victories. We know that none of the old strategies—electoral campaigns (of social democrats), spontaneous uprising (the anarchist favorite), or professional planning by a revolutionary party elite (the Leninist formula) have succeeded in doing anything more than forcing modifications in capitalism. Of course, modifications matter. Forced changes in the composition of class forces and shifts in the balance of class power that improve our ability to craft new struggles are essential if we are ever to get rid of the chains that bind us. An argument can be made that while we have not, so far, freed ourselves from Leviathan, we have at least established a secular trend in the right direction. While historical experience suggests that no new strategy or tactics are likely to achieve quick and final success, we do know that we have found in the past, and can certainly find in the future, ways to rupture the dialectics of capitalism and improve our chances. The trick, it would seem, is to find strategies and tactics that will enable us not just to momentarily rupture those dialectics but, in the process, to approach progressively the goal of getting rid of capitalism completely. Therefore, in what follows I will not lay out a "program" of struggle, suggesting precisely what methods we should use or which battles are key to accomplishing our ultimate goal, but take up the old conundrum of "reform or revolution."

First, however, I'd like to emphasize that I think getting rid of money and markets entirely is not only a necessary condition for getting rid of capitalism but also desirable in its own right. I think that many utopians have been quite right to imagine worlds without money.[1] I reject all programs that propose to transcend capitalism but retain money and markets as supposedly efficient methods of allocating resources in a new and better society—whether they be of socialist or anarchist or libertarian inspiration. Understanding the constraints that capitalism puts on our lives clarifies what we do not want and therefore what we want to get rid of. Many of those constraints have been associated with money—in all its roles, even those we have been able momentarily to *détourne* to our advantage. Every proposal I have seen for some kind of "market socialism" would retain those constraints. It is way past time to transcend them once and for all.

Why do I think getting rid of money and markets is desirable? Because together they have been the means for replacing a rich array of meanings—that have varied over time and cultures—with one singular measure by which everything and every action is evaluated. By passing through markets, everything becomes a commodity with a "value" designated by the money price at which it is exchanged. Although economists insist that the determination of the demand side of markets is the result of endlessly varying

---

1   See, for example, some of the classical utopian literature such as Thomas Moore's *Utopia* (1516), Edward Bellamy's *Looking Backwards* (1888), and William Morris's *News from Nowhere* (1891). Then dream along with Peter Tosh's song "The Day the Dollar Die," on his album *Mystic Man* (1979), available on YouTube. Or, for those with a taste for science fiction, revisit *Star Trek* where, following Gene Roddenberry's vision, humanity has dispensed with money, and only pseudo-capitalists such as the Ferengi remain preoccupied with its accumulation. One particularly amusing episode is "The Neutral Zone" (1988), in which a cryogenically frozen financier from 1994 is revived and discovers, to his horror, that neither money nor finance still exist in human society.

"preferences," or individual judgments of the value of the goods or services they find in markets, the effect of market pricing—and the array of marketing and advertising tools that shape those preferences—is to impose the same measure of value on everything.[2] Commodities with higher prices are not only worth more in terms of money, but there is also a distinct tendency for them to be judged more desirable. Higher priced cars are "better" than lower priced ones; higher priced houses are "better" than lower priced ones. To be sure, advertising touts this or that characteristic of the commodities being offered on the market, partly because it's necessary for "product differentiation," by which firms try to convince potential customers that their product is not only different from others but more desirable, and partly because people are not stupid and do purchase commodities for their particular use-values. But one of those use-values is the price when higher is equated with better. It is not only businesses that cultivate the importance of prices as measures of value but a whole array of institutions. One that I find particularly both revealing and obnoxious is Public Television's *Antiques Roadshow*. The punch line to the evaluation of every antique discussed on the show, the line that provokes the most reaction—delight or resignation—is the final announcement of the item's likely market price.[3] (Fortunately, and amusingly, from time to time, the person whose item has just been given a stunningly high market value says, "No, thanks. This thing has far too much sentimental value in my life [or the history of my family] to sell it.")

With money the measure of everything—capital's universal equivalent—the result, inevitably, is money fetishism and the idea that having more of it is better. From being viewed as merely a means of purchase, obtaining ever more of it becomes a goal in itself. One result is the tendency to judge more highly paid

---

2 Certainly one of the most poisonous and deceptive ideas peddled by economists under the rubric of "consumer sovereignty" is the false idea that the capitalist market merely responds to our desires and produces what we need and want.

3 An even more vulgar version of the *Antiques Roadshow* was the (thankfully) short-lived NBC game show *It's Worth What?* in which teams competed to judge the "worth" of antiques in purely monetary terms. Like most other game shows, the excitement came from the anticipation and success in winning ever larger sums of money.

and wealthier individuals as "better" than lower paid ones and less wealthy ones—while measuring "wealth" in purely monetary terms. Capitalism has not only retained and utilized the patriarchal hierarchy that generally values (and pays) men more than women but has also promulgated—in literature, theater, film, and television—ranking the relative value of men and women in terms of their income, wealth, and credit rating. All too often we have internalized such carefully cultivated cultural norms and judge our own worth in precisely these ways. Such focus, of course, diverts attention from other differences, including the class roles played by individuals. It is emphasized in academia by sociologists' preference to discuss social differences in terms of income "stratification" rather than class and economists' preference to measure inequality—from individuals through firms to countries—using purely monetary measures (e.g., individual income, net worth, stock value, and Gross National Product).

As with other aspects of capitalism, this preoccupation with market value—the money price of things and the monetary worth of individuals—has been mocked and critiqued throughout its history. Just as the privileging of monetary value has been manifest in every dimension of culture, so have attacks on that privileging. After all, the preoccupation with income and wealth was already present in many of those societies in which capitalism arose, so there was already a history of criticism that has grown as capitalism has forced more and more people into its labor markets, while commodifying more and more of life, attaching money prices to more and more things and actions. Some of those critiques have been reactionary—juxtaposing the imagined virtues of various pre-capitalist systems of domination to their absence in capitalism—for example, the noblesse oblige of feudal lords who supposedly took care of those who served them as opposed to heartless capitalists who ruthlessly use and discard their workers.[4] Other critiques have highlighted the capitalist displacement, subordination, or absolute abandonment of this or that value judged worthwhile.

So imagine living without money, markets, or prices. Liberating our lives from them would free us from considerable

---

4   This myth was integral to the story lines of *Downton Abbey*, as time and again the kindhearted Crawleys looked out for those of their servants who got into trouble.

unpleasantness and eliminate a great many ways in which our time and energy are wasted. No more being defined by our wage (or lack of it) or its size. Instead we can define ourselves and be defined by others according to our abilities, to how we choose to utilize them, and by the nature of our relationships. No more having our relationships with others (and with the rest of nature) mediated by money. Instead we can elaborate more direct and meaningful forms of interaction, of myriad sorts. No more those with a lot of money having the power to impose work on those with less. Instead we can decide collectively what needs to be done, who will do it, and how to do it. No more endless working for profit. Instead we can organize to actually meet our needs and satisfy our desires. No more money, no more commodities, no more cash, no more credit cards, no more wallets, no more checks, no more checkbooks to balance, no more stocks, no more bonds, no more brokers, no more derivatives, no more finance, no more banks, no more bankers, no more financialization, no more speculation, no more speculators, no more financial crisis, no more casinos, no more gambling, no more taxes, and no more crime and imprisonment associated with money.

In one of his earliest, and too long neglected, writings, Friedrich Engels waxed eloquent on the vast amount of human time and energy wasted within capitalism by myriad social roles tied to its particular characteristics.[5] Some of his illustrations related to roles associated with money, especially the array of "middlemen" involved in the financing, speculating, and profiting from manufacturing and trade, but he also pointed to other wastes of time and energy involved in the huge judiciary and police forces required to protect capitalist property relationships, standing armies required to keep order and impose capitalist relationships abroad, and, of course, widespread unemployment where those in dire need of income are denied jobs by the dynamics of the economy. Transcending

---

5   Those neglected writings are versions of speeches Engels gave in Elberfeld, Germany, in 1845. See "Speeches in Elberfeld, February 8, 1845," in Marx and Engels, *Collected Works*, vol. 4, 243–51. In those speeches, he framed his argument by juxtaposing the situation within capitalism with that possible within a hypothetical communist society. A similar perspective framed Baran and Sweezy's critique of capitalist irrationality.

capitalism, its property relations, and the endless war of all against all, he argued, could dramatically reduce the amount and kinds of work required by society. Moreover, the freeing of people from all those wasteful activities would make them available to share in whatever labor is still required to meet people's needs and desires—thus reducing the amount of work per individual. In this period of financialization, the reductions in work possible through the progressive elimination of money—for example, the end of brokerage, banking, speculating, and the whole array of jobs associated directly and indirectly with such activities—are obviously vast.

There is a lovely passage in the first chapter of the *Grundrisse*, the chapter on money, where Marx makes clear that transcending money requires transcending capitalism. He is in the midst of critiquing Proudhon's followers—"Darimon and consorts"—who kept proposing ways to reform the money system. Had they addressed the problem of "the periodic depreciation of money," he argued, "the problem would have reduced itself to: how to overcome the rise and fall of prices. The way to do this: abolish prices. And how? By doing away with exchange value. But this problem arises: exchange value corresponds to the bourgeois organization of society. Hence one last problem: to revolutionize bourgeois society economically."[6]

True then, true now. Getting rid of money—and with it exchange value and markets—requires getting rid of capitalism. Therefore, in order for efforts to achieve the former to be successful, they must contribute to the latter. Along the way, progressively getting rid of both will facilitate our efforts to create the future in the present, crafting and experimenting with alternative and more appealing kinds of social relationships.

This idea of getting rid of money was not new with Marx, but he demonstrated more clearly than any before him how a fully developed money system was an inextricable part of capitalism. Indeed, many who would "revolutionize" (i.e., abolish) capitalism have conceived of its replacement by a society in which the things and services people need would be produced and distributed directly without the mediation of money and markets. Some years back Maximilien Rubel and John Crump edited a collection of historical essays about such visions that they grouped under the

6   Marx, *Grundrisse*, 134.

rubric of "non-market socialism."[7] The abolition of money is only one of many ideas touched upon in those essays, but they situate that idea among others in useful ways. Moreover, these surveys of the ideas and platforms of individuals and groups in the nineteenth and twentieth centuries are detailed and well footnoted. As such, they provide a useful point of departure for anyone interested in exploring the history of the intellectual battle against money within the context of the struggle against capitalism.

More recently, the objective of freeing society from the bonds of money has been placed center stage in another collection of essays—*Life without Money* (2011)—designed to contribute to the "building of fair and sustainable economies."[8] The editors of that collection, Anitra Nelson and Frans Timmerman, explicitly associate their ideas with Rubel and Crump's "non-market socialism" and anchor their critique of money in Marx's analysis. In a similar manner, Andreas Exner has recently surveyed support for "demonetization" while critiquing ideas supporting "market socialism" or the effort to create "non-capitalist market economies" through such means as local currencies. He too roots his critique in a reading of Marx that focuses on the inextricable link between money and capitalism.[9]

Marx's logic in the above quotation from the *Grundrisse*—how getting rid of prices requires getting rid of exchange value (money), which requires getting rid of capitalism—sweeps forward swiftly to the penultimate goal, but, as with Engels's exhortations at Elberfeld, there is no discussion of how such a trajectory, however logical, might be constructed. As a result, it could be dismissed as a young revolutionary's rhetorical *pronunciamento*, disparaging reforms and simply constituting a call to arms and immediate revolution. It was not, however, his final word on the subject.

In the course of his political work, that included the Communist League (1847–52), his and Engels's participation in the

---

7   Maximilien Rubel and John Crump, eds., *Non-Market Socialism in the Nineteenth and Twentieth Centuries* (New York: St. Martin's Press, 1987).

8   Anitra Nelson and Frans Timmerman, eds., *Life without Money: Building Fair and Sustainable Economies* (London: Pluto Press, 2011).

9   Andreas Exner, "Degrowth and Demonetization: On the Limits of a Non-Capitalist Market Economy," *Capitalism Nature Socialism* 25, no. 3 (2014), 9–27.

German Revolution of 1848, and later the International Working-men's Association, or First International (1864–76), the question of what to do next was frequently front and center. Because the upheavals throughout Europe in 1848 had followed a serious economic downturn in 1847, Marx was always hopeful that the next major economic crisis would bring a new round of revolutionary insurrection.[10] But even if that were to occur, the question still remained of what to do today and to what degree today's choices would prepare the next rising to be more successful. Organizing—in the Communist League and in the First International—was part of his answer. But organizing for what kinds of demands in the interim?

---

10   Indeed, hopes of a forthcoming upheaval, spurred by the economic crisis of 1857, motivated the urgency with which he pulled together his work in the *Grundrisse* notebooks. As it turned out, those hopes were disappointed.

REFORMS AND REVOLUTION

The disparagement of reform, and its juxtaposition to revolution, has a long history in the Marxist tradition. After Marx's death in 1883, the years of the Second International (1898–1914) saw sustained debate between social democratic Marxists who pursued reforms through electoral politics and self-styled revolutionary Marxists who thought armed revolt would be necessary. *Reform or Revolution* (1899) by Rosa Luxemburg (1871–1919), which attacked social democratic reformism in both its trade-unionist and parliamentary guises, is probably the most incisive classic text of the debates.[1] When the German Social Democratic Party voted to support war in 1914—a war most working-class members of the Second International had adamantly opposed—the dangers of opportunism inherent in parliamentary politics was graphically illustrated. From that point on, the rejection of reformism has been prevalent in Marxist circles hoping or organizing for revolution.

Marx himself supported many reforms. His problem with Proudhon and his followers—and others—was not that they were merely reformers but that he judged that their proposed reforms, even if enacted, would not get the workers of his time any closer to their greater goals. Whether he was correct in that judgment, I'll leave to others to judge. But his willingness to support reforms that *do* get us closer to where we want to go—seems sound to me.

We can see that willingness in Marx's own political practice. Examples of reforms that he supported were less work, safer work, higher wages, and greater legal rights. Volume 1 of *Capital* contains ample evidence of his support for the first two "reformist" goals. His argument against Weston made his support for wage struggles quite clear.[2] His and Engels's support of Chartism—the fight for a workers' bill of rights and universal suffrage—was equally clear.[3] None of these objectives would end capitalism, but mak-

---

1   Rosa Luxemburg, *Reform and Revolution and Other Writings* (Mineola, N.Y.: Dover Publications, 2006).

2   Karl Marx, "Value, Price and Profit," speech to the First International Working Men's Association, June 1865, in Marx and Engels, *Collected Works*, vol. 20, 101–49.

3   Karl Marx, "The Chartist Movement," *New York Tribune*, August 25, 1852,

ing gains in each of these battles would strengthen workers, rupture existing forms of capitalist command and exploitation, and bring about material transformations in the organization of class relationships. It was the success of workers' struggles in forcing down the length of the working day, he argued in chapter 15 of volume 1, that drove capitalists to invest more heavily in machinery, reducing the amount of work required to produce each unit, and at least potentially reducing the amount of work required to meet workers' needs. Success in increasing wages could have the same effect. Struggles to either raise wages or limit capitalist efforts to reduce them could not only preserve the material grounds of workers' strength but also provide experience in self-organization and militant action that would facilitate future struggles.

At the same time, Marx's analysis of this technological consequence of workers' success in achieving their reformist demands for shorter working days and higher wages demonstrated his understanding of the difficulties of realizing all the potential benefits. First, his analysis of relative surplus value revealed how increased productivity resulted in more surplus value and thus more investment and more work. Second, he saw how capitalists' choices of new productivity-raising technology and the manner of implementation were used to get workers to work more intensely in their shorter hours—thus undermining their efforts to work less.[4] As a result, he demonstrated how these capitalist methods undermined the struggle for less work and thwarted long-standing dreams and desires to free humans from undesirable labor.

> "If," dreamed Aristotle, the greatest thinker of antiquity, "if every tool, when summoned, or even by intelligent anticipation, could do the work that befits it, just as the creations of Daedalus moved of themselves, or the tripods of Hephaestus went of their own accord to their sacred work, if the weavers' shuttles were to weave of

---

republished in the Chartist *People's Paper*, October 9, 1852, in Marx and Engels, *Collected Works*, vol. 11, 333–41.

4   Capitalists had already learned how the introduction of machinery could be used to extend the working day, but once that strategy was defeated they still used new production methods to intensify the rhythm of work—by increasing the speed of their machines and making workers work on more machines.

themselves, then there would be no need either of apprentices for the master craftsmen, or of slaves for the lords." And Antipater, a Greek poet of the time of Cicero, hailed the water-wheel for grinding corn, that most basic form of all productive machinery, as the liberator of female slaves and the restorer of the golden age.[5]

What Aristotle and Antipater dreamed, workers of Marx's time were struggling to bring about. That capitalists found and continue to seek methods to undermine such reformist struggles did not deter Marx from supporting them.

While avoiding a lengthy examination of Marx's position on each reformist issue that he addressed, I do want to dwell briefly on one of his most famous interventions, one that set the stage for much of the debate that followed. That intervention was his response to the Gotha Program, the party platform adopted by the United Workers' Party of Germany at its initial congress in 1875. The program was drawn up with no input from Marx or Engels; their response was severely critical. The most systematic presentation of their critique was penned by Marx that same year and sent off to allies; it consisted of a series of excerpts from the program, with each followed by objections to the ideas set forth and sometimes alternative formulations.[6] The part I want to focus on here are a few paragraphs in the first section, in which Marx discussed the emergence of communist society out of capitalism. Calling for the transcendence of capitalism, as he repeatedly did, necessarily prompted a series of questions: what aspects of society are to be abolished, what will replace them, and through what processes shall their replacement proceed? Because he rejected utopian projects of designing and offering blueprints for a post-capitalist society, his answers to those questions tended to be quite general and based on his analysis of the general tendencies manifested in workers' struggles. Indeed, from as early as their joint unpublished work *The German Ideology* (1845–46), he and Engels had argued: "Communism is for us not a *state of affairs* which is to

---

5   Marx, *Capital*, vol. 1, 532.

6   *The Critique of the Gotha Program*, as it was eventually published by Engels in 1891, consisted of Marx's scathing commentary on the program, a letter he wrote accompanying his commentary, and a letter by Engels, written at the time, providing some of the political background to both the program and their criticisms of it.

be established, an *ideal* to which reality [will] have to adjust itself. We call communism the *real* movement which abolishes the present state of things."[7]

He was not loath, however, to critique proposals set forth by others, including the authors of the Gotha Program. Although many of the specific proposals in the Gotha Program and many of his critiques are long since moot, Marx did enunciate elements of a general vision of communism as "the real movement" that bear on the issue of abolishing money.

As communism emerges, he wrote, it is "still stamped with the birthmarks of the old society." Among those birthmarks are the ideas of equal exchange and that each should receive from society "exactly what he gives" to it in the form of labor.[8] Therefore, the individual producer "receives a certificate from society that he has furnished such-and-such an amount of labor (after deducting his labor for the common funds); and with this certificate, he draws from the social stock of means of consumption as much as the same amount of labor cost."

This was the kind of proposal, put forward by the Proudhonists, that Marx had critiqued years before in the *Grundrisse*. Here it is discussed as a possible transitional choice. Against such a mode of distribution, Marx evokes a "higher phase of communist society," when certain criteria have been met, in which society will be able to "inscribe on its banners" the old communist dictum: "From each according to his ability, to each according to his needs!"

The reason these passages are historically important is because they have been interpreted by many Marxists as amounting to a sketch of the one proper path to full-fledged communism.

Marx goes on, in the fourth section of his commentary, to state the following: "Between capitalist and communist society there lies the period of the revolutionary transformation of the one into the other. Corresponding to this is also a political transition period, in

---

7   Marx and Engels, *Collected Works*, vol. 5, 49.

8   Despite the way it hides exploitation, it is worth noting that the standard microeconomic assertion that wages are equal to the marginal value product of labor amounts to much the same thing. The only exploitation recognized by that theory is the narrow one of "Joan Robinson exploitation"—in which, due to imperfect competition (which she analyzed), wages are less than the value product of labor.

which the state can be nothing but *the revolutionary dictatorship of the proletariat*."

In the accompanying discussion, Marx raises the question, but does not answer it, as to "what social functions will remain in existence [in communist society] that are analogous to present state functions?"

Reading this text, I find four things. First is a general prophesy that capitalism—a mode of social organization that itself took centuries to transform, to some degree, virtually every nook and cranny of society—will not be done away with all at once.

Second, a proper theoretical understanding of the characteristics of capitalism is essential to figuring out how to progressively achieve a new transformation. Unfortunately, the Bolsheviks' (and subsequent Marxist-Leninists') narrow understanding of capitalism in terms of *private* property and profit meant that the only transformation they were able to achieve was the creation of a form of *state* capitalism based on continuing the endless imposition of work, exploitation, and the political repression of resisting peasants and workers to prevent *them* from dictating policy.[9]

Third, orthodox Leninists have framed their interpretation of the "dictatorship of the proletariat" only in terms of state forms and quickly reduced the concept to the dictatorship of their party—a situation that obtained in the Soviet Union until Communist Party rule was ended in 1991.[10] If we read Marx's phrase "the

---

9 Despite its willingness to use police state repression, the power of the Communist Party of the USSR can be, and often has been, overstated. Resistance was widespread and constant, overt when possible, covert when necessary. As a result, many changes in official policy can be traced to workers' demands, made felt through their struggles. Violent repression was not the regime's only response—especially in the post-Stalin era, in which efforts to respond positively to workers' demands came to resemble a kind of Soviet Keynesianism.

10 The evolution of party doctrine and policies in the USSR was internally contested, complex, and not easily summarized. However detached the party was from any ability of workers and peasants to control it—as an actual instrument of their rule—nevertheless, a whole series of debates unfolded within it. Those debates even included a short-lived consideration of the possibility of eliminating money and exchange. Some aspects of these debates are briefly summarized by Anitra Nelson in *Life without Money*, 33–37, drawing mostly on E. H. Carr's *The Bolshevik*

dictatorship of the proletariat" as meaning the actual ability of the proletariat to dictate (i.e., having the power to determine elements of transformation and new alternatives), we can see how that ability has been exercised in many different ways, down through the years. We have often successfully struggled to transform aspects of the capitalist world to better meet our needs and desires. We have also, repeatedly, crafted more appealing alternatives. That we have not succeeded in transforming all, or even most, aspects of capitalism and that we have sometimes been unable to prevent our alternatives being either crushed or co-opted, should neither blind us to our successes nor prevent us from building on them to further transform "the present state of things."

Fourth, Marx did not specify those "social functions" that will remain that are "analogous to present state functions." He also continued to refuse to specify other aspects of that "communist society" that communism—defined as "the *real* movement which abolishes the present state of things"—will create and elaborate.

In its response to the financial crisis of 2007–2008, the Midnight Notes Collective and friends, drawing on the work of Massimo de Angelis and Chris Carlsson, usefully reformulated the dichotomization of struggles as either reformist or revolutionary into a juxtaposition of being either *inside* capitalism (i.e., consistent with its dynamic) or *outside* of it (i.e., *autonomous*, constituting real alternatives).[11] They recognized explicitly how drawing such a distinction can often be difficult, because inside struggles can lay the basis for autonomous ones, and struggles to build autonomous alternatives can be co-opted and neutralized. But the category "autonomous" doesn't just replace "revolutionary," it evokes the only content of struggles that make them revolutionary in the sense of not just combating the evils of capitalism but of creating alternatives. Thus,

---

Revolution 1917–23, vol. 2 (London: Penguin, 1966). Nelson also recounts, as briefly, similar debates within the Cuban Communist Party after the revolution in that country, drawing mostly on Che Guevara's writings.

11 De Angelis, *The Beginning of History*; Chris Carlsson, *Nowtopia: How Pirate Programmers, Outlaw Bicyclists, and Vacant-Lot Gardeners Are Inventing the Future Today!* (Oakland: AK Press, 2008).

autonomous struggles strive to create social spaces and relations
that are as independent of and opposed to capitalist social relations as possible. They may directly confront or seek to take over
and reorganize capitalist institutions (a factory, for example) or
create new spaces outside those institutions (e.g., urban gardening or a housing cooperative) or access resources that should
be common. They foster collective, non-commodified relations,
processes, and products that function to some real degree outside of capitalist relations and give power to the working class in
its efforts to create alternatives to capital.[12]

The evocation of "non-commodified relations, processes, and
products" returns us to the project of abolishing money. If Marx's
perception was correct, and I think our historical experience since
his time has confirmed it, we are no more likely to be able to abolish money all at once than we are to abolish capitalism as a whole.
If so, then it seems to me, the most practical and productive way to
proceed is to examine the steps that we have taken in the past, and
that we might take in the future, to figure out how to advance progressively toward both objectives. Those steps include both those
that restrict the sphere of money and exchange—while expanding
spheres free of it—and those that involve the diversion of money
for our own purposes, including funding programs designed to reduce or eliminate the need for it. As we strive to marginalize and
ultimately squeeze money, exchange, markets, and capitalism entirely out of our lives, both kinds of steps constitute a subversion of
capital's own use of money.

---

12 Midnight Notes Collective, *Promissory Notes*, 13. Characterizing struggles as
"autonomous" carries many of the same connotations as those evoked by concepts
of "self-valorizing" or "constituent" struggles.

OUR USE OF MONEY

While struggling to restrict and ultimately eliminate capital's use of money against us, it continues to play all of the roles Marx analyzed in chapter 3 of volume 1 of *Capital*: measure of value, standard of price, medium of circulation, and means of payment. More generally, it remains a prime universal mediator of the antagonistic social relationships we seek to abolish and escape. Therefore, we need to explore how, as long as this situation encumbers us, we can best use money against capital and for our own purposes.

Money as Measure of Value?

As discussed in part 1, money embodies "value" to capital as a means to put us to work. Inversely, money provides us with means to refuse that work. Access to sources of money gives us the power to resist being exploited at work—with all the alienation it involves—by buying time away from it (e.g., weekends and vacations that are more than mere recuperation), by buying time to struggle (e.g., strikes and political organizing), or by buying time to invent alternatives (e.g., new modes of collective decision-making and new kinds of decisions). Such power is a good reason for both those of us with wages and those of us without to fight for more money. However much we may properly denounce money as one "root of all evil," success in raising wages and salaries and success in obtaining money income for the unwaged increases the power to refuse the work capital seeks to impose. It buys us moments of that "disposable time" that Marx imagined could replace labor— open-ended time for the invention of new values. Capital knows this, and it is one basic reason why it seeks to restrict our access to money.[1] In short, money has value for us, in this sense, in a way diametrically opposed to the value it has for capital. It can be a weapon for us to wield in order to obtain a limited freedom from capitalist domination via work. The more we have, the more powerful that weapon.

---

1   As Pink Floyd sing in "Money" on *The Dark Side of the Moon* (1972), "Money, so they say / is the root of all evil today. / But if you ask for a raise, it's no surprise / that they're giving none away."

At the same time, because essential elements of capitalist ideology are reverence for money and a tendency to value highly those who seek and obtain a lot of it—higher income, higher status—the denunciation of such ideological buttresses to money as a measure of the value of individuals has long been an element of anti-capitalist efforts. The recurrent cartoon caricature of Mr. Moneybags, poems, songs, novels, and art have all provided critiques of the evils of such capitalist ideology and its embrace.[2] Valuing money for the power it gives to refuse work and denouncing the power it conveys to impose work or measure the value of individuals are complementary positions.

Money as Standard of Price and Medium of Circulation

The "price" of things, capital insists, is the amount of money one must give up to obtain them. As I have pointed out, capital's commentary stops there—and its enforcers (police and the judiciary) lurk to make sure we don't obtain them through other means (e.g., direct appropriation—taking stuff on the job, shoplifting in retail outlets, and so on).[3] But while capital's commentary is limited to surface appearances, we know not only from Marx but from experience that the real "price" of goods is the labor we must expend to obtain the money necessary to buy them. Labor may have value for capital as a means of social control, but for us, when we work

---

2   Such denunciation in all its various forms predates capitalism and has invariably been an element of critique and resistance in every historical social system whose rulers and apologists have valorized money and its accumulation. Reflections of this can be found in virtually every important, ancient religious text. If you doubt this, take to the Internet where today you can search such documents as the Quran and the Old and New Testaments online. While situations have obviously differed from hierarchical social system to hierarchical social system, the common element of critique of the love of and greed for money and wealth is recurrent and—as liberation theologians and other progressive clergy have often pointed out—has continuing relevance to our contemporary struggles.

3   Business is well aware that the prices it puts on things are purely theoretical until it actually succeeds in obtaining money in exchange (and the amount may or may not be identical to the "sticker price"). The avoidance of direct appropriation requires whole industries of surveillance to deter or identify those who would bypass prices and take what they need.

for wages or salaries or go through the annoying steps necessary to obtain welfare payments or unemployment compensation, the value of money is measured by the use-values of the commodities we are able to purchase. Because capital has been so thorough in its enclosure of land, tools, and information, money is all too often our only means to obtain all those things (available as commodities) that we can't grow or raise or make for ourselves. Because there are a great many such things (and services), obtaining and having money haunts the lives of many.

The most obvious ways in which we have been able to obtain money and the powers it embodies have been via our wages and salaries, and, in recent times, monetary transfers exacted from the government (e.g., welfare, unemployment compensation, family allocations, and social security).[4] We use money immediately accessible to us to purchase the things and services we need and desire. Such purchases often strengthen our ability to struggle—although they do not always do this, given capitalist manipulation of our desires through such means as advertising and the cultural cultivation of the obsession with "more" and "the latest" stuff. Similarly, the long-standing demand for "full employment" is rarely a demand for work; it is rather a demand for wages—to make life easier, despite the sacrifice involved in working for some employer.

The demand for higher wages (including benefits and pensions) amounts to a demand to divert money from capitalist profit to our uses. In Marx's jargon, value is shifted from surplus value (S) to variable capital (V), which, *ceteris paribus*, not only reduces the rate of exploitation (S/V) and rate of profit [$S/(C+V)$] but also facilitates the diversion of money from being expended as V—from financing the reproduction of labor power (LP^*)—to struggle and, through access to disposable time, to the self-valorizing improvement of our lives (i.e., to the very negation of its role as the embodiment of value). The same can be true for other sources of money

---

4   In the best of circumstances, unfortunately rare, the government gets the tax revenue that it transfers to workers from taxes on capitalists. More commonly, the source is other workers—a situation that lends itself to the conservative ideological ploy of playing taxpayers against transfer recipients by appealing to the selfishness of the former and denouncing the lazy greed of the latter.

246 Rupturing the Dialectic

income—for example, unemployment insurance, Supplemental Security Income, and so on.

Although for the most part we spend our income for goods and services that benefit us directly, there are two ways in which we employ our money for indirect benefits. First, if we have enough money to spare, we often donate to "good causes"—sometimes organized by nongovernmental organizations (NGOs), sometimes by governmental ones (e.g., UNICEF). In a few cases, they may benefit us or people we know directly, but for the most part we donate to support activities that we feel improve some aspect of the world we live in and thus our own lives. Such causes are those of ecological protection, human or animal rights, alternative media, medical research, public libraries, disaster relief, campaigns against gender and racial discrimination, and so on.

Second, we pay taxes. Some only pay taxes because they have to, but probably most of us pay taxes because we feel they fund vital public services that are in our interest, in that of society as a whole, and sometimes of our world as a whole. They constitute— within capitalism and its institutions of the state and of money— part of our contribution to the management of human affairs and of human relationships with the rest of nature. We pay despite an awareness that too much of our taxes are channeled into programs of which we do *not* approve (such as military aggression and the research and development that supports it, systems of repressive policing, injustice and punishment, and so on) and constitute vast subsidies to capitalists, facilitating their efforts to control and exploit us.[5]

On this terrain of what economists call "fiscal policy," there are two kinds of battles: over who pays how much taxes and how those tax monies are spent. As has been abundantly demonstrated over the last thirty years or so, repeated neoliberal "tax cuts"—supposedly undertaken to benefit everyone by stimulating investment and growth—have instead been structured to primarily benefit capital and its functionaries at the expense of working people who have

---

5   A few, on the left and on the right, refuse to pay taxes at all in protest against those part of taxes that are expended on programs to which they are opposed. But, for the most part, such protests are not directed against taxes as such but against their specific uses.

accordingly paid an ever larger share of taxes. This has been one cause of the growing inequality in income and wealth of those years. As a result, there have been growing demands for increasing taxes on corporations and on those wealthy, high-income individuals who have profited from previous cuts.

Battles over the expenditure of tax monies—increasingly, because of biased tax cuts, drawn from our wages and salaries (and thus reducing variable capital)—have involved demands for the funding of government policies and programs that help us, and the defunding of those subsidizing capital. Some helpful expenditures may benefit us directly. Unemployment compensation and welfare put tax money back into our hands and compensate us for the work of looking for jobs and for rearing children.[6] Pensions, disability, and social security compensate us for work we have already performed in the past. All such programs effectively increase variable capital, while facilitating its subversion.[7]

Beyond such government programs that put money directly into our hands are all those that benefit us indirectly. Such programs include those created for the continued elaboration of an extensive system of public health services. These include local public hospitals and clinics, the provision of clean water and sewage treatment, and the organization of federal programs such as the Centers for Disease Control and Prevention (CDC), the Food and Drug Administration (FDA), the Occupational Safety and Health Administration (OSHA), and the Environmental Protection Agency (EPA). We have supported such programs because of their obvious benefits. At the same time, close examination has long since revealed the ambiguity of such benefits in class terms. While we

---

6   In the United States, Aid to Families with Dependent Children (1935–96) and Temporary Assistance for Needy Families (1997–) have long been the major component of welfare expenditures.

7   The degree to which these things are true depends on how they have been organized and what becomes of them. To some degree, pensions and social security merely restore money previously deducted from our paychecks. But pensions—assuming they haven't been defaulted on by unscrupulous companies—usually also contain monies contributed by our past employers. Disability payments may result from insurance financed to varying degrees by ourselves, our employers, or by the government (e.g., SSI and social security).

have benefited from public health programs, so too, at times, has capital. Some programs are largely the result of our struggles (e.g., OSHA); others are primarily the result of the efforts by capitalists to improve our productivity and their profits (e.g., disease control).[8] On the other hand, recent neoliberal cutbacks of state expenditures on health services or water supplies amount to unambiguous reductions in variable capital and attacks on our health—as in the continuing efforts to defund women's health services and the disastrous "cost-saving" changes in the water supply of Flint, Michigan, that has poisoned the people of that city, increasing the medical and human costs to thousands of lives for years to come. Among those costs are the increased work involved in longer travel times to sources of health services, in coping with inadequate water supplies and in the present and future care for those poisoned.

Critics of virtually all government regulatory agencies—including the CDC, the FDA, OSHA and the EPA—have pointed out how they have all too regularly failed to adequately restrict capitalist activities that undermine our well-being. Too many epidemiological problems have been ignored by the CDC because of political pressure (e.g., the unregulated proliferation of guns). The FDA has allowed too many drugs onto the market with inadequate testing. Similarly, too many inadequately tested chemicals have been allowed in farming, in the processing of food, and in the production of far too many other kinds of products. The battles against capitalist firms genetically engineering and releasing organisms whose impact on humans and the rest of the ecology remain unstudied are well known. So too are current attempts to ban pesticides toxic not only to unwanted parasites but to humans and bees—whose role in pollination is essential to our current and future food supply. Even leaving aside the efforts of conservative governments to defund regulatory efforts (e.g., the Reagan administration's efforts to cripple the EPA), chronic inadequate funding—at the behest of

8 I have discussed self-interested capitalist support, or the withdrawal of support, for disease control elsewhere. See Cleaver, "Malaria, the Politics of Public Health, and the International Crisis." Also see Herbert K. Abrams, "A Short History of Occupational Health," *Journal of Public Health Policy* 22, no. 1 (2001), 34–80; Peter Linebaugh, *Lizard Talk: Or, Ten Plagues and Another: A Historical Reprise in Celebration of the Anniversary of Boston ACT UP* (Midnight Notes, 1989).

corporations opposed to any limits on their activities—has dramatically limited the extent of enforcement, even when our pressure has forced the creation of regulations.

Limitations and attacks of this sort have made it easy for some to ignore the restrictions we have won and to dismiss such agencies and programs as being more in service to the industries they are supposed to regulate than constraints on their activities.[9] Yet those of us who have fought and continue to fight to overcome those limitations and tighten the constraints have made these confrontations between capitalist profit-making and our welfare terrains of class struggle essential to the well-being of millions and ultimately of our planetary ecology. These battles around our health unfold on only one terrain of many in the struggle over "fiscal policy."

Money as Means of Payment

As discussed in part 2, when we have enough money income—and enough wealth, valued in money terms—we can also obtain money via credit. I have already discussed the contradictory nature of credit. It enables us to obtain money that we can use in all of the ways just mentioned. But it can also be a vehicle of capitalist exploitation and control. Whether we obtain and employ credit for our own individual or family purposes, the system of credit constitutes a macro terrain of both vulnerability and opportunity. This becomes obvious when we understand the institutions capital has put in place at both the national and international level for the manipulation of credit and debt against us.

Turning from fiscal policy to monetary policy moves us onto a murkier terrain of class struggle. "Monetary policy" normally means the manipulation by central banks of the overall supply of

---

9   One of the useful things advocacy groups often do is to regularly inform their supporters not only of battles in progress but of successes and failures. They often constitute, therefore, invaluable sources of information on how we are doing on various fronts of the class war. With the rise of the Internet, the petition has become a form of struggle that makes it easy for thousands, even millions, to participate in efforts to achieve desirable changes or block undesirable ones. Those who organize such petitions—as one part of struggles that also, often, include direct action—commonly report the results of their efforts to signatories. Done well, such reporting facilitates the discovery of both the usefulness and the limitations of that form of intervention.

money through various means. In the case of the United States, those means include changing the cost of borrowing from the Federal Reserve System to meet legal requirements on monetary reserves, changes in those reserve requirements, and the buying and selling of government securities (debt)—for example, treasury bills issued and sold to raise cash to cover shortfalls in tax revenues vis-à-vis government expenditures. More recently monetary policy has also included the purchase or sale of financial assets from private financial institutions. Reducing required reserves and the cost of borrowing means banks can loan out more money, effectively expanding the money supply. Buying back government debt or purchasing private securities—called quantitative easing—have the same effect, injecting more money into the economy. Inversely, raising reserve requirements and costs of borrowing and selling securities reduces the supply of money.

Exactly how such manipulations affect the economy as a whole has long been subject to considerable debate. Keynesians—who dominated monetary policy throughout the post–World War II decades—argued that the primary result was to change interest rates and thus influence the amount of corporate investment and consumer spending. Lower rates would make more investment possibilities profitable and the acquisition of consumer durables (things bought on credit) less costly, thus stimulating demand, inducing investment, and facilitating growth in employment and output. Higher rates would dampen both kinds of expenditures. Monetarists—the predecessors of neoliberalism—and neoliberals have argued that expanding the money supply to lower interest rates risks the generation of inflation and that preventing disruptive inflation should be the primary goal of monetary policy.

According to law and prevalent mythology, central banks choose monetary policies in the interest of the general welfare. Macroeconomics 101 teaches that whether monetary policy is Keynesian (and dedicated to keeping interest rates low and stimulating investment and consumer expenditures in order to achieve something like full employment) or neoliberal and preoccupied with limiting inflation, those policies aim to "keep the economy healthy," which is supposedly in the interests of everyone. Similar mythology surrounds the behavior of supranational monetary institutions such as the International Monetary Fund, the World

Bank, and the European Central Bank. All supposedly act in the interests of the citizens of member countries. In reality, as countless studies have shown, both national central banks and such supranational institutions are fundamentally organized to preserve and promulgate capitalism and to oppose and repress—through their manipulation of money—struggles that threaten or actually rupture its expanded reproduction. "Keeping the economy healthy" means maintaining a balance of class power in favor of continued capitalist command over our lives. Nevertheless, Marx's observation that although we make history, how we do so depends on the situation in which we find ourselves, also applies to those formulating and imposing monetary policy against us.[10]

During the Keynesian era, a period in which monetarism was largely marginalized, the Federal Reserve geared monetary policy to stimulating investment. It did so not just in the general capitalist interest of facilitating expanded reproduction, but also as a result of workers' struggles in the 1930s and 1940s. Workers' organized efforts had imposed industry-wide labor unions in key industries, social security, unemployment compensation, and finally a mandate to prevent depression, high unemployment, and falling wages, which was codified legally in the Full Employment Act of 1946. Low interest rates in the postwar period gave business access to money to cope with these new constraints, while they sought to purge militant workers, suborn labor union leaders, limit the right to strike, et cetera. The expansion of consumer spending facilitated by low interest rates was, as I have argued above, entirely the result of the success of our struggles to raise wages and salaries. That success gave us access to more credit and the possibilities of obtaining things like costly consumer durables that most of us can only pay for over time.

During the 1960s, the height of the Keynesian period, two powerful waves of struggle undermined the monetary strategy of low interest rates and resulted in new attention to monetarists' insistence on using monetary policy to control inflation. First, wage and

---

10   "Men make their own history, but they do not make it as they please; they do not make it under self-selected circumstances, but under circumstances existing already, given and transmitted from the past." Marx, "The 18th Brumaire of Louis Bonaparte."

salary demands, coupled with growing resistance to work, under-mined the "productivity deals" through which labor relations had been managed and produced upward pressure on prices—to pro-tect profits. Second, when the civil rights movement, begun during the previous decade, mutated into even more militant forms (e.g., Black Power, dramatic uprisings in major US cities, widespread Chicano organizing in fields and cities, and the rebirth of the wom-en's movement), when discontent with US government's wars in Indochina gave rise to an antiwar movement, and when revulsion against consumerism gave birth to an anti-work, pro-cultural rev-olution, the government responded with expanded expenditures—on food stamps and other forms of welfare that made up "the war on poverty," on the war, on student aid, and on COINTELPRO re-pression.[11] Afraid that offsetting these expanded expenditures with increased taxes would produce even more unrest, the Fed adopted an "accommodating" monetary policy that facilitated the growth of the money supply, making accelerating inflation possible.

During the neoliberal era, in which we are currently living, the overwhelming preoccupation with limiting inflation has been the direct result of the perceived influence of rising wages (and labor costs more generally) on prices and the desire to repress such in-creases. Marginalized during most of the Keynesian period, the acceleration of inflation in the late 1960s and the failure *to use* in-flation in the early 1970s and higher unemployment in the mid-1970s to undermine average real wages, monetarism came roaring back during the decade. It became full-blown neoliberalism with the Federal Reserve's dramatic restriction of the money supply and resulting double-digit interest rates at the end of the Jimmy Carter administration and the beginning of Ronald Reagan's first

---

11   COINTELPRO is an acronym for "counterintelligence program." Operations under such programs have been carried out by virtually all intelligence agencies—including the FBI, which is legally charged with domestic police work, and those agencies legally charged to deal only with foreign threats—against left-wing, an-tiwar, and militant activist groups. Today they continue not only against a hyped threat of terrorism but also against such domestic activists as those involved in an-imal rights and environmental struggles. See Ward Churchill and Jim Vander Wall, eds., *The COINTELPRO Papers: Documents from the FBI's Secret Wars against Dis-sent in the United States* (Boston: South End Press, 1990).

term—as the former appointed the and latter retained Paul Volcker as Fed chairman and architect of this new policy. The application of such restrictive monetary policy was part of an all-out counter-attack on workers' power that included parallel efforts to impose fiscal austerity through the reduction in government expenditures on "social services," to reduce regulations that limited corporate profit making, and to reverse the cultural revolution of the 1960s.

That shift in monetary policy also facilitated processes of financialization. Remember: the first rationalizations offered in support of financial deregulation included not only the need to fight inflation but also the need to eliminate negative real interest rates that were crippling creditor profits. Thus, the rush to wipe out anti-usury laws and deregulate finance proceeded in tandem with restrictive monetary policies that dramatically raised interest rates (and the value of creditors' loan assets) and with fiscal austerity. Each of these policy changes was aimed at liberating financial institutions from restrictions previously imposed on them by workers' struggles. In extreme cases, such as the New York City fiscal crisis of the mid-1970s and the more recent Detroit case, deregulation has been complemented by direct state intervention to remove governance from elected officials in order to impose policies demanded by creditors and from which only they have profited.[12]

Given the influence of the United States on capitalism worldwide, these changes were replicated to varying degrees by monetary authorities in other countries and in the supranational institutions they had jointly created. Indeed, the International Monetary Fund became a sort of global enforcer of neoliberal policy changes on any and all member governments that turned to it for support in the midst of the global depression and international debt crisis brought on in the 1980s by sky-high American and then international interest rates. Such policies are still with us several decades later. They are at the heart of both fiscal crises and debt crises plaguing countries in both the Global North and Global South. As a result, our struggles against them continue—more obviously in places such as Greece, less obviously but no less tenaciously elsewhere. And continue they must. Without our resistance, capitalist

---

12   See Darrell Preston and Chris Christoff, "Only Wall Street Wins in Detroit Crisis Reaping $474 Million Fee," *Bloomberg*, March 13, 2013, www.bloomberg.com/.

policy makers will achieve their apparent objective: a global victory in which the vast numbers of us see our wages, salaries, and standards of living dramatically reduced and capital's ability to exploit us dramatically enhanced.

RESTRICTING THE NEED FOR MONEY

There are two obvious approaches to restricting the need for money. One involves reducing the need for things for which money is necessary. The second is making things and services available at lower prices or for free.

The first approach has been shared both by monastic traditions in some religions and by some in reaction to capitalists' constant and omnipresent efforts to get people to buy products and services and to undertake the endless work required to be able to do so. In both cases, self-imposed austerity is chosen for the freedom it creates for pursuits other than working for money, shopping, display, and status. Monks in monasteries limit both their material requirements and the work involved in meeting them in order to free themselves for spiritual development. Others, who choose small houses, limited wardrobes, bicycles instead of cars, and so on, free themselves for all sorts of activities, both individual and collective—including the struggle to further escape the imposition of work, money, markets, and all their negative consequences.

The second approach usually involves collective efforts to craft and impose policies that restrict money's various roles as universal mediator. For example, reducing the prices of commodities reduces the need for money to buy them. Replacing prices and markets with rules for distributing goods and services eliminates recipients' need for money completely. To what degree is it feasible to get rid of *some* prices, and then *some other* prices, thus excluding money from a growing number of transactions and in the process progressively constricting the role of exchange value, money, markets, and capitalism?

Post–World War II agricultural and energy policies in the United States kept food prices low and reduced the need for money to eat—especially for low-income folks who spend a higher percentage of their money on food. Making government-stockpiled food—generated by subsidies to agricultural production—available for free school lunches or famine relief wiped out the need of many students for "lunch money" and that of starving people for wages that are no longer paid in the midst of disaster.¹ Obviously, in both cases, money continued to play its roles elsewhere, in the financing of food production, storage, transportation, and processing, but its role was at least marginally restricted.

Later, in the early 1970s, such policies were reversed, and the government, through secret deals with private international grain companies and the Soviet Union, engineered an increase in food prices. The initial reaction of workers in the United States—in both the sphere of production and that of consumption—was outrage, protest, and recourse to expanded gardening to supply their own needs.² Over the last few decades, subsistence agriculture, widespread in the Global South, has also been making a comeback against industrial agribusiness in the Global North. A whole movement has developed in reaction not only to high food prices but also to repeated revelations of the outrageous practices of corporate food production (from the mistreatment of animals and the land to the inclusion of poisons in food products). In the community gardening movement, food grown is distributed among the gardeners and their neighbors (and sometimes schools), often with no setting of prices and no exchange of money.³

When we look back, it is not hard to find battles we have won to restrict both the sphere of money and exchange value and the capitalist use of money against us. Restricting the sphere of money and exchange has occurred in each situation in which the role or influence of capitalist market forces on production,

---

1   Despite such useful results, the supplying of free grain to starving people in the Global South was mostly motivated by foreign policy goals—such as opening countries to US corporate investment. See "U.S. Grain Arsenal," *NACLA's Latin America and Empire Report*, October 1975. An opposite and very capitalist mode of famine relief is the distribution of money to those who can't afford to buy food. During the widespread intense famine in the Sahel in Africa in the early 1970s, such "relief" was supplied in the form of hard cash, carried into famine areas in suitcases. Such an approach, of course, rewards those who have monopolized available food and jacked up prices to extortionate levels.

2   See James Trager, *Amber Waves of Grain* (New York: Arthur Fields, 1973).

3   Patricia Hynes, *A Patch of Eden: America's Inner-City Gardeners* (White River, Vt.: Chelsea Green, 1996). See also chapter 5 ("Vacant-Lot Gardeners") in Chris Carlsson, *Nowtopia*.

distribution, or reproduction have been reduced and spheres of activity of collective importance created. Such spheres we might call "new commons"—as differentiated from more traditional, long-standing commons. Leaving aside earlier history, and limiting ourselves to the twentieth and twenty-first centuries in the United States, we can see such reductions in policies that have either withheld or removed resources and activities from the realm of private capitalist exploitation. Every such removal, even when supported by some capitalists, has been contested by other capitalists who have often sought to reverse such policies in order to acquire new means of exploitation.

One such policy has been the preservation of huge tracts of land from capitalist investment through the creation of state and national parks. That preservation emerged from a continuing struggle over some capitalists' efforts to turn every possible aspect of nature into "resources" (exploiting workers extracting those resources as quickly as profitable), a struggle between pro-capitalist conservationists who wanted to manage such extraction to maximize its possibilities over the long term and those who have sought to preserve the wild forever as a part of a national commons. President Theodore Roosevelt is generally considered to have led the conservation movement in the twentieth century by creating 150 national forests and establishing the US Forest Service to regulate the private extraction of timber. He also institutionalized a vast expansion of the commons by creating national parks and national monuments— both of which preserved land and its contents indefinitely.

Before and since, the struggle over such commons has gone on, including both remote areas of wilderness and urban spaces (e.g., city parks). On the one side, there is capitalist pressure to exploit; on the other, battles rage to preserve or expand land available for our common use. Battles have erupted repeatedly over capitalist plans to undertake profit-making ventures that threaten public lands. Threats to national parks constitute one set of examples—such as current efforts to overturn a 2012 federal moratorium on mining in the Grand Canyon watershed. That moratorium, achieved by a coalition of Native Americans, conservationists, and environmental activists, is under attack by corporations and their friends in the government of Arizona, who want to mine uranium in the area—a process that dumps radioactive wastes into the environment.

Recurrent efforts by ranchers and right-wing extremists to achieve the privatization of pieces of our commons constitute another set of examples, as in the recent armed seizure of the Malheur National Wildlife Refuge in Oregon. Because resistance to such pressure and proactive attempts to enlarge such commons are generally organized by environmentalist NGOs, such efforts are not often considered forms of working-class struggle. But if we recognize how most of us struggle not only against our exploitation and alienation but to create better worlds, then such efforts can be understood as one dimension of those positive struggles. Expanding the commons today not only increasingly restricts capitalist exploitation, but also makes progress in accomplishing the vast task of transforming every aspect of capitalist society into new kinds of relationships among humans and between humans and the rest of nature.

A second policy—subject to similar class conflicts—has entailed the creation and preservation of public school systems in every state. This huge endeavor, free from *direct* capitalist investment and exploitation, burgeoned in the Progressive era early in the twentieth century. It was a response to workers' successful demands that their children be freed from waged labor (via passage of laws restricting their direct exploitation in production). To maintain its control over this sizeable part of the population, capital corralled those freed children in schools structured to condition them into being able and willing to submit to the wills of future employers. Thus, as a result of often conflicting demands and efforts, public school systems have become terrains of endless struggle, in which conflicts over the roles of money have been prominent.[4]

---

4   Money was never completely absent in pre-capitalist scenarios of education. In ancient times, families paid some fee for their offspring to study with teachers, such as Socrates or Confucius, although money was not the only way of paying such a fee. According to Confucius's words, recorded on the bamboo strips that make up the *Analects*, he "never failed to instruct students who, using their own resources, could only afford a gift of dried meat." Roger T. Ames and Henry Rosemont Jr., *The Analects of Confucius: A Philosophical Translation*, book 7, (New York: Ballantine Books, 1998), 112. In more recent centuries, governesses and tutors were long hired by well-to-do families to prepare their offspring to take their places in the ruling class. The children of crafters were sometimes paid at least some wages while they learned their trade as apprentices.

The success of working-class families in freeing their children from waged labor and demanding free access to public education dramatically limited the opportunities for private investment and private profit making in the sphere of education. A few capitalists responded by building private schools for profit. More generally, capitalists used their influence on government to impose on public education huge factory-like schools, built at high cost, with legions of waged staff and instructors to manage classrooms and impose authoritarian discipline. While Marx's "schoolmasters" have not escaped the wage—and many have organized like other workers to fight to raise it—millions have avoided working directly "to increase the money of the entrepreneur who owns the knowledge-mongering institution." Unable to exploit most teachers directly, capitalist policy makers for the most part have succeeded in avoiding the costs of this incarceration by imposing them on the rest of us. Instead of paying apprentice wages to students, their families and other members of their class have been made to pay—either directly, through the necessity of buying school supplies for younger students and of paying tuition and fees for older ones, or indirectly through taxation.[5] In recent years, those costs have been rising rapidly. Moreover, scholarships and fellowships that mitigate monetary costs have been largely replaced by loans and debt for the many. Short-term grants have been largely replaced by long-term debt peonage. Struggles in the 1960s to open higher education to those previously unable to afford it won monetary subsidies from the government. Unfortunately, those subsidies have mainly taken the form of access to credit—burdening those least able to afford it with just such peonage.

Yet there have been at least two creative responses aimed at reducing the subordination of education and learning to monetary constraints in the United States in recent years. The first has been homeschooling. Although sometimes originating in reactionary efforts to keep children out of segregated schools or to ensure preferred religious training, homeschooling has spread in

---

5   Despite being denied the direct control involved in private schools, capitalists have profited from building those taxpayer-funded edu-factories and from the imposition of carefully selected, standardized school supplies, especially textbooks based on a common curriculum and standardized tests.

reaction both to the rising costs of education and to its ever more oppressive character as speedup, standardized tests, and policing have been inflicted on students. As more and more progressive parents have become involved, homeschooling has increasingly involved social networking—the organization of collective activities by parents that break out of the home and provide their children with opportunities for social interaction, play, and collective learning. Through such activities, the home becomes less an alternative form of incarceration and more a point of departure for learning. The confinement of children at home by fanatic parents is less and less the paradigm of homeschooling.[6] The term "homeschooling" would seem to be an increasingly inadequate descriptor of how such learning opportunities are organized outside of schools. What is involved sounds somewhat more like the "deschooling" Ivan Illich once evoked.[7] The obvious questions include to what degree does homeschooling—carried on collectively through the elaboration of social networks—constitute a subversion of capitalist control and the demonetization of education, and in what ways and to what degree can such reorganization of learning contribute to further such efforts in other domains? Are those who have learned in such environments less likely to submit to school-factory discipline elsewhere? Does the escape from money in this domain lead to a desire to avoid it in others? I don't have the answer to these questions, but such experiences would seem to be worth examining and evaluating.

Refusal is a second creative response to recent capitalist efforts to impose even more monetary restraints through the imposition of costs so high as to force millions to borrow and enter into long-term debt peonage. Some are demanding the cancelation of already accrued debt and the permanent liberation of schooling from future debt by making it free. Although such refusal is

---

6   The recent documentary *Wolf Pack* (2015) recounts the story of one such family that imposed not only homeschooling but the isolation of their children from the world—until some of them escaped.

7   Ivan Illich, *Deschooling Society* (New York: Harper & Row, 1971). Illich's proposals met with widespread discussion and critique. He was not always happy with the way his ideas were appropriated. See his essay in the follow-up book *After Deschooling, What?* (New York: Perennial Library, 1973).

relatively recent in the United States, such struggles have been fierce elsewhere in the world, as students and their families have resisted higher costs and demanded reductions, up to and including free education. The 1999 strike at the National Autonomous University of Mexico was to preserve free access to higher education. Energetic student protest in Chile in 2011 demanded this—despite tuition costs supposedly equal to a whopping 2 percent of the country's GNP.

Different approaches to such refusal in the United States have been proliferating. Some ex-students who have been defrauded by now-failed private schools have demanded cancellation of all debt acquired to finance their non-education. Others—such as the Strike Debt movement—have been organizing resistance to all kinds of debts, including student debt.

These demands have been so well organized as to force politicians to offer or embrace policies accepting at least part of these demands. The student protests in Chile led to candidate (and later president) Michelle Bachelet embracing free higher education. Efforts in both Germany and Austria to impose tuition have been largely rolled back as a result of widespread protest. As of this writing, the most recent response to the growing chorus of demands for free education in the United States has been that of various Democrats whose policy advisors have crafted a variety of proposals for either "debt-free" college or some reduction in student debt. In some of the proposals, the costs would be shifted to taxpayers, although the liberal Democrats have usually called for the tax burden to be saddled on those high-income folks who have benefited so greatly from all of the neoliberal tax cuts passed in recent years. In another proposal, part of the funding would come from taxing financial transactions—an anti-speculation policy dating from economist James Tobin's original 1972 suggestion of a marginal tax on currency conversion, designed to stabilize exchange rates but subsequently considered, and even experimented with, on other financial transactions. The various proposals would not remove money from the educational system, nor do they include provisions for helping finance learning outside that system, but they would—to some degree—reduce the money required by students and their families to pay for schooling. As students around the world have been proclaiming, free access to learning should be a human right, just like free access to health care—which evokes...

A third set of policies that have largely provided vital public services outside the domain of profit-maximizing corporations are those previously mentioned that have created an extensive system of public health services. These services range from public hospitals and clinics through the provision of clean water and sewage treatment to the organization of federal programs such as the CDC, the FDA, OSHA, and the EPA. Additional policies have continued the provision of national public postal, road, and rail services, both locally (e.g., bus and subway systems) and nationally (e.g., AMTRAK).

Although most of these services are provided by government institutions and thus are, in principle, public services provided to meet collective needs, that hasn't prevented those institutions from frequently acting like capitalists and turning those services into commodities available only through purchase with money. While, say, CDC efforts to identify and thwart epidemic disease are carried out without any direct charge (being entirely funded by taxes), local health and water supplies are usually furnished only on the basis of monetary payment—payment when possible at public hospitals for services rendered and regular utility bills for the supply of water. Such demands for payments are rationalized on the basis of the usual economic arguments about markets being efficient means for allocating scarce resources. The results are the usual ones: Those who can pay, get. Those who can pay more, get more. Those who can't pay, don't get any at all. In this period of neoliberal austerity and increased unemployment, challenges to this logic have been forthcoming from those denied vital services, such as water, just because they live in areas subject to underdevelopment, high unemployment, and low wages. Examples are the 2014–2015 battles over water shutoffs in Detroit and Baltimore and the longer-standing war over water privatization in Bolivia.[8] As in the case of food production, some have had recourse

---

8   The struggle over the right to water in Bolivia burst into international public awareness in 2000 due to reporting on public protests against water privatization in Cochabamba. There, as a result of pressure from the World Bank and in exchange for some debt relief, the city's municipal water company was sold to a

to autonomous methods for meeting their needs. "Frustrated with both the private and public water management models, residents of Cochabamba's southern zones are increasingly relying on traditional community-run water systems as an alternative," Emily Actenberg reported.[9]

Challenges to these policies and programs have restricted the capitalist use of money and exchange against us. How those battles unfold in determining the degree to which restriction actually occurs also determines the degree to which the tax monies used to fund them are serving our purposes or theirs. The diversion of tax dollars from subsidizing capitalist enterprise to placing restraints on their activities, restraints that are to our benefit, amounts to the subversion of those monies. They are, in Marx's jargon, monies diverted from their potential role as money capital into money-as-revenue, money spent to obtain and provide use-values to people. That they are spent by the state, instead of by the wage-earning taxpayers from whom those monies were taken, is secondary. The key issue here, as elsewhere, is whether capital is able to use money to control and exploit us or whether we are able (in these cases through the state) to meet our needs and limit capitalist valorization.

That all these policies and programs have constricted the freedom of private capital is clearly demonstrated by the sustained efforts on the part of industry to reduce the constraints and of neoliberal policy makers to try to eliminate or privatize these government programs. Such efforts to enclose and privatize such domains of both old and new commons were a central component of the austerity programs imposed by financial creditors, the IMF, and the US government during the international debt crisis of the 1980s and 1990s. They can be seen in the United States in such examples as the long-standing efforts to subvert and privatize the

multinational consortium controlled by Bechtel, a consortium that immediately raised water prices, outraging citizens. The intense clash between people's right to water and corporate profits that followed became known as the Cochabamba (or Bolivian) Water War.

9   See Emily Achtenberg, "From Water Wars to Water Scarcity: Bolivia's Cautionary Tale," *ReVista: Harvard Review of Latin America* 12, no. 2 (Winter 2013), 39–42.

postal service and public rail. They also characterize more recent efforts to privatize roads (e.g., the creation of toll roads for private profit) and water (i.e., the handing over of public water networks to private companies, as in the case of Cochabamba, Bolivia, mentioned above).[10]

---

10 Due to the refusal to recognize the inherent interrelationship between "surface" water (e.g., rivers and lakes) and "ground" water (e.g., aquifers), the latter has remained largely private and unregulated. The intensification of drought conditions in recent years—quite possibly related to global warming, accelerated by capitalist resistance to the abandonment of currently profitable fossil fuels—is bringing the need for such recognition and pressure to regulate groundwater to the fore.

CONCLUSION

As I hope the above discussion makes clear, I don't think any of the old privileged strategies of attacking the state with the objective of abolishing it immediately and in toto, or trying to build a cadre of professional revolutionaries to talk everyone else into uniting to overthrow the government and seize state power, are likely to be any more effective in getting us beyond capitalism in the future than they have been in the past. Instead it seems to me that the best we can do is to be clear about what, concretely, we want to get rid of, and then set about trying to do so, while simultaneously fighting for more time, space, and resources to experiment with, and elaborate alternatives to virtually every aspect of capitalist society. In the place of such old, comprehensive strategies, I prefer to consider some general ideas to help inform our struggles against capitalism as we seek to elaborate better futures for ourselves.

One such set of general ideas was offered by the Midnight Notes Collective and friends in the aforementioned pamphlet *Promissory Notes*. As one of those friends—who had some marginal input in the drafting of that text—I found the suggested characteristics of struggles whose presence qualify them as "revolutionary," in the sense of autonomous from capitalism, to provide useful, indeed vital, criteria for evaluating both social democratic "inside" and autonomous "outside" struggles. Two of the characteristics suggested are of particular relevance to my concerns here. The first is that struggles "lead toward more time outside of capitalist control"—"In particular this means a shorter work week for the waged and unwaged."[1] The second is that struggles "strengthen the commons and expand de-commodified relationships and spaces."[2] Allow me to discuss the first, then the second.

Less Work

Given that I have argued here that the most fundamental means of capitalist domination—the way it shapes our lives to function within its own set of rules by imposing so much work that we have little

---

1   Midnight Notes Collective, *Promissory Notes*, 15.

2   Ibid., 14.

time and energy to resist those rules or to develop alternatives, the
first of these is, for me, of essential importance. It seems to me that
we do best to frame *all* of our struggles, as much as possible, to help
reduce the subordination of all our lives to work, with the ultimate
aim of ending that subordination.

Where possible, we can struggle for direct reductions in work
time, not just for shorter workweeks, but also for shorter working
days (e.g., less or no overtime), years (e.g., more vacation time), and
lives (e.g., earlier retirement). We can also demand the adjustment
of what work time we are forced to perform to meet our needs,
through flexible subordination of work time to the times we need
for other things (e.g., taking care of the young and the old, seeing doctors, taking care of legal matters, taking time to vote, and
so on).[3] In general, we can demand the subordination of both the
amount and the timing of obligatory work to our needs, individual
and collective—the exact opposite of what capital tries to achieve.

Whatever concrete struggles we undertake, in every domain
dominated by work-for-capital, whether it be within forms of
waged and salaried labor or within forms of unwaged labor, we
need to pose the question of whether, how, and to what degree
those struggles will help free us from work.

For example, as I have pointed out, successful struggle for income may provide more resources for reducing work in many ways,
but circumstances may have a bearing on the particular kinds of
demands we make. Given the huge variety of ways in which work is
imposed, I will not try to discuss all possible situations of struggle,
but I can give some examples of taking the principle of seeking to
reduce work into account.

For those with salaried jobs, the simple demand for more money (and benefits) may often make sense. However, one of the advantages of salaried labor to capital is the opportunity it provides
to impose work without fixed time limits—in such a manner as to
result in unpaid overtime work. In such circumstances, the demand for more money (and benefits) might be conceded only in return for more work and more unpaid overtime—with the net result

---

3   There are ongoing struggles around all of these. Perhaps the best known at the
moment are those for maternity and paternity leave, for paid sick leave, and for paid
(or even unpaid but unpunished) time to vote.

of not only more work but lower pay per hour of labor. Recognizing that possibility might result in different kinds of demands—for example, ones that would reduce workloads directly and effectively increase income per hour of work.

For those with waged jobs, the demands might be different, such as increased pay not just for regular work but also for overtime work—that is, extra hours of labor. Employers often prefer to employ their workers longer hours rather than hire extra workers—particularly in periods of rising demand after slumps. When employers have been successful in reducing real wages, workers sometimes want more paid hours to compensate. Higher regular and overtime pay reduces workers' need for overtime hours; higher overtime pay reduces the incentive of employers to demand or impose it. Struggles around overtime pay have developed in recent years, especially among those finding themselves saddled with overtime work but with no extra pay at all. Forcing employers to pay overtime has the same effects as forcing them to pay more for overtime hours. These examples illustrate how struggles for higher salaries and wages can be, if appropriately formulated, consistent with efforts to reduce work and with it capital's hold on our lives.

However, when we pull back from our local struggles and put them in a wider perspective, we are forced to recognize that our ability to fight for less work, directly and indirectly, is limited by the abilities of others elsewhere. Long hours and exhausting work are two of the many reasons why workers move from place to place, including crossing borders; they seek jobs that require less work. That motivation may lead them to accept what are for them shorter, less intense hours, that nevertheless involve more work than that normal for local workers and in the process undermine the struggles of the latter. It is also why multinational corporations relocate production to areas and countries where they can impose longer and more intense hours of work. Clearly, the only way to overcome such problems is to impose more or less universal labor standards everywhere. In other words, our ability to win less work locally depends on the ability of others to do the same. Thus the absolute necessity of international working-class solidarity that organizes the struggle for less work, as for so many other objectives, at the same global level at which capital is organized. This necessity has long been recognized among workers—from the time of the First International on—even if so far progress has been limited.

Social democratic efforts in this direction have included a pre–World War I International Association for Labour Legislation that brought together those who believed in the possibility of forming international legal standards. After World War I, the International Labour Organization (ILO) was formed, in 1919, first within the League of Nations and then as part of the United Nations, with the purpose of pushing for international labor rights and standards that would protect all workers, throughout the global wage hierarchy.[4] However, neither the ILO nor other social democratic efforts to institutionalize such rights and standards internationally have ever had any effective enforcement powers. As a result, they have been largely limited to documenting the conditions of labor and the lack of (or violation of) labor rights while propagandizing for their institution or enforcement. Where such rights and standards have been included in international trade agreements (e.g., NAFTA), there has also been virtually no enforcement. This is, of course, not surprising given that such agreements have been sponsored by and formulated for the benefit of precisely those multinational corporations that benefit from an international hierarchy that pits workers in one country against those in others.

At another level, major trade union federations, such as the AFL-CIO in the United States and the International Federation of Trade Unions (IFTU), have for the most part only paid lip service to the internationalization of workers' struggles, including those to reduce work. In the worst cases, some, such as the AFL-CIO, have actually undercut such internationalization by cooperating with Cold War governmental efforts to limit or destroy progressive labor organizations abroad under the rubric of anticommunism.[5]

However, we did see an encouraging shift during the run-up to NAFTA, when many Canadian, US, and Mexican labor locals came together across borders to discuss the likely costs and benefits of

---

4   See Jasmien Van Daele, "Engineering Social Peace: Networks, Ideas and the Founding of the International Labour Organization," *International Review of Social History* 50, no. 3 (2005), 435–66.

5   In the 1960s, awareness of their role was so well known that the AFL-CIO was often referred to by militants as the AFL-CIA.

the agreement. We saw much less such collaboration in the efforts that killed the Trans-Pacific Partnership—an even broader trade pact certainly aimed, as NAFTA was, at undermining workers' strength everywhere. Yet such organization is imperative if we are to develop the capacity to counter the ability of capital to plan and operate at a global level.

At the same time, what the experience of organizing resistance to NAFTA demonstrated was that the required collaboration goes far beyond trade unionism. A great many people involved in all sorts of struggles came together in Canada, the United States, and Mexico and in cross-border meetings to discuss the likely costs and benefits of that proposed pact and how to organize against it. Although the effort failed and NAFTA was passed, the collaborations constituted useful examples of the kind of organizing that provides some hope of countering capital's international strategies to impose more work and enhance its profits and control.[6] There are a number of other examples of international working-class collaboration that deserve study to discover both their limitations and what can be learned for use the next time around.[7] A useful survey of the recent evolution of internationalism among activists in both labor and social justice movements was published in the journal *Interface* in 2014.[8]

---

6   The seriousness of the threat capitalist policy analysts perceive in such collaboration can be seen in their efforts to discover ways to counter it. See, for example, Cathryn Thorup, "The Politics of Free Trade and the Dynamics of Cross-Border Coalitions in U.S. Mexican Relations," *Columbia Journal of World Business* 26, no. 11 (Summer 1991), 12–26; John Arquilla and David Ronfeldt, "Cyberwar Is Coming!" *Comparative Strategy* 12, no. 2 (1993), 141–65; Arquilla and Ronfeldt, *The Advent of Netwar* (Santa Monica: RAND, 1996); Arquilla and Ronfeldt, *Networks and Netwars: The future of Terror, Crime and Militancy* (Santa Monica: RAND, 2001).

7   Among other examples of mobilization against particular capitalist efforts were those against the OECD Multilateral Investment Agreement (MAI) that succeeded in killing it, and those against the Maastricht Treaty in Europe and against the World Trade Organization that did not. See Wendy Varney and Brian Martin, "Net Resistance, Net Benefits: Opposing MAI," *Social Alternatives* 19, no. 1 (January 2000), 47–51.

8   See the introduction by Peter Waterman and Laurence Cox, "Movement Internationalism/s," *Interface: A Journal for and about Social Movements* 6, no. 2 (November 2014), 1–14, and the other articles in that issue.

The principle of evaluating the impact of various demands on the amount of imposed work can also be brought to bear when we examine the struggles over the work of the unwaged (e.g., housework and schoolwork). For many years, unwaged women—who have long borne most of the burden of housework—have fought for less work by demanding the diversion of family income (or government resources) into labor-saving domestic devices and services (e.g., running water, gas, water heaters, electricity, washing machines, and so on).[9] It may not be obvious to those born and raised where running water, natural gas, and electricity have been readily available, but millions of women, especially those living in the Global South, spend long hours daily fetching and hauling water for drinking, cooking, and cleaning, and firewood or dried dung for cooking and heating. As a result, women have been among those most active in fighting for such public services in both rural and urban areas.[10]

In the Global North, the loss of jobs, wages and homes imposed by the latest financial crisis have all reduced access to domestic labor-saving devices and services and imposed more unwaged work. Searching for new jobs, dealing with the bureaucratic obstacles to obtaining unemployment compensation or welfare and finding new housing have all required more unwaged labor. Such hardships have been intensified by the imposition of austerity, which has included reductions in social services and cutoffs of water supplies. Such cutoffs have meant extra work obtaining bottled water and extra work trying to cook and wash—family members, dishes, and clothes—with dramatically limited amounts of water.

At a global level, by all serious accounts, global warming and climate change are accentuating the problems of access to adequate, especially potable, water for millions around the world— even as capitalists push to monopolize water sources and privatize

---

9   The capitalist response to success in such struggles was to increase standards of cleanliness (e.g., no "ring around the collar," no dust on the shelves, and no pet hair under the table) and by so doing imposed more cleaning work and more waged work to be able to purchase all the supposedly necessary cleaning materials.

10   For an example of women's struggles to dramatically reduce their workload by forcing the government to provide piped water supplies, see Vivienne Bennett, *The Politics of Water: Urban Protest, Gender, and Power in Monterrey, Mexico* (Pittsburgh: University of Pittsburgh Press 1995).

control over access. Efforts to avoid or end such monopolization and the diversion of water into unnecessary and environmentally destructive profit-making projects such as bottling in plastic containers and the landscaping of production and sales facilities have been emerging as water scarcity is being increasingly recognized as artificially increased by such practices. Eliminating such projects would not only make more water available for better purposes but would directly benefit the environment and reduce work.[11]

A different kind of technological fix for reducing housework, for which women have also fought, with widely varying degrees of success, has been access to various methods of birth control to reduce procreation and all the work that follows from it. Where women have made substantial strides—mainly in the Global North—birth rates have plummeted, family size has dropped precipitously, and the amount of housework substantially reduced. The result, other things held equal, is a slowdown in the growth of the labor force, a reduction in the number of workers seeking jobs, and increased leverage for those with jobs in fighting for things like reduced working hours.[12] Unfortunately, other things are

---

11   One of the obvious ways in which the elimination of such projects would reduce work is by eliminating the work of those currently employed on them. Unfortunately, the counterpart to the social gain of reducing work is the loss of income by those who lose their jobs in the process. The same is true of the replacement of hydrocarbon energy sources such as coal with renewable ones; the inevitable decline in the demand for coal will cost thousands of workers their jobs. In trying to sell renewable energy to capitalists, supporters have long argued that the development of new energy sources would create new jobs—offsetting such losses. For an early example, see Amory B. Lovins, "Energy Strategy: The Road Not Taken?" *Foreign Affairs 55, no. 1* (October 1976), 65–96. While such job replacement may help capitalists continue to impose work overall, it does not address the immediate problems faced by displaced workers. In such cases, in which job losses are caused by public policy decisions, the costs of supporting the income of displaced workers should be borne by the state via taxation—a burden that would be lightened by another decision to shorten all working hours and spread the work. Any finite amount of work can always be redistributed over a finite number of people—the only question is how.

12   This impact on the size of the labor force has been offset to some degree as reduced housework has made it easier for women to escape wagelessness by finding and holding waged and salaried jobs.

rarely equal, and the lesser ability of many women to gain control over their own bodies through access to birth control technologies—especially in the Global South—has not only meant continued heavy workloads for them but also the ability of capital to pit them against women elsewhere. Their large families augment local labor supplies, keep hours of waged labor long and wages low, and spin off out-migration by family members moving to areas where conditions appear better. Such movement often provides immigrant workers to capitalists in areas where women have been more successful, workers that they pit against local workers, including women who with fewer children have been able to obtain waged jobs, undermining their struggles for higher wages and less work. Fortunately, because most such immigrant workers have been men who commonly send part of their income back to their families in their communities of origin, the recipients of that income have often been the women left behind. Such women effectively command the repatriated part of those wages, a command that often improves their own ability to struggle for less work.[13]

The interdependence of women's struggles against unwaged housework in different parts of the world makes evident the same need for the internationalization of those struggles as in the case of the struggles of waged and salaried workers discussed above. Fortunately, there has been organizing in that direction, organizing that has increased the ability of women to overcome the hidden character of unwaged housework and to force recognition of both its extent and nature on those who have long refused to recognize it as a form of labor just as important as waged and salaried labor. Such refusal has been characteristic not only of men in general but also of the labor movement, whose organizers have defined their movement purely in terms of labor paid for by employers. Nevertheless, pressure from women around the world has succeeded in

---

13 A seminal article analyzing the various relationships between women's work and emigration was Mariarosa Dalla Costa, "Riproduzione e emigrazione," in A. Serafini, et al., *L'Operaio multinazionale in Europa* (Milan: Feltrinelli Editore, 1974), 207–42. In that article she examined the effects on women left behind during male out-migration from both southern Italy to the north and from Africa into Italy. An English translation, "Reproduction and Emigration" is now available online at www.zerowork.org.

obtaining recognition from some men and from some governments such as to redistribute the burden of housework in the former case and to receive various forms of compensation in the latter (e.g., those welfare payments and family allocations mentioned earlier). Unfortunately, such recognition, changes in behavior, and compensation are extremely unequal around the world, which results in some women being exploited more than others at home and in the ability of capital to exploit women who are willing to migrate to improve their working conditions (e.g., Thai women working in bars from Bangkok to Tokyo and Filipino women working as domestic laborers throughout the world). Such disparities have produced solidarity movements to support women in less favorable situations and cross-border feminist dialogues within Global Women's Strike, the World Social Forum, the World March of Women, and Encuentros Feministas in Latin America. But, as far as I have found, no organizations on the order of the ILO have been created, nor has international organizing developed the capacity to enforce substantial equalization in the ability of women to reduce their housework.

The cultural revolution of the 1960s and early 1970s around the world included the revolt by students against the structures and constraints of schooling.[14] In various countries, student struggles circulated nationwide through organizations such as the Students for a Democratic Society in the United States and the Union Nationale des Étudiants de France. Within the United States, battles against the constraints on student self-activity included not only demands for free speech and an end to racial discrimination in admittance but also resistance to their factory-like unwaged work—imposed through top-down curriculum. To the degree that they were successful in reducing their workload, they used the time set free to struggle against other constraints and to develop alternative modes of learning.

Such alternatives, from teach-ins to demonstrations to alternative courses, thrived both on campus and off. Teach-ins and demonstrations were forums for learning about such things as

---

14   For a sense of the worldwide scope of rebellion in that period, see George Katsiaficas, *The Imagination of the New Left: A Global Analysis of 1968* (Boston: South End Press, 1999).

university complicity with war-making, the repressive structures of education, and movements for civil rights. Alternative courses provided historical background to such phenomena and opportunities to explore modes of living not based on competition and monetary gain (e.g., communal forms of self-valorization). Some such courses were eventually incorporated into curriculum modified by students to meet their needs, such as the kind of courses that have constituted "Black Studies" and "Chicano Studies." Others survived as informal alternatives both on and off campus. The neoliberal counterattack on those gains has involved attacks on such curriculum, increased unemployment, falling wages, and a shift from grants to loans, all of which have imposed such anxiety and worry about future income as to push many students into "practical" (i.e., job-oriented) courses, diverting their time and energy from the kind of coursework and extracurricular activities developed to inform their resistance to work and capitalism more generally.

Success by the current campaigns to dramatically reduce the costs of education, perhaps even to make it free, with access to learning understood as a civil right, would certainly reduce pressure on students and hours of imposed study. At the same time, without struggles that succeed in altering the job-income environment within which student efforts unfold, their success is likely to be limited. It is worth remembering that the "movement" of those earlier years was partly financed by grants and scholarships for students and facilitated by historically low levels of unemployment that gave most college students confidence that their future income was safe, regardless of how much of their time and energy they diverted into struggle within and against schools.

De-commodification in Action and Language

Let me turn now to the other characteristic that interests me here among those proposed in *Promissory Notes* as being essential aspects of autonomous "outside" struggles, namely that they "strengthen the commons and expand de-commodified relationships and spaces."

> The commons is a non-commodified space shared by the community. Social democratic versions include such things as health

care, education, social security—however imperfectly realized. However, does the struggle also support bringing the bottom up, expanding inclusiveness and participatory control? On the other hand, are autonomous sectors able to avoid commodification (avoid being turned into business products or services for sale)? Even if they cannot do so completely, can they maintain a political stance and active behavior that pushes towards non-commodity forms? More generally, how can the working class on small or large scales create forms of exchange that are or tend toward being de-commodified? Create markets (forms of exchange) that do not rule lives and livelihoods? Reduce the reach of commodification and capitalist markets on people's life?[15]

There are a number of important concepts packed into the above statement. The two most obvious that have received relatively little attention in this book are those of the commons and "bringing the bottom up, expanding inclusiveness and participatory control." Although both have been evoked, neither has received the treatment it deserves. Here I have been focused on using the labor theory of value to illuminate struggles against work and against money. Therefore, my primary interest in the above statement, at present, is the emphasis on de-commodification.

In Marx's theory of capitalism, as I have explained earlier, commodities are goods, services, or labor power that are sold, in the process becoming exchange-values and eventually use-values as they are consumed. *Commodification* has been the processes through which capitalists have 1) converted every aspect of reality possible into goods and services to be bought or sold at prices that realize a profit and 2) shaped human attitudes into the willingness work for them and abilities into those that fit their needs. *De-commodification* therefore involves the bypassing of sales and exchange-value in favor of folks directly realizing the use-values of goods, services, and their own abilities. Such a bypassing happens *sporadically*, when goods and services are directly appropriated by workers, on the job or off, and it happens much more *systematically* in activities such as peer-to-peer (P2P) file sharing, especially

15 Midnight Notes Collective, *Promissory Notes*, 14.

of software, music, video, and film.[16] Such activities, by appropriating goods directly, remove them from the market and undermine the ability of capitalists to realize surplus value and profits,
and thus the continuing value of the labor employed as a means
of social control. The adaptation and diversion of workers' abilities to their own autonomous pursuits also undermines their employers' control. Thus, the intensity of business's countermeasures:
endless surveillance of customers and workers, jailing shoplifters
and those caught "stealing" on the job while prosecuting file and
software sharers, both individuals and institutions. In this period
when so many commodities' essential inputs are imagination and
creativity, as with software, music, video games, and film, much
of the corporate push for "intellectual property rights" is aimed at
criminalizing the direct appropriation of such products.[17]

---

16 While on-the-job appropriation, shoplifting, and P2P file sharing are common
enough practices in the Global North, crop seizures during harvest periods are one
lesser-known recourse of poor peasants in the Global South. While visiting villages
in the Indian state of Bihar, during the state of emergency declared by Indira Gand-
hi in the mid-1970s, I heard many stories of such seizures from peasants who had
tried other forms of resistance to falling agricultural prices and rising input prices
but had been violently repressed.

17 Capitalist interest in intellectual property rights also seeks to protect corporate
profits by curbing competition. The pursuit, in recent years, of international trea-
ties guaranteeing intellectual property rights has been aimed primarily at "piracy,"
wherein a capitalist firm copies the designs of another and produces "knockoffs"—
identical products that it sells at lower prices. The same method has been used by
poor artisans—on a much smaller scale—in the informal sector. (I discovered one example of such appropriation in Tepito, a Mexico City community known not only for
its fierce political independence but also for the illegal peddling of untaxed goods.
Artisanal shoemakers copied upscale European designs, manufactured them, and
sold them at dramatically lower prices.) Another side to intellectual property rights
is the interest of creative workers in protecting income from the fruits of their efforts (e.g., writers of various sorts copyrighting their work or scientists and inventors
seeking patents). Such individual interest in turning what might otherwise simply
be a gift to the community into private property derives purely from the absence
of other sources of income. Alternative sources of income, that do not involve such
property rights have included wealthy patrons and state (taxpayer) support. More
recently, crowd-sourcing has emerged as yet another alternative—an arrangement

Another kind of bypassing takes place when we undertake to meet our needs and satisfy our desires directly—without the mediation of money, markets, or commodities—in ways that go beyond the mere reproduction of our lives as labor power to be sold in some capitalist labor market for a wage or salary. On a small scale, such direct meeting of needs has a long history, especially in small rural communities, not only in the behavior of families but also in collective collaboration for raising houses and barns, sharing seeds, gathering crops, or fishing. In cities there have always been communities, especially immigrant working-class ones, where folks help each other out in a variety of ways, many of which involve no money or exchange. When people collaborate to meet their needs, whether those of an individual, a single family, or a community, their cooperation with one another can be called "mutual aid." That was the term used by Peter Kropotkin (1842–1921), the Russian noble turned anarchist. His experiences, first in Siberia during a military assignment and then in western Europe among Swiss watchmakers, led him to research and write a whole book illustrating the history of mutual aid among humans and its presence among other animals.[18] Whereas Marx limited his most extensive analysis of cooperation, in chapter 14 of volume 1 of *Capital*, to recognizing its productive power and how capitalists expropriated it for their own benefit, Kropotkin sought out and reported many, many examples of mutual aid down through the centuries. They both clearly projected the liberation of cooperation from capitalism, and Kropotkin imagined its role in post-capitalist communities. Although his discourse did not turn on the concept of the "commons," he saw that most wealth in society was the result of collective collaboration and should be liberated from private property to be enjoyed in common.[19]

---

through which those who appreciate various creations donate money to support the creators. As one might expect, this has become a new terrain of struggle as capitalists are also using this approach to raise funds for profit-making ventures.

18   Originally published in 1902, partly as a counterweight to social Darwinist theories, his book is currently available as Peter Kropotkin, *Mutual Aid: A Factor of Evolution* (London: Freedom Press, 2006) and online as a Project Gutenberg e-text.

19   Kropotkin's ideas about the potentials of mutual aid were further elaborated in his books *The Conquest of Bread* (1892) and *Fields, Factories and Workshops* (1889).

Efforts to organize such mutual aid in ways that bypass the market have never been easy. Perhaps the most obvious recurrent difficulties have been those faced by workers who have organized themselves in self-managed cooperatives—whether producer or consumer cooperatives.[20] Self-management avoids capitalist bosses and usually has involved collective decision-making. In producer cooperatives such decision-making involves the organization of work, the sharing of income, collective decisions about investment, and relationships with the surrounding community. In consumer cooperatives, it also includes members collectively choosing the kinds of consumer goods they desire.[21]

In small-scale projects, such as community gardens—a form of producer cooperative—members can largely dispense with markets and simply share the tasks involved in growing food and share the fruits of their efforts.[22] However, for the most part, both producer and consumer cooperatives—no matter how well organized internally as a "labor common"—still have to engage with markets.[23] Producer cooperatives must buy the equipment and

---

20 Some cooperatives exist almost purely as collective interventions in markets. Examples are farmer grain cooperatives that maintain storage silos and allow member farmers to gain better prices for their produce and thus higher income for themselves.

21 There are many sorts of consumer cooperatives, ranging from retail food co-ops through housing, health-care, and insurance co-ops to credit unions.

22 Obviously, things like seeds and tools may be bought—with money donated by members—but organic gardening methods characteristic of such projects tend to minimize such recourse to markets. As opposition to genetically modified organisms has grown, so too has the use and propagation of "heritage" seeds by the gardeners themselves. Such practices further reduce the need for engagement with markets.

23 Nick Dyer-Witheford, as part of an interesting theorization of how isolated commons might circulate and multiply to constitute an ever-growing alternative to capitalist ways of organizing our lives, has differentiated three potentially interactive moments in such circulation of commons: labor commons, eco-social commons, and networked commons. "By labour commons," he writes, "we mean the democratized organization of productive and reproductive work." See Nick Dyer-Witheford, "The Circulation of the Common," talk given in the "Future of the Commons" series, University of Minnesota, October 29, 2009; Greig de Peuter and Nick Dyer-Witheford, "Commons and Cooperatives," *Affinities: A Journal of Radical Theory, Culture and Action* 4, no. 1 (Summer 2010), 30–56.

materials required to produce, and then, as a general rule, they must find markets where they can sell what they have produced. They also tend to pay their members money wages and salaries. Expanding membership involves hiring labor power, but assuming new members participate as fully as the old, the ability to work includes not only technical skills but also managerial ones (or, at least the willingness to learn them). Consumer cooperatives must buy whatever goods their members require and then sell them to those members. Within this context, both producer and consumer cooperatives have obvious advantages to their members. The former provide income and collective control over their work. The latter provide lower consumer prices and higher real income. In other words, such cooperatives still operate very much within the market economy. For those who visualize a post-capitalist society as still involving markets, the problems with this situation are limited to such things as how the capitalist markets with which they must engage put pressure on the worker-members of the cooperatives to impose more work on themselves and cut costs (even their own wages) in order to compete successfully. But if our goal is to do away with money and markets, as I have argued it should be, then the question arises: what bypassing of markets, if any, is possible?

One response to market competition, by members of some cooperatives, embraced by many supporters, has been to link up with other cooperatives in as integrated a manner as possible—so that some provide inputs to others. In this process, however, markets are only internalized, not bypassed. Buying and selling among a growing number of networked cooperatives parallels what goes on within vertically integrated capitalist corporations.[24] Although most cooperatives are relatively isolated operations, such networks do exist. One of the largest and most famous cooperative efforts, the Basque Mondragón Corporación Cooperativa, made up of over a hundred networked cooperatives, has expanded to the point of becoming a multinational corporation employing waged labor in

---

24 Whereas capitalist corporations are well known for manipulating "transfer prices" among subsidiaries so that profits show up mainly in the accounts of those located in low-tax countries, one can imagine cooperatives carrying out a similar manipulation to obtain a greater equality in the income available to members.

China and eastern Europe, minimizing its costs and maximizing its profits.[25]

Nowadays, some of the kinds of collective activities character-istic of cooperatives are discussed under the rubric of "sharing" or "social and solidarity" economies. I say "some" because those terms have been used quite loosely and, although originating in collec-tive activities of mutual aid, have frequently been applied both to endeavors such as producer and consumer cooperatives and to businesses such as Uber (which profits from the organization of informal taxi services) or Airbnb (which profits from operating a peer-to-peer lodging service).[26]

It is worth remembering that one of the originators of coopera-tives was the Welsh capitalist reformer Robert Owens (1771–1858), who proposed production cooperatives as a solution to unemploy-ment—a way of putting the unemployed to work productively rath-er than just confining them in unproductive workhouses.[27] Owens's plan, if enacted, would have removed workers from the "reserve

25 For the history of the Cooperativa, see William Whyte and Kathleen Whyte, *Making Mondragon: The Growth and Dynamics of the Worker Cooperative Com-plex* (Ithaca: ILR Press, 1988). For a critical assessment of its functioning, see Shar-ryn Kasmir, *The Myth of Mondragon: Cooperatives, Politics and Working Class Life in a Basque Town* (Albany: State University of New York Press, 1996).

26 See, for example, Neal Gorenflo, "The New Sharing Economy," Shareable, www.shareable.net/blog/the-new-sharing-economy. See also Anitra Nelson's cri-tique of the associated concepts and projects of a "social and solidarity economy" in her essay "An Impossible Marriage: Solidarity Economy and Monetary Economy," presented to an UNRISD Conference on "Potential and Limits of Social and Soli-darity Economy" in 2010. Those limits are inherent not only in the continued use of money and markets but in the very concept of "an economy" of any sort whatsoever.

27 Owens has been called a "utopian socialist" because of his various efforts to improve the lives of workers (in his own mills and community at New Lanark, Scot-land, and then more broadly), to form broad-based labor unions, and eventually to found whole communities embodying his ideas about better ways to organize social life. On his proposals for cooperative villages for the unemployed, see Robert Owen, *Report to the Committee of the Association for the Relief of the Manufacturing and Labouring Poor* (1817) and *Report to the County of Lanark* (1820). Both of these re-ports are included in Gregory Claeys, ed., *Selected Works of Robert Owen, vol. 1, Ear-ly Writings* (London: William Pickering, 1993), 143–55 and 287–332 respectively.

army of the unemployed" and by so doing put upward pressure on
wages—one reason, perhaps, why capitalist policy makers of his
day rejected it. Workers, however, saw its advantages to them in
terms of income, and it was to them that Owens turned when re-
buffed by his fellow capitalists.

Certainly, one motivation behind worker interest in forming
cooperatives and other "sharing" projects has been the opportunities they have offered for alternative sources of income (in the
case of producer cooperatives) or for ways to stretch limited income (in the case of consumer cooperatives). For those in need,
"sharing" can be just another way to gain access to, and better real
income from, the economy. But interest and participation in cooperatives and other modern forms of "sharing" have also derived
from many other motives, including the desire for alternatives to
capitalist institutions.[28]

Such desire has been manifested in the collective decision-
making practices of many cooperatives—practices intentionally
more democratic than the vertical managerial hierarchies typical
of capitalist institutions. Efforts to design, implement, and sustain
practices of "workers' control" or "self-management" have been
recurrent in the history of cooperatives.[29] Self-management has
typically been aimed not only at improving everyone's income but
also at improving working conditions, including gaining the dig-
nity associated with taking control over an important part of one's
life. Such self-management has repeatedly demonstrated that we
are quite capable of organizing our own work collectively without
any capitalist boss telling us what to do. Certainly this was one reason why Marx was, at certain points, enthusiastic about producer cooperatives. For example, in 1864 he wrote of a "great victory"

---

28   See the discussion of motives in Juliet Schor, "Debating the Sharing Economy,"
Great Transition Initiative, October 2014, www.greattransition.org/publication/
debating-the-sharing-economy. Schor's essay, based on three years of empirical research, illustrates the diversity of activities loosely considered part of the "sharing
economy," with many concrete examples.

29   For an excellent history of cooperative efforts in the United States that illustrates many of these goals and problems, see the second edition of John Curl, *For All
the People: Uncovering the Hidden History of Cooperation, Cooperative Movements
and Communalism in America* (Oakland: PM Press, 2012).

of the "political economy of labor over the political economy of property": "We speak of the co-operative movement, especially of the co-operative factories raised by the unassisted efforts of a few bold 'hands'. The value of these great social experiments cannot be over-rated. By deed, instead of by argument, they have shown that production on a large scale, and in accord with the best of modern science, may be carried on without the existence of a class of masters employing a class of hands."[30]

Such practices have also been common in many recent instances of workers taking over and operating either businesses about to be closed down or enterprises in which they previously worked but from which they have been locked out. Perhaps best known, these days, are the many worker-run businesses of Argentina, recuperated in the wake of the huge financial crisis in 2001–2002. That crisis led to dozens of seizures by unemployed—and often unpaid—workers of their former places of employment, seizures supported by people in the local communities and followed by their reopening and operation as cooperatives by the workers themselves.[31] Although the first wave of seizures were primarily of industrial factories, their success and subsequent legal victories have led to takeovers in a variety of service sectors (e.g., printing, hotels, restaurants, retail, health care, media, and education).[32] The experiences of such *empresas recuperadas* have since been circulated far beyond Argentina.

One example is Vio.Me, a one-time capitalist firm in Greece producing building materials (e.g., glues), taken over by its workers and converted into an operation for making things like soap—using locally grown components. The takeover occurred in the midst of

30 Karl Marx, "Inaugural Address of the Working Men's International Association," November 1864, in Marx and Engels, *Collected Works*, vol. 20 (New York: International Publishers, 1985), 11.

31 See Marina Sitrin, *Horizontalism: Voices of Popular Power in Argentina* (Oakland: AK Press, 2007); Lavaca Collective, *Sin Patron: Stories from Argentina's Worker-Run Factories*, (Chicago: Haymarket Books, 2007); Marina Sitrin, *Everyday Revolutions: Horizontalism and Autonomy in Argentina* (London: Zed Books, 2012).

32 Andrés Ruggeri and Marcelo Vieta, "Argentina's Worker-Recuperated Enterprises, 2010–2013: A Synthesis of Recent Empirical Findings," *Journal of Entrepreneurial and Organizational Diversity* 4, no. 1 (2014), 75–103.

the contemporary crisis over Greek debt and the imposition of austerity measures. Within a widespread situation of high unemployment and plummeting standards of living—similar to the context of worker seizures in Argentina—the takeover was supported by the surrounding community that has continued to defend Vio.Me against recurrent efforts by the previous owners to sell the property and evict the workers.[33] In principle, the left-wing SYRIZA government has a policy supporting such efforts, but it has so far not intervened on the workers' behalf. As with so many of its other promises, it remains to be seen whether it ever will.[34]

One source of confusion, which makes it difficult to differentiate "sharing" projects that struggle valiantly to elaborate alternatives to capitalism from those that merely modify its forms, lies in the continuing use of the concepts and language of capitalism when analyzing different projects. Among the most important of those concepts that we need to escape is that of "the economy." Attempts to imagine and elaborate alternatives to capitalism in terms of some kind of alternative economy have a history that demonstrates the limitations of some current discourses. By accepting economists' myths that economies have always existed and will always exist and that economics is an ever-applicable ahistorical science that can be used to understand the past and imagine post-capitalist futures just as effectively as it can be used to understand capitalism, generations of would-be reformers and revolutionaries have limited their ability to imagine true alternatives.

This was the case in the nineteenth century when efforts began to imagine new "socialist" alternatives to capitalism. At that time, economists defined the economy as including the production, distribution, and consumption of wealth. Adam Smith had titled his seminal work on the economy *The Wealth of Nations* (1776) and focused, at great length, on those processes that he saw as contributing to or constricting the expansion of wealth. So, by the time the term "socialism" appeared in 1832, efforts to imagine alternatives were already focused on alternative methods of production,

---

33 For similar examples elsewhere in Europe, see Marina Sitrin, "Recuperating Work and Life," *Roar Magazine* no. 0 (Winter 2015), roarmag.org/.

34 Vio.Me now has its own website (www.viome.org) with materials about its struggles in several languages.

distribution, and consumption.[35] Results varied from utopian blue-prints—that Marx enjoyed but rejected—through the Gotha Program—that he critiqued (as I discussed above)—to the construction of actual *socialist economies* in the USSR and China in the wake of the Bolshevik seizure of power and the Chinese communists' defeat of Chang Kai-shek and his warlords. Revisiting those histories will show how framing the project of inventing alternatives to capitalism in terms of building a new kind of economy led inevitably not to alternatives but to mere variations. Although state ownership and control largely displaced private ownership and control, the very capitalist preoccupations with maximizing the imposition of work, the extraction of a surplus, and its use to finance investment (i.e., more work), resulted in changes in the forms of accumulation but not in its essential character. Those "socialist" economies, by continuing the capitalist imposition of work as their primary mode of social control, retained an antagonistic class structure and became so fraught with workers' opposition and resistance as to require methods of police state repression such as judicial and ex-trajudicial killings and incarceration—not all that different from those in other capitalist countries.[36]

To destroy the myth that the "economy" is an inescapable human phenomenon, we need to study the concepts and language of economists to discover how they denote phenomena specific to capitalism rather than human activities in general. As with the

---

35   The term "socialism" was apparently first used in France that year by Pierre Leroux, a disciple of Saint-Simon, in his journal *La Globe*. For a discussion of many of the contradictory historical conceptions of "socialism," see Harry Cleaver, "Socialism?" in Wolfgang Sachs, ed., *The Development Dictionary: Knowledge as Power* (London: Zed Books, 1992), 233–49.

36   The need of the Soviet and other socialist regimes for police state repression was due, in part, to the rigidities of their adaptations of several Western institutions—for example, electoral political systems, labor organizing, and the inculcation of cultural hegemony through the monopolization of education and the mass media. At the same time, it is worth remembering that Cold War, anticommunist propaganda condemning the Soviet Gulag conveniently distracted attention from such Western phenomena as the genocide of indigenous peoples, the enslavement of Africans, the barbarities of colonialism, mass incarceration (especially of minorities), and forced prison labor at home.

concept of economy, most of the concepts deployed by economists in their analysis are generic; they are theoretical concepts abstracted from particular, concrete phenomena. The example that I discussed in Part I of this book was the concept of labor, or work. Such a concept, I argued, makes sense within capitalism because all of those varied concrete activities that capitalism succeeds in imposing on people with the objective of producing commodities have a common characteristic—they are the means through which capitalists achieve social control. To the degree that we are able to liberate those concrete activities from capitalist domination, they lose that common characteristic and become, once again, particular activities in which we choose to engage or not.

Something similar can be said about terms such as "production," "distribution," and "consumption," those terms that denote what nineteenth-century economists considered to be key elements of the "economy." "Production" occurs when workers "produce" a "product"; all of these terms denote activities specific to capitalist imposition of work. People are not put to work in just any old way but rather in "production" processes specifically designed to "produce" "products" for sale. These terms are so hegemonic that we are tempted to apply them in all sorts of completely different situations. When we grow food in the backyard or collectively in community gardens, or so raise flocks or herds, are we engaged in "production"? Are we "producing" food? Is the food we harvest a "product"? Certainly not in the capitalist sense, if we are growing food for our own, and perhaps our neighbors', enjoyment and nutrition.

We know that economists theorize "production" with mathematical functions. In the general function $Q = f(K,L,N)$, output (Q) is viewed as the result of the input labor (L) combined with other inputs—in this case, capital (K) and land (N). Particular functions are intended to represent particular technologies. Such functions abstract almost completely from the actual concrete activity of growing plants or raising animals, not only by being a mathematical simplification that fails to grasp the complexity of gardening or husbandry but also by completely missing the personal and social significances of the activity. Gardening and raising animals, like traditional farming, necessarily involves a connection with the earth and with nature more generally. At the very least, we are intimately involved in the cycle of life. We prepare soil and

plant seed. We care for growing plants, providing them with nu-
trients and water; we remove competitors by weeding. We harvest
their fruits, literally and figuratively. And, if we are smart, we return their remains to enrich the soil from which they sprang. We
tend to the birth of animals. We take care of them by feeding them
and tending to their health as they grow. And, if we are smart, we
not only care for them but we honor them as vital companions. We
harvest food from them, be it milk, eggs, or wool, or, through their
death, meat, hides, or feathers. In all these, we must take into account the ecological complexity of our intertwined lives, eschewing
practices that undermine both them and us.

For many, such activities amount to much more. Within the
widespread movement to create urban gardens, they provide a
connection to neighbors and a space of community building. In
some traditional cases, they constitute a religious link to the cosmos. For example, Mayan peasants' *milpas*—cornfields—are vital
affirmations of their place as "people of the corn" since the time of
creation.[37] Although their story differs, corn and its cultivation and
consumption are also at the center of Hopi spirituality and culture.[38] Capitalism and its economists snuff out such significances
as they turn these aspects of our connection to the rest of nature
into the simple production of food. Capitalism does so from the
subordination of once independent farmers' activities through
corporate dictated contracts to industrial agribusiness practices,
where the choice of inputs and outputs is determined through
cost-benefit studies of how to maximize profits. Capitalist factory
farming manipulates and mistreats soil, plants, animals, and labor—to their detriment and to the detriment of the wider ecology
and us. The results: the de-valorization of the human connection to
the earth and the poisoning of earth, plants, animals, and humans.

---

37 In ancient Mayan mythology—still alive to a surprising degree long centuries
after the imposition of Catholicism by the invading Spanish—the gods created humans from corn. See the classic remaining text of Mayan mythology, *Popol Vuh: The
Mayan Book of the Dawn of Life*, rev. ed., translated by Dennis Tedlock (New York:
Touchstone, 1996).

38 See Dennis Wall and Virgil Masayesva, "People of the Corn: Teaching in Hopi
Traditional Agriculture, Spirituality and Sustainability, *American Indian Quarterly*
28, nos. 3–4 (Summer/Fall 2004), 435–53.

Discovering and elaborating ways of cultivating plants and caring
for animals that are healthier for them, the earth, and ourselves
must be vital components of our efforts to craft new worlds beyond
capitalism.

As we divert our efforts from working for capital to meeting
our needs and satisfying our desires directly, let us also abandon
its language (and the jargon Marx elaborated to understand capitalism) and find new ways to talk about the worlds we are crafting.
Instead of speaking of *producing*, let us speak of making (things)
or doing this or that (singing, sewing, growing, coding, helping,
etc.) Instead of *products*, let us speak of the things we make or the
results of our doing. Instead of speaking of *services*, let us speak
of helping each other. Instead of speaking of *productivity*, let us
speak of the complex results of our actions. Instead of speaking of
labor power, let us speak of our desires and abilities to do all kinds
of things, alone and together. Instead of speaking of *working*, we
can speak instead of how we invent, create, and make things, how
we help each other, and how we elaborate our desires and abilities
throughout our lives.[39] These are ways I choose to talk about the
diverse kinds of activities that I find in Chris Carlsson's many concrete examples of "a new politics of work."[40]

All of the above involve our activities as social individuals.
Our behaviors are shaped by our experiences among others and
sometimes among individuals acting together as collectivities or
communities. At the same time, whatever our common experiences and interactions, as individuals we have differing needs and
desires. Because it is neither possible nor desirable for us to meet

---

39 The project of escaping from the language of domination was at the heart of a
collective process that generated the contents of Sachs, ed., *The Development Dictionary*—a compilation of essays on various words, common in the discussion of
"development," both among capitalist policy makers and those seeking alternative
paths. See Jean Robert's essay ("Production," pp. 177–91) in that collection for a
historical evaluation and critique of the concept of production that juxtaposes capitalist "economic production" to traditional activities such as the cultivation of the
Mexican *milpa*. Although he misinterprets Marx, his essay provides good reasons
for setting aside capitalist concepts when we want to think through the creation of
alternatives and evaluate projects for their elaboration.

40 Carlsson, *Nowtopia*.

all our needs or satisfy all our desires through our own actions, we need the help of others, and we need to help others. Within capitalism, such de facto *mutual aid* is mostly organized through a division of labor and the market exchange of commodities and services produced by that labor. Within a post-capitalist community, or commons, we can organize such mutual aid quite differently.

We can find examples of alternative ways of organizing mutual aid in both the past and the present. Historians and anthropologists have identified a variety of non-market ways in which communities, ancient and recent, large and small, have organized the sharing of the fruits of individual and small groups' different activities.[41] They range from informal systems of reciprocity to formalized pooling and redistribution. An examination of contemporary commons, both old and new, can reveal current approaches to such organization.

Here we have another problem with language. Both participants and observers of contemporary commons are often tempted to use the familiar economic term "exchange" to describe the relationships among people involved in organizing commons. However, using that term has become questionable because it has been so closely associated with exchanges in markets (e.g., money for goods or services or vice versa), whether we speak of "equal" or "unequal" exchange. Even extracted from the context of markets, most people think of exchange in terms of *trading*—one individual (or group) transfers something to another individual (or group) only under the condition that the other transfer something back. However, *sharing* the fruits of one's activities does not necessarily involve a trade—it can take the form of simply giving to "to each according to their needs"—that is, one-way transfers. We can find better terms as we construct our paths from the economy into new worlds.

One thing I like about the wording in the *Promissory Notes* passage above is the sense of de-commodification as a process, getting from here (working for capital, producing commodities) to there (making things, helping each other, elaborating our desires

41 Beside Kropotkin's book, see for example, chapter 4 ("Societies and Economic Systems") of Karl Polanyi's *The Great Transformation: The Political and Economic Origins of Our Time* (New York: Amereon House, 1944).

and abilities). As long as much that we need and desire is available only through markets, it is difficult to escape them entirely.[42] The authors write of the creation of markets (or forms of exchange) "that do not rule our lives." It sounds good. However, making one's *goal* to be such markets is a formulation that evokes, for me, "market socialism." I prefer the notion of progressively marginalizing both markets and exchange—as I have suggested in the previous chapter's discussion of restricting the need for money.

To sum up: if Marx's labor theory of value teaches us that the fundamental source of capitalist control and of much misery in our lives is the endless imposition of far more work than we either need or desire, then to undermine that control and to free ourselves from the associated misery, all of our struggles, to the degree possible, must include the reduction of work—both on the job and off. Only through the reduction of work can we gain the free time and energy necessary for the discovery and elaboration of alternative, more agreeable ways of organizing our lives—individually and collectively. As money and markets are not only key elements of the capitalist imposition of work but cultivate undesirable social attitudes and relationships, so too must our struggles, to the degree possible, find ways to marginalize those institutions and construct alternatives. The reduction in the roles of, and eventual elimination of, work, money, and markets are not just utopian dreams, nor need they be limited to "nowtopian" experiments. They are all possible. It is only a matter of finding the best paths to doing so.

With respect to the reduction of work as we know it, we can—as Engels argued long ago—eliminate huge amounts of labor by progressively dispensing with work necessitated only by the existence of capitalist institutions and the enforcement of capitalist rules. At the same time, by systematically and successfully fighting

---

42 A romantic withdrawal from society at large, to create entirely self-sufficient communes, not only separates those who do from wider struggles but involves giving up a great many things that the working class has invented and developed in the past to meet its needs and desires. The process is akin, on a small scale, to the proposal put forward by some *dependistas* for whole countries to withdraw from the world market and go it alone. Both projects just lead to vastly more work for those involved.

for the fruits of rising productivity to be enjoyed in the form of less work as well as more wealth, the amount of labor necessary to meet our needs and desires can be steadily reduced toward zero.

With respect to the marginalization and elimination of money and markets, we need only invent and impose rules to replace them. A great many such rules already exist; we need only identify others that we require, invent them and fight for their use. Given that one of the noxious aspects of money and markets is the reductionism they involve—especially the reduction of myriad human values held in different communities to exchange value measured by money, the elaboration of alternative rules can be as diverse as those communities themselves. We are no longer talking about replacing one world with another, but one world with many.

BIBLIOGRAPHY

Abrams, Herbert K. "A Short History of Occupational Health." *Journal of Public Health Policy* 22, no. 1 (2001): 34–80.

Achtenberg, Emily. "From Water Wars to Water Scarcity: Bolivia's Cautionary Tale." *ReVista: Harvard Review of Latin America* 12, no. 2 (Winter 2013): 39–41. http://revista.drclas.harvard.edu/files/revista/files/water_0.pdf.

Alquati, Romano. *Sulla FIAT e Altri Scritti*, Milan: Feltrinelli Editore, 1975.

Ames, Roger T., and Henry Rosemont, Jr. *The Analects of Confucius: A Philosophical Translation*. New York: Ballantine Books, Random House, 1998.

Arendt, Hannah. *The Human Condition*. Chicago: The University of Chicago Press, 1958.

Arquilla, John and David Ronfeldt. "Cyberwar is Coming!" *Comparative Strategy* 12, no. 2 (1993): 141–165.

———. *Networks and Netwars: The Future of Terror, Crime and Militancy*. Santa Monica: RAND, 2001.

———. *The Advent of Netwar*. Santa Monica: RAND, 1996.

Bagehot, Walter. *Lombard Street: A Description of the Money Market*. New York: Charles Scribner's Sons, 1873, 1897.

Bahadur, Nina. "'Femvertising' Ads are Empowering Women—and Making Money for Brands." *The Huffington Post*, October 3, 1014. http://www.huffingtonpost.com/2014/10/02/femvertising-advertising-empowering-women_n_5921000.html.

Baran, Paul. *The Political Economy of Growth*. New York: Monthly Review Press, 1957.

Barber, William. *Designs within Disorder: Franklin D. Roosevelt, the Economists, and the Shaping of American Economic Policy, 1933–1945*. New York: Cambridge University Press, 1996.

Becker, Gary S. *Human Capital: A Theoretical and Empirical Analysis, with Special Reference to Education*. National Bureau of Economic Research, 1964.

Bellamy, Edward. *Looking Backwards* (1888). New York: New American Library, 1960.

Bennett, Vivienne. *The Politics of Water: Urban Protest, Gender, and Power in Monterrey, Mexico*. Pittsburgh: University of Pittsburg Press, 1995.

Berle, Adolf and Gardiner Means. *The Modern Corporation and Private Property*. New York: Macmillan, 1932.

Bianco, Anthony. "The Casino Society: Playing with Fire." *Business Week*, September 16 (1985): 78ff.

Billy Budd. Directed by Peter Ustinov. Los Angeles: Allied Artists Pictures, 1962. Film.

Bobrow-Strain, Aaron. *Intimate Enemies: Landowners, Power, and Violence in Chiapas.* Durham: Duke University Press, 2007.
Boddy, Raford and James Crotty. "Class Conflict and Macro-Policy: The Political Business Cycle." *Review of Radical Political Economics 7,* no. 1 (April 1975): 1–10.
Bologna, Sergio. "Composizione di classe e teoria del partito alle origini del movimento consiliare." In *Operai e Stato: Lotte operaie e riforma dello stato capitalistico tra revoluzione d'ottobre e New Deal,* Sergio Bologna, G.P. Rawick, M. Gobbini, A. Negri, L. Ferrari Bravo, and F. Gambino. Milano: Feltrinelli, 1972, 13–46. In English: "Class Composition and the Theory of the Party at the Origin of the Workers' Council Movement." *Telos,* no. 13 (Fall 1972): 4–27.
——. "The Theory and History of the Mass Worker in Italy." *Common Sense: Journal of the Edinburgh Conference of Socialist Economists,* nos. 11 and 12 (1991): 16–29 and 52–78.
Braverman, Harry. *Labor and Monopoly Capital: The Degradation of Work in the Twentieth Century,* New York: Monthly Review Press, 1974. In Italian: *Lavoro e capitale monopolistico. La degradazione del lavoro nel XX secolo,* Torino: Einaudi Editore, 1978.
Brophy, Enda. "Language put to Work: Cognitive Capitalism, Call Center Labor and Worker Inquiry," *Journal of Communication Inquiry 34,* no. 4 (2011): 410–416.
——. "The Subterranean Stream: Communicative Capitalism and Call Centre Labour," *ephemera: theory & politics in organization* 10, nos. 3 and 4, 2010. http://www.ephemerajournal.org/contribution/subterranean-stream-communicative-capitalism-and-call-centre-labour.
Bukharin, Nikolai. *Imperialism and the World Economy* (1917). New York: Monthly Review Classics, n.d.
——. *The Economic Theory of the Leisure Class* (1914). New York: Monthly Review Press, 1972.
Caffentzis, George. "The End of Work or the Renaissance of Slavery? A Critique of Rifkin and Negri." *Common Sense: Journal of the Edinburgh Conference of Socialist Economists,* no. 24 (December 1998): 20–38. Reprinted in *In Letters of Blood and Fire: Work, Machines and the Crisis of Capitalism,* George Caffentzis. Oakland and Brooklyn: PM Press, Common Notions, and Autonomedia, 2013, 66–81.
——. "Essay: Dealing with Debt," *Red Pepper,* August 2014. http://www.redpepper.org.uk/essay-dealing-with-debt.
——. "Marxism after the Death of Gold" in Marcel van der Linden and Karl Heinz Roth (eds) *Beyond Marx: Theorizing the Global Labour Relations of the Twenty-First Century.* Chicago: Haymarket Books, 2014, 395–415.
——. *From Capitalist Crisis to Proletarian Slavery: An Introduction to Class Struggle in the US, 1973–1998.* Jamaica Plain, Mass.: Midnight

Notes, 1999.

———. "The Student Loan Debt Abolition Movement in the United States." In *Generation of Debt: The University in Default and the Undoing of Campus Life.* Pamphlet by *Reclamations Journal,* August–September 2011, 31–41.

Callahan, Raymond E. *Education and the Cult of Efficiency: A Study of the Social Forces That Have Shaped the Administration of the Public Schools.* Chicago: University of Chicago Press, 1962.

Captain Philips. Directed by Paul Greengrass. Los Angeles: Columbia Pictures, 2013. Film.

Caraway, Brett. "Audience Labor in the New Media Environment. A Marxian Revisiting of the Audience Commodity." *Media, Culture & Society* 33, no. 5 (2011): 693–708.

———. "Crisis of Command: Theorizing Value in New Media." *Communication Theory* 26, no. 1 (February 2016): 64–81.

Cariappa, Cheeyakapuvanda. *The Unruly Masses in the Development of Economic Thought.* Ph.D. dissertation, University of Texas at Austin, August 2003. Available through ProQuest., UMI#3116273.

Carlsson, Chris. *Nowtopia: How Pirate Programmers, Outlaw Bicyclists, and Vacant-Lot Gardeners are Inventing the Future Today!* Oakland: AK Press, 2008.

Carpignano, Paolo. "US Class Composition in the Sixties" *Zerowork,* no.1 (December 1975): 7–32.

Carr, E. H. *The Bolshevik Revolution 1917–23,* Vol. 2. London: Penguin, 1966.

Chamberlin, Edward. "Monopolistic Competition Revisited." *Economica,* New Series 18, no. 72 (November 1951): 343–362.

———. *The Theory of Monopolistic Competition: A Re-orientation of the Theory of Value.* Boston: Harvard University Press, 1933.

Chandler, Alfred D. *The Visible Hand: The Managerial Revolution in American Business.* Cambridge: Belknap Press, 1993.

Churchill, Ward and Jim Vander Wall, eds. *The COINTELPRO Papers: Documents from the FBI's Secret Wars Against Dissent in the United States.* Boston: South End Press, 1990, 2002.

Cleaver, Harry. "Close the IMF, Abolish Debt and End Development: A Class Analysis of the International Debt Crisis." *Capital & Class,* no. 39 (Winter 1989): 17–50.

———. "Competition or Cooperation?" *Common Sense,* no. 9 (April 1990): 20–22.

———. "The Contradictions of the Green Revolution." *Monthly Review* 24, no. 2 (June 1972): 80–111.

———. "Domestic Labor and Value in Mariarosa Dalla Costa's 'Women and the Subversion of the Community'" (1971). http://la.utexas.edu/users/hcleaver/357k/HMCDallaCostaDomesticLaborAndValue.htm.

294

————. "Genesis of Zerowork #1." https://www.academia.edu/7363142/
Genesis_of_Zerowork_1.
————. "Karl Marx: Economist or Revolutionary?" In *Marx, Schumpeter &
Keynes: A Centenary Celebration of Dissent*, edited by Suzanne W.
Helburn and David F. Bramhall. Armonk, NY: M.E. Sharpe, 1986,
121–146.
————. "Malaria, the Politics of Public Health, and the International Crisis"
in the *Review of Radical Political Economics* 9, no. 1 (April 1997):
97–99.
————. "On Schoolwork and the Struggle Against It" (2006). http://la
.utexas.edu/users/hcleaver/OnSchoolwork200606.pdf.
————. "Socialism?" In *The Development Dictionary: Knowledge as Power*,
edited by Wolfgang Sachs. London: Zed Books, 1992, 233–249.
————. "The Uses of an Earthquake." *Midnight Notes*, no. 9 (May 1988):
10–14.
————. "Vorwort zur deutschen Übersetzung." In *"Das Kapital" Politisch
Lesen: Eine alternative Interpretation des Marxschen Hauptwerks*.
Wien: Mandelbaum Kritik & Utopie, 2012, 9–41.
————. "Work Is Still the Central Issue! New Words for New Worlds." In
*The Labour Debate: An Investigation into the Theory and Reality
of Capitalist Work*, edited by Ana Dinerstein and Michael Leary.
Hampshire: Ashgate, 2002, 135–148.
————. "Work, Value and Domination: On the Continuing Relevance of the
Marxian Labor Theory of Value in the Crisis of the Keynesian Planner
State" (1989). Published as: "Lavoro, Valore e Dominio: Sull'attuale
rilevanza della teoria di Marx del laboro-valore nella crisi dello sta-
to piano Keynesiano." *Vis a Vis: Quaderni per l'autonomia di classe*
(Bologna), no. 2 (Spring 1994): 73–90.
Cleaver, William. "Wildcats in the Appalachian Coal Fields." *Zerowork*, no.
1 (1975): 113–126.
Conference of Socialist Economists. *The Labor Process & Class Strategies*.
CSE Pamphlet no. 1, 1976.
Curl, John. *For all the People: Uncovering the Hidden History of Coopera-
tion, Cooperative Movements and Communalism in America*. Oak-
land: PM Press, 2012.
Curry, Timothy and Lynn Shibut. "The Cost of the Savings and Loan Cri-
sis." *FDIC Banking Review* 13, no. 2 (2000): 26–35.
Dalla Costa, Mariarosa. "Donne e sovversione sociale" ("Women and the
Subversion of the Community"). In *Potere femminile e sovversione
sociale*, 33–71. Padova, Italy: Marsilio editori, 1972.
————. *Famiglia, welfare e stato tra Progressismo e New Deal*, Milano:
FrancoAngeli, 1983. English translation: *Family, Welfare and the
State: Between Progressivism and the New Deal*. Brooklyn: Common
Notions, 2015.
————. "Riproduzione e emigrazione." In *L'Operaio multinazionale in*

Europa, A. Serafini, et al, 207–242. Milano: Feltrinelli Editore, 1974. In English: "Reproduction and Emigration." *Zerowork*, no. 3, Special Issue on Immigration. http://www.zerowork.org/Dalla CostaReproductionEmigrationA.html

Dalla Costa, Mariarosa and Monica Chilese. *Our Mother Ocean: Enclosure, Commons, and the Global Fishermen's Movement.* Brooklyn: Common Notions, 2014.

Darity, Sandy and Bobbie Horn. *The Loan Pushers: The Role of Commercial Banks in the International Debt Crisis.* New York: Ballinger, 1988.

De Angelis, Massimo. *The Beginning of History: Value Struggles and Global Capital.* London: Pluto Press, 2007.

De Angelis, Massimo, and David Harvie. "Cognitive Capitalism and the Rat Race: How Capital Measures Ideas and Affects in UK Higher Education." *Historical Materialism* 17 (2009): 3–30.

De Kadt, Maarten. "Insurance: A Clerical Work Factory." In *Case Studies on the Labor Process*, edited by Andrew Zimbalist, 242–256. New York: Monthly Review Press, 1979.

De Paula, Joao Antonio et al. "Marx in 1869: Notebook B113, *The Economist* and *The Money Market Review*." Belo Horizonte, Brazil: UFMG/CEDEPLAR, 2011.

De Peuter, Greig, and Nick Dyer-Witheford. "Commons and Cooperatives." *Affinities: A Journal of Radical Theory, Culture and Action* 4, no. 1 (Summer 2010): 30–56.

De Soto, Hernando. *The Other Path: The Invisible Revolution in the Third World.* New York: Harper & Row, 1989.

Demac, Donna, and Philip Mattera. "Developing and Underdeveloping New York: The 'Fiscal Crisis' and the Imposition of Austerity." *Zerowork*, no. 2 (1977): 113–139.

Dickens, Charles. *A Tale of Two Cities* (1859). New York: Penguin Classics, 2003.

Dyer-Witheford, Nick. "The Circulation of the Common." A talk given in the "Future of the Commons" series, University of Minnesota, October 29, 2009. https://commonism.wordpress.com/2009/11/30/the-circulation-of-the-common/.

———. *Cyber-proletariat: Global Labor in the Digital Vortex.* London: Pluto Press, 2015.

Dylan, Bob. "Only a Pawn in Their Game." *The Times They Are a-Changin'* Columbia, 1964. Album.

Eagleton, Terry. "Communism: Lear or Gonzalo?" In *The Idea of Communism*, edited by Costas Douzinas and Slavoj Žižek. New York: Verso 2010, 101–110.

Economic Report of the President for 2015. Washington, D.C.: GPO, 2015. https://www.whitehouse.gov/sites/default/files/docs/cea_2015_erp_complete.pdf.

Elk, Mike, and Bob Sloan. "The Hidden History of ALEC and Prison Labor." *The Nation*, August 1, 2011. https://www.thenation.com/article
/hidden-history-alec-and-prison-labor/.

Engels, Friedrich. "Speeches in Elberfeld" (February 8, 1845). In Karl
Marx and Friedrich Engels, *Collected Works*, Vol. 4, 243–251. London: Lawrence and Wishart, 1975.

Esteva, Gustavo. "Regenerating People's Space." *Alternatives* 12 (1987):
125–152.

Exner, Andreas. "Degrowth and Demonetization: On the Limits of a
Non-Capitalist Market Economy." *Capitalism Nature Socialism* 25,
no. 3 (2014): 9–27.

Farmelant, James. "Obituary of Gerald Allan Cohen (1941–2009)." *MR-
Zine*, August 8, 2009. http://mrzine.monthlyreview.org/2009/
farmelant080809.html.

Fast Food Nation. Directed by Richard Linklater. Century City, CA: Fox
Searchlight Pictures, 2006. Film.

Faux, Jeff. "The Austerity Trap and the Growth Alternative." *World Policy
Journal* 5, no. 3 (Summer 1988): 367–413.

FDIC. *2013 FDIC National Survey of Unbanked and Underbanked Households*. October 2014.

Fishing Without Nets. Directed by Cutter Hodierne. Cleveland: Think Media Studios, 2014. Film.

Foster, John Bellamy. "Memorial for Paul Sweezy, February 27, 2004."
Monthly Review. http://monthlyreview.org/commentary/memorial
-service-for-paul-marlor-sweezy-1910-2004/.

———. *The Theory of Monopoly Capitalism: An Elaboration of Marxian
Political Economy* (New Edition). New York: Monthly Review Press,
2014.

Foster, John Bellamy and Fred Magdoff. *The Great Financial Crisis:
Causes and Consequences*. New York: Monthly Review Press, 2009.

Foucault, Michel. *Folie et deraison: Historire de la folie a l'age classique*.
Paris: Gallimard, 1972. In English: *History of Madness*. New York:
Routledge, 2006.

———. *Naissance de la Clinique: Une archéologie du regard médical*. Par-
is: Presses Universitaires de France, 1963. In English: *Birth of the
Clinic: An Archeology of Medical Perception*. New York: Pantheon
Books, 1973.

———. "The Politics of Health in the Eighteenth Century." *Foucault Studies*, no. 18 (October 2014): 113–127.

———. *Surveiller et punir: Naissance de la Prison*. Paris: Gallimard, 1975.
In English: *Discipline and Punish: The Birth of the Prison*. New
York: Vintage Books, 1995.

Fuchs, Christian. "Dallas Smythe Today—The Audience Commodity, the
Digital Labour Debate, Marxist Political Economy and Critical
Theory. Prolegomena to a Digital Labour Theory of Value." *Triple*

C: Open Access Journal for a Global Sustainable Information Society 10, no. 2 (2012): 692–740. http://www.triple-c.at/index.php/tripleC/article/download/443/414.

Gardner, Richard. *Grito! Tijerina and the New Mexico Land Grant War of 1967*. Indianapolis: Bobbs-Merrill Company, 1970.

Gaskell, Elizabeth. *Mary Barton: A Tale of Manchester Life* (1848). New York: Penguin, 1988.

Glaberman, Martin. *Union Committeemen and Wildcat Strikes*. Detroit: Correspondence, 1955.

Glenn, Evelyn Nakano and Roslyn L. Feldberg. "Proletarianizing Clerical Work: Technology and Organizational Control in the Office." In *Case Studies on the Labor Process*, edited by Andrew Zimbalist, 51–72. New York: Monthly Review Press, 1979.

Gómez, Alan Eladio. *People's Power, Educational Democracy and Low Intensity War: The UNAM Student Strike, 1999–2000*. M.A. Thesis, University of Texas at Austin, 2002.

Gorenflo, Neal. "The New Sharing Economy." Shareable.net, December 24, 2010. http://www.shareable.net/blog/the-new-sharing-economy.

Gramsci, Antonio. "Americanism and Fordism" (1934). In *Selections from the Prison Notebooks*. New York: International Publishers, 1971, 279–318.

Guattari, Felix. *La revolution moleculaire*. Fontenay-Sous-Bois: Recherches, 1977.

Guha, Ranajit, and Gayatri Spivak, eds. *Selected Subaltern Studies*. Delhi: Oxford University Press, 1988.

Gunn, Richard, and Adrian Wilding. "Revolutionary or Less-than-revolutionary Recognition?" Heathwood Institute and Press, July 24, 2013. http://www.heathwoodpress.com/revolutionary-less-than-revolutionary-recognition/.

Gutman, Herbert, ed. *Work, Culture, and Society in Industrializing America*. New York: Knopf, 1976.

Hanusch, Horst, and Andreas Pyka, eds. *Elgar Companion to Neo-Schumpeterian Economics*. Northampton, Mass.: Edward Elgar Publishing, 2007.

Haraszti, Miklos. *A Worker in a Worker's State*. London: Penguin, 1977.

Hardt, Michael, and Antonio Negri. *Empire*. Cambridge: Harvard University Press, 2000.

Harris, Wess. ed. *Truth be Told: Perspectives on The Great West Virginia Mine War, 1890 to Present*. Gay, West Virginia: Appalachian Community Services, 2015.

Hegel, Friedrich. *Grundlinien der Philosophie des Rechts* (1821). In English: *Philosophy of Right*, T. M. Knox's translation, Oxford: Clarendon Press, 1952, and Stephen Houlgate, Oxford: Oxford University Press, 2008.

———. *The Science of Logic*, W. H. Johnston and L. G. Struthers translation,

New York: The MacMillan Company, 1929; A. V. Miller translation, New York: Humanities Press, 1969; and George di Giovanni translation, Cambridge: Cambridge University Press, 2010.

Helman, Christopher. "The Profits of Piracy." *Forbes*, April 15, 2010. http://www.forbes.com/2010/04/15/pirates-somalia-shipping -insurance-business-logistics-piracy.html.

Hicks, John. *Value and Capital* (1939). London: Oxford University Press, 1946.

A Highjacking. Directed by Tobias Lindholm. Copenhagen: Nordisk Film, 2012. Film.

Hilferding, Rudolf. *Finance Capital: A Study of the Latest Phase of Capitalist Development*. Boston: Routledge & Kegan Paul, 1981.

Hobson, John A. *Imperialism: A Study* (1902). Ann Arbor: University of Michigan Press, 1965.

Hobson, John A., and A. F. Mummery. *The Physiology of Industry* (1889). Boston: Routledge Reprint edition, 2013.

Hribal, Jason. "Animals are Part of the Working Class: A Challenge to Labor History." *Labor History* 44, no. 4 (2003): 435–453.

———. *Fear of the Animal Planet. The Hidden History of Animal Resistance*. Petrolia/Oakland: Counterpunch/AK Press, 2010.

Hynes, Patricia. *A Patch of Eden: America's Inner-City Gardeners*. White River, Vermont: Chelsea Green, 1996.

Hyppolite, Jean. *Phénoménologie de L'Esprit*. Paris: Editions Montaigne, 1947.

Illich, Ivan. *After Deschooling, What?* London: Writers and Readers Publishing Co-operative, 1974.

———. *Deschooling Society*. New York: Harper & Row, 1971.

———. *Medical Nemesis*. London: Calder & Boyars, 1974.

———. *Toward a History of Needs*. New York: Pantheon Books, 1978.

ILO. *ILO Global Estimate of Forced Labor: Results and Methodology*. 2012. http://www.ilo.org/global/topics/forced-labour/publications/ WCMS_182004/lang--en/index.htm.

Kasmir, Sharryn. *The Myth of Mondragon: Cooperatives, Politics and Working Class Life in a Basque Town*. Albany: State University of New York Press, 1996.

Katsiaficas, George. *The Imagination of the New Left: A Global Analysis of 1968*. Boston: South End Press, 1999.

Kaye, Harvey. *The British Marxist Historians*. London: Palgrave Macmillan (new edition), 1995.

Keynes, John Maynard. *General Theory of Employment, Interest and Money* (1936). New York: Harcourt, Brace & World, 1965.

Kilgore, James. "The Myth of Prison Slave Labor Camps in the U.S." *Counterpunch*, August 9–11, 2013. http://www.counterpunch .org/2013/08/09/the-myth-of-prison-slave-labor-camps-in-the -u-s.

Kindleberger, Charles. *Manias, Panics, and Crashes: A History of Financial Crises*. London: Macmillan, 1978.

The Kinks. *Soap Opera*. RCA, 1975. Album.

Kropotkin, Peter. *The Conquest of Bread* (1892). Montreal: Black Rose Books, 1990.

———. *Fields, Factories and Workshops Tomorrow* (1889). London: Freedom Press, 1985.

———. *Mutual Aid: A Factor of Evolution* (1902). London: Freedom Press, 2006.

Lamphere, Louise. "Fighting the Piece-Rate System: New Dimensions of an Old Struggle in the Apparel Industry." In *Case Studies on the Labor Process*, edited by Andrew Zimbalist, 257–276. New York: Monthly Review Press, 1979.

Lavaca Collective. *Sin Patron: Stories from Argentina's Worker-Run Factories*. Chicago: Haymarket Books, 2007.

Lazzarato, Maurizio. *The Making of the Indebted Man*. South Pasadena: Semiotext(e), 2012.

Lazzarato, Maurizio, and Joshua David Jordan. *Governing by Debt*. South Pasadena: Semiotext(e), 2013.

Le Goff, Jacques. *Your Money or Your Life: Economy and Religion in the Middle Ages*. New York: Zone Books, 1988.

Lenin, Vladimir Ilyich. *Imperialism: The Highest Stage of Capitalism, A Popular Outline* (1917). Moscow: International Publishing, 1952.

Lichten, Eric. *Class, Power and Austerity: The New York City Fiscal Crisis*. South Hadley, Mass.: Bergin & Garvey, 1986.

Linebaugh, Peter. "Karl Marx, The Theft of Wood, and Working Class Composition: A Contribution to the Current Debate." *Crime and Social Justice*, 6 (Fall–Winter 1976): 5–16.

———. *Lizard Talk: Or, Ten Plagues and Another: A Historical Reprise in Celebration of the Anniversary of Boston ACT UP*. Jamaica Plain, Mass.: Midnight Notes, 1989.

———. *The London Hanged: Crime and Civil Society in the Eighteenth Century*, London: Allen Lane (Penguin Group), 1991.

Linebaugh, Peter, and Marcus Rediker. *The Many-Headed Hydra: Sailors, Slaves, Commoners and the Hidden History of the Revolutionary Atlantic*. Boston: Beacon Press, 2001.

Lovins, Amory B. "Energy Strategy: The Road Not Taken?" *Foreign Affairs* 55, no. 1 (October 1976): 65–96.

Luxemburg, Rosa. *Reform and Revolution and Other Writings*, Mineola, NY: Dover Publications, 2006.

Magdoff, Fred and John Bellamy Foster. "Stagnation and Financialization: The Nature of the Contradiction." *Monthly Review* 66, no. 1 (May 2014): 1–24.

Mandel, Ernest. *Marxist Economic Theory*, Vols. 1–2. New York: Monthly Review Press, 1968.

Mao Tse-tung. "How to Differentiate the Classes in the Rural Areas" (1933). In *Selected Works of Mao Tse-tung*, 137–139. Peking: Foreign Languages Press, 1967.

Marazzi, Christian. *The Violence of Financial Capitalism*. Los Angeles: Semiotext(e), 2010.

Marris, Robin. *The Economic Theory of 'Managerial' Capitalism*. London: Macmillan, 1964.

Marshall, Alfred, and Mary Paley. *The Economics of Industry*. London: Macmillan And Co., 1879.

Marx, Karl. *Capital* (1867), Vol. 1. New York: Penguin Books, 1990.

——. *Capital* (1893), Vol. 2. New York: Penguin Books, 1978.

——. *Capital* (1894), Vol. 3. New York: Penguin Books, 1990.

——. "The Chartist Movement" (1852). In Karl Marx and Friedrich Engels, *Collected Works*, Vol. 11. New York: International Publishers, 333–341.

——. "Class Struggles in France" (1850). In Karl Marx and Friedrich Engels, *Collected Works*, Vol. 10. New York: International Publishers, 45–145.

——. "The Critique of the Gotha Program" (1891). In Karl Marx and Friedrich Engels, *Collected Works*, Vol. 24. New York: International Publishers, 75–99.

——. *Dispatches for the New York Tribune: Selected Journalism of Karl Marx*. New York: Penguin Classics, 2008.

——. "The Eighteenth Brumaire of Louis Bonaparte" (1851–52). In Karl Marx and Friedrich Engels, *Collected Works*, Vol. 11. New York: International Publishers, 99–197.

——. *Grundrisse* (1859). The Pelican Marx Library. Harmondsworth, UK: Penguin Books, 1973.

——. "Inaugural Address of the Working Men's International Association" (1864). In Karl Marx and Friedrich Engels, *Collected Works*, Vol. 20. New York: International Publishers, 1985, 5–13.

——. "Proceedings of the Sixth Rhine Province Assembly. Third Article. Debates on the Law of the Theft of Wood" (1842). In Karl Marx and Friedrich Engels, *Collected Works*, Vol. 1. New York: International Publishers, 224–263.

——. "To Abraham Lincoln, President of the United States of America," (1864). Karl Marx and Friedrich Engels, *Collected Works*, Vol. 20. New York: International Publishers, 19–21.

——. "Value, Price and Profit," (1865), Karl Marx and Friedrich Engels, *Collected Works*, Vol. 20. New York: International Publishers, 101–149.

——. *A Workers' Inquiry* 1880, *New International*, December 1938, 379–381.

Marx, Karl to Engels, June 22, 1867. In Karl Marx and Friedrich Engels, *Collected Works*, Vol. 42. New York: International Publishers,

383–386.

Marx, Karl to Sigfrid Meyer and August Vogt (1870). In Karl Marx and Friedrich Engels, *Collected Works*, Vol. 43. New York: International Publishers, 471–476.

Marx, Karl, and Friedrich Engels *Communist Manifesto* (1848). In Karl Marx and Friedrich Engels, *Collected Works*, Vol. 6. New York: International Publishers, 477–519.

———. *German Ideology* (1845–46). In Karl Marx and Friedrich Engels, *Collected Works*, Vol. 5. New York: International Publishers, 19–539.

Mattera, Philip. "National Liberation, Socialism and the Struggle against Work: The Case of Vietnam." Zerowork, no. 2 (1977): 71–89.

Mattick, Paul. *Marx and Keynes: The Limits of the Mixed Economy*. Boston: Porter Sargent Publisher, 1969.

Meek, Ronald. *Studies in the Labor Theory of Value*. New York: Monthly Review Press, 1956.

Mellencamp, John Cougar. "Rain on the Scarecrow." *Scarecrow*. Mercury, 1985. Album.

Melville, Herman. *Billy Budd, Sailor: An Inside Narrative* (1888), Chicago: University of Chicago Press, 1962.

———. *Moby Dick: or, The Whale* (1851). Norton Critical Edition, New York: W.W. Norton, 1967.

Midnight Notes. *The Work/Energy Crisis and the Apocalypse* (1981). Reprinted in *In Letters of Blood and Fire: Work, Machines, and the Crisis of Capitalism*, George Caffentzis. Oakland: PM Press, 2013, 11–57.

Midnight Notes Collective and Friends. *Promissory Notes: From Crisis to Commons*. Jamaica Plain, Mass.: Midnight Notes, 2009.

Modern Times. Directed by Charlie Chaplin. 1936. Criterion Collection, 2010. DVD.

Moore, Sir Thomas. *Utopia* (1516). http://www.gutenberg.org/ebooks/2130.

Morishima, Michio. "The Fundamental Marxian Theorem: A Reply to Samuelson." *Journal of Economic Literature* 12, no. 1 (March 1974): 71–74.

———. "Marx in the Light of Modern Economic Theory." *Econometrica* 42, no. 4 (July 1974): 611–632.

———. *Marx's Economics: A Dual Theory of Value and Growth*. Cambridge: Cambridge University Press, 1978.

Morishima, Michio, and F. Seton. "Aggregation in Leontief Matrices and the Labour Theory of Value." *Econometrica* 29, no. 2 (April 1961): 203–220.

Morris, William. *News from Nowhere; Or, An Epoch of Rest* (1891). http://www.gutenberg.org/ebooks/3261.

Negri, Antonio. "Crisi dello Stato-Piano: comunismo e organizzazione rivoluzionaria." *Potere Operaio*, no. 45 (September 25,1971). In English: "Crisis of the Planner-State: Communism and Revolutionary

Organization." In *Revolution Retrieved: Selected Writings on Marx, Keynes, Capitalist Crisis and New Social Subjects*, 97–148. London: Red Notes, 1989.

———. *Marx au-dela Marx: cahiers de travail sur les "Grundrisse."* Paris: Christian Bourgois, 1979. In Italian: *Marx Oltra Marx: Quaderno di lavoro sui Grundrisse*. Milano: Feltrinelli, 1979. In English: *Marx beyond Marx: Lessons of the Grundrisse*. South Hadley, Mass.: Bergin & Garvey Publishers, 1984.

———. "Valeur-travail: crise et problèmes de reconstruction dans le post-moderne." *Futur antérieur*, no. 10, (1992): 30–36.

Nelson, Anitra. "An Impossible Marriage: Solidarity Economy and Monetary Economy." Presented to an UNRISD Conference on "Potential and Limits of Social and Solidarity Economy" in 2010. http://www.unrisd.org/unrisd/website/newsview.nsf/(httpNews)/B98423E686C1FEBEC1257B3A00493CAC.

Nelson, Anitra, and Frans Timmerman, eds. *Life Without Money: Building Fair and Sustainable Economies*. London: Pluto Press, 2011.

"New York Banker to Join Faculty." *The Stanford Daily* 115, no. 24, April 1, 1949: 1. http://stanforddailyarchive.com/cgi-bin/stanford?a=d&d=stanford19490401-01.2.8&srpos=1&e=-------en-20--1--txt-txIN-New+York+Banker+to+Join+Faculty------.

Nietzsche, Friedrich. "On the Future of Our Educational Institutions" (1872). http://www.thenietzschechannel.com/lectures/fed/fed-eng.htm.

Owen, Robert. *Report to the Committee of the Association for the Relief of the Manufacturing and Labouring Poor* (1817) and *Report to the County of Lanark* (1820). In *Selected Works of Robert Owen, Vol 1, Early Writings*, edited by Gregory Claeys. London: William Pickering, 1993, 143–155 and 287–332 respectively.

Palazzini, Karen L. *Women's Work in Lauro de Freitas, Bahia, Brazil: Marginalization or Autonomous Development*. Ph.D. Dissertation, University of Texas at Austin, 1997.

Panzieri, Raniero. "Plusvalore e pianificazione: Appunti di lettura del Capitale." *Quaderni rossi* 4 : 257–288. In English: "Surplus-value and planning: notes on the reading of Capital." *The Labour Process & Class Strategies*, CSE Pamphlet no. 1, London: Stage 1, 1976, 4–25.

———. "Sull'uso capitalistico delle macchine nel neocapitalismo." *Quaderni rossi*, no. 1 (1961): 53–72. Reprinted in *La ripresa del marxismo leninismo in Italia*, Sapere Ed. 1975, 148–169. In English: "The Capitalist Use of Machinery: Marx Versus the 'Objectivists.'" In *Outlines of a Critique of Technology*, edited by Phil Slater, 44–68. Atlantic Highlands, NJ: Humanities Press, 1980.

Parton, Dolly. "9 to 5." *9 to 5 and Odd Jobs*. RCA, 1980. Album.

Peterson, Peter G. *Facing Up: How to Rescue the Economy from Crushing Debt and Restore the American Dream*. New York: Simon &

Schuster, 1993.
———. "The Morning After." *The Atlantic* (October 1987): 43–65.
Pink Floyd. "Money." *The Dark Side of the Moon*. Harvest, 1972. Album.
The Pirates of Somalia: The Untold Story. Directed by Neil Bell. 2011. Sweden: Robotat in association with Somali Tribal Rights Watch, 2015. DVD.
Piven, Francis Fox, and Richard Cloward. *Poor People's Movements: Why They Succeed and How They Fail*. New York: Pantheon, 1977.
Polanyi, Karl. *The Great Transformation: The Political and Economic Origins of Our Time* (1944). Boston: Beacon Press, 1971/2001.
Popol Vuh: The Mayan Book of the Dawn of Life. Translated by Dennis Tedlock. Revised edition. New York: Touchstone, 1996.
Preston, Darrell, and Chris Christoff. "Only Wall Street Wins in Detroit Crisis Reaping $474 Million Fee." *BloombergBusiness*, March 13, 2013. https://www.bloomberg.com/news/articles/2013-03-14/only-wall-street-wins-in-detroit-crisis-reaping-474-million-fee.
Rediker, Marcus. *Between the Devil and the Deep Blue Sea: Merchant Seamen, Pirates and the Anglo-American Maritime World, 1700–1750*. New York: Cambridge University Press, 1987.
———. *Outlaws of the Atlantic: Sailors, Pirates and Motley Crews in the Age of Sail*. Boston: Beacon Press, 2015.
———. *Villains of All Nations: Atlantic Pirates in the Golden Age*. Boston: Beacon Press, 2004.
Robinson, Joan. *The Economics of Imperfect Competition*. London: Macmillan and Co., 1933.
———. *An Essay on Marxian Economics*. London: Macmillan and Co., 1942.
Roemer, John. *Analytical Foundations of Marxian Economic Theory*. Cambridge: Cambridge University Press, 1981.
———. *Free to Lose: An Introduction to Marxist Economic Philosophy*. Cambridge, Mass.: Harvard University Press, 1988.
———. *A General Theory of Exploitation and Class*. Cambridge, Mass.: Harvard University Press, 1982.
———. *Value, Exploitation and Class*. Reading: Harwood Academic Publishers, 1986. New edition: Taylor & Francis, 2013.
Roett, Riordan. *Mexico-Political Update*. January 13, 1995. http://www.hartford-hwp.com/archives/46/027.html
Romano, Paul (Paul Singer), and Ria Stone (Grace Lee, later Boggs) *The American Worker* (1947). Detroit: Bewick/ED, 1972.
Ross, John. *Rebellion from the Roots: Indian Uprising in Chiapas*. Monroe, ME: Common Courage Press, 1995.
Rubel, Maximilien, and John Crump, eds. *Non-Market Socialism in the Nineteenth and Twentieth Centuries*. New York: St. Martin's Press, 1987.
Ruggeri, Andrés, and Marcelo Vieta. "Argentina's Worker-Recuperated

Enterprises, 2010–2013: A Synthesis of Recent Empirical Findings."
Journal of Entrepreneurial and Organizational Diversity 4, no. 1
(2014): 75–103.

Sachs, Wolfgang. *The Development Dictionary: A Guide to Knowledge as Power.*
New York: St. Martin's Press, 1992.

Sartre, Jean Paul. *Critique de la raison dialectique: Tome I, Théorie des
ensembles pratiques.* Paris: Gallimard, 1960. In English: *Critique of
Dialectical Reason* 1. London and New York: Verso, 1991, 2004.

———. *Critique de la raison dialectique: Tome II: L'intelligibilite de l'histoire.* Paris: Gallimard, 1985. In English: *Critique of Dialectical Reason* 2. London and New York: Verso, 2006.

Schor, Juliet. "Debating the Sharing Economy." The Great Transition Initiative, October 2014. http://www.greattransition.org/publication/
debating-the-sharing-economy.

Schultz, Theodore W. "Investment in Human Capital." *The American Economic Review* 51, no. 1 (March 1961): 1–17.

Schumpeter, Joseph. *Capitalism, Socialism and Democracy* (1942). New
York: Harper & Row, 1962.

———. *The Theory of Economic Development* (1912), Oxford: University of
Oxford Press, 1962.

Segal, Lynne. *Out of Time: The Pleasures and Perils of Ageing.* London:
Verso, 2014.

Shaikh, Anwar. "Political Economy and Capitalism: Notes on Dobb's Theory of Crisis." *Cambridge Journal of Economics* 2, no. 2 (June 1978):
233–251.

Shapiro-Perl, Nina. "The Piece Rate: Class Struggle on the Shop Floor.
Evidence from the Costume Jewelry Industry in Providence, Rhode
Island." In *Case Studies on the Labor Process*, edited by Andrew Zim-
balist, 277–298. New York: Monthly Review Press, 1979.

Shaviro, Steven. *No Speed Limit: Three Essays on Accelerationism.* Minneapolis: University of Minnesota Press, 2015.

Silver-Greenberg, Jessica. "Debtor Arrests Criticized." *Wall Street Journal*,
November 22, 2011. http://www.wsj.com/articles/SB100014240529
70203710704577052373900992432.

Sinclair, Upton *The Jungle* (1906). Chicago: University of Illinois Press,
1988.

Sitrin, Marina *Everyday Revolutions: Horizontalism and Autonomy in
Argentina.* London: Zed Books, 2012.

———. *Horizontalism: Voices of Popular Power in Argentina.* Oakland: AK
Press, 2007.

———. "Recuperating Work and Life." *Roar Magazine*, no. 0 (Winter   2015):   153–166.   https://roarmag.org/magazine/marina
-sitrin-recuperated-workplaces/.

Smith, Adam. *An Inquiry into the Nature and Causes of the Wealth of Nations* (1776). New York: Modern Library, 1937.

Smythe, Dallas. "Communications: Blindspot of Western Marxism." *Canadian Journal of Political and Social Theory* 1, no. 3 (Fall 1977).
———. *Dependency Road*. Norwood, NJ: Ablex, 1981.
Solow, Robert. "Technical Change and the Aggregate Production Function." *The Review of Economics and Statistics* 39, no. 3 (August 1957): 312–320.
Steindl, Josef. *Maturity and Stagnation in American Capitalism*. Oxford: Basil Blackwell, 1952.
Star Trek: The Next Generation. "The Neutral Zone." Season 1, Episode 26. Directed by James L. Conway. CBS, May 16, 1988. Television.
Stolen Seas. Directed by Thymaya Payne. Los Angeles: Brainstorm Media, 2012. Film.
Strange, Susan. *Casino Capitalism*, New York: Basil Blackwell, 1986.
Strike Debt. *Debt Resisters' Operations Manual*. Oakland/Brooklyn: PM Press/ Common Notions/Autonomedia, 2014.
Subcomandante Marcos. *Conversations with Durito: Stories of the Zapatistas and Neoliberalism*. New York: Autonomedia, 2005.
Suen, Hoi K., and Lan Yu. "Chronic Consequences of High-States Testing? Lessons from the Chinese Civil Service Exam." *Comparative Education Review* 50, no. 1 (February 2006): 46–65.
Sweezy, Paul. "Some Problems in the Theory of Capital Accumulation." *Monthly Review* 26, no. 1 (May 1974): 38–55.
———. *The Theory of Capitalist Development: Principles of Marxian Political Economy* (1942). New York: Monthly Review Press, 1968.
———. "The Triumph of Finance Capital." *Monthly Review* 46, no. 2 (June 1994): 1–11.
Sweezy, Paul, and Paul Baran. *Monopoly Capital: An Essay on the American Economic and Social Order*. New York: Monthly Review Press, 1966.
Sweezy, Paul M., and Harry Magdoff. *Economic History as it Happened, Volume IV, Stagnation and Financial Explosion*. New York: Monthly Review Press, 2009.
———. "The Financial Explosion." *Monthly Review* 37, no. 7 (December 1985): 1–10.
———. "Production and Finance." *Monthly Review* 35, no. 1 (May 1983): 1–13.
Texas Appleseed. *Class, Not Court: Reconsidering Texas' Criminalization of Truancy*. March 2015. https://www.texasappleseed.org/sites/default/files/TruancyReport_All_FINAL_SinglePages.pdf.
Thompson, Edward. "Time, Work-Discipline and Industrial Capitalism." *Past & Present* 38, no. 1 (1963): 56–97.
Thorup, Cathryn. "The Politics of Free Trade and the Dynamics of Cross-Border Coalitions in U.S. Mexican Relations." *Columbia Journal of World Business* 26, no. 11 (Summer 1991): 12–26.
Tijerina, Reies Lopez. *They Called Me "King Tiger": My Struggle for the*

Land and Our Rights. Houston: Arte Publico Press, 2000.

Tosh, Peter. "The Day the Dollar Die." *Mystic Man.* EMI, 1979. Album.

Trager, James. *Amber Waves of Grain.* New York: Arthur Fields Books, 1973.

Tronti, Mario. "La fabbrica e la società." *Quaderni rossi* 2, giugno 1962: 1–31.

———. "Il piano del capitale." *Quaderni rossi,* 3 (April 1963): 44–73. Reprinted in Mario Tronti, *Operai e Capitale,* 267–311. Turin: Einaudi, 1966, 1971. In English: "Social Capital." *Telos,* no. 17 (Fall 1973): 98–121.

"U.S. Grain Arsenal." *NACLA's Latin America and Empire Report* 9, no. 7 (October 1975): 1–11.

Van Daele, Jasmien. "Engineering Social Peace: Networks, Ideas and the Founding of the International Labour Organization." *International Review of Social History* 50, no. 3 (2005): 435–466.

Varney, Wendy, and Brian Martin. "Net Resistance, Net Benefits: Opposing MAI." *Social Alternatives* 19, no. 1 (January 2000): 47–51.

Varoufakis, Yanis. "How I Became an Erratic Marxist." *The Guardian,* February 18, 2015. https://www.theguardian.com/news/2015/feb/18/yanis-varoufakis-how-i-became-an-erratic-marxist.

Veblen, Thorstein. *The Higher Learning in America: A Memorandum on the Conduct of Universities by Businessmen* (1918). Reprints of Economic Classics. New York: Augustus M. Kelley, Bookseller, 1965.

———. *The Theory of the Leisure Class: An Economic Study of Institutions* (1899). New York: The Macmillan Co., 1953.

Virno, Paolo. "Virtuosity and Revolution: The Political Theory of Exodus." In *Radical Thought in Italy: A Potential Politics,* Paolo Virno and Michael Hardt, 189–209. Minneapolis: University of Minnesota Press, 1996.

Wahl, Maurice. *La France aux colonies.* Paris: Librairies-Imprimeries Réunies, 1896.

Walk-Free Foundation. *The Global Slavery Index.* 2016. https://www.globalslaveryindex.org/.

Wall, Dennis, and Virgil Masayesva. "People of the Corn: Teaching in Hopi Traditional Agriculture, Spirituality and Sustainability." *American Indian Quarterly* 28, Nos. 3–4 (Summer–Fall 2004): 435–453.

Wallace, William. *Hegel's Logic.* Oxford: Clarendon Press, 1975.

Waterman, Peter, and Laurence Cox. "Movement Internationalism/s." *Interface: A Journal for and about Social Movements* 6, no. 2 (November 2014): 1–14.

Watson, Bill. "Counter-planning on the Shopfloor." *Radical America* (May–June 1971): 77–85.

Whyte, William, and Kathleen Whyte. *Making Mondragon: The Growth and Dynamics of the Worker Cooperative Complex.* Ithaca: Cornell International Industrial and Labor Relations Reports, 1988/1991.

Wolf Pack. Directed by Crystal Mosselle. New York: Magnolia Pictures, 2015. Film.

Wright, Steve. "Revolution from Above? Money and Class Composition in Italian Operaismo." In *Beyond Marx: Theorizing the Global Labour Relations of the Twenty-First Century*, edited by Marcel van der Linden and Karl Heinz Roth, 369–394. Chicago: Haymarket Books, 2014.

———. *Storming Heaven: Class Composition and Struggle in Italian Autonomist Marxism.* New York: Pluto Press, 2002.

Yates, Michael D. "Braverman and the Class Struggle." *Monthly Review* 50, no. 8 (January 1999): 2–11.

Young, Jeffrey R. "Grades Out, Badges In." *Chronicle of Higher Education,* October 14, 2012. http://chronicle.com/article/Grades -Out-Badges-In/135056.

Zimbalist, Andrew, ed. *Case Studies on the Labor Process,* New York: Monthly Review Press, 1979.

INDEX

international trade. *See* trade,
  international
International Workingmen's
  Association, 234
Internet, 85, 103, petitions, 249n9
investment, 24–26 passim, 66, 150–
  52 passim, 156–69 passim, 176–81
  passim, 186–98 passim, 202–10
  passim, 284; Depression-era
  regulations, 165; diminishment of,
  18, 77, 204, 209, 210; government,
  136–37, 141, 182n3; in machinery, 133n38, 236; Marx views,
  139–40, 150–52 passim, 156–57,
  161–69 passim, 236; of profits, 3,
  135; resistance to, 257–59 passim,
  269n7; stimulation of, 246, 250,
  251. *See also* foreign investment;
  reinvestment
Iranian Revolution, 24
iron, 109
Israel, 23
Italy, 56–61, 213–14n55

J

Jobless Future (Aronowitz), 62
Johnson-Forest Tendency, 120n16,
  195n23
judiciary, 81n18, 114, 118, 222, 231

K

*Karl Marx's Theory of History: A
  Defense* (Cohen), 53
Keynes, John Maynard, 44, 45n14,
  47, 48
Keynesianism, 19, 22, 52, 93n10,
  209, 250; Soviet Union, 239n9.
  See also neo-Keynesians
Kristol, Irving, 82; *Two Cheers for
  Capitalism*, 66
Kropotkin, Peter, 277, 288n41
Krugman, Paul: "Stagnation and
  Financialization," 204–6

L

"labor" (word), 20–21
labor, abstract. *See* abstract labor
labor, affective. *See* affective labor
labor, as social control. 71-86 passim,
  131n34

labor, child. *See* child labor
labor, clerical. *See* clerical work
labor, division of. *See* division of
  labor
labor, forced. *See* forced labor
labor, household. *See* housework
labor, immaterial. *See* immaterial
  labor
labor, migrant. *See* migrant labor
labor, quality of. *See* quality of labor
labor, "skilled" and "unskilled." *See*
  "skilled" and "unskilled" labor
labor, surplus. *See* surplus labor
labor, unproductive. *See* unproductive labor
labor, unwaged. *See* unwaged labor
labor, utility theory of. *See* utility
  theory of labor
Labor and Monopoly Capitalism
  (Braverman), 48n24, 213–16
  passim
labor contracts, 8n5, 102, 126,
  176n46
labor deregulation. *See* deregulation,
  labor
labor force reproduction. *See* reproduction of labor force
labor power (LP), 66, 78, 79, 110,
  138–40, 171, 206–8 passim, 245;
  credit and, 173; value, 133, 134
labor quality. *See* quality of labor
labor theory of value (Marx), 8, 11,
  12, 13, 17–18, 27–69 passim, 81–85
  passim, 107, 108, 289; as theory
  of the value of labor to capital,
  13, 17, 27, 65, 66, 82, 84, 90,
  180; *Reading* Capital *Politically*
  interpretation, 12–13, 18, 28, 65;
  Sweezy and Meek interpretation,
  44–52 passim, 89–90, 186–87, 192
labor unions. *See* unions
land, theft and occupation of. *See*
  colonization and colonialism
land enclosure. *See* enclosure of land
landlords and rent. *See* rent and
  landlords
Latin America, 261–64 passim; debt
  crisis, 25. See also Argentina;
  Mexico
layoffs, 25, 77, 129, 134, 176n46

Lazzarato, Mauricio, 105, 157
leisure, 4, 34, 79, 97
lending of money. *See* credit and debt
Lenin, Vladimir, 40, 87n1;
    Imperialism, 186, 188; *"Left-
    Wing" Communism*, 41–42; theory
    of imperialism, 185–91 passim;
    view of union leaders, 189n13
Leninists and Leninism, 39, 51, 227,
    239
Leontief, Wassily, 43n10, 53n37
lesbian, gay, bisexual, and transgen-
    der (LGBT) people, 118
Life without Money (Nelson and
    Timmerman), 233
Linebaugh, Peter, 85n24, 113n10,
    114n11, 124n22,23, 154n15, 248n8,
    299
loans. *See* credit and debt
lumpenproletariat, 113
Luxemburg, Rosa: *Reform or
    Revolution*, 235

M

Maastricht Treaty, 27, 269n7
machinery, introduction of. *See*
    mechanization
macroeconomics, 19n4, 44, 48, 52,
    134, 165, 192, 250
Magdoff, Fred: *Great Financial
    Crisis*, 201–4; "Stagnation and
    Financialization," 204–6
Magdoff, Harry, 45, 193–94, 205
Malthus, Thomas, 10n6
management, industrial. *See* indus-
    trial management
managerial positions, 5, 8n5
Mandel, Ernest: *Marxist Economic
    Theory*, 48n24
Marazzi, Christian, 95, 157
Marcuse, Herbert, 42, 184
market bubbles. *See* financial
    bubbles
"market socialism," 228, 233, 289
marriage, 5, 118, 128, 130
Marx, Karl, 9, 40, 96, 107–14 passim,
    119–27 passim; "abstract labor,"
    49; analysis of cooperation,
    277; analysis of finance, 144;
    Communist Manifesto, 155n17;

*Contribution to the Critique of
    Political Economy*, 49; *German
    Ideology*, 42, 237–38; *Grundrisse*,
    62, 63–64, 232, 234n10; Hegel
    and, 131n34, 137; Lenin and
    Leninist interpretation, 39, 40;
    on producer cooperatives, 281; re-
    formism, 235–41 passim; response
    to Gotha Program, 237, 238, 284;
    study of strikes and insurrections,
    119; "unproductive" labor, 179;
    view of history, 251; view of lib-
    eration, 67; views of finance, 156,
    161–69 passim; views of value,
    107–15 passim, 119–42 passim,
    179, 236, 245; *Workers' Inquiry*,
    57n50. See also *Capital* (Marx);
    labor theory of value (Marx)
Marxist Economic Theory (Mandel),
    48n24
Marxists and Marxism, 97, 119–20,
    219; abandonment of labor theory
    of value, 39–69 passim; "autono-
    mist," 123; dialectics, 72n2; views
    of credit, 157–58, 167. *See also*
    "analytical Marxism"; *Monthly
    Review*/Monthly Review Press
*Marx's Economics: A Dual Theory of
    Value and Growth* (Morishima),
    53
master-slave relationship, 11, 110
Mattick, Paul, 42
mechanization, 3, 75, 88–93 passim,
    104, 113n10, 133n38, 236, 270;
    Marx views, 62–63, 88, 92, 96;
    Panzieri on, 59. *See also* assembly
    lines; automation
media, alternative. *See* alternative
    press
media, corporate/mass, 98, 126, 220,
    229. *See also* television
media, social. *See* social media
media, underground, 117n15
media consumers, 97
Meek, Ronald, 77, 78, 89, 90; *Studies
    in the Labor Theory of Value*,
    48–51 passim
mental labor, 96
mercantilists, 10, 168
Merchant of Venice (Shakespeare),

stimulation, economic. *See* economic
  stimulation
stocks and bonds, 25, 152, 156,
  160–61, 163, 175, 218; market
  collapse, 221
strikes, 77, 104, 117–20 passim, 141,
  152, 251; credit and, 160; students',
  130, 261. *See also* wildcat strikes
student aid, 136, 252
student debt, 147, 150, 182, 259,
  260–61
student movements, 119, 136, 273–74
students' homework. *See* homework,
  students'
Studies in the Labor Theory of Value
  (Meek), 48–51 passim
subsidies, 26, 136, 182, 255, 263
subsistence, 114, 132, 135, 138, 168n,
  256
superrich, 221
supply and demand, 32–33, 34, 44,
  165
Supreme Court, 222
surplus, 47, 48n23; Baran and
  Sweezy treatment, 192; in monopoly, 191; peasants', 138; production, 135
surplus labor, 56, 66, 83, 156
surplus value, 83, 98; in financial
  work, 213; Marx views, 66, 68,
  151, 157, 167–70 passim, 197, 236;
  over-accumulation and, 204
surveillance, 98, 100, 216, 244n3,
  276
Sweezy, Paul, 44–52 passim, 77, 78,
  89, 90, 205; on Depression, 193–
  94; *Monopoly Capital*, 46, 47n21,
  51n32, 184, 186, 191–96; *Theory
  of Capital Development*, 44–51
  passim, 185–91, 205; "Triumph of
  Financial Capital," 198–201; view
  of Hilferding, 156; view of union
  leaders, 189n13
SYRIZA Party (Greece), 16, 283

T

taxation, 27, 163, 164, 174, 193, 222,
  245n4, 263; cuts, 135n40, 182,
  246–47; in education policy, 261;
  fear of raising, 210, 252; higher

education spending and, 136;
  "negative income tax" idea, 137;
  revenue shortfalls, 250
Taylor, Frederick, 91n8
teach-ins, 273–74
technological development, 36n9,
  59, 271. *See also* mechanization
television, 96, 229, 230
testing, standardized. *See* standardized testing
Texas, criminalization of truancy in,
  81n18
textile industry, 109
theft, 129, 135, 244n3, 276. *See also*
  bank robbery
The Theory of Capital Development
  (Sweezy), 44–51 passim, 185–91,
  205
Third International. *See* Communist
  International
Third World. *See* Global South/Third
  World
Thompson, Edward, 88
time. *See* clock time and machine
  time; socially necessary labor time
  (SNLT); work hours
Timmerman, Frans: *Life without
  Money*, 233
Tobin, James, 261
totalization, capitalist. *See* capitalist
  totalization
trade, international, 25, 153–54,
  160, 212, 268, 269; Global South,
  121n18; grain, 23. *See also* exports;
  imports
transportation, 171–72, 262, 264. *See
  also* shipping industry
transportation, penal, 189
Tronti, Mario, 60, 215n58
Trotskyists, 40, 48n24, 51
truancy, 81n18
Trump, Donald, 225n67
Tsipras, Alexis, 15, 16
Two Cheers for Capitalism (Kristol),
  66

U

under-consumption, 18, 155, 186n7,
  188
unemployment, 22, 25, 62, 93, 95,

143, 231, 252; compensation,
128–29, 247; cooperatives and,
280; factory takeovers and, 282;
France, 189n12; low levels, 274;
need for, 155; prevention, 251;
strikes and, 77
UNI Finance Global Union, 217
Union for Radical Political
Economics (URPE), 52
unions, 102, 126, 129, 189n13, 194,
222, 251; bank workers, 217;
college teachers, 118, 119, 129;
federations, 268; Italy, 56; pension
funds, 141, 162. *See also* strikes
United East India Company. *See*
Dutch East India Company
United Kingdom. *See* Great Britain
universities. *See* colleges and
universities
unproductive labor, 170, 171, 179. *See*
also mental labor
unwaged labor, 83, 86, 100–101,
111–18 passim, 127, 128, 270, 272
uranium, 255
use-value, 21, 65–67 passim, 71, 124,
156, 158, 229; of credit/borrowed
money, 166, 167; in transportation, 172
US Supreme Court. *See* Supreme
Court
usury, 19n6, 24, 174, 253
utility theory of labor, 32–35 passim,
44

V

vacation, 82n20, 92, 141, 243, 266
value, 77–78, 89–90; exchange
and money as, 107–42 passim,
228–30 passim, 290; measure of,
77, 87–105, 243–44; price and,
33, 229. *See also* exchange value;
labor theory of value (Marx);
surplus value; use-value; values,
human
Value, Exploitation and Class
(Roemer), 54, 55
values, human, 65–66
Varoufakis, Yanis, 15, 16
Veblen, Thorstein, 101
Vio.Me, 282–83

Virno, Paolo, 64, 95, 171
Vietnam War, 121, 136, 141, 197–98,
210, 252. *See also* antiwar movement: Vietnam War
Volcker, Paul, 24, 196, 223

W

wages and salaries, 22–26, 126, 208,
223, 224, 251–52; colonial, 190;
consumption and, 140–41; credit
and, 158, 202, 203; cuts, 183; family and, 128; Ford, 91n7; financing,
150; hierarchy/inequality, 101,
127, 134, 229–30, 244; increases,
18, 22–26 passim, 133, 134, 180,
236, 245; microeconomic view,
238n8; payment in kind, 124,
131n35; self-identification and,
111; shareholder and, 162; supply
and demand and, 34; teachers and
professors, 118; unemployment
and, 155
walkouts, 7, 86, 119, 120, 130
war and wars, 208, 209; financing,
163n27; university complicity,
273–74. *See also* Vietnam War
water supply, 248, 262–63, 264,
270–71
welfare, 129, 134, 136, 137, 245, 247,
252
welfare rights movement, 22, 84, 129
wildcat strikes, 23, 129
women, 84–86 passim; advertising
and, 76; birth control, 271, 272;
domestic labor, 74–75, 85, 86, 118,
270, 272, 273; exploitation, 273;
Mexico, 117n15; rape, 159
women's movement, 84, 117n15, 118,
130
work (word), 20–21
work, as social control. *See* labor as
social control
work, clerical. *See* clerical work
work, organization of society, 71n1
work, resistance to. *See* resistance to
work
work, unwaged. *See* unwaged labor
workaholism: workaholics, 4; capitalist devil, 8
workday, 88, 98–99, 236, 266

worker factory takeovers. *See* factory
takeovers
workerism. See *operaismo*
(workerism)
worker promotions, refusal of. *See*
promotions, refusal of
workers, industrial. *See* industrial
workers
workers' councils, 41
workers' creativity and innovation.
See creativity and innovation,
workers'
A Workers' Inquiry (Marx), 57n50
workers' self-organization, 56, 59,
236
workforce, reproduction of. *See*
reproduction of labor force
work hours, 82, 87n1, 88, 133n38,
265–74. *See also* overtime; workday; workweek
working class, 112, 117, 122–23, 126,
133; Baran and Sweezy overlook-
ing of, 194, 198, 199; de-commodification, 275; racism and, 127n26;
solidarity, 267; stocks and bonds
and, 162. *See also* class struggle;
class war
working day. *See* workday
work pace. *See* pace of work
workplace shirking. *See* shirking
workweek, 82n20, 265, 266
World Bank, 25, 145, 199, 203,
223n66, 250–51
World Trade Organization, 203,
269n7

Y
Yates, Michael, 216

Z
Zapatistas, 26, 117n15, 130, 141nn45–
46, 149, 162, 200, 201n36, 205
Zimbalist, Andrews: *Case Studies on
the Labor Process*, 214–15

AK Press is small, in terms of staff and resources, but we also manage to be one of the world's most productive anarchist publishing houses. We publish close to twenty books every year, and distribute thousands of other titles published by like-minded independent presses and projects from around the globe. We're entirely worker-run and democratically managed. We operate without a corporate structure—no boss, no managers, no bullshit.

The Friends of AK program is a way you can directly contribute to the continued existence of AK Press, and ensure that we're able to keep publishing books like this one! Friends pay $25 a month directly into our publishing account ($30 for Canada, $35 for international), and receive a copy of every book AK Press publishes for the duration of their membership! Friends also receive a discount on anything they order from our website or buy at a table: 50% on AK titles, and 20% on everything else. We have a Friends of AK ebook program as well: $15 a month gets you an electronic copy of every book we publish for the duration of your membership. You can even sponsor a very discounted membership for someone in prison.

Email friendsofak@akpress.org for more info, or visit the Friends of AK Press website: https://www.akpress.org/friends.html

There are always great book projects in the works—so sign up now to become a Friend of AK Press, and let the presses roll!